# Representations of Musical Signals

# Representations of Musical Signals

edited by Giovanni De Poli, Aldo Piccialli, and Curtis Roads

The MIT Press
Cambridge, Massachusetts
London, England

© 1991 Massachusetts Institute of Technology

This book was set in Times Roman by Asco Trade Typesetting Ltd., Hong Kong and printed and bound by Halliday Lithograph in the United States of America.

Library of Congress Cataloging-in-Publication Data

Representations of musical signals / edited by Giovanni De Poli, Aldo Piccialli, and Curtis Roads.
    p.  cm.
  Includes bibliographical references and indexes.
  ISBN 0-262-04113-8 (hc)
  1. Music—Data processing. I. De Poli, Giovanni. II. Piccialli, Aldo. III. Roads, Curtis.
ML74.R46  1991
780′.285—dc20
                                              90-44203
                                                CIP
                                                  MN

**In Memoriam**

My work for this book is dedicated to Sergio Ravarino, whom I worked with and whose indispensable help and insight I had the privilege of appreciating.

Aldo Piccialli

# Contents

# Contributors

**Jean-Marie Adrien**, IRCAM, 31, rue S. Merri, F-75004 Paris, France

**Daniel Arfib**, Laboratory of Mechanics and Acoustics and Faculté des Sciences de Luminy, 31 chemin Joseph Aiguier, F-13402 Marseille, Cedex 09 France

**Claude Cadoz**, ACROE (Association pour la Création et la Recherche surs les Outils d'Expression, Ministère de la Culture et de la Communication) and LIFIA (Laboratoire d'Informatique Fondamentale et d'Intelligence Artificielle, Institut National Polytechnique de Grenoble), 46 avenue Felix Viallet, F-38000 Grenoble, France

**Sergio Cavaliere**, IRIS, Spl., Parco La Selva, 03018 Paliano (FR) Italy, and Department of Physics, University of Naples, Mostra d'Oltremare, Pad. 20, I-800125 Naples, Italy

**Roberto D'Autilia**, Department of Physics "La Sapienza," Piazzale Aldo Moro, 2, I-00185 Rome, Italy

**Giovanni De Poli**, Department of Electronics and Informatics, University of Padua, Via Gradenigo 6/A, I-35131 Padua, Italy

**Gianpaolo Evangelista**, Department of Electrical Engineering, University of California, Irvine, California 92717 U.S.A.

**Jean-Loup Florens**, ACROE (Association pour la Création et la Recherche surs les Outils d'Expression, Ministère de la Culture et de la Communication) and LIFIA (Laboratoire d'Informatique Fondamentale et d'Intelligence Artificielle, Institut National Polytechnique de Grenoble), 46 avenue Felix Viallet, F-38000 Grenoble, France

**Guy E. Garnett**, Center for New Music and Art Technologies, Department of Music, University of California, Berkeley, 1750 Arch Street, Berkeley, California 94709 U.S.A.

**Alex Grossman**, C. N. R. S. Center for Theoretical Physics II, Faculté des Sciences de Luminy, Case 907, F-13288 Marseille, Cedex 09, France

**Francesco Guerra**, Department of Physics "La Sapienza," Piazzale Aldo Moro, 2, I-00185 Rome (Roma), Italy

**Kurt Hebel**, CERL Music Project, 252 Engineering Research Laboratory, 103 South Mathews Street, University of Ilinois, Urbana, Illinois 61801-2977 U.S.A.

**Richard Kronland-Martinet**, C. N. R. S. Laboratory of Mechanics and Acoustics and Faculté des Sciences de Luminy, 31 chemin Joseph Aiguier, F-13402 Marseille, Cedex 09 France.

**Christoph Lischka**, Institute for Applied Information Technology, Gesellschaft für Mathematik und Datenverarbeitung mbH, Schloss Birlinghoven, Postfach 1240, D-5205 St. Augustin 1, Federal Republic of Germany

**Aldo Piccialli**, Department of Physics, University of Naples, Mostra d'Oltremare, Pad. 20, I-800125 Naples, Italy

**Jean-Claude Risset**, C. N. R. S. Laboratory of Mechanics and Acoustics and Faculté des Sciences de Luminy, 31 chemin Joseph Aiguier, F-13402 Marseille, Cedex 09 France

**Curtis Roads**, E39-346, M.I.T., Cambridge, Massachusetts 02139 U.S.A.

**Carla Scaletti**, CERL Music Project, 252 Engineering Research Laboratory, 103 South Mathews Street, University of Illinois, Urbana, Illinois 61801-2977 U.S.A.

**Johan Sundberg**, Department of Speech Communication and Music Acoustics, K. T. H., Royal Institute of Technology, S-10044, Stockholm, Sweden

# Preface

A fundamental issue in digital audio and computer music is the question of how to represent musical signals in software and digital hardware. Four closely related questions are

• How should we display musical signals to musicians, engineers, and scientists who want to work with them?

• How can we operate on (interact with) the representations to accomplish musical tasks?

• How can we design systems that let us work with multiple views of the same signal?

• How should we organize the representations for efficient communication of musical signals between devices?

Two separate views of signals have dominated past research: *time-domain* and *frequency-domain* representations. A simple oscilloscope display presents a time-domain representation (showing the amplitude of a signal versus time). The histograms of a spectrum analyzer show the frequency-domain, which displays the magnitude of each frequency component (or band) of the spectrum.

Recent advances in theory have converged with powerful signal processing hardware and programming techniques to make possible a new generation of musical representations. A characteristic of many of these methods is the combination of time- and frequency-domain views in one representation, such as *grains* or *wavelets*. Increased computational power allows another approach, that of representing the signal in terms of a mathematical (physical) model of the sound production mechanism. Software advances, such as the use of visual programming, object-oriented languages, and artificial intelligence techniques like neural networks, give us new "handles" for working with musical sounds. Indeed, for composers, perhaps the most important aspect of thse developments is that they suggest new and interesting ways of organizing musical structure.

The goal of *Representations of Musical Signals* is to expose the state of the art in representations of musical signals, and in particular those methods that innovate in

• Integrated time- and frequency-domain representations

• Physical models of sound production mechanisms

• Visual programming and advanced user interfaces

• Incorporation of musical knowledge via artificial intelligence techniques and neural networks

We have gathered together a set of contributions from a diverse group of authors, experts in the fields of music, digital signal processing, phonetics, psychoacoustics, musical acoustics, theoretical physics, computer science, and the cognitive sciences. We have divided the material into five parts, each of which addresses a major theme in the representation of musical signals. The overviews for each of the parts explain the basic issues and place the articles into historical perspective. Within each part is a collection of both theoretical and empirical papers, reflecting both sides of the research agenda. In addition there are several surveys that also serve as tutorials. Musical, philosophical, and aesthetic considerations are intertwined with technical discussions in many of the papers.

*Representations of Musical Signals* is aimed at the expanding group of musicians, engineers, and scientists who are interested in innovative approaches to digital audio and computer music. We expect that this book will be useful in undergraduate and graduate courses in computer music, musical acoustics, and digital audio signal processing.

## Origins of this Book

*Representations of Musical Signals* has its origins in an international workshop of the same name, held in Sorrento, Italy in October 1988. (See the report in *Computer Music Journal* 13[2]: 90–92, 1989.) This workshop was organized by the authors and Alvise Vidolin (Venice), with local assistance from Camilla DeFelice and Giancarlo Sica of the University of Naples.

One goal of organizing the workshop was to broaden the participants' perspective and thereby enrich the content of this book. *Representations of Musical Signals*, however, is not a proceedings volume. These chapters include a selection from the topics explored at the workshop, but they also include several invited texts written after the workshop at the request of the editors.

The final manuscripts were contributed a year after the events in Sorrento, and the entire book has benefited from several stages of editing. When the first draft contributions were received, all three editors provided feedback. In some cases this led to substantive revisions. In early 1990 Curtis Roads edited the final drafts to improve their organization and smooth out wrinkles in the translations. Katherine Arnoldi and Laura Radin at The MIT Press performed a final production edit on all of the manuscripts in preparation for typesetting.

Finally, we thank Terry Ehling of The MIT Press for her kind assistance in the publication of this book.

# I TIME-FREQUENCY REPRESENTATIONS OF MUSICAL SIGNALS

# Overview

## Aldo Piccialli

Analysis and synthesis methods play a leading role in the representation of musical signals. This part deals with the subject from various points of view, with particular emphasis on time-frequency representations and their time-scale versions.

There are two distinct approaches on which analysis and synthesis can be based: nonparametric methods, which in this part are extensively discussed, and parametric methods. Nonparametric methods generally ignore traditional sound production mechanisms, and thus no hypothesis is advanced on the possible mechanical-acoustical structure of the signal analyzed; therefore nonparametric methods may be considered as completely general and objective representations. As such, it is difficult for them to supply precise information about a specific idiomatic sound structure.

On the other hand, parametric methods allow compact representations, generally by means of a reduced number of coefficients, and take advantage of certain a priori information: for example, a known production model of the sound of certain instruments (the voice, for example) has a parametric representation. Parametric methods are extremely interesting for computer music because they allow a wide range of hypothetical choices on the nature of the sound to be analyzed or synthesized, ranging from psychoacoustic data to the physical structure of the instrument. Conversely nonparametric methods are the bases of musically significant modifications for the composer, and they are extremely useful tools from an analysis viewpoint for estimating the parameters of a suggested model.

What is a time-frequency representation? Let us consider some basic concepts: If we have a periodic acoustic event (temporal representation), it could be useful to have a different representation in the frequency domain. The algorithm that is most often used is the well-known Fourier series. If we wish to find a counterpart for this algorithm in the digital version (which incidentally is the one used in computer music) we use the discrete Fourier transform (DFT). In such a representation $N$ samples specified in time generate $N$ samples in the frequency domain; then we can say that the transform supplies a unique description of the signal with coefficients that are independent among themselves. What has been described above is a stationary signal (in a deterministic sense), that is, a signal the characteristics of which do not vary in time. Obviously the transformation introduced cannot supply information on signals having time-varying spectral contents, but under the proper constraints it can be useful for handling analysis problems of nonstationary signals.

The voice and musical sounds must use time-dependent variables that can represent dynamic sounds, those having a spectral content that develops in time. Numerous solutions have been suggested in the field of digital signal processing. The most popular is the one called short-time Fourier transform (STFT) in its two equivalent implementations, by means of the fast Fourier transform (FFT) or equispaced filter banks. The use of time-shifted short-time analysis windows allows us to characterize the development of the signal in time by means of a set of parameters.

The duration of the window is a critical element in sound analysis; already forty years ago Gabor understood that the temporal location of the signal by means of short windows supplies undetermined measures of the analyzed frequency and vice versa. This type of analysis is well known in phonetics, where we adapt the window to the type of information we wish to view.

At this point two comments can be made: Contrary to what was observed in the analysis of a stationary system, using the DFT the approach called short-time Fourier analysis (or equivalent methods) does not supply a uniquely defined description of the signal: For each window duration there is a different representation.

The second point regards the use of STFT for voice and musical sound analysis: The basis of the analysis and synthesis system consists of a hypothesis of quasi-stationariness (systems varying slowly in time), which is justified for the voice, at least as a first approximation according to the knowledge of the production mechanisms of sound. This hypothesis is also widely used in models of musical production, allowing us to analyze a dynamic signal using stationary analysis by means of the DFT. Techniques justified by this hypothesis have had excellent results in computer music and in phonetics; additive synthesis is an example.

Nevertheless we can also speculate: Facing a model that presumes quasi-stationariness of the signals considered, are all sounds (and voice itself) characterized by this restrictive hypothesis? The answer can only be negative, and the introduction of time-scale representation (wavelets) constitutes a way of overcoming the limits set by the STFT. In its interpretation as a bank of constant Q filters, the wavelet transform creates analysis systems that are able to adapt the measuring window according to the frequency content of the signal. On the other hand, a wavelet representation is subject to various realizations according to the kernel used in the transform (the choice of the analyzing wavelet). We can formulate different structures suitable for the type of information we want to obtain.

This is a brief summary of the points discussed by the authors in this part. Interdisciplinary aspects of computer music and the use of analysis and synthesis methods are discussed in a broad cultural context by Risset in chapter 1. Particularly useful are the many examples supplied from the wide musical experiences of the author.

Next Kronland-Martinet and Grossmann introduce the wavelet transform in an integral sense along with its properties. The technique is well described through many examples and applications.

Arfib, in chapter 3, illustrates time-frequency representations seen from the point of view of their musical application.

Finally, Evangelista presents a digital version of the wavelets implemented by means of quadrature mirror filters together with some interesting examples.

## References

Bastiaans, M. J. 1982. "Gabor's signal expansion into elementary signals." *Proceedings of the IEEE* 68(4): 1223–1229.

Crochiere, R., and L. Rabiner. 1981. *Multirate Digital Signal Processing.* Englewood Cliffs: Prentice-Hall.

Daubechies, I. 1988. "Orthonormal bases of compactly supported wavelets." *Communications on Pure and Applied Mathematics* 41: 909–996.

Fallside, F., and W. A. Woods. 1985. *Computer Speech Processing.* Englewood Cliffs: Prentice-Hall.

Flanagan, J. L. 1972. *Speech Analysis, Synthesis and Perception.* New York: Springer-Verlag.

Flandrin, P. 1989. "Some aspects of non-stationary signal processing with emphasis on time-frequency and time-scale methods." *Proceedings of the 1989 International Wavelet Conference.* New York: Springer-Verlag, pp. 68–97.

Gabor, D. 1946. "Theory of communication." *Journal of the IEE* 93: 429–441.

Grossmann, A., R. Kronland-Martinet, and J. Morlet. 1987. "Reading and understanding continuous wavelet transform." *Proceedings of the 1987 International Wavelet Conference.* New York: Springer-Verlag.

Makoul, J. 1975. "Linear prediction: a tutorial review." *Proceedings of the IEEE* 63: 561–580.

Moorer, J. A. 1977. "Signal processing aspects of computer music: a survey." *Proceedings of the IEEE* 65(8): 1108–1137.

Moorer, J. A. 1978. "The use of the phase vocoder in computer music applications." *Journal of the Audio Engineering Society* 26(1/2): 42–45.

Risset, J. C. 1986. "Musical sound models for digital signals." *Proceedings of ICASSP 86*. New York: IEEE, pp. 1269–1271.

Roads, C., and J. Strawn, eds. 1985. *Foundations of Computer Music*. Cambridge, Massachusetts: MIT Press.

Smith, M. I. T., and T. P. Barnwell III. 1986. "Exact reconstruction techniques for tree-structured subband coders." *IEEE Transactions on Acoustics, Speech and Signal Processing* 34(3): 434–441.

Strawn, J. 1987. "Analysis and synthesis of musical transitions using the DSFT." *Journal of the Audio Engineering Society* 35 (1/2): 3–14.

Youngberg, J. E. 1978. "Constant-Q analysis and synthesis." *Proceedings of ICASSP 78*. New York: IEEE, pp. 375–378.

# 1 Timbre Analysis by Synthesis: Representations, Imitations, and Variants for Musical Composition

**Jean-Claude Risset**

In this chapter, I stress the use of sound analysis as a tool for music synthesis. Digital sound synthesis has potentially infinite resources. It lends itself to unprecedently refined control, allowing composers to extend their compositional activity down to the level of sound structure, to compose the sonic microstructure as well as the musical macrostructure. As Varèse pointed out many decades ago, new sonic materials suggest new musical architectures.

In chemistry, analysis is essential to understand how to obtain new compounds from the chemical elements. Similarly, in acoustics, analysis is essential to help synthesis, in particular imitative synthesis. In addition analysis can yield musically useful representations of sound. And synthesis is essential to ascertain the aural significance of the elements extracted in the analysis. Although it is clear that analysis methods should imply both the time domain and the frequency domain, it is fair to say that there is no generally optimal process for either analysis or synthesis. Methods must be evaluated in terms of economy, but also of perceptual validity and of significance for the musical goal at hand.

I discuss these issues in general terms, but also with specific examples drawn from my own work in two related fields—computer research in the acoustics of musical sound and musical composition with computer-generated sounds. I first recall some historical precedents for both analysis and synthesis. Then I describe some early experiments on instrument simulation by computer, which exemplified the method of timbre study by analysis and synthesis. The main goal of synthesis is not instrument imitation; rather its main interest lies in its flexibility, which makes it easy to produce sonic variants. I elaborate on this topic with examples from my pieces, where representations of sound were used as an aid to composition and also performance. I then recall the most frequently used synthesis models, and I stress the difficulty of finding the parameters to feed a model so as to yield any given sound. This will lead to analysis-synthesis models, such that the parameters extracted from a given sound by analysis permit to reconstruct an accurate copy of this sound by synthesis. Analysis-synthesis techniques can help give more flexibility to sound processing, permitting intimate sonic transformations. I give some examples of such possibilities; which I have applied in recent compositions. I conclude by discussing representations as compositional tools, focusing on the issue of specificity versus generality.

## Historical Precedents for Analysis, Synthesis, and Representation

*Analysis* refers to decomposition into elements. The notion of atoms as the simplest elements of matter goes back to Democritus (b. ca. 460 B.C.). Lucretius (96–55 B.C.) justified this conception as a necessity for the mind.

*Synthesis* refers to the operation of putting the elements together, going from these elements to the whole, from the simple to the compound.

These seemingly speculative notions have become completely practical since modern chemistry established the existence of stable chemical elements from which any chemical substance can in principle be synthesized. I am not sure when analysis and synthesis were first clearly conceived regarding sound. Apparently Democritus considered perception as a somewhat obscure operation, induced by contacts, through the sensory organs, between outside atoms and the mind's atoms. Pythagoras's (d. ca. 497 B.C.) experiments with the sonometer deal with sound relations rather than sound structure. Greek music with lyra and aulos—a double-reed pipe— does not appear as elementary as the voice; it is already a kind of synthesis. So is the sound of the Cheng, the Chinese mouth organ, with its many pipes.

*Representation* of something makes it present, visible—to the eye or to the mind. It offers a substitute similar in some ways to the real thing. Going back to Aristotle, representation was thought of mostly as a way of knowledge; but it has also an operational value, in that it suggests actions. Western musical notation, introduced in Europe in the Middle Ages, was intended for memorization; but the graphic representation suggested transformation of the musical phrases through spatial translations and symmetries, which are fundamental in counterpoint. Certain trends in contemporary mathematical physics propose to replace space, as the locus and representation of objects, by operators—to consider function rather than structure.

Organs were built centuries before the time of Jesus Christ, but initially each sound was produced by only one pipe. Polyphony appeared in the Western world through the Middle Ages; it may be considered a form of synthesis. In particular, melodic phrases were often sung by parallel voices at intervals of octaves, fifths, or thirds; this is akin to harmonic synthesis. Harmonic synthesis was truly realized in the mutation stops of the pipe organ in France and in Germany, probably before the fifteenth century. The technique is fully described in the famous treatise of Dom Bedos, *L'Art du Facteur d'orgues*, written at the end of the eighteenth century. In 1636

Galileo and Mersenne ascribed pitch to frequency. Around 1700 Sauveur invented a method to count acoustic vibrations, and he understood clearly the harmonics—"simple" components of frequencies $f$, $2f$, $3f$, and so on as components of a periodic sound of frequency $f$. This concept strongly influenced Rameau's theory on the fundamental bass in music. At the end of his life, the great mathematician Euler was blind, but he was very good at analyzing by ear the harmonic components present in a sustained instrumental sound. This may have led him to propose a wave theory of light, in which he assigned each color to a specific frequency of vibration.

In the mutation stops of the organ, a given pitch, triggered by a single key of the keyboard, is obtained by simultaneously sounding several pipes, tuned so that each pipe alone vibrates at a frequency corresponding to one harmonic of the pitch intended. The sounds of these pipes tend to fuse (not always perfectly) and to yield a specific timbre that depends on which harmonics have been added. This is genuine harmonic synthesis. It was done by ear—and soon by tradition—without recourse to any analysis other than aural introspection.

Although they did not really perform synthesis, many ingenious devices stored time sequences: sequences of pitches in the Kircher music machines or in the barrel organs and sequences of sound events in the Vaucanson artificial duck. In Van Kempelen's speaking machine the operator moves with his hand various flexible cavities that are excited by a reed, so as to imitate speech. This variable filtering effect could be termed *subtractive synthesis*.

The nineteenth century saw the blooming of chemical analysis and synthesis. Atomic theory was thoroughly confirmed from Lavoisier to Liebig and Berthelot. Sound analysis began to come of age at that time. J. B. J. Fourier's theorem was not demonstrated in the context of acoustics; nonetheless it gave a mathematical foundation to the notion of harmonic components. The theorem states that any regular periodic function of frequency $f$ can be reconstituted as the sum of an infinite series of sinusoidal components of frequencies $f$, $2f$, $3f$, and so on. Given a periodic waveshape, a problem of harmonic analysis is then to find the amplitudes and phases of the Fourier series that converges toward this waveshape. If this can be solved, it means that one can synthesize any waveshape by adding sinewave components. The coefficients of the successive harmonics form what is called the *harmonic spectrum*; the phases of the successive harmonics form the *phase spectrum*. Both spectra form what is called a *frequency-domain*

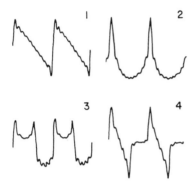

**Figure 1.1**
Waveforms 1 to 4 correspond to the same amplitude spectrum but to different phase
spectra. These periodic waveforms all sound the same to the ear. Thus the time-domain
representation is not very meaningful.

representation (because the frequencies can be read at first sight on this
representation), as opposed to *time-domain* representations, directly related
with the waveform.

The frequency-domain representation of periodic sounds was studied by
the scientists Ohm, Helmholtz, and Hermann in particular. Ohm stated
that changes in the phase spectrum, although they altered the waveshape,
did not affect its aural effect. Helmholtz developed a method of harmonic
analysis with acoustic resonators. According to these studies, the ear is
"phase-deaf," and timbre is determined exclusively by the spectrum. Thus,
although the time-domain representation is not very meaningful, the description in term of spectrum alone is concise and adequate (figure 1.1).
Such conclusions are still considered essentially valid—for periodic sounds
only because Fourier series analysis-synthesis works only for those. This
is a major restriction because one cannot always reduce musical sounds to
periodic sounds.

Various Fourier analyzers were developed so that the spectra of the
steady-state portion of the sound of musical instruments could be determined. Different sounds had different spectra; quite naturally the spectrum
was considered to be the "recipe" for harmonic resynthesis. As for atomic
theory, however, this was only speculation until synthesis could verify it.
One crucially needs tests to confirm or invalidate speculations, otherwise the theory is not falsifiable, in Karl Popper's terms. (Long before
Copernicus, Aristarque from Samos had proposed a heliocentric model of
the universe; but without a telescope, he could not prove it.)

Around 1875 two inventions took place that were to deeply change our possibilities of dealing with sound. In 1877 Edison realized the first sound recording using mechanical devices. Two years earlier Bell had invented the telephone, where electricity conveys vibrations that come from sounds or that can make sounds.

Once they are recorded, sounds can be saved, observed at leisure, and analyzed in various ways. And electroacoustic technology (amplifiers, loudspeakers) lets us produce sounds that escape acoustic constraints. Before electroacoustic technology, sounds were usually produced by the vibrations of stable structures, so that sound identity was always linked to its origin. For instance, the timbre of musical sounds were characterized by specifying the instrument and the way to play it (for example, cello pizzicato). But a loudspeaker is a rather general sound source, so that the sounds that emanate from it have to be characterized otherwise. They must be represented in some way, perhaps through the specification of the process of electrical generation synthesis, or alternately through a pattern extracted from an analysis—for instance, the Fourier spectrum.

At the turn of the twentieth century, Cahill built the Telharmonium, or Dynamophone, a huge sound-making machine that looked like an electric power station and used dynamos to produce electrical vibrations. This first serious attempt to take advantage of electricity for producing sounds was impractical; electronic technology was needed. Lee de Forest invented the triode vacuum tube in 1906, hoping to use it to build an electronic music instrument. Starting around 1920, several pioneers indeed realized electronic music instruments, where the instrumentalist can shape the vibration by modifying the electrical elements of an oscillating circuit. In 1921 Leon Termen (or Theremin), who is still alive, demonstrated his "singing antenna" to Lenin in Moscow. Later the Ondes Martenot, the Dynaphone, the Trautonium, and the Ondioline met some success.

Hundreds of musical scores, notably from from Arthur Honegger, Olivier Messiaen, Andre Jolivet, and Tristan Murail, use the Ondes Martenot. (I call for two of them in my piece *Aventure de ligne*, written in 1982 for the Itinéraire ensemble for electronic instruments and computer-generated tape.) Recording techniques have also been "perverted" for creating sounds, for instance, by drawing pictures on the optical tracks of films, as explored by McLaren, Cholpo, Arma, and Grainger, or by modifying phonographs to perform unusual transformations on recorded material, as tried by Varèse, Toch, Honegger, and John Cage—the latter realized in 1939

*Imaginary Landscape Number 1*, probably the first musical work existing only as a recording.

After World War II the possibilities open to musical creation by electroacoustic techniques were explored in a more systematic way. *Musique concrète*, initiated in Paris by Schaeffer in 1948, started with acoustically generated sounds, recorded on disk or on tape; this initial material was then submitted to transformations—looping, splicing, changing tape speed, filtering, adding echoes and reverberation; the resulting material was edited and mixed to produce the piece. The process was purposely empirical, under the aural control of the composer.

*Electronic music*, pioneered by Eimert, Meyer-Eppler, and Stockhausen in Cologne around 1951, was initially intent on realizing precisely into sound a given score, conceived a priori with specific formal constraints in the vein of serial music. For some time it used exclusively electronically generated sound material, with physical parameters precisely specified by the score. (*Music for Tape*, developed by Ussachevsky and Luening in New York at the same time, did not display such clear-cut exclusive choices because it used both recorded and electronic sounds.)

The advent of digital sound synthesis and processing, initiated and developed mainly by Max V. Mathews on the computer, was a turning point, bringing within reach the infinite wealth of sonic possibilities that one hoped for from electrical sound. Modular programs, such as Mathews's Music V, permit users to construct their own synthesis process. They have to specify this process in complete detail, which amounts to specifying the physical structure of the desired sound. This program was extended to also perform processing of sampled sounds. One can incorporate—or use instead—one's own software, implementing whatever process can be thought of and formulated explicitly.

Microelectronics have made computers compact and inexpensive, available as individual tools, and special digital hardware can be built to synthesize or process even complex sounds digitally in real time. The limitations are no longer technical, stemming from hardware problems, but intellectual, related to the software, the data bases, and the know-how. For instance, it is a difficult challenge to design musically useful programs and digital hardware devices. One can be hopeful, though, because everything is replicable, and know-how on sound synthesis and processing can be accumulated and transmitted. But a great deal of thought must be spent on the issues of analysis, synthesis, and representation for musical purposes, especially when idiosyncrasies of perception must also be taken into account.

The difference between the attitudes of practitioners of musique concrète and of musique électronique was crystallized by the respective technical limitations of the two media. With computers and digital processing, technical limitations are no longer determinant. Yet the two attitudes remain with the computer, now corresponding to electing digital synthesis or processing of sound. Only now can one hope to bridge the gap between synthesis, which affords to the composer more intimate control of the sound structure, and processing, which starts with sounds already endowed with identity and richness, but which has difficulty transforming them as intimately.

## Timbre Imitation by Analysis and Synthesis

Computer music pioneers did not initially strive to imitate existing sounds because they had faith in the potential of sound synthesis to give access to a new world of sound. The initial results, however, were disappointing: By specifying parameters in ways that were thought untypical, one did not obtain really new and interesting sounds. Most quasi-periodic or randomly modulated sounds were dull; they lacked life and identity. In fact the identity of certain instrumental sounds could not even be suggested by their computer-synthesized imitation. Early imitations were based on the replication of their frequency-domain "recipe," their harmonic spectrum. Of course real sounds are not truly periodic—they grow and decay, and they have transients. Pierre Schaeffer distinguished between *form*, related to the amplitude envelope, and *matter*, linked with the spectral aspects. However, even introducing a proper time envelope was not sufficient for certain types of sounds, especially brass sounds and bowed string sounds.

In 1964, at the suggestion of Max Mathews, I investigated the timbre of trumpet tones. Attempts to imitate brass sounds from spectra and attack and decay times found in the literature were a complete failure. They did not evoke, even remotely, the brassy quality. Thus it cannot be assumed that brass sounds have a fixed spectrum, as would be the case if they were periodic or quasi-periodic; one must take into account the variations of the waveshape in the course of a note, which can be seen on the oscillogram—a time-domain representation (figure 1.2). Clearly a combined time- and frequency-domain representation is needed. I performed analyses of trum-

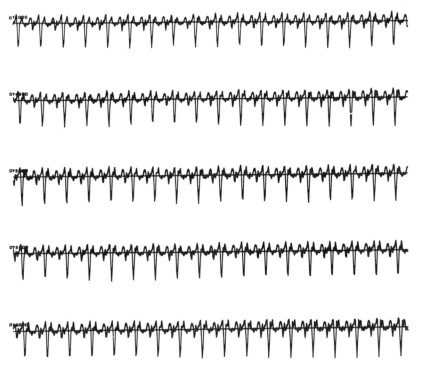

**Figure 1.2**
Digital oscillogram of a fragment of an F4 trumpet tone. Each line corresponds to 50 ms. If one looks closely, one can see that the waveshape gradually changes.

pet tones, beginning with the sound spectrograph, which yields displays of a running short-time Fourier spectrum. The displays present frequencies as a function of time. The amplitude of a frequency component at a given time is indicated by the level of gray—between light and dark. At a given time one can also obtain sections that indicate more precisely the frequency spectrum at this instant. It could be seen on the spectrograms of trumpet tones that spectra often vary throughout a note. Most of the energy is concentrated in the harmonic lines, although a burst of inharmonicity is often visible at the onset of the sound (figure 1.3).

This suggested that I turn to another method of analysis and display that would take advantage of that concentration. This was *pitch-synchronous analysis*, implemented by Mathews and Miller. In pitch-synchronous analysis the wave is segmented into *pseudoperiods*. For each pseudoperiod the

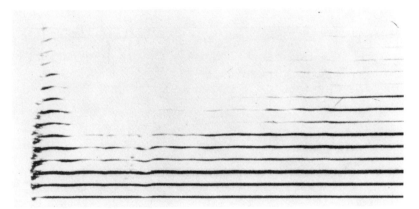

**Figure 1.3**
Sound spectrogram of an A4 trumpet tone with evolving dynamics, described by the
markings *sf p cresc ... f*. This represents frequency versus time—the portion represented
lasts 1.7 s and goes up to 7.0 kHz in frequency. The amplitude of a component at a given
time is indicated by its darkness. One can also see that the spectrum extends with loudness.

pitch is measured, and the Fourier spectrum is calculated as though the
sound were periodic, repeating that period. Each period spectrum is then
plotted so that one gets for successive period numbers the evolution of the
amplitude of the first harmonic, the second harmonic, and so on. If the
frequency is constant, this gives plots of the amplitude of each harmonic
as a function of time.

Pitch-synchronous analysis suggested that one should resynthesize the
analyzed tones by specifying different envelopes for each harmonic component, with each envelope corresponding to the curves extracted from the
analysis. This can be described as additive synthesis—specifying separately
the evolution of the components and summing them together. I simplified
the curves by approximating them as *piecewise linear functions* (made up
of line segments), and used the simpler curves from synthesis (figure 1.4).
The synthesis, at last, gave good results. This method was later pursued
and extended by Moorer and Grey (1977), who published a "lexicon of
analyzed tones" that gives data for adequate resynthesis.

There remains a major problem, though: Figure 1.4, which displays the
"simplified curves" for a tone of about 0.25 s, shows that even a simplified
description can be very complex. The simplification was done "by hand,"
and this set of curves only works for a single tone. It would not be
satisfactory to use these curves for other tones of different pitches, different
durations, or loudnesses. Grey later developed programs to perform auto-

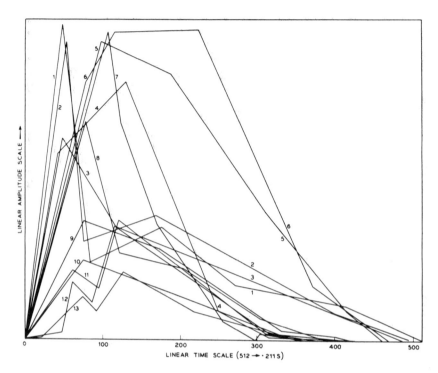

**Figure 1.4**
Plot of functions schematizing the envelopes of individual harmonics for a D4 trumpet tone
of duration 0.21 s. These functions are drawn with a linear amplitude scale. They are made
up of line segments. These functions have been used to control the harmonic amplitudes of
synthetic tones.

matic extraction of such curves, going in the direction of a genuine analysis-
synthesis system for additive synthesis of quasi-periodic tones. This procedure requires a great deal of computation, and the amount of information
describing the sounds is voluminous—one needs a unique set of envelope
data for each different tone.

I looked for a more compact description, hoping to find some kind of
invariant that would characterize the specific timbre of the trumpet, which
after all remains typical throughout the various tones. I systematically
studied the audibility of certain details found in the analysis. Some could
be discarded, because although they were physically present in the real tone,
their absence in the synthesized tone did not make any difference to the
ear. This is the case of amplitude fluctuations for the trumpet (whereas these

seem relevant for the flute). Some features were, on the contrary, important cues to the identity of the sound. In the case of the trumpet, I isolated a characteristic property: When the tone gets louder, the spectrum gets richer in high-order harmonic components. In particular, during the initial 30 to 50 ms, this property causes the frequency components to be asynchronous, with the low-order components building up earlier. This asynchrony is relevant to the ear. This feature can be recognized in figure 1.3, and the physical reasons for it can be understood by studying the acoustic generation of trumpet tones. However, the point of interest here is that this asynchrony is a significant aural cue for brassy tones. It allows us to synthesize brasslike tones "by rule," that is, by programming a set of rules that automatically take care of computing the many parameters needed (such as the evolving amplitudes for all the harmonics). It accepts as input parameters the pitch, one amplitude envelope, and the duration, and it generates sound algorithmically, generating for each different synthesized tone a new set of data extracted by analysis from a different original tone.

Starting with a fixed spectrum, one could never obtain an accurate imitation of a brass sound because it is a typical spectral variation with amplitude that is characteristic to the ear. This property is not truly an invariant but a consistent relation between two different aspects of the sound. Such a relation is more robust than the structure of a fixed spectrum. It also explains how one can appreciate the loudness at which the sound has been produced regardless of the intensity at which the sound reaches the ear. The latter is of course a function of the distance of the instrument. I implemented this property using additive synthesis with a degenerate version of the oscillator of the Music IV program, so that it would generate as output a prescribed function of the input. I made the amplitude of each harmonic a function of the amplitude of the first harmonic, such that the higher the harmonic order, the steeper the slope of the function. Thus the only data required for synthesis is the envelope of the first harmonic. The instantaneous amplitudes of the other harmonics are then determined automatically, "by rule," by means of a lookup of these functions in arrays in computer memory. This method was a bit heavy computationally, though. Fortunately I realized that the details of the amplitude evolution of high-order harmonics were often irrelevant. I could group together several harmonics, imposing on them a parallel envelope, without badly impairing the quality of the synthesis. I stress this here, because it relates to the constant $\Delta f/f$ spacing of the channels in a *wavelet* analysis and synthesis. In most practical cases a $\Delta f/f$ spacing is probably more adequate to give a good practical compromise than the constant $\Delta f$ spacing in the phase vocoder of the Gabor transform. (The data on some of my brass synthesis, together with many other synthesis data, can be found in my 1969 "computer sound catalog.")

This characteristic brass property was also implemented using other synthesis processes. In the context of analog synthesizers, Robert Moog devised a voltage-controlled lowpass filter that would admit a proportion of high harmonic energy growing with the input voltage. By sending as input a voltage proportional to the amplitude envelope, one obtains the desired brassy quality. Using digital computers, John Chowning (1973) implemented the property in an elegant fashion through his frequency modulation technique, by linking the value of the modulation index to the envelope. To get optimal brassy sounds, Dexter Morrill and David Bristow refined this technique somewhat to avoid the diminution of the energy in the fundamental when the modulation index increases.

From these studies I draw two conclusions: First, there does not seem to be any general and optimal paradigm to either analyze or synthesize any type of sound. One has to scrutinize the structure of the sound—quasi-periodic, sum of inharmonic components, noisy, quickly or slowly evolving—and also investigate to find out which features of the sound are relevant to the ear. Such investigations can point to efficient types of analysis and advantageous synthesis models. But to extract from analysis the optimal parameters for a given synthesis model is not easy: It is a genuine research project involving trial and error. It requires signal processing and musical sound know-how, insight, and above all a good ear. John Chowning (1973) has shown evidence of such research in his early work on the use of the frequency modulation (FM) technique. Then he used data from Johan Sundberg (see chapter 9) and from his own spectral analyses to implement variants of FM synthesis models (combining in effect FM and additive synthesis) that could yield remarkable imitations of the singing voice (Chowning 1980).

Second, a useful method to characterize a given type of timbre is *analysis by synthesis*, that is, building up a synthesis model, discarding aurally irrelevant features, and deciding from the subjective quality of the synthesis whether the simplified synthesis model retains the information essential to the identification of that timbre. There is much to be said for physical models, which attempt to synthesize sound with algorithms that simulate the physical behavior of the acoustic device producing the instrument (chapters 7 and 8; see also Cadoz, Luciani, and Florens 1984, Adrien and Rodet 1985). However, physical models are difficult and costly to implement. In timbre analysis by synthesis, the criterion is perceptual: The validity of the model can be ascertained only when the synthesis is submitted to the foolproof test of listening. One can thus take advantage of some limitations of hearing to propose relatively simple production models with psychoacoustic validity.

## The Flexibility of Synthesis: Producing Variants

Analysis by synthesis leads to models for synthesizing certain types of sound. The interest of such models goes beyond mere imitation. Such models, together with their parameters corresponding to specific sounds, constitute in effect a representation of those sounds. As stated initially, a representation suggests possibilities for action. Here, by changing the parameters of the synthesis models, one can produce *variants*. Variants can be intriguing because they can be very close to the original sound in some ways and yet quite different in other ways.

In my 1969 "computer sound catalog," I enumerated a number of examples of computer synthesis, using mostly additive synthesis-based models. In general such models can be represented by

$$s(t) = \Sigma_i A_i(t) \sin(2\pi f_i(t) + j_i),$$

where the $f_i$ are often chosen as constant or as modulated globally by the same frequency-controlling function (to introduce vibrato, for example). The envelopes $A_i(t)$ and the frequency-controlling functions $f_i(t)$ can be specified by stored functions in a synthesis program like Music V. These models can also be implemented with certain digital synthesizers (Risset 1969, Alles and DiGiugno 1977, Lawson and Mathews 1977).

With additive synthesis a percussive sound can be changed to something completely different merely by changing the envelopes. Thus bell-like sounds can be transformed into fluid textures that retain the same basic harmonic structure. I have used this process in my pieces *Little Boy* (1968), *Mutations* (1969), and mostly *Inharmonique* (1977). I synthesized bell-like sounds by additive synthesis as a sum of exponentially decaying sinusoids at inharmonic frequencies. If the decays are synchronous, the sound is quite

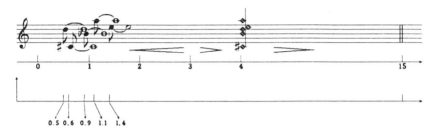

**Figure 1.5**
Schematic score of the beginning of *Mutations*. An arpeggiated chord is echoed after
4 s by a gonglike synthetic sound that has components of the same frequencies as the
fundamentals of the chords. Although the gonglike sound is not heard as a chord, but
rather as a timbre, one can hear clearly that this timbre is a prolongation, a shadow of the
chord harmony.

unnatural, reminiscent of an electronic chime. In natural bells, as a general
rule, the lower the component frequency, the longer the decay, although
this is not always strictly true. One can use the frequencies of real bells or
other frequencies as well. Indeed I often "compose" my synthetic "bells" or
other inharmonic sounds as one composes a chord—so that timbre can be
related to the harmony, appearing as the "shadow" of the chord. Although
it is hard to analyze aurally the components of the inharmonic sounds,
which tend to fuse, one can clearly notice this relation—a prolongation of
harmony into timbre. This can be heard at the beginning of *Mutations* or
in *Dialogues* (figure 1.5).

A reasonable bell approximation can be generated with only one envelope shape—a sharp attack and an exponential decay—using different
decay times for the different frequency components. With such a model a
"bell" is thus defined by an envelope shape and a set of frequencies (the $f_i$)
and durations, those of the components (figure 1.6a). If I change the
envelope shape, which is the same of all components (only the duration
differs), to one that gradually swells and then decays (figure 1.6b), listeners
will no longer gather the impression of a bell. Rather they will hear a fluid
texture that is harmonically related to the bell. The attack is no longer
synchronous, which helped to aurally fuse the components. The sound no
longer sustains the illusion that it is emanating from a single object—an
imaginary bell. Instead the maximum amplitude is reached at different
times for different components. This influences listeners so that they hear
the components separately; the components disperse just as a prism disperses

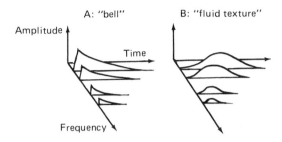

**Figure 1.6**
Transformation of a bell-like sound (A) into a fluid texture (B) by changing the shape of the amplitude envelope

white light (Risset 1989). I have often used this transformation, notably in *Mutations* (1969), *Inharmonique* (1977), *Passages* (1982), *Profils* (1983), and *Contours* (1983).

I have used a similar dispersion for chords. Each tone of the chord comprises a series of harmonic components: Instead of sounding together, these harmonics can be made to come in and out at different times, either with sharp attacks or with slow, insidious envelopes. For instance, in *Little Boy* (1968), notably at the beginning, I have used what I call *spectral analysis of a chord*. The harmonics come in and die out in order (or in reverse order), as though one was hearing them through a frequency window moving up (or down). (figure 1.7).

Both for "bells" and harmonics, condensed representations appear as a musical tool, suggesting transformations. Indeed I used graphic representations for the overlaps of harmonics, and I wrote a subroutine to manage these harmonic shifts. The specifications given to the program appear also as a kind of representation, of structural notation, which can be viewed as facilitating specific musical operations.

Such variants are musically interesting because they correspond to very intimate and novel sound transformations. Similar effects cannot usually be obtained with acoustic instruments because their structure is much less flexible. Extensions beyond usual ranges are easy. In his *Studies for trumpet and computer*, Dexter Morrill (1975) has synthesized trumpetlike sounds that have a much wider frequency range than actual trumpets. John Chowning synthesized very low singinglike sounds—*basso profundissimo*—which can be heard in his piece *Phōnē*. In Chowning's *Sabelithe* and *Turenas*, one can hear timbral transitions between two different timbres—

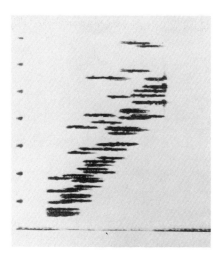

**Figure 1.7**
Harmonic arpeggio: For each note of an initial chord, harmonics 1, 2, 3, and so on appear
in time succession, at different time intervals for the different notes. This is akin to viewing
all the harmonics of the chord through a frequency window moving up.

from dry percussion to brass, for instance. These were obtained by gradually changing the synthesis data, interpolating between those corresponding to the initial and the final timbre. John Grey performed similar transitions between sounds synthesized by additive synthesis. The envelopes
controlling the evolution of each harmonic were approximated by piecewise linear functions, and the coordinates of the breakpoints were interpolated. He could thus produce the impression that a clarinet gradually
gets turned into a cello, which then is metamorphosed into a horn. Again,
such effects cannot be obtained with instruments. Orchestrators have tried
to perform transitions between instrumental timbres by the equivalent of
slide projector fade-in and fade-out, but one then hears two sounds in the
intermediary stage.

I mentioned Morrill's *Studies,* in which a live trumpet player engages in
dialog with computer-synthesized sounds that are often get very similar to
trumpet tones. The same year, 1975, I realized *Dialogues.* As the name
suggests, it tries to manage close encounters between two different worlds:
the real world of instrumentalists live on stage and the imaginary, illusory
world of synthesized sounds. The imaginary world sometimes contrasts
with the instruments, sometimes fuses with them, and sometimes comple-

**Figure 1.8**
A plot of the frequency content versus time for the beginning of my piece *Moments Newtoniens*, number 3. Here about one minute is represented. The frequency content is split into three parts: The lowest one corresponds to the range 50 to 500 Hz, the one above it corresponds to the range 200 to 2000 Hz, and the highest one corresponds to the range 1000 to 10000 Hz. The section represented shows gliding sounds that are difficult to draw on a score. A representation like the ordinary spectrogram might be easier to read, however, this was proposed to display the information in a more detailed way. The incentive here was to propose representations that could serve for copyright purposes as scores for electronic or computer sounds, which are realized directly into sound. (Courtesy of J. Appleton; author unknown)

ments them, for instance, by prolonging harmony into inharmonic timbres or into harmonic clouds (similar to the process of spectral analysis of chords mentioned for *Little Boy*). A number of hybrid pieces of this kind have been produced since (this is also the case of *Inharmonique*, in which a soprano interacts with the computer-generated music).

The human soloists usually need a score with a representation of the tape part to follow it accurately. Sometimes this representation can be a very crude simplification, or even a single symbol or warning. However, it is often interesting to offer a rather faithful picture of what is happening in the tape. Doing it by hand, from listening to the tape recording and timing it, is boring and time consuming. Here the best solution seems to be the sound-spectrogram–like representations, showing the frequency content as a function of time (figure 1.8) (or wavelet plots of scale versus time, which look similar if one uses Morlet-like wavelets) (chapter 2). Depending on the musical purpose, one may want either a linear frequency scale, to recognize harmonics, or a logarithmic frequency scale, to have musical intervals look invariant over the frequency scale (see figure 1.10).

Meaningful representations of complex sound structures offer other interests. Leipp insisted that the eye can track significant features on a sound spectrogram. Such representations can help detect musical plagiarism, which the possibilities of sampling and processing have made easier.

They also offer the possibility of different scales of view, from the macro-scopic to detailed images of musical works, either instrumental or classical, which can spark revealing insights about the musical structure, as Robert Cogan (1984) has shown.

## Toward Automatic Parameter Identification for Specific Sound Models?

As we have seen, finding synthesis models capable of mimicking existing sounds is intriguing because such models can suggest musically interesting variants. Certain synthesis processes have proved very useful, especially (1) additive synthesis, where one sums the contributions of components that are controlled separately, (2) subtractive synthesis, where one starts from a complex source and filters out the unwanted components, (3) frequency modulation, where the frequency of a sine wave is modulated at an audio rate by another sine wave, generating a complex spectrum depending on the parameters of the modulation, and (4) nonlinear distortion (or wave-shaping), where a sine wave is submitted to nonlinear distortion, and the resulting complex spectrum depends on the distortion function and the input amplitude.

Many of these synthesis processes can be implemented on fast special-purpose digital hardware devices. For instance, additive synthesis with individual control of each component's amplitude and frequency could be realized on the 4B processor, realized at IRCAM by Alles and DiGiugno (1977, Lawson and Mathews 1977). The relatively inexpensive DX or TX digital synthesizers implement many FM-derived models, and there are now powerful additive synthesis processors.

The different synthesis processes are by no means equivalent. Certain kinds of sound are much easier to obtain with certain techniques. The sonic territory of any of these techniques is much larger than people generally believe, but only a small area of this territory will be reached if one uses the technique in a simple, stereotypical way. For example, FM does not necessarily "sound like FM": Chowning, Schottstaedt, McNabb, Serra, and others have shown that elaborate uses of FM can give extremely varied types of sound. Moreover the territories of various synthesis techniques overlap a great deal. Let me quote a sentence from a review of my piece *Inharmonic Soundscapes* (which appears in the record *New Directions of Music*): "The piece appears to be mostly the result of FM synthesis."

Actually I use almost only additive synthesis. It is certainly true that certain techniques are more conducive to certain kinds of control. Refined control of the synthesis parameters is essential. The synthesis model must be elaborate to allow for such supple, not-too-repetitive time patterns in the sound itself.

However, it is often a hard problem or a tedious job to find interesting parameter values for these models. Hence it would be of great interest to develop automatic analysis procedures that could, starting with a given sound, identify the parameter values of a given sound model that yield a more or less faithful imitation of this sound. The problem was seen clearly by James Tenney in 1965. Tenney defined a model for sound synthesis involving both periodic and random amplitude and (slow) frequency modulation. He proposed the idea of "demodulation" of existing sounds to reveal the modulation parameters that would provide an imitation of these sounds.

Efforts continue in that direction, although few become practical realizations. I have already mentioned the Grey's efforts to develop programs that extract simplified harmonic envelopes for harmonic resynthesis. James Justice (1979) has worked toward a similar goal, as have Mian and Tisato (1984). It appears that Julius Smith is devising procedures to identify, from existing sounds, the parameters of his model based on traveling waveguides.

I shall mention here some attempts in this direction made in our laboratory in Marseille—even though this is work in progress, proposing processes that are far from being automatic yet.

Working on nonlinear distortion synthesis, Daniel Arfib (1979) has set up an elegant process to determine the distortion that will yield a given frequency spectrum for a certain value of the input amplitude of the distorted wave. (Distortion produces a spectrum that becomes richer when the input amplitude increases; hence this amplitude is often used as a timbre index, and the model then involves an amplitude compensation so that actual output amplitude can be decoupled from this index.) If the amplitude of the harmonics in the spectrum are $a1, a2, \ldots, ap$, the distorting function is simply the sum of the first $p$ Chebychev polynomials, respectively weighted by $a1, a2, \ldots, ap$. Patrick Sanchez has implemented a set of programs that perform various operations of sonic "microsurgery" on IBM PC–compatible computers. The programs make it easy to isolate a period in a waveform, to measure the Fourier spectrum by the first Fourier transform, and then to generate the distortion function producing that same spectrum. The problem is now to try to find an envelope for the timbre index that causes in the synthetic sound a spectral evolution not too different from that in the real sound. In general the solution cannot be very good because distortion with a given function varies in its own way with the timbre index, and it does not give all possible spectra. The identification has nevertheless been tried by taking as a criterion the *centroid*—the center of gravity of the spectrum. By choosing at each point a timbre index such that the synthetic spectrum centroid matches that of the real sound, one obtains data for an amplitude envelope. Sanchez has thus sometimes obtained interesting results, for example, synthetic sounds that mimic bass clarinet tones.

Sanchez has also implemented an original way to detect *formants*, assuming that the tones studied have a formant structure. (A formant is a peak in the spectrum that, for traditional instruments, usually corresponds to resonances in the instrument.) We see formants, for example, in bowed strings and in tones sung on a given vowel. Sanchez's method implies recording a chromatic scale (sung or played). The scale scanning reveals the formant structure by representing the spectra of the notes of the scale properly registered (figure 1.9). From such data Sanchez devises an inverse filter that will compensate for the formant structure. One can then restore a source spectrum, using the differences between the curves corresponding to the successive harmonics. This works well for synthetic sounds generated with a formant structure. With real sounds that possess this structure, one obtains some interesting results despite the irregularities in the playing or singing. Models of sound involving a source excitation and a resonance seem to have a real significance to the ear (Huggins 1952).

Concerning subtractive synthesis, Pierre Dutilleux has implemented "state variable" digital filters that have several desirable features. They can provide for very sharp (high Q) filtering, and their parameters can be varied dynamically. One can thus interpolate between various filters. Stability is preserved in the intermediary filters, which would be problematic with ordinary digital filters. The filters have been implemented on the SYTER audio processor, and the filtering characteristics can be changed in real time through the Musical Instrument Digital Interface (MIDI) protocol. These filters lend themselves to subtractive synthesis, and the parameters could be gathered from real sounds by obtaining the successive short-time spectra through the fast Fourier transform and setting the successive cor-

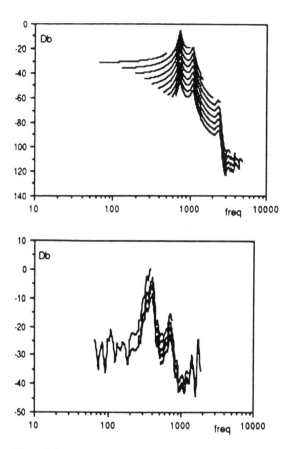

**Figure 1.9**
Spectral plots realized by Patrick Sanchez, obtained from chromatic scales of sounds with a
formant structure: The formants appear on the plots. The upper one corresponds to a test
signal, and the lower one corresponds to a singer singing the same vowel while going up the
scale.

responding filters. The prospects are very appealing from a musical stand-point, and I shall use this process for my piece *Electron-positron*.

In chapter 2 Richard Kronland-Martinet and Alex Grossmann speak at length about the wavelet transform. I mention it here, anticipating the next paragraph, because wavelet analysis with the Morlet waveform automatically gives data for additive resynthesis. The additive synthesis reconstruction is akin to the *phase vocoder* (Dolson 1986). The analysis yields functions that are the envelopes of the sinusoidal components. However, the components are no longer equally spaced in frequency but spaced at $\Delta f/f$ intervals, which can save data. This is the way Kronland-Martinet actually reconstructed most of his sounds analyzed through the wavelet technique—the genuine "granular" wavelet reconstruction was first realized by Frédéric Boyer.

Recently, on a suggestion by Bernard Escudié, Kronland-Martinet has implemented a method to extract *ridges* or *skeletons* from the wavelet transform. (For details, see chapter 2.) The idea is to approximate the integral of an oscillating function to the contributions of the portions with stationary phase. The method gives indications on the amplitude and frequency modulations imposed on a simple signal, as Nathalie Delprat could demonstrate by realizing some automatic frequency "demodulation" on specially designed synthetic signals. This technique seems promising, and it may help find from a signal the parameters of an elaborate FM model that would give approximations to that signal.

It must be stressed that this research is quite introductory. The issue of automatic parameter identification for specific sound models is important because the aim is to endow synthetic sounds with the richness existing in many natural sounds. But the problem is difficult, perhaps too difficult for certain synthesis models.

## Analysis-Synthesis Models

Fortunately it is possible to analyze sounds in terms of certain basic functions that are "complete" in the sense that a faithful reconstruction of the original waveform is possible from this analysis. (I do not mean here an imitation that sounds faithful to the ear. The criterion is now objective; it implies that the reconstructed wave is very close mathematically to the original wave). When one limits oneself to periodic functions, Fourier's theorem states that the analysis in terms of harmonic sinusoidal components is complete. Of course a perfect reconstruction requires that we sum an infinite number of terms, so that one can actually obtain only an approximate reconstruction; but it may be very close to the original, and the ear may be tolerant to minute differences. The ear has its idiosyncrasies, and it may be very touchy about some fine differences and indifferent to other apparently gross differences. In the case of periodic sounds, a change in the relative phase of the components is ignored by the ear, whereas it can completely modify the waveform. On the other hand the addition of a high-frequency component of small amplitude can go almost unnoticed when looking at the waveform, but not when listening to it!

The Fourier transform is a complete representation of a sound, which in some sense generalizes the Fourier series, with its amplitude and phase spectra. However, it is not a very useful one: for instance, it does not display the evolution in time of the sound, whereas the ear does follow it. The Fourier transform has been developed into a short-time Fourier spectrum. Time windows are imposed to limit the duration of the signal considered at a time; one then computes the Fourier spectrum of this limited signal. The sound spectrograph displays running short-time Fourier spectra. This representation of the frequency domain is very useful (figures 1.3, 1.8, and 1.10). It does not give enough information, though, to allow the reconstruction of the original wave.

The Walsh-Hadamard transform involves analysis in terms of square waves of different frequencies. It seems convenient from a purely computational standpoint. It is, however, generally grossly inadequate for sound because "it does not deteriorate gracefully," as Andy Moorer has put it. For instance, the approximation of a sine wave will stay jagged until a very high number of terms is used, and this will give to the corresponding sound a typical "unsinusoidal" and generally objectionable quality. The basic functions of the Walsh-Hadamard analysis do not sound elementary to the ear.

Indeed it is a paradox to try to express a sound with finite duration in terms of sounds with infinite duration, such as sine waves. A genuine sine wave—one that was always there in the past, that will always be there in the future—has a single Fourier component. But as soon as one limits this sine wave to a segment of time, the only way it can be considered the sum of functions that are nonzero on a boundless interval is by summing many of those functions such that they cancel each other out of this interval. (This can be conceived as starting with two beating sine waves and diminishing the frequency spacing.) So any departure from periodicity—including

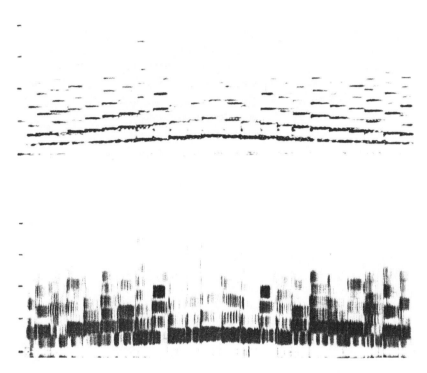

**Figure 1.10**
Two spectrograms of a rapid chromatic scale played on a piano and going up and down
one octave. The upper diagram corresponds to a bandwidth of 50 Hz: The individual
harmonics (or nearly harmonic components) can clearly be resolved. This is no longer the
case in the lower diagram, realized with the 300 Hz filter; but on this diagram, with a better
time resolution, one can count the beats. The frequency scale is linear; on the upper
diagram one can see that the harmonics are equally spaced, but that the octave between the
two lower components looks larger in the middle than on the left or on the right.

drastic temporal evolution—translates into the widening of spectral lines. This is rather impractical for synthesis.

As early as 1933 Szasz demonstrated the completeness of complex exponentials (sine waves with an exponential decaying envelope), which may have been used almost two centuries ago by Prony (Marple 1982, Laroche 1987). Around 1960 Dolansky and Huggins used decomposition in terms of exponentially decaying sine waves—each such function is a formant when one looks at it in the frequency domain. Around 1975 Rodet used similar functions—*formant-wave-functions*—to perform synthesis in an ingenious way. The program CHANT is based on those functions (Rodet, Potard, and Barriére 1984). There are data bases for CHANT synthesis that allow us to produce varied quasi-periodic and even noisy sounds, but until recently (d'Alessandro and Rodet 1989, Liénard 1987), it did not constitute an analysis-synthesis system.

At about the same time Andy Moorer applied *linear prediction* to musical purposes. This technique uses a model for synthesis with a quasi-periodic or noisy source exciting an evolving resonance given by a complex evolving recursive filter. Apart from details in the excitation, this is a fair model of actual speech production. The parameters for synthesis can be extracted from a given sound by optimizing the similarity of the signal and the predicted reconstruction (hence one often uses the name *predictive coding*). Thus predictive coding can be used as an analysis-synthesis model. Between the analysis and synthesis stages, the user can alter the parameters so as to perform intimate transformations. Moorer has taken advantage of the possibility to modify separately the parameters for the source and the resonance to change the rate of recorded speech, getting the famous Donald Duck effect (speeding up also moves the formants up). He has also realized an impressive piece of "concrete poetry," *Lions Are Growing*, where the originally recorded poem is submitted to a number of transformations, for instance, slowing down up to a factor of 27. Moorer has also performed cross-synthesis, which had first been realized with vocoders, by using the excitation data of one sound and the resonance data of another one. Recently cross-synthesis was implemented on a Synclavier synthesizer at Groupe de Musique Expérimentale de Marseille by Richard Kronland-Martinet, David Hagège, Jacques Diennet, and Jérôme Decque.

I used cross-synthesis in my piece *Sud*, realized at the studios of the Groupe de Recherches Musicales in Paris in 1985, using linear prediction programs implemented by Benedict Mailliard. I thus hybridized sounds of pianos and metal chimes, cellos and birds, harpsichords and sea waves. My musical incentive was partly to try to evoke chimeras, but mostly to imprint onto certain recognizable sound textures energy contours and fluxes issued from other types of sound (for example, to suggest waves of harpsichords).

Actually, in that piece the energy flux of the initial sea wave sounds permeates various aspects of the composition. In the piece the natural sounds, initially very different, tend to gradually merge with the synthetic sound. I tried to achieve this in several ways—through conventional mixing of course, but in a more unusual way, which I might call *subtractive cross-synthesis*. Although many natural sounds (the sea, the wind) have a continuous frequency spectrum, I used synthetic harmonic arpeggios and scales with sharply defined pitches (in particular a major-minor scale, G, B, E, F-sharp, G-sharp, B, E, F-natural, G-natural, B, E, F-sharp, G-sharp ...). Then I used resonant filters tuned to these pitches to filter natural sounds. If the resonance is damped, it just colors the original sounds, which retain much of their identity. If the filters are sharply tuned and thus resonant, one gets the feeling of a harp tuned to those pitches and set into vibration by the sounds, which only leave the trace of their energy flux. Thus, in the third movement, there is a "bird's raga": the bird's song is sharply filtered, and only the pitches of the scale—the raga—remain, with rhythms and with quantized frequency contours originating from the bird's song. I also used such resonant filters, implemented by Daniel Arfib in the Music V program, to filter Michel Portal's clarinet in my composition *Attracteurs Etranges*, realized in Marseille in 1988.

Linear prediction synthesis parameters provide an encoding scheme that is usually more economical than the original unencoded waveform. Linear predictive coding (LPC) was used in the first commercial speaking machines, such as the Texas Instruments "Speak and Spell" toy for children. However, LPC is really manageable as an analysis-synthesis system only insofar as the sound to be analyzed is appropriate to the specific model embodied—which is the case for speech and various other types of quasi-periodic sounds. Otherwise LPC analysis leads to an information explosion. Similarly the phase vocoder (Moorer 1978, Dolson 1986) lets us resynthesize and alter the time-scale for quasi-periodic tones, but it takes quite a bit of computation.

Around 1946 Gabor wrote several landmark articles in which he criticized the conventional representation of signals as continuous functions of time. He proposed to represent signals as a function of both time and frequency.

Considering the finite information present in actual signals, he divided this "information plane" into *cells*. Each signal can be represented in many ways; he proposed to consider them as the sum of what are now often called *Gabor grains*, that is, bell-like Gaussian curves modulated in amplitude by sinusoids. Bacry, Grossmann, and Zak (1975) and Bastiaans (1980) have proved that this expansion is complete, permitting faithful reconstruction. Iannis Xenakis (1971) had been inspired by Gabor to compose music in terms of grains of sound, and he made some suggestions to use those grains for computer sound synthesis. Although his proposals seemed to be problematic (Smith 1973), they motivated Roads (1978; see also chapter 5) and later Truax (1988) to perform granular synthesis of sound by digital computer. This was not analysis-synthesis, though.

Daniel Arfib (chaper 3) was probably the first to program a computer to perform analysis-synthesis in terms of the Gabor grains. The reconstruction is quasi-perfect, and it also lends itself to intimate modifications. For instance, by increasing the grain separations (and speeding the phase rotation, as he explains), he can slow down a speech utterance without transposition—which he did up to a factor of 128. I took advantage of these developments in *Attracteurs Etranges*. The clarinetist Michel Portal (also a brilliant jazzman and composer) recorded a number of prewritten musical phrases and sound effects. Some recorded segments were transformed in various ways—complex editing; spatialization, filtering, and mixing through our augmented version of Music V (written by Daniel Arfib for IBM PC-compatible computers); and adding echoes, spatialization, and harmonization (implemented by Pierre Dutilleux on the SYTER real-time audio processor). But I also used in a number of places recorded phrases speeded up or slowed down using Arfib's technique with Gabor grains.

The wavelet transform seems to hold considerable promise as an analysis-synthesis process (Combes, Grossmann, and Tchamitchian 1989). Kronland-Martinet and Grossmann (chapter 2) give many details about the method, which was introduced by Morlet and formalized by Grossmann. Originally the wavelet transform looked like a derivation of the Gabor method, but a very significant one that offered better numerical convergence and stability. Moreover the formalism of the method is still valid with a variety of basic wavelets that must only fill certain acceptability conditions, but that do not look at all like Gabor grains. The method goes beyond sound signals and time-frequency representation. It truly provides a time-scale representation, and the nontime axis can correspond to a logarithmic frequency scale, if a Gabor-Morlet type grain is used, but to different notions as well.

In Marseille Kronland-Martinet, in collaboration with Grossmann, has taken advantage of the speed of the SYTER audio processor to undertake a broad scientific exploration of the wavelet transform. This has left little time to develop specific musical applications. The analyses, however, were quite revealing—discontinuities are very obvious on the phase spectrum. Also the analysis can be changed in many ways to meet different needs. Kronland-Martinet has realized several interesting musical transformations, for instance, one akin to wave dispersion. So did Frédéric Boyer, who performed granular wavelet resynthesis with many channels (whereas the reconstruction can work well with only one channel per octave, provided the bandwidth of the analyzing wavelet is over one octave). For instance, using twelve channels per octave, Boyer has performed analysis-synthesis of the spoken voice. For the resynthesis he dropped many channels, keeping only those forming, for instance, a perfect chord (or a diminished seventh chord, or whatever), thus giving the strange impression of a voice with a specific musical chord in the vocal cords!

Redundancy exists within a wavelet transform, so that by performing an arbitrary modification on the parameters derived from wavelet analysis, one obtains what may well not be the legitimate wavelet analysis of any wave. Such arbitrary modifications may or may not generate artifacts that are musically interesting, but one should be aware of them. This is made clearer with the notion of *reproducing kernel*, explained by Arfib (chapter 3) as well as Kronland-Martinet and Grossmann (chapter 2).

## Generality and Specificity: Representation as a Compositional Tool

In principle all analysis-synthesis methods should give the same final result, that is, a perfect reconstruction. But perfect reconstruction is no more than a recording, unless one takes advantage of analysis-synthesis in other ways.

The analysis should be useful; it should display a representation so that important events become obvious. What does important mean here? It is all a function of the task at hand.

One may want a representation that emphasizes whatever stands out for the ear. In this case frequency-versus-time or log frequency-versus-time displays are meaningful because hearing has the capability to perform running frequency analyses. Although I cannot go into great detail on this here, auditory perception is an extremely elaborate and specific process, which has evolved so as to take advantage of the properties of sound waves to extract information about the changes in the environment (Gibson 1966, Kubovy and Pomerantz 1981, McAdams and Bregman 1979, Risset 1973, 1988). For instance, the ear performs a preliminary frequency analysis, which helps it cope with sounds emitted simultaneously by different sources. A complex sorting of the frequency components is performed by the brain. Those that are in harmonic relation tend to fuse, unless they undergo asynchronous modulations. Sounds in time succession are also processed in intricate ways, and the auditory input is "segregated" into several "streams," which are tentatively assigned to different sources. Subjective scales tend to correspond grossly to logarithms of the corresponding physical variable. For instance, a loudness progression in decibels seems relatively regular. This permits the ear to embrace a larger dynamics. Similarly a musical interval correspond to a fixed frequency ratio (2/1 for an octave).

It would thus seem that a log frequency representation would be more adequate— as in musical scores. On such a representation, however, the fact that certain components are in harmonic relation is not evident. It is not clear either that one must use a frequency channel bandwidth approximating the critical band, for example, the spectral resolution of the ear, which is roughly a third octave above 800 Hz (Carterette and Friedman 1978). For instance, speech researchers tend to use spectrograms with a wide channel bandwidth (300 Hz), which does not resolve the individual harmonics, but which makes formants stand out. For music displays a narrow bandwidth—30 to 50 Hz—is usually recommended, despite the imprecision in time entailed (figure 1.10).

Alternatively one might also want the analysis to reveal aspects that are perhaps not the most obvious to the ear. Then the representation must be selected accordingly. Frequency-domain representations traditionally are used to predict the effect of a transmission system characterized by amplitude-versus-frequency response curves. One may want the representation to stress flaws or information-bearing elements. For instance, the phase display of the wavelet transform strongly emphasizes discontinuities in the wave or its derivatives. This could be useful to automatically detect scratches in old recordings. Kronland-Martinet has shown that one can take advantage of a wavelet with a specific structure—for instance, that of a musical interval; then the amplitude display of the analysis with this basic wavelet will emphasize occurrences of this musical interval.

For certain types of sounds one can find compact and useful representations that would not work for other sounds. For instance, quasi-periodic sounds can be represented by the amplitude evolution of quasi-harmonics. This can be used to perform reconstructions and intimate transformations. In this case it would be useless to keep continuous spectra. However, such a simplified model may have to be qualified by introducing, for instance, a burst of noise at the onset of the tone, as figure 1.3 would suggest. It may be better to abandon generality here for models that can be quite specific and ad hoc.

When one thinks of using analysis-synthesis for intimate transformations of sound, it should be clear that each analysis-synthesis process can perform certain things more easily than it can others. Even though the Morlet wavelet analysis seems to compact information in a way that is well suited to the characteristics of hearing, it does not work as easily as the use of Gabor grains for altering independently frequency and speed. Hence the value of this or that method is contingent on the musical purpose. Indeed to realize various types of intimate sonic modification, one have may have to go out of the general framework and resort to more specific models. For example, it is of great musical interest to merge synthetic sounds with sounds derived from natural sounds. That is, we want to be able to merge the specific sound synthesis model approach, which opens a certain domain of flexible variations, with a more or less general analysis-synthesis approach, which brings more immediate results, but which has more rigid constraints.

As Barry Truax wisely said, generality is at the expense of strength. Special-purpose tools designed for a particular task are usually more efficient than general-purpose tools applied to the same task. This also applies to criteria such as computing efficiency and compactness of coding. It is true that, for instance, the wavelet transform does not create an information explosion as linear predictive coding does. But it brings no information reduction either, at least not until one can take advantage of specifics: the purpose at hand, the particular structure of the sounds processed, and the tolerance of aural perception for this or that simplification. To attain the ultimate degree of information reduction, one has to know clearly in what context the information dropped is really irrelevant.

This is important when one tries to design special-purpose hardware to speed up digital sound processing: Compromises have to be made for ease of use, efficiency, and economy. These compromises are limitations that are really valid only in certain contexts: Their implications should be clear and explicit. A few years ago commercial digital synthesizers were limited to the pitches of the tempered scale. Technological progress and commercial logic should not entail musical regression. When musical systems are made too user friendly, too easy to use, they usually restrict the possibilities to a menu of operations that may severely hinder creativity. Composers must involve themselves in all the aspects that they want to really control in their music. As a complement to ready-made hardware, the flexibility of software remains precious to preserve boundless possibilities. It is important to be specific, but the musician must be able to decide which specificity.

Representations of musical signals have played and will continue to play a great role in transmitting know-how, so that experience can accumulate. Just as the composition student analyzes scores, the composer who wants to control sound structure can now look at graphics. The input for a synthesis program can be a genuine score of the sound structure, containing all the desirable information and permitting the replication of the sounds.

Specific representations of musical signals can suggest new types of musical operations. Here the purpose of representations is to stimulate invention. The notation does not have to be accurate or complete but rather suggestive, stimulating, or heuristic. Indeed this discussion could be extended beyond isolated sounds. David Wessel's (1979) representation of timbral space can be inspirational to the composer. Also it will become gradually easier to benefit from the combinatorial power of the computer and from the possibilities of advanced programming languages—object-oriented languages or logic programming. Proper representations within this framework may considerably extend the musical role of structural notation.

In any case, for some time to come it will remain a difficult challenge to design effective digital music systems. For the goal is not only to make good sounds but to provide composers with the possibility of various levels on which they can act and react, choosing their own representations, shaping their own special tools of analysis and synthesis, to explore or invent their own territory and build their own sonic architectures.

## Bibliography

Adrien, J., and X. Rodet. 1985. "Physical models of instruments, a modular approach: application to strings." In B. Truax ed. *Proceedings of the 1985 International Computer Music Conference.* San Francisco: Computer Music Association, pp. 85–89.

d'Alessandro, C., and X. Rodet 1989. "Synthèse et analyse-synthèse par fonctions d'ondes formantiques." *Journal d'Acoustique* 2: 163–169.

Allen, J. B., and L. R. Rabiner 1977. "A unified approach to short-time Fourier analysis and synthesis." *Proceedings of the IEEE* 65: 1558–1564.

Alles, H., and G. DiGiugno. 1977. "The 4B: a one-card 64 channel digital synthesizer." *Computer Music Journal* 1(4): 7–9. Reprinted in C. Roads and J. Strawn, eds. 1985. *Foundations of Computer Music*. Cambridge, Massachusetts: MIT Press, pp. 250–256.

Arfib, D. 1979. "Digital synthesis of complex spectra by means of multiplication of non-linear distorted sine waves." *Journal of the Audio Engineering Society* 27: 757–768.

Bacry, A., A. Grossmann, and J. Zak. 1975. "Proof of the completeness of lattice states in the $kq$-representation." *Physical Review* B12: 1118.

Barrière, J.-B., Y. Potard, and P. F. Baisnée. 1985. "Models of continuity between synthesis and processing for the elaboration and control of timbre structure." In B. Truax, ed. *Proceedings of the 1985 International Computer Music Conference*. San Francisco: Computer Music Association, pp. 193–198.

Bastiaans, M. 1980. "Gabor's expansion of a signal into gaussian elementary signals." *Proceedings of the IEEE* 68: 538–539.

Battier, M., and B. Truax, eds. 1980. *Computer Music*. UNESCO report, Canadian Commission for UNESCO.

Cadoz, C., A. Luciani, and J. Florens. 1984. "Responsive input devices and sound synthesis by simulation of instrumental mechanisms: the Cordis system." *Computer Music Journal* 8(3): 60–73. Reprinted in C. Roads, ed. 1989. *The Music Machine*. Cambridge, Massachusetts: MIT Press, pp. 495–508.

Campanella, S., and G. S. Robinson. 1971. "A comparison of orthogonal transformations for digital speech processing." *IEEE Transactions on Communication Technology* COM-19: 1045–1050.

Carterette, E., and M. P. Friedman, 1978. *Handbook of Perception, Vol. IV: Hearing*. Orlando: Academic Press.

Chamberlin, H. 1980. *Musical Applications of Microprocessors*. Rochelle Park: Hayden Book Company.

Charbonneau, G. 1981. "Timbre and perceptual effect of three types of data reduction." *Computer Music Journal* 5(2): 10–19.

Chouinard, L., L. N. Bélanger, and H. T. Huynh. 1985. "A computer-based harmonic analysis additive/synthesis system." In B. Truax, ed. *Proceedings of the 1985 International Computer Music Conference*. San Francisco: Computer Music Association.

Chowning, J. 1973. "The synthesis of complex audio spectra by means of frequency modulation." *Journal of the audio Engineering Society* 21: 526–534. Reprinted in C. Roads and J. Strawn, eds. 1985. *Foundations of Computer Music*. Cambridge, Massachusetts: MIT Press, pp. 6–29.

Chowning, J. 1980. "The synthesis of the singing voice." In J. Sundberg. ed. *Sound Generation in Winds, Strings, Computers*. Stockholm: Royal Swedish Academy of Music.

Chowning, J., and D. Bristow. 1986. *FM Theory and Applications*. Tokyo: Yamaha Music Foundation.

Cogan, R. 1984. *New Images of Musical Sound*. Harvard University Press.

Combes, J., A. Grossmann, and P. Tchamitchian, eds. 1989. *Wavelets: Time-frequency Methods and Phase Space*. New York: Springer-Verlag.

De Poli, G. 1983. "A tutorial on sound synthesis techniques." *Computer Music Journal* 7(4): 8–26. Reprinted in C. Roads, ed. 1989. *The Music Machine.* Cambridge, Massachusetts: MIT Press, pp. 429–448.

Deutsch, D. ed. 1982. *The Psychology of Music.* Orlando: Academic Press.

DiGiugno, G., and J. Kott. 1981. "Présentation du système 4X." *IRCAM Report Number 32.* IRCAM: Paris.

Dodge, C., and T. A. Jerse. 1985. *Computer Music: Synthesis, Composition and Performance.* New York: Schirmer.

Dolansky, L. 1959. "A novel method of speech-sounds analysis and synthesis." Ph.D. dissertation. Cambridge, Massachusetts: Department of Applied Mathematics, Harvard University. See also *IRE Transactions on Audio* AU-8(6): 221, 1960.

Dolson, M. 1986. "The phase vocoder: a tutorial. *Computer Music Journal* 10(4): 14–27.

Fano, R. 1950. "Short-time autocorrelation functions and power spectra." *Journal of the Acoustical Society of America* 22: 546–550.

Flanagan, J. L. 1972. *Speech Analysis, Synthesis and Perception.* New York: Springer-Verlag.

Gabor, D. 1946. "Theory of communication." *Journal of the IEE* 93: 429–457.

Gabor, D. 1947. "Acoustical quanta and the theory of hearing." *Nature* 159: 303.

Gabor, D. 1947. "New possibilities in speech transmission." *Journal of the IEE* 94: 369–387.

Gabor, D. 1948. "Recherches sur quelques problèmes de télécommunications et d'acoustique." *L'Onde Electrique* 28: 433–439.

Gabor, D. 1951. "La théorie des communications et la physique." In L. de Broglie, ed. *La cybernétique–théorie du signal et de l'information.* Paris: Editions de la revue d'optique, pp. 114–149. (See also articles by Aigrain, Blanc-Lapierre, Fortet, Marcou, and Ville in the same volume.)

Gibson, J. J. 1966. *The Senses Considered as Perceptual Systems.* Boston: Houghton Mifflin.

Grey, J. 1975. "An exploration of musical timbre." Report STAN-M-2. Stanford: Stanford University Department of Music.

Grey, J., and J. A. Moorer. 1977. "Perceptual evaluation of synthesized musical instrument tones." *Journal of the Acoustical Society of America* 62: 454–462.

Grossman, A., and J. Morlet 1984. "Decomposition of Hardy functions into square integrable wavelets of constant shape." *SIAM Journal of Mathematical Analysis* 15: 723–736.

Grossman, A., R. Kronland-Martinet, and J. Morlet. 1987. "Analysis of sound patterns through wavelet transforms." *International Journal of Pattern Recognition and Artificial Intelligence* 1(2).

Grossman, A., and R. Kronland-Martinet. 1988. "Time-and-scale representations obtained through continuous wavelet transforms." *Signal Processing IV: Theories and Applications.* Amsterdam: Elsevier Science Publishers.

Hiller, L., and P. Ruiz. 1971. "Synthesizing sound by solving the wave equation for vibrating objects." *Journal of the Audio Engineering Society* 19: 463–470.

Howe, H. S., Jr. 1975. *Electronic Music Synthesis.* New York: Norton.

Huggins, W. 1952. "A phase principle for complex frequency analysis and its implications in auditory theory." *Journal of the Acoustical Society of America* 24: 582–589.

Huggins, W. 1957. "Representation and analysis of signals. Part 1: the use of orthogonalized exponentials." John Hopkins University Report AFCRC TR-57 357. Baltimore: Johns Hopkins University.

Huggins, W. 1956. "Signal theory." *IRE Transactions on Circuit Theory* CT 3(4): 210.

Hartmann, W. 1985. "The frequency-domain grating." *Journal of the Acoustical Society of America* 78: 1421–1425.

Justice, J. 1979. "Analytic signal processing in music computation." *IEEE Transactions on Acoustics, Speech, and Signal Proceeding* ASSP-27: 670–684.

LeBrun, M. 1979. "Digital waveshaping synthesis." *Journal of the Audio Engineering Society* 27: 250–266.

Koenig, W., H. K. Dunn, and L. Y. Lacey. 1946. "The sound spectrograph." *Journal of the Acoustical Society of America* 18: 19–49.

Kronland-Martinet, R. 1989. "Analyse, synthèse et modification de signaux sonores: application de la transformée en ondelettes." Marseille: Thèse d'Etat de l'Université d'Aix-Marseille II.

Kronland-Martinet, R., J. Morlet and A. Grosmann. 1987. Analysis of sound patterns through wavelet transforms." *International Journal of Pattern Recognition and Artificial Intelligence* 1: 273–302.

Kubovy, M., and J. R. Pomerantz, ed. 1981. *Perceptual Organization*. Hillsdale: Erlbaum.

Lansky, P., and K. Steiglitz 1981. "Synthesis of timbral families by warped linear prediction." *Computer Music Journal* 5(3): 45–49. Reprinted in C. Roads, ed. 1989. *The Music Machine*. Cambridge, Massachusetts: MIT Press, pp. 531–536.

Laroche, J. 1987. "Etude d'un système d'analyse-synthèse utilisant la méthode de Prony. Application aux instruments de musique de type percussif." Rapport ENST. Paris: ENST.

Lawson, J., and M. V. Mathews. 1977. "Computer program to control a digital real-time synthesizer." *Computer Music Journal* 1(4): 16–21.

Liénard, J. 1987. "Speech analysis and reconstruction using short-time, elementary waveforms." In *Proceedings of the International Conference on Acoustics, Speech, and Signal Processing*. New York: IEEE.

Leipp, E. 1971/1984. *Acoustique et Musique*. Paris: Masson.

Loy, G. 1985. "Musicians make a standard: the MIDI phenomenon." *Computer Music Journal* 9(4): 8–26. Reprinted in C. Roads. 1989. *The Music Machine*. Cambridge, Massachusetts: MIT Press, pp. 181–198.

Marple, S. 1982. "Spectral time analysis via a fast Prony algorithm. *Proceedings of the IEEE* 70: 1375–1378.

Mathews, M. V. 1969. *The Technology of Computer Music*. Cambridge, Massachusetts: MIT Press.

Mathews, M., and J. Kohut 1973. "Electronic simulation of violin resonances." *Journal of the Acoustical Society of America* 53: 1620–1626.

Mathews, M., and J. R. Pierce, ed. 1989. *Current Directions in Computer Music Research*. Cambridge, Massachusetts: MIT Press.

McAdams, S., and A. S. Bregman 1979. "Hearing musical streams. *Computer Music Journal* 3(4): 26–43, 60, 63. Reprinted in C. Roads and J. Strawn, ed. 1985. *Foundations of Computer Music*. Cambridge, Massachusetts: MIT Press, pp. 658–698.

Mian, A., and G. Tisato. 1984. "Sound structuring techniques using parameters derived from a voice analysis/synthesis system." In D. Wessel, ed. 1984. *Proceedings of the 1984 International Music Conference*. San Francisco: Computer Music Association.

Meyer, E., and G. Buchmann. 1931. *Die klangspektren der Musikinstrumente*. Berlin.

Moorer, J. A. 1977. "Signal processing aspects of computer music: a survey." *Proceedings of the IEEE* 65: 1108–1137. Reprinted in J. Strawn, ed. 1985. *Digital Audio Signal Processing: An Anthology*. Madison: A-R Editions.

Moorer, J. A. 1978. "The use of the phase vocoder in computer music applications." *Journal of the Audio Engineering Society* 26: 42–45.

Moorer, J. A. 1979. "About this reverberation business." *Computer Music Journal* 3(2): 13–28. Reprinted in C. Roads and J. Strawn, eds. 1985. *Foundations of Computer Music*. Cambridge, Massachusetts: MIT Press, pp. 605–639.

Moorer, J. A., and J. M. Grey 1977. "Lexicon of analyzed tons. Part I: a violin tone." *Computer Music Journal* 1(2): 39–45. "Part II: clarinet and oboe tones." *Computer Music Journal* 1(3): 12–29.

Morrill, D. 1977. "Trumpet algorithms for music composition." *Computer Music Journal* 1(1): 46–52. Reprinted in C. Roads and J. Strawn, eds. 1985. *Foundations of Computer Music*. Cambridge, Massachusetts: MIT Press, pp. 30–44.

Morrill, D. forthcoming. *The Little Book of Computer Music Instruments*. Madison: A-R Editions.

Oppenheim, A. 1969. "Speech analysis-synthesis system based on homomorphic filtering. *Journal of the Acoustical Society of America* 45.

Petersen, T. 1976. "Analysis-synthesis as a tool for creating new families of sound." Preprint 1104 (D-3). *54th Convention of the Audio Engineering Society*. New York: Audio Engineering Society.

Paley, R., and N. Wiener. 1934. *Fourier Transforms in the Complex Domain*. Publications 19. New York: American Mathematical Society Colloquium.

Pierce, J. R. 1983. *The Science of Musical Sound*. New York: Scientific American Library, Freeman (with disks of sound examples).

Risset, J.-C. 1966. "Computer study of trumpet tones (with sound examples)." Bell Laboratories Report. Murray Hill: Bell Laboratories.

Risset, J.-C. 1969. "An introductory catalog of computer synthesized sounds (with sound examples)." Bell Laboratories Report. Murray Hill: Bell Laboratories.

Risset, J.-C. 1973. "Sons." *Encyclopedia Universalis* 13: 168–171.

Risset, J.-C. 1978. "Paradoxes de hauteur." IRCAM Report 10. (Includes cassette of sound examples.) Paris: IRCAM.

Risset, J.-C. 1985. "Computer music experiments 1964–...." *Computer Music Journal* 9(1): 11–18. Reprinted in C. Roads, ed. 1989. *The Music Machine*. Cambridge, Massachusetts: MIT Press, 67–74.

Risset, J.-C. 1986. "Musical sound models for digital synthesis." *Proceedings of the International Conference on Acoustics, Speech, and Signal Processing*. New York: IEEE. pp. 1269–1271.

Risset, J.-C. 1986. "Pitch and rhythm paradoxes: Comments on 'Auditory paradox based on a fractal waveform'." *Journal of the Acoustical Society of America* 80: 961–962.

Risset, J.-C. 1988. "Perception, environnement, musiques." *Inharmoniques* 3: 10–42.

Risset, J.-C. 1989. "Additive synthesis of inharmonic tones." In M. Mathews and J. R. Pierce. 1989. *Current Directions in Computer Music Research*. Cambridge, Massachusetts: MIT Press, pp. 159–164.

Risset, J.-C., and M. V. Mathews. 1969. "Analysis of instrument tones." *Physics Today* 22(2): 23–30.

Risset, J.-C., and D. L. Wessel. 1982. "Exploration of timbre by analysis and synthesis." In D. Deutsch, ed. *The Psychology of Music*. Orlando: Academic, pp. 25–58.

Roads, C. 1978. "Automated granular synthesis of sound." *Computer Music Journal* 2(2): 61–62. Revised version published as "Granular synthesis of sound" in C. Roads and J. Strawn, eds. 1985. *Foundations of Computer Music*. Cambridge, Massachusetts: MIT Press, pp. 145–159.

Roads, C. ed. 1985. *Composers and the Computer*. Madison: A-R Editions.

Roads, C. ed. 1989. *The Music Machine*. Cambridge, Massachusetts: MIT Press.

Roads, C., and J. Strawn, eds. 1985. *Foundations of Computer Music*. Cambridge, Massachusetts: MIT Press.

Rodet, X., and Y. Cointe. 1984. "FORMES: composition and scheduling of processes." *Computer Music Journal* 8(3): 32–50. Reprinted in C. Roads, ed. 1989. *The Music Machine*. Cambridge, Massachusetts: MIT Press, pp. 405–423.

Rodet, X., Y. Potard, and J. B. Barrière. 1984. "The CHANT Project: from the synthesis of the singing voice to synthesis in general." *Computer Music Journal* 8(3): 15–31. Reprinted in C. Roads, ed. 1989. *The Music Machine*. Cambridge, Massachusetts: MIT Press, pp. 449–466.

Schaeffer, P. 1966. *Traité des objets musicaux*. Paris: Editions du Seuil.

Schottstaedt, W. 1977. "The simulation of natural instrument tones using frequency modulation with a complex modulating wave." *Computer Music Journal* 1(4): 46–50. Reprinted in C. Roads and J. Strawn, eds. 1985. *Foundations of Computer Music*. Cambridge, Massachusetts: MIT Press, pp. 54–64.

Schottstaedt, W. 1983. "Pla: a composer's idea of a language." *Computer Music Journal* 7(1): 11–20. Reprinted in C. Roads, ed. 1989. *The Music Machine*. Cambridge, Massachusetts: MIT Press, pp. 285–294.

Schroeder, M., and B. S. Atal. 1962. "Generalized short-time power spectra and autocorrelation functions." *Journal of the Acoustical Society of America* 34: 1679–1683.

Smith, S. 1973. *Perspectives of New Music* Fall 1972/Spring 1973: 269–277.

Stapleton, J., and S. C. Bass. 1988. "Synthesis of musical tones based on the Karhunen-Loève transform." *IEEE Transactions on Acoustics, Speech, and Signal Processing* ASSP-36: 305–319.

Strawn, J., ed. 1985. *Digital Audio Signal Processing: An Anthology*. Madison: A-R Editions.

Tenney, J. 1965. "The physical correlates of timbre." *Gravesaner Blätter* 26: 106–109.

Truax, B. 1988. "Real-time granular synthesis with a digital signal processing computer." *Computer Music Journal* 12(2): 14–26.

Vidolin, A. ed. 1980. *Musica e Elaboratore*. Venice: Biennale di Venezia.

Vidolin, A., and R. Doati. 1986. *Nuova Atlantide: il continente della musica elettronica*. Venice: Biennale di Venezia (with two cassettes of musical works).

Ville, J. 1948. "Théorie et applications de la notion de signal analytique." *Câbles et transmissions* 61: 74.

Weinreich, G. 1981. "Synthesis of piano tones from first principles." *Journal of the Acoustical Society of America* 69: 588.

Wessel, D. 1979. "Timbre space as a musical control structure." *Computer Music Journal* 3(2): 45–52. Reprinted in C. Roads and J. Strawn, eds. 1985. *Foundations of Computer Music*. Cambridge, Massachusetts: MIT Press, pp. 640–657.

Wessel, D., and J. C. Risset. 1979. "Les illusions auditives." *Universalia* (*Encyclopedia Universalis*) pp. 167–171.

Xenakis, I 1971. *Formalized Music*. Bloomington: Indiana University Press.

## Discography

*L'IRCAM: un portrait*. IRCAM 0001, Paris.

M. Mathews, J. R. Pierce, J.-C. Risset, W. Slawson, J. Tenney. *Music from Mathematics*. Decca DL710180.

E. Ghent, J. Olive, T. Petersen, J.-C. Risset, D. Wessel. *New Directions in Music*. Tulsa Studios, Tulsa, Oklahoma.

S. Korde, C. Lippe. D. Mabry, J.-C. Risset, A. Rubin, G. Scelsi, I. Xenakis. *Neuma New Music Series, Volume 1*. Neuma CD-450-71.

J.-C. Risset. *Sud, Mutations, Dialogues, Inharmonique*. INA C003.

J.-C. Risset. *Songes, Passages, Little Boy, Sud*. Wergo 2013-50.

J.-C. Risset. *Moment Newtonien numero 3*. In *Mille et un poèmes*. Planète 1.

# 2 Application of Time-Frequency and Time-Scale Methods (Wavelet Transforms) to the Analysis, Synthesis, and Transformation of Natural Sounds

## Richard Kronland-Martinet and Alex Grossmann

One of the critical problems in the use of digital synthesis of sound, whether in real time or deffered time, is the establishment of a correspondence between synthetic and natural sounds. Since 1957 the digital synthesis of sound has been successfully used in the domains of speech and music; it became clear, however, that one of the main problems would be to relate it with natural sound. The first synthetic sounds were obtained with calculations of samples given by simple mathematical models without direct reference to real sounds. However, it is musically interesting to be able to synthesize sounds that imitate or refer to natural sounds. These sounds would have the richness and distinctiveness of natural sounds and could still be manipulated as is done in all systems of synthesis.

To approach such a problem, it is necessary to bring two complementary aspects into play: the *analysis* and the *resynthesis* of signals (natural sound waves). This leads to the setting up of relationships between the physical (or psychoacoustic) parameters extracted from the analysis and the parameters of synthesis corresponding to a mathematical algorithm.

The analysis aspect should take into account significant parameters such as frequency, time envelopes, microvariations (accidental noise, random or regular modulations), and the distribution of partials. But it should also encompass *data reduction* resulting from the characteristics of auditory perception. For instance, the subjective notion of timbre cannot be always modeled with the help of the Fourier transform of the signal only. In the case of instruments with formants, it is useful to separate the contributions of the *resonances* of the physical system (the modes of the piano, resonant modes of the voice, and so on) from the effects of the system of *excitation* (the struck or plucked string, vibrating vocal chords, and the like).

The synthesis aspect consists of the creation of digitally and musically efficient algorithms. However, the parameters that determine the production of sound only rarely come from existing natural sounds. There are, however, cases where synthesis gives convincing results (for example, with trumpet or voice). Some methods, such as additive or subtractive synthesis, frequency modulation, or waveshaping can give adequate results, particularly if they are completed by adding microvariations or combined with other methods.

The work we present is an approach to the problem of extracting parameters for synthesis and sound modification based on the use of analysis and synthesis methods that combine time and frequency information. In this framework we deal with digital synthesis and analysis of signals by parametric and nonparametric methods. We stress in particular the exploration of acoustic applications of a new method of signal decomposition, the *wavelet transform*. This method, which is strictly speaking "time-scale" rather than "time-frequency," has turned out to be very fruitful, especially in the area of analysis-synthesis.

When one speaks of analysis, one thinks in general about a mathematical representation—as faithful as possible—of a physical phenomenon described in mathematical form. The parameters appearing in the representation must consequently be related in a straightforward way to physical parameters that represent the real world. In the case of audible signals, the "real world" is not limited to the phenomena of sound production and propagation but includes also a biological captor of the greatest importance: our ear. Although many studies in psychoacoustics have contributed to our understanding of the auditory system, it is nevertheless true that the only criterion for deciding on the auditory relevance of a physical parameter is still the ear. Using this criterion, Jean-Claude Risset has developed a powerful technique, *analysis by synthesis*, which consists of refining and characterizing the parameters of a method of synthesis on the basis of its psychoacoustical effect. These results have been quite conclusive, especially in the analysis of the timbre of the trumpet, pointing out the importance of the temporal aspect associated with the evolution of the spectral components.

Methods of digital synthesis attempt to simulate the sometimes rapid evolutions of sound through the manipulation of parameters that should—if possible—have psychoacoustical relevance. Relating those parameters to parameters coming out of analysis requires time-frequency analysis methods, so that the time evolutions of spectral properties of the analyzed signal can be described.

Time-frequency methods can be divided into two types: parametric methods and nonparametric methods.

Methods of the first kind consist of the determination of parameters in a specific model of sound production. Therefore they require some a priori knowledge about the signal being analyzed. In this chapter we are mostly concerned with "blind" analysis and so with nonparametric methods, supplemented when necessary by parametric methods after a "precharacterization" phase. However, in some situations (signals with formants) parametric methods are very useful. This will be illustrated by the example of cross-synthesis of two natural sounds. In cross-synthesis the characteristics of one source sound are used to drive a system whose response is based on another source sound.

## An Example of Parametric Analysis: Linear Prediction

Generally speaking, digital analysis and synthesis of natural sound signals requires the determination of a certain number of physical parameters. It is important to be able to isolate the ones that are most significant or relevant from an auditory point of view. When analyzing a natural sound, one is often led to distinguish between the contribution of the source of excitation and the contribution of the mechanical resonance of the system, which can be modeled by means of a filter. Both aspects are almost always present, but there are situations where the separation between excitation and resonance is not clear-cut. This is the case, for instance, in some percussive systems. Nevertheless in many cases one hopes to find a model of resynthesis by designing a digital filter, starting from a knowledge of the physics of the system that produces or analyzes the sound (figure 2.1).

If $s(t)$ is a real signal (the natural sound wave), then this model is described by a convolution,

$$s(t) = (e * r)(t) = \int e(u)r(t - u)\, du,$$

where $e(t)$ is the excitation or "source" signal, and $r(t)$ is the impulse response of the filter, taking into account propagation within the structure.

This model is then fully characterized by its *impulse response $r(t)$*.

In most cases the impulse response may be considered as fixed, for example, in "rigid" instruments. However, there exist signals that are produced by varying systems. Such signals give rise to time-varying filters (speech).

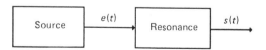

**Figure 2.1**
Schematic view of physical model synthesis. A source component generates an excitation signal $e(t)$ that is processed by a resonator to create the output signal $s(t)$.

In what follows we discuss this latter kind of signal and show how to apply automatic techniques for identification of the characteristics of time-varying filters and for resynthesis of signals.

We limit ourselves here to the case of filters that vary slowly, so that their frequency response can be considered stable over a time interval $T$. For the human voice $T$ is usually between 10 and 20 ms. This is an experimental estimate, generally accepted in speech processing (Rabiner et al. 1971, Flanagan et al. 1970).

At this point let us also note that "resonance" and "excitation" can originate from different sources, so that we could perform cross-synthesis.

### Analysis by Linear Prediction

The linear prediction technique was originally developed for the purposes of analysis and synthesis of speech (Atal and Hananer 1971). It consists of representing the system in terms of a recursive filter of order $p$ with multiple resonances (figure 2.2). The transfer function is

$$R(z) = \frac{S(z)}{E(z)} = \frac{1}{1 - \sum_{k=0}^{p} a_k z^{-k}}$$

Here $E(z)$ is the $z$ transform of the input signal $e$. For a voice it can be expressed as $e$ = pulse train (voiced sounds such as vowels) or $e$ = gaussian white noise (nonvoiced sounds such as consonants).

The analysis of a signal then consists of the determination of the coefficients $a_k$, which can be performed as follows (let us suppose that $e(t)$ is a white gaussian noise):

The system is characterized by

$$s(n) = \sum_{k=1}^{P} a_k \cdot s(n - k) + e(n).$$

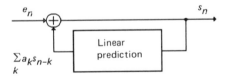

**Figure 2.2**
Schematic view of linear predictive analysis by means of a recursive filter

Let $\tilde{s}(n)$ be the estimated value of $s(n)$. We write $\tilde{s}(n)$ in the form

$$\tilde{s}(n) = \sum \tilde{a}_k \cdot s(n - k)$$

The prediction error is

$$C(n) = s(n) - \tilde{s}(n) = s(n) - \sum \tilde{a}_k \cdot s(n - k).$$

The $\tilde{a}_k$ are chosen so as to minimize the mean square error:

$$\langle C(n)^2 \rangle = \sum_n \left( s(n) - \sum_k \tilde{a}_k \cdot s(n - k) \right)^2. \tag{1}$$

Differentiating equation 1 with respect to $\tilde{a}_j$, $j = 1 \ldots p$, and setting the derivatives equal to zero, we obtain a system of $p$ equations with $p$ unknowns:

$$\sum_n \tilde{a}_k \sum_n s(n - k) \cdot s(n - j) = \sum_n s(n) \cdot s(n - j) \qquad j = 1 \ldots p. \tag{2}$$

We can write equation 2 in matrix form:

$$\Phi[a] = \psi.$$

Here $\Phi$ is the autocorrelation matrix of the signal,

$$\Phi_{i,j} = \sum s(n - i) \cdot s(n - j),$$

$\psi$ is the autocorrelation vector of the signal,

$$\psi_j = \Phi_{i,j}$$

and $[a]$ is the vector of components $\tilde{a}_k$.

In practice one has to calculate the matrix $\Phi$ for every time interval compatible with the evolution of the signal and then solve the corresponding system of equations so as to obtain the prediction coefficients that characterize the resonance aspects of the system (Makhoul 1975, Kronland-Martinet 1988a, 1988b).

### Subtractive Resynthesis by Predictive Filtering

Having identified the discrete evolution of the filter that serves as model for the instrument, we can perform the resynthesis by

$$s(n) = \sum a_k s_{n-k} + e(n)$$

The excitatory signal $e$ can be obtained from the signal $s(t)$ either by inverse filtering (Moorer 1979) or else—if the mechanism of sound production is simple enough—by mathematical modeling (such as a simplified plucked string).

It is important to also notice the possibility of modeling $e(t)$ with the help of parameters of global synthesis (frequency modulation, amplitude modulation, waveshaping). This procedure yields—in addition to a significant reduction in the volume of data—a possibility of simplified control of the time-dependence of the signal.

Next we examine the possibility of using an excitation signal different from the one that corresponds to the instrument under consideration or its model. We shall now see an application of this possibility, which generalizes the notion of subtractive synthesis and opens up broad prospects for the synthesis of musical sound.

**Transformation of Sound: Cross-Synthesis**

The cross-synthesis of two sound signals is the construction of a hybrid signal that combines the resonant and the excitation aspects of two distinct sounds (Risset and Wessel 1982). We give here an example of cross-synthesis between voice and cymbal. This example was obtained in collaboration with the Groupe de Musique Expérimentale de Marseille (GMEM). Of course this is just one example out of various possible hybrids (voice + cello, voice + voice, and so forth).

The figures that follow are the spectral representations of, respectively, the voice signal (figure 2.3), the cymbal signal (figure 2.4), and the result of cross-synthesis (figure 2.5).

Here the cross-synthesized signal has been obtained by using the unfiltered cymbal signal as the excitation. This is justified by the fact that such cymbals do not present pronounced resonances.

We can see that resulting signal combines the excitation information of the cymbal (the distribution of partials) and the resonances of the voice (the spectral envelope). The resulting auditory effect is a "talking cymbal."

Parametric analysis obviously has the advantage of considerably reducing the amount of data necessary for the description of sound. Parametric analysis, however, is valid only if the parametric model corresponds to the actual sound generation mechanism. If this is not the case, the results obtained cannot be exploited and, in general, give rise to unstable filters. We shall not discuss here this delicate problem.

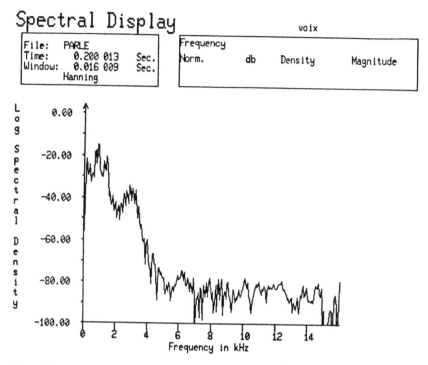

**Figure 2.3**
Spectral representation of a voice signal

## Nonparametric Analysis

Nonparametric analysis methods often use the concept of *local spectrum*, where the signal is decomposed into a sum of complex exponentials (as in the short-time Fourier transform), weighted by a function that plays the role of a time localization window. This procedure is well suited for the identification of quasi-periodic structures in the signal; however, it is not appropriate for the study of rapid transients because events of short duration are delocalized, and their energy is distributed over a region determined by the width of the window.

Taking into account a simplified model of the auditory system, which consists of the representation of the receivers (ears) as a bank of filters with constant $\delta f/f$ for frequencies higher than about 800 Hz, we are tempted to look for a technique of analysis that stresses the time aspect at high

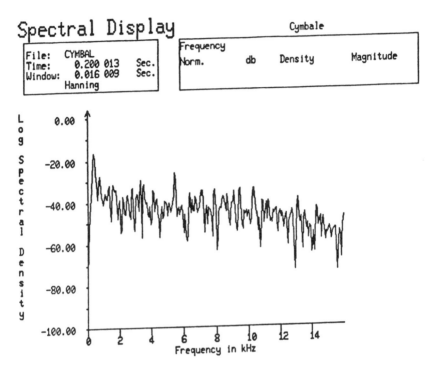

**Figure 2.4**
Spectral representation of a cymbal signal

frequencies and the frequency aspect at low frequencies. These requirements are satisfied by a new technique of analysis and synthesis, namely, the wavelet transform.

The wavelet transform is a linear transformation that consists of decomposing an arbitrary signal into elementary contributions. Those contributions called wavelets are generated by dilation and translation from a *mother function* called the *analyzing wavelet*.

One of the advantages of such a transform is the fact that one can choose (and consequently adapt) the analyzing wavelet depending on the information in the signal that one wants to point out. The choice of analyzing wavelet is subject only to some mathematical admissibility conditions that are not very restrictive in practice. The wavelet transform associates to a real signal (a real-valued function of time), a function depending on two variables (time and scale). Hence it gives rise to a two-dimensional represen-

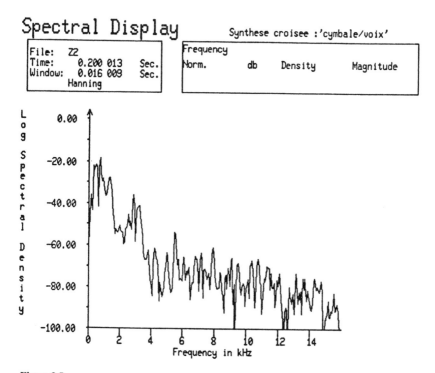

**Figure 2.5**
Spectral representation of cross-synthesis with a cymbal and a voice

tation (picture) that contains all the information carried by the signal. Because the transform is invertible, one can interpret these pictures as acoustic signatures of the sound. Our experience has indicated that it is useful to assume that the analyzing wavelet is "progressive," that is, that its Fourier components for negative frequencies vanish. Under these conditions the wavelet transform is complex valued. It can be suitably described by its modulus and its phase.

This double representation is interesting on several accounts, in particular because it establishes a relation between the result of the wavelet transform and physical parameters associated with the signal. Indeed the conservation of energy by wavelet transforms makes possible the interpretation of the square of the modulus of the transform as an energy density localized in regions of the time-scale half-plane that depend on the choice of the analyzing wavelet. Furthermore the phase of the wavelet transform can be used to define an *instantaneous frequency* at a given scale. Finally, the wavelet transform can be used to localize discontinuities and to extract modulation laws.

Before applying this method to the analysis, synthesis, and modification of real sounds, we describe the corresponding mathematical formalism. It is convenient to discuss in parallel wavelet transforms and the well-known short-time Fourier transform used in the phase vocoder because the two methods have many points in common as well as significant differences.

### Elementary Functions: Grains

The underlying idea of any linear transformation associating a two-dimensional representation to a signal is the decomposition of this signal in terms of elementary grains, such that their sum, multiplied by appropriate coefficients, allows the reconstruction of the original signal (Gabor 1946). Such an approach is clearly useful if every coefficient has a physical or, even better, psychoacoustical interpretation. This interpretation depends strongly on the choice of the basic grains used and in particular on their behavior under variations of the parameters that define the representation.

To obtain decompositions of the kind that we mention, we have to define a family of elementary functions, preferably well localized with respect to the two variables of the representation.

In the case of wavelet transform, the elementary functions are copies of a mother function $g(t)$ (figure 2.6) that have been translated and dilated (or contracted, that is, subjected to a change of scale):

$$g_{\tau,a}(t) = \frac{1}{\sqrt{a}} g\left(\frac{t - \tau}{a}\right). \tag{3}$$

Here $\tau$ is the parameter of translation in time, and $a$ is the rescaling (or dilation) parameter. $\tau$ is any real number, and $a$ is necessarily positive. The function $g(t)$ is called the *analyzing wavelet*.

The localization in time of function 3 is its effective support region. The frequency localization of this grain is given by the Fourier transform of $g_{\tau,a}(t)$:

$$\hat{g}_{\tau,a}(\omega) = \sqrt{a}\hat{g}(a\omega)e^{i\omega\tau}, \tag{4}$$

where $\hat{g}$ is the Fourier transform of $g$.

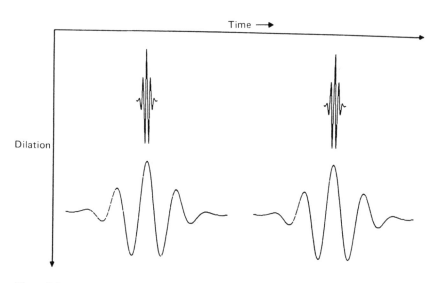

**Figure 2.6**
Elementary wavelets used for the wavelet transform in the time-dilation domain. The number of cycles in the wavelet does not change.

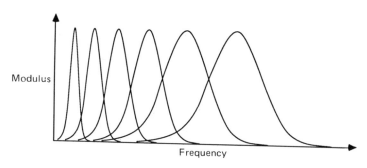

**Figure 2.7**
This family of curves represents the Fourier transform of the wavelet taken for various values of the scale parameter. The ratio $\Delta f/f$ does not change.

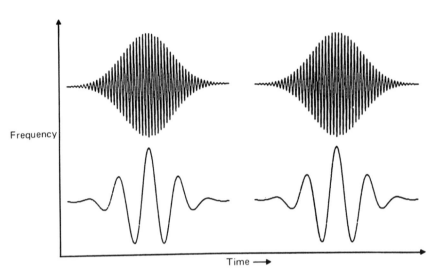

**Figure 2.8**
Elementary wavelets used for the Gabor expansion in the time-frequency domain

This localization depends on the parameter $a$ (figure 2.7). The resulting decomposition will consequently be at $\Delta\omega/\omega = \text{constant}$. Consequently wavelets can be interpreted as impulse responses of constant-$Q$ filters.

The short-time Fourier transform uses elementary grains that are translations in time and in frequency of a mother function $h(t)$ (figure 2.8):

$$h_{\tau,\omega_0}(t) = h(t - \tau)e^{i\omega_0 t}, \tag{5}$$

where $\tau$ is the time translation parameter, $\omega_0$ is the frequency translation parameter, and $h(t)$ is the window that ensures the time and frequency localization of equation 5.

In this case the time localization is given by the effective region of $h(t)$, and the frequency localization is given by the Fourier transform $\hat{h}(\omega)$ of the window. One has

$$\hat{h}_{\tau,\omega_0}(\omega) = \hat{h}(\omega - \omega_0)e^{i\omega\tau}. \tag{6}$$

An important aspect of this construction is that the localization width of equation 6 does not depend on $\omega_0$ (figure 2.9). The resulting decomposition is consequently of $\Delta\omega = \text{constant}$ type. The elementary grains can be interpreted as impulse responses of filters of constant width.

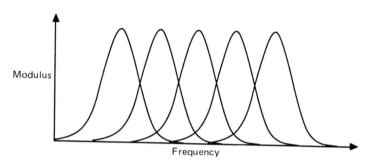

**Figure 2.9**
This family of curves represents the Fourier transform of the elementary wavelet used for the Gabor expansion. They are obtained from each other by frequency shift. The width $\Delta f$ is constant.

## Decompositions of an Arbitrary Signal

The time-scale and time-frequency transforms are obtained by decomposition of a signal of finite energy into *elementary grains*. The coefficients of this decomposition can be calculated in general as scalar products (correlation) between the signal and the grains, and represent the "weight" associated with each one of them. This is not immediately obvious because the grains are not mutually orthogonal, but is nevertheless true (Grossmann and Morlet 1985).

Consequently the wavelet transform is given by

$$S(\tau, a) = \langle g_{\tau,a} | s \rangle = \int \bar{g}_{\tau,a}(t)s(t)\,dt = \frac{1}{\sqrt{a}} \int \bar{g}\left(\frac{t-\tau}{a}\right)s(t)\,dt, \tag{7}$$

where the bar denotes complex conjugation.

In view of the Parseval relation, an expression equivalent to equation 7 and written in terms of Fourier transform is given by

$$S(\tau, a) = \langle g_{\tau,a} | s \rangle = \langle \hat{g}_{\tau,a} | \hat{s} \rangle = \int \bar{\hat{g}}_{\tau,a}(\omega)\hat{s}(\omega)\,d\omega$$

$$= \sqrt{a} \int \bar{\hat{g}}(a\omega)\hat{s}(\omega)e^{i\omega\tau}\,d\omega. \tag{8}$$

Similarly the short-time Fourier transform is given by

$$T(\tau, \omega_0) = \langle h_{\tau, \omega_0} | s \rangle = \int \overline{h}_{\tau, \omega_0}(t) s(t)\, dt = \int e^{i\omega_0 t} \overline{h}(t - \tau) s(t)\, dt, \tag{9}$$

$$T(\tau, \omega_0) = \langle \hat{h}_{\tau, \omega_0} | \hat{s} \rangle = \int \overline{\hat{h}}_{\tau, \omega_0}(\omega) \hat{s}(\omega)\, d\omega. \tag{10}$$

Let us define a voice as the restriction of the wavelet transform (or, respectively, the short-time Fourier transform) to a fixed value of the scale parameter $a$ (respectively, the frequency $\omega_0$). In other words a voice is the output of a filter with impulse response given by the corresponding grain. The transform so defined can be represented by a *continuous filter bank* with constant Q (wavelet) or with constant width (as in the short-time Fourier transform).

### Inversion: Admissibility Conditions

Because the transforms just shown are linear, we may ask for an inversion (or resynthesis) formula by "resummation" of elementary grains weighted by the coefficients (granular synthesis).

In the case of the wavelet transform, we obtain (for progressive wavelets, see "Analysis of Signals: Graphical Representations")

$$s(t) = \frac{1}{c_g} \int S(\tau, a) g_{\tau, a}(t) \frac{d\tau\, da}{a^2}, \tag{11}$$

where $c_g$ is a constant that depends on the choice of the analyzing wavelet:

$$c_g = 2\pi \int \frac{|\hat{g}(\omega)|^2}{\omega}\, d\omega. \tag{12}$$

Looking at equation 11, we notice that inversion is possible only if $c_g$ exists, that is, if the integral in equation 12 converges. This condition that an analyzing wavelet has to satisfy is called the *admissibility condition*. In practice this condition reduces to

$$-E_g = \int |g(t)|^2\, dt < +\infty \quad (g \text{ has finite energy}),$$

$$-\hat{g}(0) = \int g(t)\, dt = 0 \qquad (g \text{ has zero mean value, that is, no DC bias}).$$

There exist other formulas for the inversion of wavelet transforms. One of them is useful because of its simplicity and consists of a reconstruction of the signal by appropriate summation of coefficients at a fixed time:

$$s(t) = k_g \int S(t, a) \frac{da}{a^{3/2}}, \tag{11'}$$

where $k_g$ is a constant that depends on the choice of the wavelet $g$.

In the case of the short-time Fourier transform, we obtain

$$s(t) = \frac{1}{c} \int T(\tau, \omega_0) h_{\tau, \omega_0}(t) \, d\tau \, d\omega_0, \tag{13}$$

where $c = 1/2\pi$ is now independent of the choice of $h(t)$. However, $h(t)$ has to be of finite energy.

$$E_h = \int |h(t)|^2 \, dt < +\infty \tag{14}$$

### Properties of the Wavelet Transform

**Linearity**   The wavelet transform and the short-time Fourier transform are linear. This property is very useful. It means that the transform of the sum of signals is the sum of their transforms, which is convenient for the analysis of polyphonic signals. It should be remarked that the well-known Wigner Ville time-frequency representation is not linear but rather bilinear.

**Conservation of Energy**   The total energy of the signal can be expressed in term of the values of the transforms by

$$E_s = \int |s(t)|^2 \, dt = \frac{1}{c_g} \int |S(\tau, a)|^2 \frac{d\tau \, da}{a^2}$$

$$= \frac{1}{2\pi E_h} \int |T(\tau, \omega_0)|^2 \, d\tau \, d\omega_0, \tag{15}$$

where $E_h = \int |h(t)|^2 \, dt$.

These expressions allow us to interpret the square of the modulus of the transforms as a density of energy distributed over the domains of representation. In the case of the short-time Fourier transform, this representation is well known; it is the *spectrogram*.

**Constraints on the Coefficients**   The elementary grains are, in general, not orthogonal:

$$\langle g_{\tau,a}|g_{\tau',a'}\rangle = \int \bar{g}_{\tau,a}(t)g_{\tau',a'}(t)\,dt \neq 0,$$

(16)

$$\langle h_{\tau,\omega_0}|h_{\tau',\omega_0'}\rangle = \int \bar{h}_{\tau,\omega_0}(t)h_{\tau',\omega_0'}(t)\,dt \neq 0.$$

The coefficients of the transform are constrained to satisfy

$$S(\tau,a) = \int p_g(\tau,a;\tau',a')S(\tau',a')\frac{da'\,d\tau'}{a'^2},$$

(17)

where $p_g(\tau,a;\tau',a') = (1/c_g)\langle g_{\tau,a}|g_{\tau',a'}\rangle$.

For the coefficients of the short-time Fourier transform, one has

$$T(\tau,\omega) = \int p_h(\tau,\omega;\tau',\omega')T(\tau',\omega')\,d\omega'\,d\tau',$$

(18)

where $p_h(\tau,\omega;\tau',\omega') = (1/2\pi E_h)\langle h_{\tau,\omega}|h_{\tau',\omega'}\rangle$.

The relations in equations 17 and 18 are important in the interpretation of the transform. One can show that it is possible to find a grid such that the analysis coefficients at the points of the grid allow an arbitrarily accurate reconstruction of the coefficients on the representation plane.

For wavelet transform the points of such a grid are of the form shown in figure 2.10A, that is, $\{a_0^j; k\tau_0 a_0^j\}$, where $j$ and $k$ are integers, and $a_0$ and $\tau_0$ are real numbers that depend on the choice of the wavelet (Daubechies 1988).

For the short-time Fourier transform, the grid is of the form shown in figure 2.10B, that is, $\{m\tau_0; n\omega_0\}$, where $m$ and $n$ are integers, and $\omega_0$ and $\tau_0$ are real numbers that depend on the choice of the window $h(t)$.

Under certain conditions imposed on the grains, it is possible to construct orthonormal bases corresponding to some of the grids just defined. In the wavelet case the grids are dyadic ($a_0 = 2$). For details, see Meyer (1989).

The relations in equations 17 and 18 show that an arbitrary function of two variables need not be the transform of a signal. This may seem restrictive, if one wants to perform a synthesis starting from a picture that has been arbitrarily constructed or obtained by deformation of an existing transform. However, it can be shown that the inversion formula (equation 11) automatically projects into the appropriate subspace of functions that are wavelet transforms of signals.

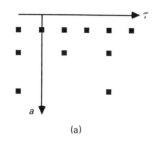

(a)

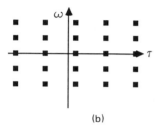

(b)

**Figure 2.10**
Comparison of analysis grids for the wavelet transform (A) and the short-time Fourier transform (B)

## Behavior of the Transform under Translation and Dilation of the Signal

The wavelet transform of a signal changes in a simple way if the signal is translated or rescaled. Let $s(t) \to S(\tau, a)$, that is, let $S(\tau, a)$ be the wavelet transform of $s(t)$. Then $s(t - t_0) \to S(\tau - t_0, a)$ that is, the wavelet transform of the shifted signal can be obtained by a natural shift of the original transform. Also one has

$$\frac{1}{\sqrt{\lambda}} s\left(\frac{t}{\lambda}\right) \to S\left(\frac{\tau}{\lambda}, \frac{a}{\lambda}\right).$$

The short-time Fourier transform is covariant under translation in frequency. Let $s(t) \to T(\tau, \omega)$, then $s(t)e^{i\omega_0 t} \to T(\tau, \omega - \omega_0)$. However, it is not covariant under translation in time $s(t - \tau_0) \to T(\tau - \tau_0, \omega)e^{-i\omega_0 t}$.

It is often preferable to be covariant under time translations rather than under frequency translations. This can be achieved by using the modified grain:

$$\tilde{h}_{\tau, \omega}(t) = h(t - \tau)e^{i(t - \tau)\omega}.$$

This is the grain to be used in the section "Analysis of Signals: Graphical Representations."

**Localization**   One of the aims of time-frequency representations is to associate to the coefficients some information about the signal that is simultaneously localized in time and in frequency. In the case of wavelets let us assume that $g(t)$ and $\hat{g}(\omega)$ are negligible, respectively, outside an interval $[t_{min}, t_{max}]$ and $I\omega_{min}, \omega_{max}]$. Then $g_{\tau,a}(t)$ and $\hat{g}_{\tau,a}(\omega)$ have, respectively, the regions $[at_{min} + \tau, at_{max} + \tau]$ and $[\omega_{min}/a, \omega_{max}/a]$. Consequently the domain of influence in time of a value $s(t_0)$ of the signal is a cone pointing toward $\tau = t_0$ and defined by the lines illustrated in figure 2.11A, that is,

$$at_{min} + t_0 = \tau, \qquad at_{max} + t_0 = \tau.$$

The domain of influence in frequency is bounded by the two horizontal lines (figure 2.11B):

$$\omega_{min}/a = \text{constant}, \qquad \omega_{max}/a = \text{constant}.$$

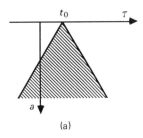

(a)

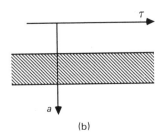

(b)

**Figure 2.11**
Wavelet domains of influence. (A) Domain of influence in time. (B) Domain of influence in frequency.

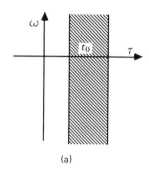

(a)

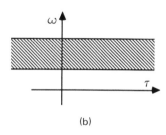

(b)

**Figure 2.12**
Short-time Fourier transform domains of influence. (A) Domain of influence in time. (B) Domain of influence in frequency.

In the case of short-time Fourier transform, let us suppose that $h(t)$ and $\hat{h}(\omega)$ are negligible, respectively, outside an interval $[t_{min}, t_{max}]$ and $[\omega_{min}, \omega_{max}]$, then $h_{\tau, \omega_0}(t)$ and $\hat{h}_{\tau, \omega_0}(\omega)$ have as a range, respectively, $[t_{min} + \tau, t_{max} + \tau]$ and $[\omega_{min} + \omega_0, \omega_{max} + \omega_0]$. Consequently the domain of influence of a point $s(t_0)$ is a strip given by (figure 2.12A)

$$\tau = t_{min} + t_0, \qquad \tau = t_{max} + t_0.$$

The domain of influence in frequency is bounded by the two horizontal lines (figure 2.12B)

$$\omega_{min} + \omega_0 = \text{constant}, \qquad \omega_{max} + \omega_0 = \text{constant}.$$

## Algorithms for the Calculation of the Wavelet Transform

The short-time Fourier transform can be easily implemented with the help of fast Fourier transform (FFT) algorithms. Because the wavelet transform is a recent method, we describe the digital techniques used in its implementation and present methods that implement the wavelet transform in real time.

Our first implementation of wavelets was done in 1987 on the SYTER real-time signal processor (Allouis and Mailliard 1981). This system consists of a host processor and a real-time processor that can implement transverse filters. This classical filtering method has been used with impulse responses given by dilated and contracted versions of wavelets. For a fixed value of the dilation parameter, equation 7 consists of a convolution between the signal and the time reversed wavelet $g(-t)$. The calculation is discretized:

$$Y(n) = \sum_i g_i X(n - 1 - i)$$

(we suppose here that the sampling rate is 1).

Here $Y(n)$ is the $n$th output sample, $g_i$ the $i$th value of the wavelet, and $X(n)$ the $n$th input sample. For each value of the dilation parameter $a$ (for each "voice"), the host processor calculates the corresponding discrete values of the wavelet and transmits them to the processor, which then calculates the wavelet transform.

This method of calculation has the disadvantage of not being compatible with real-time operation. The convolutions have to be performed on an arbitrarily large number of points because—for a fixed sampling rate—the dilated wavelet is defined on a large number of samples. This is an important consideration in the case of sound signals. If the analysis takes into account $n$ octaves (here $n$ can be of the order of 10), then the ratio of the number of samples between the most dilated and the most contracted wavelets is $2^n$. Consequently the number of operations (multiplications, additions) grows as $2^n$.

A different algorithm based on the notion of decimation of signal has been developed and implemented on SYTER, called the *algorithme à trous* ("algorithm with holes"). It allows a parallel and hierarchical structure of calculations, while keeping fixed the number of operations as the scale is changed. We give here only a sketchy indication of the method of calculation and refer the reader to Holschneider et al. 1989. The scheme is shown in figure 2.13A. The information necessary for this algorithm is, on the one hand, discrete values of the analyzing wavelet $G$ and, on the other hand, the coefficients of a filter $f$ that performs a polynomial interpolation of the

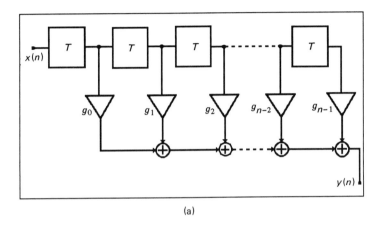

(a)

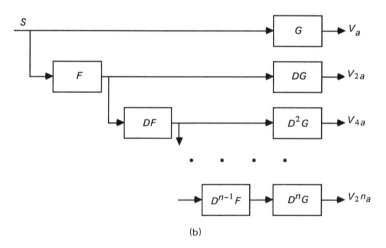

(b)

**Figure 2.13**
Implementation of the wavelet transform. (A) Transverse filter used for the calculation of the wavelet transform in the SYTER digital signal processor. $T$ is the unit time shift. (B) schematic view of the *algorithme à trous*.

wavelet. One can so construct the filter $F = 1 + TDf$, where $T$ is the unit shift, $D$ is the operation of dilation by 2:

$$Df(i) = f\left(\frac{i}{2}\right) \text{ for even } i,$$

$$= 0 \text{ for odd } i,$$

and $1$ is the identity (the filter corresponding to an impulse response that is zero everywhere except for $i = 0$, where it is 1).

A hierarchical structure enables us to use partial results calculated for higher voices (figure 2.13B).

### Analysis of Signals: Graphical Representations

Time-frequency analysis of audio signals has been the subject of numerous publications; we refer the reader to the bibliography. The aim is to extract detailed information about the behavior in time and in frequency (or scale) to help with the characterization of sound phenomena in view of reproduction or transformation of natural sounds. Although the wavelet transform and the short-time Fourier transform are conceptually closely related, they are nevertheless different in the way they cover frequency range. We have seen that the wavelet transform can be described as the output of a bank of filters with $\Delta f/f = $ constant, whereas the short-time Fourier transform performs a filtering with $\Delta f = $ constant and so can separate the harmonics of the signal (provided that $\Delta f$ is smaller than the fundamental frequency of the signal). By its very nature the short-time Fourier transform tends to decompose an arbitrary signal into harmonic components, whereas the wavelet transform allows free choice of the elementary function or grain of the decomposition.

Before visualizing the behavior of the two transforms, let us discuss the quantities to be represented. Energy conservation (see "Properties of the Wavelet Transform") is of capital importance, and we represent the modulus (or squared modulus) of the transform to obtain a physical interpretation of sound phenomena in terms of energy distribution. To obtain a realistic representation of the modulus of the transform, it is useful to separate positive and negative spectral components so as to avoid beats. This can be obtained by requiring the analyzing wavelet to the "progressive," that is, to contain only positive-frequency components.

$\hat{g}(\omega) = 0,$     if $\omega < 0$.

Such a condition is easily satisfied for wavelet transform for all $\tau$ and $a$. It cannot be satisfied for the short-time Fourier transform because it can be destroyed by translations in frequency. Figure 2.14 shows the short-time Fourier transform and the wavelet transform of a triangle function. The starting analyzing function is the same for the two transforms. Only the construction of the families is different. The starting function is a modulated gaussian:

$$f(t) = \exp(-t^2/2)\exp(i\omega_0 t) + \text{small corrections}. \tag{19}$$

In the figure the modulus of the transform is proportional to a local density of black dots. The phase is represented in the same way; this allows an easy visualization of lines of constant phases corresponding to the transition between $2\pi$ and $0$. The horizontal axis is time, and the vertical axis is frequency (respectively, the negative logarithm of the scale).

One can see in the figure that the two transforms suggest different interpretations of the phenomenon being studied. The wavelet transform allows a localization in time that improves as one progresses toward small scales. This is helpful for detection of discontinuities (Grossmann et al. 1987). On the other hand the short-time Fourier transform looks for harmonic structures in the signal showing horizontal equispaced striations in the figure.

From the point of view of psychoacoustics, wavelet transforms seem better adapted to the analysis of sound signals because they favor the temporal aspect at small scales and the frequency aspect at large scale. It is sometimes convenient to have a detailed description in terms of frequency and consequently to use a short-time Fourier transform. This aspect is developed by Arfib in chapter 3; we consequently focus more on the possibilities for analysis and synthesis provided by the wavelet transform.

**Five Examples** Interested readers will find listed in the references many articles that interpret the behavior of coefficients of wavelet transforms. Here we restrict ourselves to five examples of the wavelet transform applied to real signals. A single figure can represent both the modulus and the phase of the transform. In the original images, the modulus is coded with the help of a palette of colors represented at the top-right corner of the image. The phase is coded by a density of black dots in a way that has already been discussed.

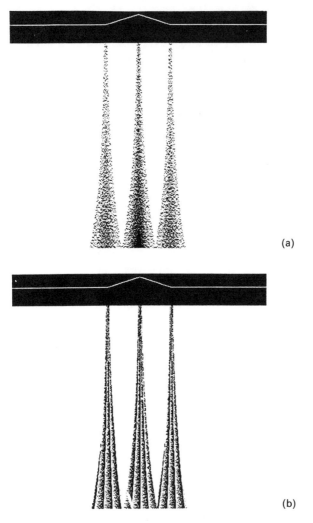

(a)

(b)

**Figure 2.14**
Transforms of a triangle function. (A) Modulus of the wavelet transform. (B) Phase of the wavelet transform. (C) Modulus of the windowed Fourier transform. (D) Phase of the windowed Fourier transform.

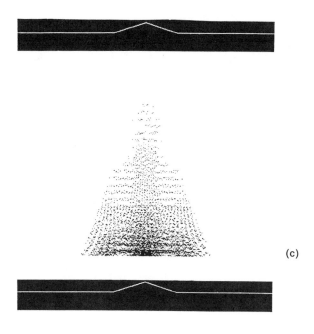

(c)

(d)

**Figure 2.14** (cont.)

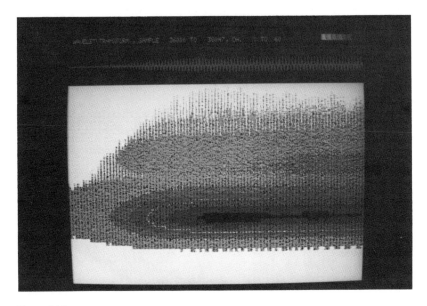

**Figure 2.15**
Wavelet transform image of the first 32 ms of a clarinet tone

Figure 2.15 represents the first 32 ms of a clarinet sound. Taking into account the domain of influence discussed in the section "Properties of the Wavelet Transform," one can conclude that successive harmonics appear at different times. There exist algorithms for the estimation of frequencies and of modulation laws associated with the components. These algorithms are based on the study of the phase of the transform (Guillemain et al. 1989) and are discussed later.

Figure 2.16 represents the same signal that has undergone a transformation realized by P. Dutilleux (Laboratoire de Mécanique et d'Acoustique, Marseille) in the framework of a study for a "sound sculpting machine" for the Museum of Music, Paris. The sound is cut into slices of equal length. To each slice one associates a linear amplitude modulation. The wavelet transform has turned out to be a very powerful tool for the visualization of the modifications so produced. In particular it provides a measure of the discontinuities introduced by the procedure and an estimation of the energy distribution generated by the modulation over the spectral components.

Figure 2.17 represents three successive notes on a trombone. Here again it is easy to interpret the distribution of the energy along the scale and time

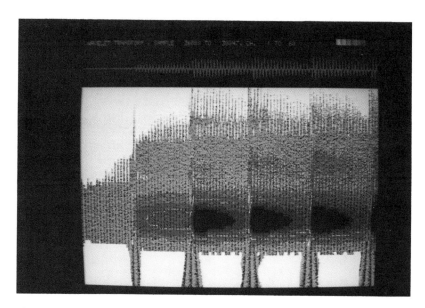

**Figure 2.16**
The same sound shown in figure 2.15, cut into equal-length slices and amplitude modulated

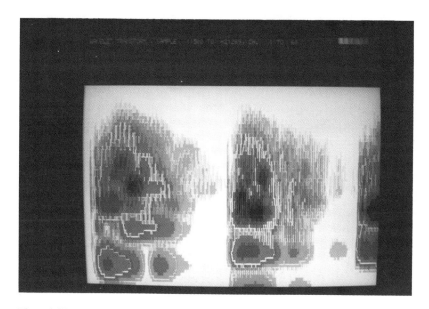

**Figure 2.17**
Wavelet transform image of three notes of a trombone

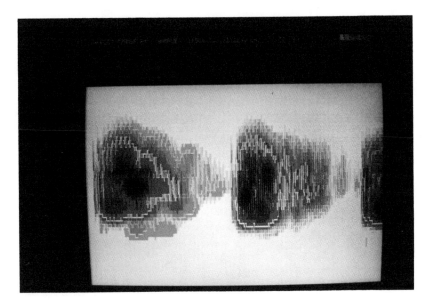

**Figure 2.18**
Same signal as in figure 2.17, processed by a bandpass filter

axes. This is shown clearly by considering the same signal filtered by a bandpass filter, shown in figure 2.18. One can so characterize the effect of the filtering on the signal and, most important, visualize possible transient effects in the case of time-varying filters.

The last example, shown in figure 2.19, is an illustration of the usefulness of a time-scale decomposition and of the difference between time-scale and time-frequency. The problem here is to detect within a signal a particular feature that can appear at an arbitrary scale. If, for instance, one wants to detect octave intervals appearing in a sound sequence, it is advantageous to decompose the signal in terms of elementary contributions that are adapted to this purpose. A wavelet with two bumps in the frequency domain at an octave distance to each other allows us to detect the occurrence of octaves. The local energy in the time-scale half-plane will be higher at times when the signal contains octaves than at other times (other parameters being equal). In such a way one can also construct wavelets adapted to detection of other chords or other predefined structures.

**Figure 2.19**
Wavelet transform adapted for octave detection. The four instances of octaves show up as
dark spots in the wavelet transform.

## Parameter Estimation with the Help of Wavelet Transforms

The information contained in the representations just described is sufficient
for an exact reconstruction of the analyzed signal. It is often useful to
extract from these representations some parameters that describe physical
phenomena occurring in the signal. Without entering into mathematical
details, we briefly describe some of the possibilities opened by wavelet
transforms in the field of detection of important features of sound signals.
A dominant role among those features is occupied by spectral components
and by frequency and amplitude modulations. They allow synthesis of the
signal by additive techniques or by frequency modulation. So far these
methods have produced convincing simulations and characterizations of
signals. The parameters so measured have not yet been used for resynthesis
of sound.

**Estimation of Spectral Lines**

The aim here is to find on the wavelet transform side the information necessary for the extraction of monochromatic components modulated in amplitude. The extraction is performed automatically, that is, it does not require a visual inspection of the two-dimensional representation described previously.

A *spectral line* is defined as a function of the form $s(t) = A(t)e^{i\omega t}$, where $A(t)$ is the amplitude modulation law, and $\omega$ is the frequency.

The search for spectral lines consists of the identification of the function $A(t)$ and of the number $\omega$. We discuss here the detection of such lines contained in signals of the form

$$s(t) = \sum_{j \text{ finite}} A_j(t)e^{i\omega_j t} + b(t),$$

where $b(t)$ is an arbitrary signal that does not contain discrete spectral components (noise).

Before we describe an iterative method that detects these parameters, let us examine the case of a monochromatic signal.

Consider the signal $Ae^{i\omega_1 t + \phi}$, whose wavelet transform is given by

$$S(\tau, a) = \sqrt{a}A\bar{g}(a\omega_1)e^{i\omega_1 \tau + \phi}, \tag{20}$$

where $\bar{g}$ is the Fourier transform of the wavelet.

To facilitate the interpretation of equation 20, we suppose that $\hat{g}(\omega)$ is real; this condition is satisfied, for example, by the wavelet equation 19. The phase of the wavelet transform is then equal to the phase of the signal itself, for every value of the scale parameter $a$. The modulus of the transform is constant on all lines of the fixed-scale parameter. In the case of real-valued monochromatic signals, the previous statement remains true, provided that $\hat{g}(\omega) = 0$ on the negative axis, so that interference phenomena are avoided. This is the motivation for the introduction of "progressive" wavelet in the section on graphical representations.

It is useful to define the instantaneous frequency of a voice $S_a(\tau)$ (the restriction of the transform to a fixed value of the scale parameter) by

$$\Omega_a(\tau) = \frac{d\varphi_a(\tau)}{d\tau},$$

where $\varphi_a(\tau)$ is the phase of $S_a(\tau)$, $S_a(\tau) = M_a(\tau)\exp(i\varphi_a(\tau))$, $M_a(\tau) = |(S_a(\tau))|$.

If the signal is monochromatic, then $\Omega_a(\tau) = \omega_1$. Consequently the instantaneous frequency obtained from the wavelet transform of such a signal is equal to the frequency of the signal and allows its determination. Furthermore the modulus of the transform of the monochromatic signal in equation 19 is given by

$$M_a = \sqrt{a}A\,|\bar{\hat{g}}(a\omega_1)|$$

Consequently, knowing the analyzing wavelet, we can also determine the value of $A$ from the wavelet transform.

More generally one can show (Guillemain et al. 1989) that it is possible to estimate the frequency of spectral components contained in a signal by taking an average of the instantaneous frequency of its wavelet transform over a suitably chosen interval. The actual method of estimation cannot be given here, and we refer the reader to Guillemain et al. 1989. Figure 2.20 represents the wavelet transform of a sum of three spectral lines. The reduced frequencies are 1, 1.75, and 2.5. One can see the instantaneous frequencies and amplitude modulation laws for values of the scale parameter that correspond to the fixed points defined previously. The estimation of frequencies and amplitude modulation laws is excellent and has already been used by P. Guillemain to extract lines in nuclear magnetic resonance (NMR) spectroscopy.

**Estimation of Modulation Laws**

The determination of the law of frequency modulation in a signal can be of major importance, particularly if one wants to use methods of resynthesis such as FM (Chowning 1973). The main idea of the method that we describe is that the information contained in the signal is not distributed uniformly over the time-scale half-plane. Consequently, for purpose of reconstruction, certain parts of the half-plane carry the essential information, and it is crucial to be able to determine these parts.

Under some mathematical assumptions that are not discussed here, one can extract from the wavelet transform its essential points (corresponding mathematically to points of stationary phase) (Escudié et al. 1989). They describe in the half-plane a trajectory called the *ridge*.

The usefulness of the ridge stems from the fact that the restriction of the wavelet transform to it is sufficient to obtain a good approximate reconstruction of the signal up to a known amplitude factor and up to a specific phase. This restriction will be called the *skeleton* of the transform. As an

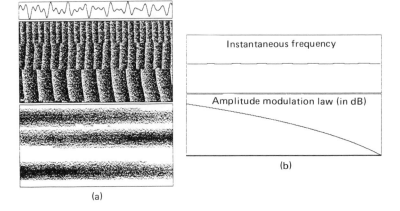

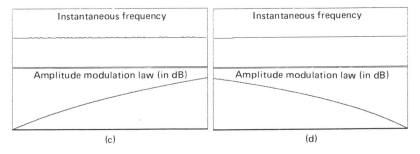

**Figure 2.20**
Extraction of spectral lines. The signal is a sum of three components with frequencies
1, 1.75, and 2.5. The amplitude modulation laws are linear. The first and the third lines
decrease; while the second increases. (A) Wavelet transform of the signal (modulus and
phase). (B, C, D) Instantaneous frequency and amplitude modulation law for each
component.

example, figure 2.21A is the ridge of a signal obtained by FM synthesis:

$$s(t) = A \sin\{\alpha t + I(t)\sin(\beta t)\}.$$

Here the modulation index $I(t)$ increases linearly.

Figure 2.21B gives the phase of the skeleton of the transform, calculated by N. Delprat (Laboratoire de Mécanique et d'Acoustique, Marseille). The linear part can easily be estimated by the linear regression method, giving the parameter $\alpha$ (the carrier). Figure 2.21C represents the phase of the skeleton after subtraction of the carrier. It is thus possible to identify the modulating frequency $\beta$ and the law of variation of the modulation index $I(t)$.

## Resynthesis by Means of Wavelets

The reconstruction formulas equations 11 and 11′, show that there are two natural methods for resynthesizing a natural sound starting from its analysis by a wavelet transform: granular synthesis and generalized additive synthesis. This section contrasts these two approaches.

### Granular Resynthesis

Equation 11 suggests an approach to resynthesis by summation over a set of dilated and translated wavelets, with complex-valued coefficients derived from the transform (figure 2.22). The digital implementation consists of associating a wavelet with an appropriate weight to each point on the analysis grid. These wavelets are *elementary grains* with overlap in time. Synthesis is then carried out as a sum of those contributions. Notice that because the coefficients associated with wavelets are in general complex, the *resynthesis grains* will in general have a different form due to phase shifts. The basic module of the instrument that perform this kind of synthesis is given by figure 2.23. The analysis is performed here with a displacement step equal to a quarter of the length of the wavelet. This requires four wavelet generators that are successively activated. The multiplexer distributes the values of the transform to the four generators of the wavelets.

F. Boyer has developed at LMA special unit generators and integrated them into the program Music V (Boyer and Kronland-Martinet 1989) to be able to use this method of synthesis. The results are very good and allow a reconstruction of almost perfect audio and digital quality using coeffi-

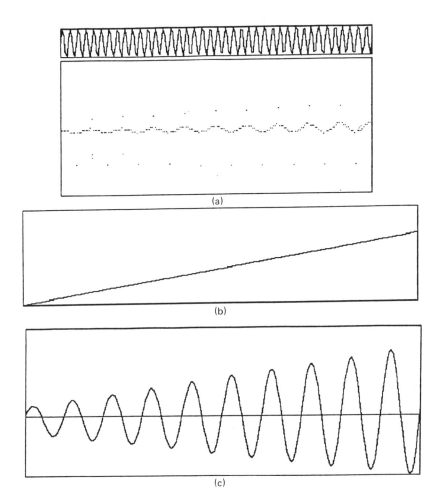

**Figure 2.21**
Estimation of modulation laws. (A) Ridge corresponding to a signal obtained by frequency
modulation synthesis. The modulation index increases linearly. (B) Unwrapped phase of the
skeleton of the transform. (C) Unwrapped phase of the skeleton after subtraction of the
carrier. It is possible to identify the modulating frequency $\beta$ and the law of variation of the
modulating index $I(t)$.

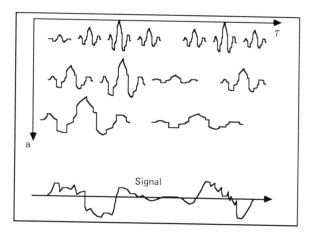

**Figure 2.22**
Granular resynthesis by summation over a set of dilated and translated wavelets with complex-valued coefficients derived from the transform

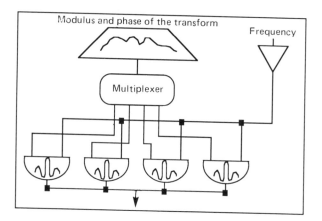

**Figure 2.23**
Module for granular resynthesis. The frequency depends only on the dilation parameters associated with the voice under consideration. The complete instrument requires as many modules as there are voices in the analysis.

cients on an appropriate grid, for example, a dyadic grid and the wavelet
of equation 19.

## Generalized Additive Synthesis

Equation 11′ allows the reconstruction of a signal at time $t$ by summation
of the values of the transform for fixed $\tau = t$. If the wavelet is complex
valued, the values of the transform are also complex, and every voice (for
fixed $a$) can be defined as

$$S_a(t) = x_a(t) + iy_a(t) = A_a(t)e^{i\varphi_a(t)},$$

where $M_a(t)$ is the modulus $M_a(t) = (x_a^2 + y_a^2)^{1/2}$, and $\varphi_a(t)$ is the instantaneous phase $\varphi_a(t) = \arctan(y_a/x_a)$.

We are here in a situation similar to the one encountered with the phase
vocoder. The same reconstruction method can be used and the problem is
reduced to the identification of instantaneous frequency or, more precisely,
to the determination of the reading increment for a sine table. Those
procedures are described by Moorer (1978).

The discretization of equation 11′ on the grid $a = 2^j$ compatible with the
wavelet of equation 19 gives

$$s(t) = k_g \sum_{a=2^j} S(t,a)a^{-1/2}$$

$$= k_g \sum_{a=2^j} A_a(t)\cos(\varphi_a(t))a^{-1/2} \qquad \text{(taking the real part).}$$

The resynthesis is then of generalized additive type because the oscillators are modulated both in amplitude and in phase. The basic module of
the instrument that realizes this kind of synthesis is given in figure 2.24.

## Transformation of Sound Signals

The resynthesis of sound signals has enabled us to verify the power of the
method by numerical tests as well as by listening. However, the main
interest of the decompositions that we studied lies in the possibilities of
characterization (by images), of modeling signals, of data reduction, and of
intimate transformation of sounds. This last aspect is very attractive for
musicians who are searching for new auditory sensations. Now we show
how wavelet transforms can be used for the modification of audio signals

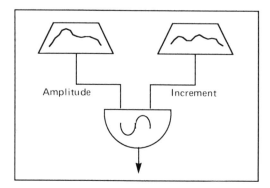

**Figure 2.24**
Module for generalized additive resynthesis. The complete instrument requires as many modules as there are voices in the analysis.

by altering the values (coefficients) between analysis or synthesis or by a deformation of the time-scale half-plane.

Among possible modifications one can distinguish between those that are obtained by linear action on the values of the transform and those that require nonlinear operators (Kronland-Martinet 1989). The latter are likely to be more interesting, but they require a more complicated mathematical formalism. We present here only the main ideas and an intuitive interpretation of the values of transform (the coefficients). These allow us to get a feel for the audio results obtained through modification.

The most obvious linear modification consists of performing a partial resynthesis by restricting the original analysis grid in time or scale or both. For instance, resynthesis that takes into account only the voices correspondig to small scales has the effect of a highpass filter, provided that the analyzing wavelet corresponds to a filter with a single resonance, or to a "high-scale" filter. More generally the interpretation of wavelet coefficients at a fixed scale as the output of a filter allows us to understand the effect of a constant gain on each of the voices. We can so obtain a "scale equalizer" with gains that can vary in time without stability problems.

Another interesting linear transform consists of time-shifting the analyzing voices with respect to each other. The physical interpretation here is that of an *acoustical wave*. The components of the wave propagate with different speeds, depending on their scale (dispersion). The resulting signal propagates in clusters, yielding an "aquatic" effect.

The nonlinear transformations we consider consist of separate modifications of the modulus and the phase of the wavelet coefficients. The results so obtained can be understood intuitively if one realizes that the modulus (or more precisely its square) plays the role of a density variable for energy. Thus it gives the distribution of the total energy in time and in scale (resonant aspects). On the other hand the phase gives the "oscillation," that is, the excitation. Such an interpretation of the coefficients allows us to make guesses concerning modifications that perform changes of the following types:

- Transpositions without change of duration (or conversely, say, stretching in time without changes in pitch)
- Harmonization or brightness effects
- Hybridization or cross-synthesis of signals.

Let us consider in a little more detail the effect of frequency transposition without changes of duration. To do this, consider first the monochromatic signal

$$s(t) = A \cos(\omega t)$$

As we saw previously, the values of its wavelet transform are given by

$$S(\tau, a) = \sqrt{a} A \bar{\hat{g}}(a\omega) e^{i\omega\tau}.$$

We have seen that the phase of the coefficients is the phase of the signal itself, provided that $\hat{g}(\omega)$ is real. A frequency transposition of ratio $n$ can thus be obtained simply by multiplying the phases of all coefficients by $n$.

Although the mathematics does not allow us to do this, we can generalize this procedure to more general signals and multiply the phases of coefficients by $n$ to obtain a transposition effect.

$$s_n(t) = k_g \sum_{a=2^j} A_a(t) \cos(n\varphi_a(t)) a^{-1/2}.$$

Notice that $n$ may depend on time; one obtains time-varying transpositions.

Similarly one can obtain brightness effects by adding harmonics at each scale in a synchronous way. One has to perform a multiple transposition with an integer ratio:

$$s_h(t) = k_g \sum_{a=2^j} A_a(t) \sum_n C_n \cos(n\varphi_a(t)) a^{-1/2}.$$

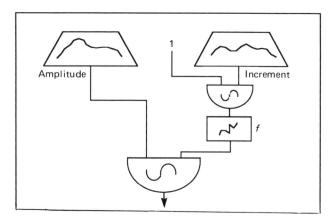

**Figure 2.25**
Resynthesis module for "brightness" effect using nonlinear distortion

The algorithm can be simplified if one notices that one is performing here a nonlinear distortion $f$, which can be written, with the help of Chebychev polynomials, as (Arfib 1979)

$$f(x) = \sum_k C_k T_k(x),$$

with $T_k(\cos \varphi(t)) = \cos(k\varphi(t))$.

The corresponding instrument Music V is represented in figure 2.25.

For a final example, we present a modification that is directly related to the cross-synthesis of two signals. The interpretation of the phase as excitation and of the module as resonance brings us naturally to "sound hybridization," by synthesis using the modulus and the phase of two distinct sounds. It is of course possible to perform other transformations as intermediate steps. Some of the examples can be heard on the soundsheet in Kronland-Martinet 1989. Almost all of the examples were realized with just one voice per octave (a total of eight voices).

## Conclusion

Wavelet analysis provides an extremely powerful tool for the analysis of audio signals. The degree of refinement of such an analysis makes it a privileged tool in many domains where it is necessary to characterize transient phenomena. The results obtained so far have confirmed the power of the method in the analysis of discontinuities and in the detection of patterns in a given signal. It has also been shown to be extremely efficient, allowing resynthesis and transformations with a small number of voices.

The use of wavelets in the synthesis and modification of signals still needs to be explored in a much more systematic way. It is reasonable to expect that the remarkable mathematical properties of the wavelet transform will turn out to be keys to many classes of applications, particularly because a fast algorithm allows us to envisage real-time approaches.

Although the nonparametric aspect of wavelet transform is seductive by its generality, it is nevertheless clear that certain parametric approaches can give rise to results that are interesting and more specific. This is proved by cross-synthesis of signals, where linear prediction gives rise to simplified implementations.

One can conclude with the truism that in matters of analysis-synthesis there is no universal panacea and that each case has its own optimal approach. However, the results presented here on wavelet transforms give a general framework for the handling of time-varying signals that corresponds to a need of musicians: a "direct" chain in which the processing of real sounds could be standardized, just as musical performance is captured by MIDI.

## References

Allouis, J. F., and B. Mailliard. 1981. "Simulation par ordinateur du studio électroacoustique et applications à la composition musicale." *Conférence des journées d'études, Festival international du son haute fidélité*. Paris: Editions SDSA, pp. 43–55.

Arfib, D. 1979. "Digital synthesis of complex spectra by means of multiplication of non-linear distorted sine waves." *Journal of the Audio Engineering Society* 27(10): 757–768.

Boyer, F., and R. Kronland-Martinet. 1989. "Granular resynthesis and transformation of sounds through wavelet transform analysis." In T. Wells and D. Butler, eds. *Proceedings of the 1989 International Computer Music Conference*. San Francisco: Computer Music Association, pp. 51–54.

Chowning, J. 1973. "The synthesis of complex audio spectra by means of frequency modulation." *Journal of the Audio Engineering Society* 21: 526–534.

Daubechies, I. 1988. "Orthonormal bases of compactly supported wavelets." *Communications in Pure and Applied Mathematics* 41: 909–996.

Daubechies, I. 1990. "The wavelet transform, time-frequency localization and signal analysis." To be published in *IEEE Transactions on Information Theory*.

Escudié, B., A. Grossmann, R. Kronland-Martinet, and B. Torrésani. 1989. "Représentation en ondelettes de signaux asymptotiques: emploi de la phase stationnaire." In *Proceedings Colloque GRETSI*. Juan les Pins.

Flanagan, J. L., C. Coker. L. Rabiner, R. Schafter, and N. Umeda. 1970. "Synthetic voices for computer." *IEEE Spectrum* 7: 22–45.

Gabor, D. 1946. "Theory of communication." *Journal of the IEE* 93: 429–441.

Grossmann, A., M. Holschneider, R. Kronland-Martinet, and J. Morlet. 1987. "Detection of abrupt changes in sound signals with the help of wavelet transforms." *Advances in Electronics and Electron Physics. Supplement 19: Inverse Problems.* Orlando: Academic Press.

Grossmann, A., and J. Morlet. 1985. "Decomposition of functions into wavelets of constant shape, and related transforms." In L. Streit, ed. *Mathematics + Physics, Lectures on Recent Results.* Singapore: World Scientific.

Guillemain, P., R. Kronland-Martinet, and B. Martens. 1989. "Application de la transformée en ondelettes en spectroscopie RMN." Note Interne 112. Marseille: Laboratoire de Mécanique et d'Acoustique.

Holschneider, M., R. Kronland-Martinet, J. Morlet, and P. Tchamitchian. 1989. "A real-time algorithm for signal analysis with the help of the wavelet transform." In J. Combes, A. Grossmann, and P. Tchamitchian, eds. *Wavelets, Time-Frequency Methods and Phase Space.* New York: Springer-Verlag, pp. 286–297.

Kronland-Martinet, R. 1988a. "Digital subtractive synthesis of signals based on the analysis of natural sounds." In *Etat de la Recherche Musicale (au 1er janvier 1989).* Aix en Provence: Editions A.R.C.A.M.

Kronland-Martinet, R. 1988b. "The use of the wavelet transform for the analysis, synthesis and processing of speech and music sounds." *Computer Music Journal* 12(4): 11–20. (Sound examples on soundsheet with 13(1) 1989.)

Kronland-Martinet, R. 1989. "Analyse, synthèse, et transformation de signaux sonores: application de la transformée en ondelettes." Marseille: Thèse d'Etat-Sciences, Faculté des Sciences de Luminy.

Makhoul, J. 1975. "Linear prediction, a tutorial review." *Proceedings of IEEE* 63: 561–580.

Meyer, Y. 1989. "Orthonormal wavelets." In J. Combes, A. Grossmann, and P. Tchamitchian, eds. *Wavelets, Time-Frequency Methods and Phase Space.* New York: Springer-Verlag.

Moorer, J. A. 1978. "The use of the phase vocoder in computer music applications." *Journal of the Audio Engineering Society* 26: 42–45.

Moorer, J. A. 1979. "The use of linear prediction of speech in computer music applications." *Journal of the Audio Engineering Society* 27: 134–140.

Rabiner, R. R., R. Schafer, and J. Flanagan. 1971. "Computer synthesis of speech by concatenation of formant-coded words." *Bell System Technical Journal* 50: 1541–1558.

Risset, J. C., and D. Wessel. 1982. "Exploration of timbre by analysis and synthesis." In D. Deutsch, ed. *The Psychology of Music.* Orlando: Academic Press, pp. 26–54.

# 3 Analysis, Transformation, and Resynthesis of Musical Sounds with the Help of a Time-Frequency Representation

Daniel Arfib

In 1946 Dennis Gabor, known for his discovery of the principle of holography, wrote a fundamental article in which he explicitly defined a *time-frequency representation* of a signal. The signal can of course be a sound. Gabor showed that, in addition to the time representation (the signal itself) and the frequency representation (the Fourier transform of the whole sound), one can construct a two-dimensional representation, where each point corresponds to both a limited interval of time and a limited interval of frequency. How can this be obtained? By taking the convolution of the signal around one point of time with a "grain," which consists of a pure frequency signal with a time-limited envelope—a *window*—applied to it. To be very clear and not misleading, this is equivalent to the well-known a *short-time Fourier transform* (STFT) approach developed later. Although it can be implemented as a sliding short-time Fourier transform, the Gabor time-frequency representaton is directly concerned with information on a two-dimensional plane and ways to transform this information in a musical way.

One essential point of the theory is that there is a reciprocal relation between the time signal and this time-frequency representation and that all the information is maintained if the values are given on a rectangular grid, that is to say, at regularly spaced time and frequency intervals. Gabor also explicitly showed (which has since become a trivial statement, but was not at that time) that there is an uncertainty principle in the frequency-time definition. Gabor worked exclusively with grains defined as pure sinusoids modulated in amplitude by gaussian envelopes. He showed that for such grains there is a limited area of influence in time and frequency. This notion has nowadays been developed under the name *reproducing kernel*. Though delicate, this notion helps us to understand what is going on when we choose grains different from the one stipulated by Gabor.

The rest of this chapter is about the use of a Gabor time-frequency representation to perform unusual transformations of sounds via the analysis and resynthesis of a signal. In particular it is possible with this analysis method to stretch independently the time axis and the frequencies of the signal (time/rate changing).

We can introduce the philosophy of this work as follows: Taking a sound, we transform it into a two-dimensional image; it can be displayed on the screen of a computer, with either the amplitude or the phase values. This image represents the short-time Fourier transform of the sound (because each point is the convolution of the signal with a grain, we can use fast Fourier transform (FFT) algorithms). After that we transform the image and try to resynthesize the signal. Hence we obtain a new sound. But the fact is that we cannot get the exact transform we would like to have because of a blurring effect during the resynthesis. A simple explanation is that each grain of reconstruction has its own Gabor transform, in a limited but unavoidable domain of time and frequency, and this reproducing kernel blurs the image of the transformation. One aim of my presentation is to try to explain how drastic these side effects can be, and how one can find ways to do better; that is, to show how one can transform time-frequency images so that they are not destroyed too much at the resynthesis.

Briefly, is the wavelet transform a Gabor time-frequency representation? Perhaps it could be if Gabor had thought about it, but he did not. As frequencies increase or decrease, wavelets are compressed or expanded in time, whereas Gabor grains keep the same duration. So there is a significant difference between the two. But what is not different is the way musicians try to use these two techniques. The fact that an arbitrary deformation of a legitimate time-frequency representation is not legitimate (it does not yield the representation of any signal) was first demonstrated on sounds by Richard Kronland-Martinet with a wavelet transform. I suggest that despite the variety of transforms, there is always this fundamental uncertainty principle that asserts that it is not possible to be precise both in time and in frequency.

## Time-Frequency Analysis Methods

This section looks at three major methods of time-frequency analysis: the long-time Fourier transform, the short-time Fourier transform, and the wavelet transform.

### Long-time Fourier Transform

The complete Fourier transform can only be applied to an infinite signal, or at least from its beginning to its end. What we usually call a Fourier transform is really a Fourier transform of a part of a sound, selected by applying a time window. At this point it is usually called a short-time Fourier transform. But let us look at the complete Fourier transform, just to see that a time-domain signal can be entirely defined in the frequency domain (without any reference to time in its expression).

First we work in the continuous domain, with a signal given from $-\infty$ to $+\infty$. The Fourier transform is defined by

$$G(\omega) = \int_{-\infty}^{+\infty} s(t)e^{j\omega t}\,dt.$$

$G(\omega)$ has some constraints. In particular, if the signal is real (which is usually the case), the negative and positive parts are conjugate:

$$G(-\omega) = \bar{G}(\omega)$$

Conversely we can obtain a time-domain signal $s(t)$ from its Fourier transform by

$$s(t) = K \int_{-\infty}^{+\infty} G(\omega)e^{-j\omega t}\,d\omega.$$

If the positive and negative parts of $G(\omega)$ are conjugate, then the signal $s(t)$ is real. Otherwise it is a complex function.

These two formulas mean that it is equivalent to give the definition of a sound by it temporal evolution or by its long-term spectral content (figure 3.1).

**Reconstruction of Sampled Sounds**     The sounds we discuss are *digitized*, like the ones taken from samplers or analog-to-digital converters (ADCs) attached to computers. A digitized sound is the equivalent of a continuous sound if and only if there are no frequencies higher than half the sampling frequency in the original continuous sound. This is what is usually called the Nyquist criterion. This is achieved by putting a strong lowpass filter before the ADC.

A way to prove the possible reconstruction from the sampled sound version is to look at what happens in the frequency domain with a long-term Fourier transform. The sampled signal is obtained by multiplying the continuous filtered signal with a train of pulses. Multiplication in time is equivalent to the convolution in frequency. The spectrum of a train of pulses is a train of pulses, so the result is the sum of the replication of the signal spectra, one around zero (so identity), and then around the sampling rate and its multiples.

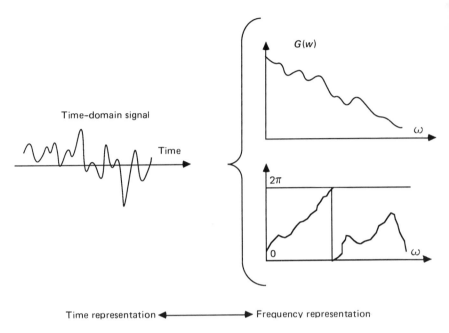

**Figure 3.1**
Time versus frequency representation of a signal

At this point it is easy to understand the Nyquist criterion: To be properly digitized and reconstructed, the sampling rate must be more than twice the maximum frequency. To reconstruct the signal after a digital-to-analog conversion, we need another strong lowpass filter. Apart from the fact that perfect lowpass filters do not exist, the entire process—filtering, analog-digital conversion, digital-analog conversion, and then again filtering—is an identity (figure 3.2).

**Fourier Transform of a Limited-Duration Sound**   Now that we know that a digital sound is a series of samples, we can again ask, What is the long-term Fourier transform of a limited-duration digital sound? An important result concerns the information that is required in the frequency domain to define a sound: If in the time domain a sound sampled at a sampling rate of $SR$ is given by its $N$ sample values, it is equivalent to define $(N + 1)/2$ complex values in the frequency domain, regularly spaced from 0 to $SR/2$ (figure 3.3).

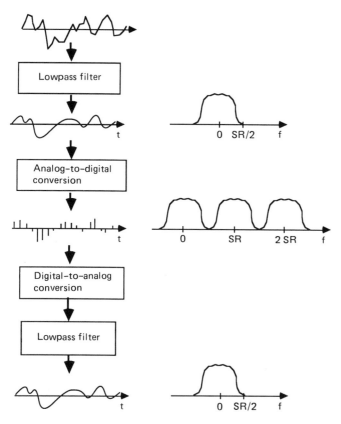

**Figure 3.2**
Sampling and reproducing a sound, from analog, to digital, to analog forms

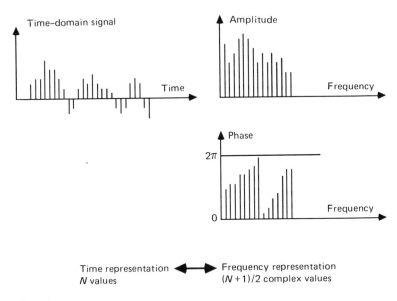

**Figure 3.3**
Discrete version of the time-frequency representation

For a brief demonstration of this fact, consider a periodic signal, a period of which is the initial sound. In this case the long-term Fourier transform consists only of the harmonics of the fundamental frequency (the inverse of the duration of the sound). This fundamental frequency is $SR/N$, and as we have to define the values of each line until $SR/2$ (because of the Nyquist theorem), we have $(N + 1)/2$ lines. Of course this could all be rendered more precise mathematically, but it is a good indication of how the things really work. Indeed it is essential to understand that a short-time Fourier transform is a long-term Fourier transform on a periodic signal, one period of which is the short-term signal.

We now see that when the sound to analyze is not infinite, it is equivalent to define a version sampled in time or in frequency.

**Short-Time Fourier Transform**

Now let us take a more precise look at what a short-time Fourier transform is. We have a signal that is a function of time, $s(t)$. At one instant, or around one instant, we extract a portion of this signal. Generally we "round" the corner of this portion by multiplying it by a window. This of course has an

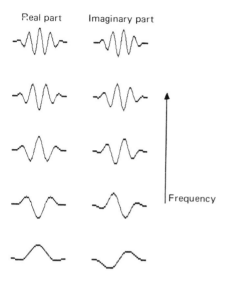

**Figure 3.4**
The series of analyzing grains in a Fourier transform

influence on the analysis, but using no window is like applying a rectangular window, which often is worse.

Though the usual algorithms do not work this way, taking the Fourier transform is equivalent to convolving this windowed signal with a series of reference signals, the envelope of which is the window, and the oscillating part is a sine or a cosine. Usually the sine part and cosine part are combined to give a complex signal (figure 3.4):

$$\cos(\omega t) + j \cdot \sin(\omega t) = e^{j\omega t}$$

It is interesting here to notice the relation with the wavelet transform. Both of them use grains of analysis, but the wavelets contract in length when the frequencies become higher. Here the grains are of the same length. A useful wavelet is the Morlet wavelet, which is the multiplication of a complex exponential by a gaussian window. Such a window can also be used, but windows of Hanning, Hamming, Blackmann type (and so on) can also be used in the Fourier analysis (Nuttall 1981). The essential fact is that this analysis uses a complex exponential, which lets us compute an instantaneous phase.

Let us turn now to practice. How can we represent musical sounds with the help of the Fourier transform? We know that sonagraphs are still widely used. The visual objects we can extract from a Fourier transform program are very close to this representation. However, it is important to notice that, with a computer, it is possible to know at each point not only the amplitude (the magnitude) but also the phase. Although phase is of no importance when we look at the spectrogramlike picture, it is fundamental when we want to reconstruct from this representation.

**Time-Frequency Diagrams with an FFT Program**   The FFT program is well known. Its algorithm can be found in the literature, and software packages exist that prevent musicians from rewriting it. So I describe only the practical points that are essential to use it musically.

The sliding FFT consists of taking a signal (which can be of infinite length), applying a time window (which restricts the time domain to a specified interval), and taking the Fourier transform of this signal (figure 3.5). For example, with a 1024-point FFT we obtain 513 complex points (because of the extrema, 0 and $SR/2$) in the frequency axis. These points can be translated into polar form, which gives an amplitude and a phase.

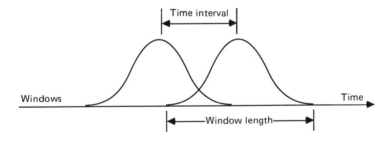

**Figure 3.5**
Elements of the sliding Fourier transform

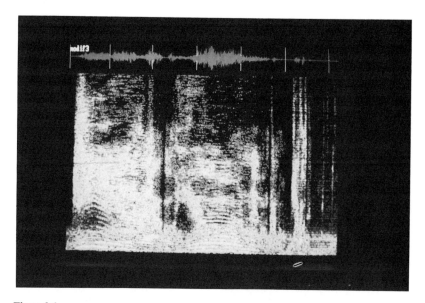

**Figure 3.6**
Sonagram of a sound (screen image), converted to black-and-white for this book.

The sonograph or sonogram is a useful tool for acoustic signal analysis. It consists of taking successive FFTs, at a certain time interval and with a specific window. I now describe a useful implementation on an inexpensive IBM PC–compatible computer. A PC screen contains $640 \times 350$ dots, which can be individually colored in 16 different shades (figure 3.6).

We would like to generate a color sonograph representation of a sound with this hardware/software configuration. Two parameters are important: the time interval between the FFTs and the length and shape of the window. The first parameter allows one to vary the resolution of the view. For instance, if we want to represent 6.4 seconds of sound on a screen, the time distance between successive FFTs is 10 milliseconds. If we use an interval of 1 millisecond, we can view only 0.64 second of sound.

The second parameter is more difficult to relate to perception. The length and shape of the window is a measure of the bandwidth that can be discriminated by the analysis. There exists a frequency/time dialectic that is the following in musical terms: To detect a pitch, we must measure on a long time window, whch tends to smooth out transients. However, if we want to be precise in the time domain, we cannot separate narrowly spaced frequency components. A good compromise for acoustic analysis is to choose a 1024-point FFT with a Hanning window. We often use in our laboratory a sampling rate of 25,600, so the bandwidth is 25 Hz. This is also a limit for the ear: When a click is repeated more than 25 times per second, it is heard as pitch and not as a repetition of sounds.

Now the problem is to assign different colors to the levels of the sound. With 16 colors we have found that a 90-db scale is fine for acoustic musical signals, so each step represents 6 db (which is a halving of the signal amplitude) (figure 3.7).

With this simple analysis we have a useful tool to show and examine sounds. Now what can use such a program for? To see a sound is not to hear it, but the program does give real insight about where the information is (Johannesma et al. 1981). The Fourier transform is a *fixed bandwidth* analyzer, so the following problem can arise: On the vertical axis the frequency scale is linear. So octaves are not well represented, but the harmonics of a sound are equally spaced. So it depends on what you want to look at: If logarithmic perception is important, other methods are better, for example, the wavelet transform. But we shall also notice that Fourier transform programs are useful for synthesis-by-analysis methods.

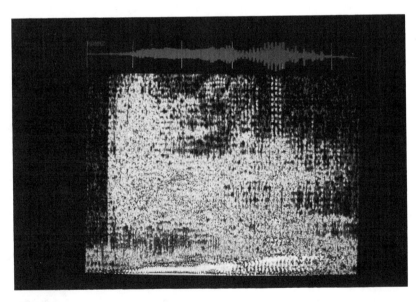

**Figure 3.7**
Sonagram of a sound using a short window (screen image)

## The Wavelet Transform

I want first to refer to Kronland-Martinet and Grossmann (chapter 2) for all signal processing details about this method. I focus only on the representation of sounds it can provide (Bacry, Grossmann, and Zak 1975, Guillemain, Kronland-Martinet, and Marthens 1989, Grossmann and Kronland-Martinet 1988).

A Fourier analysis line can be calculated as the convolution of a signal with a grain of sound that is the multiplication of the window by a complex exponential. The real term is a cosine, and the imaginary part is a sine wave. That is to say that the Fourier analysis is the result of successive convolutions with analysis grains that are all of the same length and that have equally spaced frequencies.

A wavelet transform can be viewed as the result of convolutions with analyzing grains that are of different lengths and frequencies that are on an exponential scale. This is a simplification because wavelet analysis is much more general, but for musicians it is enough to know that the analysis with a Morlet-type wavelet is at constant $DF/F$, which usually means a one-third octave analysis.

The visual representation of the wavelet transform (figure 3.8A) is different from the Fourier transform representation, for several reasons:

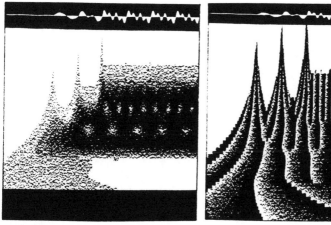

**Figure 3.8**
A wavelet representation of three sinusoids: (left) magnitude, (right) phase

• The vertical axis now has an exponential scale (which also means that octaves are equally spaced, which better respects the ear's appreciation of intervals).

• The number of channels can be much smaller: for example, 24 channels gives the equivalent of a third-octave analysis, on eight octaves.

• Much more important, the phase domain is now of great significance: as the window is narrower for high frequencies, the phase domain is accurate in the entire frequency range. Precise accidents in the sound, such as discontinuities, are obvious in the phase plane (figure 3.8B).

So which do we choose as a representation for music: the wavelet transform or a sliding Fourier transform? It depends on what you want to look at. It is well known that it is impossible to know both time and frequency as precisely as one wants. A wavelet transform or a sampled Fourier transform gives images of the time-frequency plane or the time-dilation scale. Each has constraints. The choice of the mode of representation can also be viewed as the choice of the reproducing kernel.

## Gabor-type Granular Analysis-Synthesis

We need a method that can reconstruct exactly a given analyzed signal, if desired (Bastiaans 1980). That is, starting from an analysis with the sliding Fourier transform, we would like to obtain the same sound as the original one. Gabor (1946) was first to present a coherent view of the time-frequency information contained in a sound. Although his work antedated modern signal processing using computers, his paper is a fundamental contribution to the comprehension of the link between time and frequency representations.

Gabor noticed that the best window for analysis is the gaussian window (from a mathematical point of view) because its Fourier transform leaves its shape invariant. Because I am more concerned with applications of the theory to practical sound examples, most of the time the window chosen is a Hanning window (figure 3.9). A truncated gaussian window has also been used, but it gives no practical advantage, and the computing time is longer because the window has to be larger.

If we look at the frequency domain, we can think in term of *channels*. Each grain of sound is analyzed by different filters, and the grain itself can

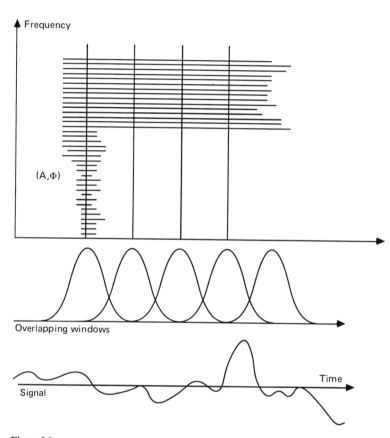

**Figure 3.9**
The elements of a rectangular grid for a perfect reconstruction

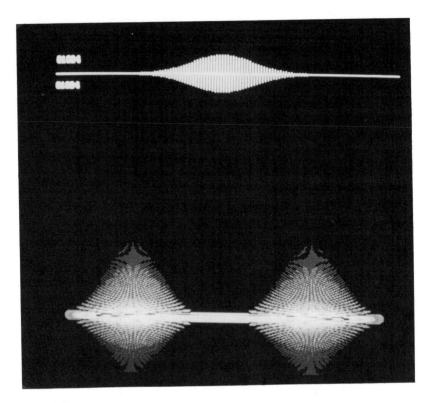

**Figure 3.10**
The reproducing kernel of a Hanning window

be reconstructed only if the sum of these filters is identity. This is true for the Fourier transform, which is reversible.

If we look at the time domain, we can think in terms of grains of sound. As can be seen in figure 3.10, it is possible to apply regularly spaced windows to a sound to obtain a series of grains. If we take the sum these tiny sounds, we will obtain the original signal if and only if the sum of the successive windows is 1. If

$$\sum_n w(t + n\Delta t) = 1,$$

then

$$\sum_n w(t + n\Delta t)\,\text{sig}(t) = \text{sig}(t),$$

where $w(t + n\Delta t)$ represents the successive windows shifted in time. For example, if the window is square, it is sufficient to take a time distance between windows that is equal to the length of this window. If we use a Hanning window, the time distance must be half its length.

If we combine the frequency and time aspects, we can say that we can achieve an exact reconstruction by taking the Fourier transform of overlapping grains of sound. If we make the sum of tiny grains containing only cosine waves with an initial phase shaped by a window, we only need to define the amplitude and phase on a rectangular grid in the time-frequency domain.

For example, if we use a 1024-point Fourier transform and a Hanning window, we must use a time interval of 512 samples (due to the Hanning shape). So we obtain our grid by having 512 amplitudes and phases at each abscissa. The reconstruction will be exact if we apply the reverse Fourier transform and sum the grains.

## Sound Transformation Applications

Now we want to deform this analysis grid and try to make this transformation realistic. For example, one difficult transformation would be to alter the time domain without changing the frequency axis. But before trying different things, it is important to state that an arbitrary transformation of the time-frequency plane cannot be similar to the analysis of an actual signal. In other words the arbitrary transformation of a legal transform is illegal. The reason for this is that the granular reconstruction from such a two-dimensional function gives a signal, the transform of which is different from the initial function. However, it can be very close, and one must not be shy for it is always possible to try something. Even if the result is not what was expected, it also can be musically interesting!

**Reproducing Kernel of a Gabor Transform**   What is the reproducing kernel of a Gabor transform? Suppose we have analyzed a sound with the help of a short-time Fourier transform, and we have the values of the amplitudes and phases of this transform on a time-frequency plane, at least on a rectangular grid. We can change the values of the amplitudes and phases and also move these points onto a different grid. Then we want to resynthesize a signal from the new image. So we assign to each point of the transform a grain of sound, called a *reconstruction grain*, with the amplitude and phase values it has on the new image.

Let us summarize what we have done: a "Gabor transform," an alteration of the image, and resynthesis to generate a new sound. But if again we take the Gabor representation of this sound, we will see that it is not equivalent to the altered image we were asking for. Why? Because during the resynthesis we applied a grain of sound at each point of the diagram, and these grains have a Gabor representation that is not a single point but that spreads over an area. The short-time Fourier transform of the window is the reproducing kernel, which is a sort of blurring sponge that we have to apply on the time-frequency blackboard to obtain the equivalent of the resynthesis.

Except for the identity, all the transforms are biased by this reproducing kernel (Griffin and Lim 1984, Portnoff 1979, 1980). It easily creates artifacts, such as comb filters and folded frequencies. And the reproducing kernel always exists; we can never avoid it. For example, if the reconstruction grain is a Dirac impulse, the reproducing kernel is a vertical bar. If it is a truncated gaussian grain, it has a more elliptical form.

We will see in following chapters that we have found some techniques to minimize the effect of the reproducing kernel of the reconstruction grains. It remains, however, the central difficulty to alter natural sounds conveniently.

**Test Sequences**   We have found it useful to examine the nonlinear transforms of natural sounds, specifically, the speaking voice and a monodic instrument (clarinet). The clarinet sounds were played by Michel Portal, and the speaking voice comes from Alex Grossmann or myself.

We have also defined synthesized sequences, which show the difficulty of separation between time and frequency. These test signals are a Dirac impulse, a long sine wave, and a gaussian window on a sine wave. The first two test sounds are degenerate versions of the third one. For example, if we test the slowing of a sound without transposition, we would want the Dirac impulse to remain a Dirac impulse and the sine wave to remain a sine wave, the envelope of which would be lengthened. But, as we will see, things are not that simple!

## Analysis-Transformation-Synthesis with Gabor Grains

A major problem in sound transformations is the fact that time and frequency are related. For example, a tape on a recorder plays frequencies that depend on its playback speed. Many attempts have been made to escape this constraint, using tools like the phase vocoder, linear prediction, and wavelets. I wanted to develop a method that could work independently of the nature of the source and that could be implemented on small, inexpensive computers. I do not claim that the method I develop here is entirely novel, but it is very simple, and it works (Portnoff 1981a, b).

Is it possible to distort the time axis without perturbing the frequency axis? In other words, can we obtain a sonogram of the altered version that is a horizontal time-warped version of the original one?

An initial idea is to take all these elementary grains and move them. This also means that it is not necessary to take an FFT and then the reverse FFT. All we have to do is to window the signal and move the big grains (figure 3.11).

For example, if we want to slow down by a factor of four, we would take our windows at regular time intervals, which are separated by only a quarter of their normal value. With the preceeding values (1024-point window) we would take the grains at a distance of 128 points and rebuild them at the normal distance of 512.

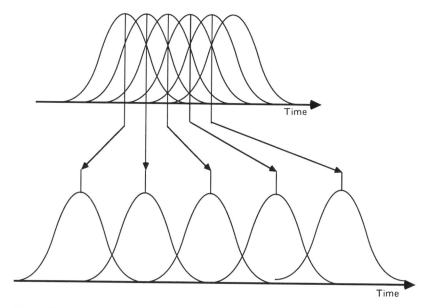

**Figure 3.11**
The classical way of warping time

In effect this is a nonlinear transformation of the grid, and it does not work. Depending on the frequencies present in the original signal, the phase scrambling that results from the time warping creates a comb filter effect.

### Temporal Deformation with an Integer Ratio (The Phase Solution)

Because the problem (and maybe the solution) is in the phase domain, let us remember that we have a rectangular grid with a value of amplitude and phase at each intersection. We can argue that the phase must "turn" when we warp the time axis. I shall not give a demonstration of the fact that it is only an approximate solution. But it works perfectly well with sine waves.

The idea is simple: If you want to slow down a sound by an integer ratio, after having windowed the sound and having obtained its FFT, multiply all the phases by this integer before doing the inverse FFT and adding the new grains well placed in time. So the suggested algorithm is as follows (figure 3.12):

- Take successive FFTs of overlapped grains.
- Bring them closer or further on the time scale according to the speed ratio.
- Multiply all the instantaneous phases by this ratio.
- Apply the inverse Fourier transform.
- Take the sum of the windowed reconstructed signals.

The constraint on the analysis grid is that at the reconstruction the grid must be tight enough to satisfy the law stating that the sum of squares of the windows is unity (as in the pure identity reconstruction). In reality a safety factor of two is preferable.

The audio result is good, be it with voice or with clarinet sounds. It has been used without any manual adjustment of parameters by Jean-Claude Risset with clarinet sounds recorded by Michel Portal: The slowed-down version had no unwanted noise.

Here are some experimental results that imply a psychoacoustical interpretation. We use a 25,600-Hz sampling rate; the original sound is a speaking voice ("gira" said by Alex Grossmann), and the slowing factor is eight. If the window length is 128 or 256, the transformation of a speaking voice will add a raucous granularity to the timbre. This may be musically interesting, but it is not what we expect from a simple slowing process.

A window size of 1024 points is our best choice for a natural-quality slowed voice. It seems to be the optimal compromise between time and

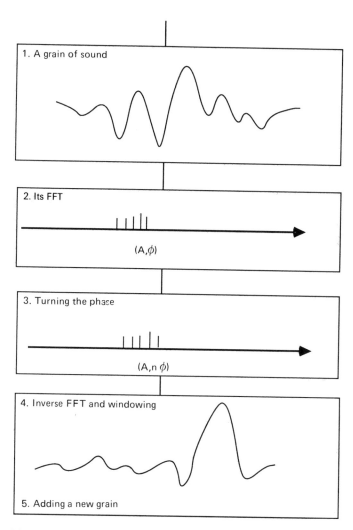

**Figure 3.12**
A better way of warping time than that shown in figure 3.11.

frequency aspects. Using 2048 or 4096 values gives a reverberation effect, more or less like successive echoes that are close enough to each other so that they are fused.

How do we interpret this? In this process we want to make a separation between the amplitude envelopes, which should be slowed down by the scale factor, and the instantaneous frequencies, which should be kept as they are. Making the phase turn faster by the scale factor ratio is identical to keeping the instantaneous frequency straight. Depending on the length of the window, the borderline between what is embodied in the amplitude terms and the frequency terms varies. We have seen in the analysis section that if we take a short window, the image creates vertical lines with the speaking voice (the amplitude envelope follows the instantaneous amplitude of the sound within each period), whereas taking a long window gives horizontal lines, indicating that the harmonics are well tracked, but then temporal accidents like transients are blurred.

Is this algorithm different from the phase vocoder (Moorer 1978)? Yes and no—not in its philosophy, but in its technique. To track phase, the phase vocoder needs an FFT at each point (in our algorithm it is only at each 128 points for a 1024-point FFT). If the phase vocoder is not followed by a bandpass filter at the reconstruction, it is as though we reconstructed only with the middle values of the inverse FFT. So it is different also from this aspect.

**Temporal Deformation with a Noninteger Ratio**

The previously described algorithm works well with integer ratios. Why? Because the phases are defined modulo $2\pi$, and the multiplication by an integer is still true modulo $2\pi$ (figure 3.13). But if the ratio is not an integer, this is obviously false.

I have tried to solve the phase problem by unwrapping the phase. It is very close to the phase vocoder problem, but here we do FFTs only at half the window rate, so the unwrapped phase can take much more than one turn between analysis. The algorithm is also very simple: We consider the phase target, starting from the preceding point, and so we know the phase advance taken during the interval. This assumes that there can be a $2\pi$ error, but if the component is really within the bandwidth, it cannot be so. Each line of the Fourier transform, on a horizontal line, can be interpreted as the result of a filtering around the central frequency of this line. So if the length of the FFT is $n$, and the order of the line is $i$, the "center phase turn"

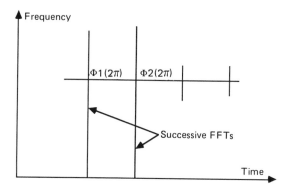

**Figure 3.13**
Unwrapped phase estimation in time warping by an integer

for a move of the sliding FFT of one sample is $(2i\pi)/n$. One can immediately deduce its vaue when the window displacement is $k$: $(2i\pi k)/n$.

Of course nothing guarantees that after $k$ samples the deviation of phase is really in a $[-\pi, \pi]$ interval around its target. But one can be sure that if it is not so its amplitude is very low. This method usually works well for any speed ratio: Only a trained ear can hear a little spark of high components when there is a failure. Of course, this does not happen with an integer ratio because what is true modulo $2n\pi$ is also true modulo $2\pi$. It is also possible to conduct a trial run with a large number of samples between windows and, if necessary, to conclude with a Fourier transform at each sample.

**Transposition without Time Alteration**

If we know how to warp time without frequency transposition, we also know how to alter frequency without time variation. One method is to time warp and then to under- or oversample this signal by the inverse ratio. It is also possible to under- or oversample before the time warping.

The usual way to under- or oversample is to interpolate with a finite-impulse-response (FIR) filter. The simplest kind is the linear interpolation between successive points, but it can create spurious components (through aliasing of the upper frequencies) if undersampling is used. A good way to avoid this is to remove the "dangerous" frequencies between the direct and inverse FFT transforms.

The musical sensation of this effect is really one of a tape recorder transposition, with its hints and drawbacks like unintelligibility of the speaking voice, but because the time axis is unchanged, many manipulations of sounds akin to *musique concrète* are now possible. This section has shown some basic ways to perform operations useful for computer music and how promising the analysis-synthesis method can be. The intermediate tool is a time-frequency representation. I have worked with the sliding FFT, but the other methods (including the wavelet transform) can be used with the same ideas. However, for the specific problem of slowing a sound without transposition, the sampled FFT works well musically, whereas the use of the wavelet transform raises difficulties here.

## Other Sound Transformations

This section deals with other techniques for sound transformation, including filtering, sound/resonance separation, and phase modifications.

### Filtering with Linear Convolution by FFT

The filtering of frequencies can be viewed at first glance as a trivial operation. In effect we obtain the values of the amplitudes provided by the analysis, and we can alter them before the resynthesis. This works only if the changes are not too drastic. We have to remember that directly altering a transform is illegal—we have to convolve it with the reproducing kernel. So the real transform we get is not the one we were expecting; that is, when we decide to alter the amplitudes one way, we obtain them another way.

There is an alternative technique, which is well known in signal processing: *linear convolution by FFT*. But first we have to speak about *circular convolution*, which is what we did by changing only the amplitudes. The algorithm for circular convolution consists of the following steps:

- Take the windowed FFT of a signal.
- Multiply by the FFT of the filter (its spectral response).
- Apply the inverse Fourier transform.
- Add the successive grains (windowed or not).

This is called circular convolution because we do the convolution of two periodic signals: one with the initial signal, and the second with the impulse response of the filter. So the modified signal is recycled due to its periodicity.

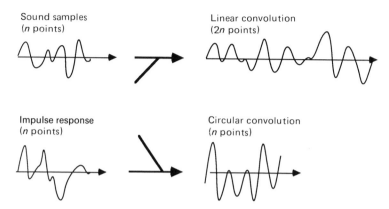

**Figure 3.14**
Difference between linear and circular convolution

Linear convolution is done by taking the multiplication of FFTs, but with a signal defined on only half of the period, so there is no overlap between one period and the successive one (figure 3.14). Both techniques can be tried when we want to filter a sound. Of course the second one takes a little bit longer to compute, but it is also more "regular."

**Source/Resonance Separation**

Among the many models of voice sound synthesis, one is very attractive: the separation of a *source* and a *resonance*. The source can be "voiced" or "unvoiced," but its characteristic spectrum is flat overall. The resonance instead determines the general envelope of the speech spectrum, but does not include the individual harmonics or more generally the accidents in the spectrum (figure 3.15). This is modeled on the natural voice mechanism, where the vocal cords act as the source, whereas the mouth and nose produce the resonance. The resonance has a continuous spectrum, and as such it filters the source. This filtering action can be simulated by a recursive IIR (infinite impulse response) or nonrecursive FIR (finite impulse response) filter.

Recall that we have an original sound, which is the sum of grains of sounds obtained by applying a sliding envelope to the signal. What we are now trying to do is to separate each grain into two grains: one that is the source grain, and a resonance that is the filter. There are some traditional techniques for doing that, the *cepstrum* being one of the most appropriate

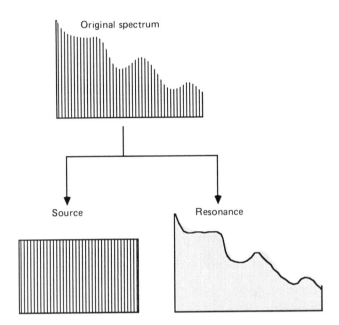

**Figure 3.15**
Source resonance separation of a periodic signal

(another is linear prediction). In our laboratory we have used an alternative technique. Very briefly it consists of taking a short-time Fourier transform, then keeping only the logarithm of the magnitude, then making this log spectrum symmetrical by duplicating its values (figure 3.16).

At this point we separate the slowly moving part and the rapidly moving part of this pseudosignal. The slowly moving part looks like the log spectrum of the formants, and the rapidly moving part looks like an approximation of the log spectrum of the source. Coming back to the initial FFT, we can easily split it into two FFTs: one for the source and one for the resonance (for example, in giving zero phase for the resonance and the initial phases for the source).

What can we do with this separation? We can independently move the two spectra. A good example of this is the octave doubling of the source, by compressing the source spectrum by a factor of two and leaving resonance spectrum unchanged. Alternative techniques exist: taking any other line, taking the sum of two successive lines, or going into the time domain and applying the compression there. Everything can be tried, the goal being only to get the physical sensation of doubling when hearing the result.

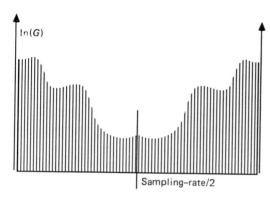

**Figure 3.16**
Making a FFT spectrum (zero phase) symmetrical

Conversely the resonance spectrum can be moved or transformed. When it is moved, "Donald Duck" or "Darth Vader" voices can result, and when it is transformed, we can whiten the sound or enhance the formants.

We can also take the source from one sound an the resonance from another to perform *cross-synthesis*. But at this point we no longer have a technique, but rather an art, because there are so many variables. It is impossible to go into details here, but spectral and musical compatibilities are required to obtain a good hybrid sound, whatever technique is used to cross them.

**Phase Modifications**

The two preceding techniques worked on the magnitude of the time-frequency diagram, and the phases were left unchanged. It is also possible to tamper with the phase values of this diagram. Some trials have been made, but work in this area is still in progress. One can, for example, set all the phases to zero after the analysis has been made on a rectangular grid. This is an elegant way to make a comb filter because at reconstruction the rays stay as they are or disappear, depending on the fact that the microscopic grains add or subtract on a horizontal line. So the comb filter effect depends on the time distance between FFTs. One can also assign a virtual phase that is different from the analyzed phase.

The main risk in applying such phase transformations is that noise may be generated. If the magnitudes are left unchanged, then the overall sensation of the envelope of the sound will remain unchanged.

The list of possible manipulations is of course endless. Choral effects or varieties of reverberation are also possible by changing values on the time-frequency diagram. Some of these manipulations are easier by other means, but even then it is a good thing to look at the image after transformation to see what has happened to the sound.

## Using Parameters Extracted from Existing Synthesis Methods

At this point we have described only transformations of sound that do not imply any synthesis model. But a good way of exploring sound transformations would be to use all the previous knowledge in synthesis to model natural sounds via a specific combination of synthesis techniques (Risset and Wessel 1982).

One often has access to a general type of computer music synthesis. At the CNRS-LMA laboratory in Marseille, as well as at the Luminy University, we use the Music V program (Mathews 1969), which has been rewritten in Turbo Pascal. This version includes many more unit generators to construct instruments, and we have tried to make it as useful as possible for musicians.

But even with such a tool one has to decide the way to perform sound synthesis. There are basically four types of synthesis: simple, additive, subtractive, and modulating or nonlinear. In broad terms simple synthesis is like taking a single object as it is, additive is like taking some particles and gluing them together, subtractive synthesis is like sculpture (the beauty was hidden in the stone . . .), and modulating can be viewed as clay modeling.

### Additive Synthesis

If we add some sounds together (figure 3.17), and if those sounds are mutually coherent to the ear, the result is one and only one sound sensation. For example, the addition of sine waves, with each having an envelope, can create harmonic sounds (if frequencies are multiples of a fundamental) or inharmonic sounds, like bells, gongs, or drums, if the partials are not in integer relations.

This method can be as precise as needed. It is time consuming, for the computer as well as for the human being, because one must describe every envelope of every partial. Of course automatic procedures can be used, but it is always a little difficult.

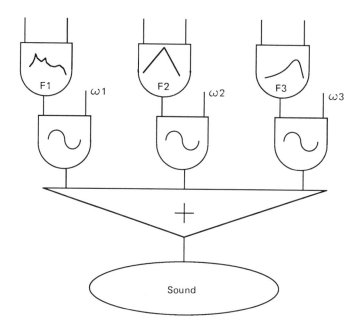

**Figure 3.17**
A Music V representation of additive synthesis

The additive method is very powerful. It requires that we separate the lines of the spectrum; the full spectrum is usually replaced by its most prominent components. The direct Fourier transform at one point only gives lines that are multiples of the sampling rate divided by the length of the FFT. By taking successive FFTs, we can model a sound as a sum of sinusoids of varying frequencies. But it must be clear that, though effective in theory, this is not what we want in practice for one harmonic of a sound is distributed among many lines of its FFT.

So what is required is a *spectral matching*. The Prony and Pissarenko algorithms are well known, but make little use of FFTs. An algorithm using wavelets has been developed by Philippe Guillemain, and we can think that this is an interesting direction. Clearly a good algorithm would be one that extracts from a grain of sound the major frequency lines.

### Subtractive Synthesis

In subtractive synthesis we remove (subtract) some parts of an initial sound (figure 3.18). This is what the mouth resonances do with the sound of the vocal cords. This method was originally developed for vocal synthesis, but

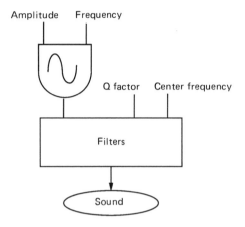

**Figure 3.18**
A Music V representation of a subtractive synthesis

it works well for instrumental simulations because the position of formants is an important cue for the ear (whenever there are formants, of course).

The subtractive method can be taken in two directions: The first one is to consider the resonance as evolving rapidly with time, like a voice model. An alternative view is to consider a musical instrument that has fixed resonances, and the problem is to extract these formants. One way has been explored by P. Sanchez at the LMA laboratory. First, one makes a recording of an entire scale played on the instrument. If there are formants, they appear as a predominance in a spectral region. A way to extract them is to take one period of each sound in its steady state and then to display the amplitude of this harmonic for each note of the musical scale. This formant structure appears well. So this is an experimental way to extract formants without knowing them in advance.

### Modulation Synthesis

During the 1970s several modulation synthesis methods appeared, such as frequency modulation (FM) (Chowning 1973) and the waveshaping method (Arfib 1979, LeBrun 1979). In each of these methods we use a mathematical formula to generate sound.

For example, the equation for FM (see figure 3.19) is

$$y = A(t)\sin(w_c t + I(t)\sin(w_m t)).$$

The equation for waveshaping plus amplitude modulation is

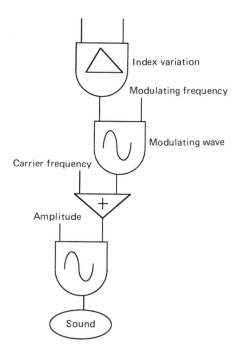

**Figure 3.19**
A Music V representation of FM synthesis

$$y = A(t)f(I(t)\sin(\omega_m t))\sin(\omega_c t).$$

A digital instrument for waveshaping plus amplitude modulation is shown in figure 3.20. The usual characteristic of these methods is to create a line spectrum, that is, frequencies that satisfy the relation $f = f_c \pm k \cdot f_m$, where $f_c$ and $f_m$ are called *carrier* and *modulating* frequencies. The spectrum also depends on the value of an index $I(t)$ in the equations.

To simulate a sound by modulation, the goal is to find the evolution of the fundamental frequency, the timbre index, and a possible post correction of amplitude. Spectral matching can be made in different ways, one of them being to identify the center of gravity of the real and synthetic sound (Beauchamp 1982).

**But Does It Work?**

The first goal is to extract values from an analysis, to feed them to a well-known synthesis method, expecting that the resulting sound will be a

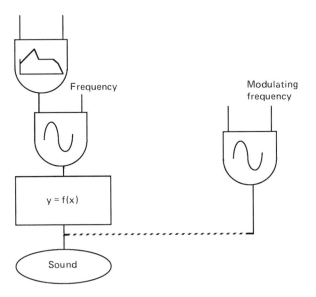

**Figure 3.20**
A Music V representation of a waveshaping synthesis with amplitude modulation

good approximation of a sound. The sound goal is to play with this model to transform this sound.

All these methods are currently under development, so it is difficult to evaluate their effectiveness. The main difference between this approach and that of direct transformation of sounds with the help of a Gabor representation is that we must have a preconceived model of the sound, whereas in direct transformation, it is of no importance. But once the model is clearly defined, the musical transformation can be particular and not general.

## Conclusion

The major points of this presentation of the time-frequency model are:

• It is possible to keep all the information of a sound in a time-frequency diagram. With a Fourier transform, this grid is rectangular.

• It is possible to use this diagram to perform unusual deformations on the sound, but these deformations are always biased by the reproducing kernel effect.

• It is possible to extract information from this diagram to feed other models that are closer to musical concepts in the way they are manipulated.

• Much work still has to be done in theory (for example, how to define "legal" transformation in one step) and, most of all, in practice (where the only limits are these of imagination).

Much of what I have discussed has been explored long before me, but I hope that the conceptual framework described here will help musicians to better understand sound processing. The bridge between natural and synthetic sounds is narrow, and I hope that it is also robust.

## References

Arfib, D. 1979. "Digital synthesis of complex spectra by means of multiplication of nonlinear distorted sine waves." *Journal of the Audio Engineering Society* 27(10): 757–768.

Bacry, H., A. Grossmann, and J. Zak. 1975. "Proof of the completeness of lattice states in the KQ representation." *Physical Review* B12: 1118.

Bastiaans, M. 1980. "Gabor's expansion of a signal into gaussian elementary signals." *Proceedings of the IEEE* 68: 538–539.

Beauchamp, J. W. 1982. "Synthesis by spectral amplitude and 'brightness' matching of analysed musical instrument tones." *Journal of the Audio Engineering Society* 30(6).

Chowning, J. 1973. "The synthesis of complex audio spectra by means of frequency modulation." *Journal of the Audio Engineering Society* 21(7): 526–534. Reprinted in C. Roads and J. Strawn, eds. 1985. *Foundations of Computer Music.* Cambridge, Massachusetts: MIT Press, pp. 6–29.

Gabor, D. 1946. "Theory of communication." *Journal of the IEE* 93: 429–441.

Griffin, D. W., and J. Lim. 1984. "Signal estimation from modified short-time Fourier transform." *IEEE Transactions on Acoustics, Speech, and Signal Processing* 32(2).

Grossmann, A., and R. Kronland-Martinet. 1988. "Time-and-scale representations obtained through continuous wavelet transforms." *Signal Processing IV: Theories and Applications.* Amsterdam: Elsevier Science Publishers.

Guillemain, P., Kronland-Martinet R., and B. Marthens. 1989. "Application de la transformée en ondelettes en spectroscopie RMN." Note Interne 112, Marseille: Laboratoire de Mécanique et d'Acoustique.

LeBrun, M. 1979. "Digital waveshaping synthesis." *Journal of the Audio Engineering Society* 27(4): 250–266.

Mathews, M. V. 1969. *The Technology of Computer Music.* Cambridge, Massachusetts: MIT Press.

Moorer, J. A. 1978. "The use of the phase vocoder in computer music applications." *Journal of the Audio Engineering Society* 26: 42–45.

Nuttall, A. H. 1981. "Some windows with good sidelobe behavior." *IEEE Transactions on Acoustics, Speech, and Signal Processing* ASSP-29: 84–91.

Portnoff, M. R. 1979. Magnitude-phase relationships for short-time Fourier transforms based on gaussian analysis windows." *ICASSP* 79. New York: IEEE, pp. 186–189.

Portnoff, M. R. 1980. "Time frequency representation of digital signals and system based on short time Fourier analysis." *IEEE Transactions on Acoustics, Speech, and Signal Processing* ASSP-28: 1.

Portnoff, M. R. 1981a. "Short time Fourier analysis of sampled speech." *IEEE Transactions on Acoustics, Speech, and Signal Processing* ASSP-29: 3.

Portnoff, M. R. 1981b. "Time scale modification of speech based on short-time Fourier analysis." *IEEE Transactions on Acoustics, Speech, and Signal processing* ASSP-29: 3.

Risset, J. C., and D. Wessel. 1982. "Exploration of timbre by analysis and synthesis." In D. Deutsch, ed. *The Psychology of Music*. Orlando: Academic Press.

# 4 Wavelet Transforms that We Can Play

**Gianpaolo Evangelista**

Additive synthesis is a classic technique for the synthesis of musical sounds (Moorer 1977). The musical signal $m(t)$ is expanded into a superposition of partials $s_k(t)$ according to some equation like

$$m(t) = \Sigma_k s_k(t). \tag{1}$$

Fourier additive synthesis is realized with quasi-periodic partials

$$s_k(t) = a_k(t)\cos(\omega_k t + \theta_k(t)), \tag{2}$$

where $a_k(t)$ and $\theta_k(t)$ are "slowly varying" functions, respectively representing amplitude and phase modulation of the otherwise uninteresting perpetual sinusoids. Amplitude and phase functions can be extracted from existing sound sources by means of a phase vocoder (see Dolson 1986 and references therein). Although a great deal of generality is contained in equation 1 with partials given as in equation 2, there are several reasons to be dissatisfied with it. In the first place the amplitude and phase of partials are not independent parameters, and indeed several pairs $\{a_k(t), \theta_k(t)\}$ may produce the same signal. This reflects the redundancy of the representation, which results in a lack of efficiency of the synthesis algorithm. This is the cause of many troubles in the analysis and identification of sounds. Moreover the rate at which the modulating functions should vary is not well defined. Notice that as a limit case the partial given in equation 2 can be thought of as a frequency modulation signal in ring modulation with $a_k(t)$.

In a celebrated paper Gabor (1946) introduced the era of combined time and frequency representations of communication signals, which is the objective of recent granular synthesis techniques in computer music (Roads 1978). According to Gabor, "Expansion into elementary signals is a process of which Fourier analysis and time description are special cases."

In a time-frequency plane one can assign to each signal a certain rectangle whose area represents its uncertainty product. This rectangle can be located around signal mean time of occurrence and spectral centroid. As extreme cases, with a sinusoid we associate a line parallel to the time axis and to a narrow pulse a line parallel to the frequency axis. Due to the uncertainty principle no signal can be assigned an area less than $\frac{1}{2}$, this minimum being achieved by gaussian-shaped envelopes of sinusoids. Gabor partitioned the time-frequency plane into identical rectangles of area $\frac{1}{2}$, called *logons* or

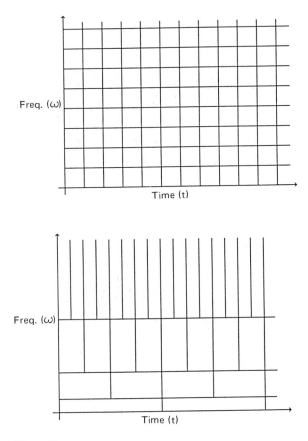

**Figure 4.1**
(Top) Gabor time-frequency grid. (Bottom) Cycle-octave time-frequency grid.

*quanta* of information, and defined the elementary signals as those associated with a minimum of uncertainty product.

Gabor's time-frequency grid is shown in figure 4.1A. Any musical waveform $m(t)$ can be expanded as a superposition of elementary signals (Gabor expansion),

$$m(t) = \Sigma_{n,k} a_{n,k} g(t - kT) e^{jn\Omega t},$$

(3)

where $g(t) = e^{-\pi t 2/\sigma}$, and $T = 2\pi/\Omega = \sigma^{1/2}$ (Bastiaans 1981). However, Gabor's partition of the time-frequency plane was somewhat arbitrary. For example, one can choose to partition the frequency axis in octave intervals and pick the nonuniform partition of the time axis that gives rectangles of area $\frac{1}{2}$, as shown in figure 4.1B. This leads to the cycle-octave representation (Grossmann and Morlet 1984) in which the elementary signals are chosen to be time translated and dilated copies of one and the same function $\psi(t)$, the so-called *wavelet*.

A problem arising in both Gabor expansions and cycle-octave representations is that the expansion coefficients are not uniquely determined; in mathematical terms the set of elementary signals is complete, but fails to be orthogonal, leading to a redundant representation. Furthermore we wish to relate a continuous-time transformation to an effective discrete-time algorithm that allows for efficient hardware or software implementations. Dropping the minimal uncertainty requirement, one can construct orthonormal wavelet bases constituted of elementary signals,

$$\psi_{n,m}(t) = 2^{-n/2} \psi(2^{-n}t - m),$$

(4)

which are characterized by a finite uncertainty product independent on the integer indices $n$ and $m$ (Daubechies 1988, Mallat 1989).

One of the advantages of orthogonal wavelet bases is that a minimum number of coefficients is required to completely represent a musical signal. Furthermore, analogous to the case of periodic waveforms in terms of Fourier series, the contributions of the partials to the overall signal are totally decoupled, and the expansion coefficients are uniquely determined as orthogonal projections. The relevance of this property is not to be underestimated because one of the reasons for the success of Fourier additive synthesis is that it represents a small perturbation of the totally uncoupled situation of pure sinusoidal partials. This fact allows the musician to associate a great deal of intuition to each signal component, starting with the simple case in which separation of effects occurs. In the sequel we shall see how orthogonal wavelet transforms can be implemented in standard digital processing structures and can be given an intuitive value as sound analysis and synthesis techniques.

## Filterbanks and Wavelet Expansions

Orthogonal wavelet transforms can be easily understood in terms of a special kind of filterbank. Roughly speaking, a structure to compute the transform consists of a bank of overlapping bandpass filters, as shown in figure 4.2. The bandwidth of each filter is approximately one octave, leading to nonuniform band splitting.

An alternate structure is shown in figure 4.3, in which bandpass filters are simply realized as cascades of lowpass and highpass frequency responses. Because the output bandwidth of each filter is approximately one-half that of the input, one can think of downsampling by a factor of two. This results in the structure of figure 4.4., in which we note that, due

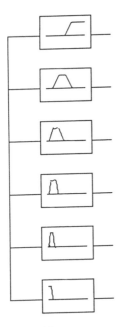

**Figure 4.2**
Filterbank

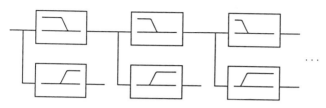

**Figure 4.3**
Filterbank realization using lowpass and highpass filters

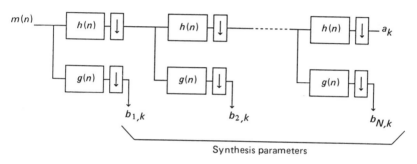

Synthesis parameters

**Figure 4.4**
Multirate filterbank

to downsampling, all the lowpass and all the highpass filters have identical transfer functions. Because practical filters have finite transition bands, however, some aliasing phenomena will occur along the way.

For resynthesis purposes we are interested in reconstructing the original signal, and here we have to do it from aliased data. Fortunately there exist highpass and lowpass filter pairs that have perfect reconstruction property (Crochiere and Rabiner 1983, Vaidyanathan 1987). These are the so-called QMFs (quadrature mirror filters). A careful look at figure 4.5 shows that the frequency responses $H(e^{j\omega})$ and $G(e^{j\omega})$ of a QMF pair satisfy the energy conservation relation

$$|H(e^{j\omega})|^2 + |G(e^{j\omega})|^2 = 1. \tag{5}$$

Together with equation 5 we can require $H$ and $G$ to satisfy the orthogonality relation

$$H(e^{j\omega})G^*(e^{j\omega}) + H(-e^{j\omega})G^*(-e^{j\omega}) = 0. \tag{6}$$

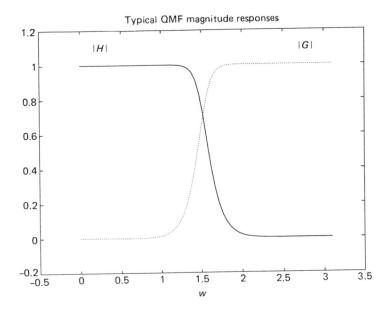

**Figure 4.5**
Typical quadrature mirror filter magnitude responses

A noncausal filter structure that allows us to reconstruct the signal is shown in figure 4.6. We baptize the impulse response of the upper lowpass branch of the synthesis structure as a *scaling function* and the impulse responses of the lower bandpass branches as wavelets. Indeed, the latter represent discrete unscaled estimations of the actual continuous-time basis functions but they well serve as basis functions of sampled signals.

More specifically, consider a depth $N$ reconstruction structure. Suppose the input to the upper branch has Fourier transform $S_0(e^{j\omega})$, then the output of the leftmost lowpass filter when all other inputs are zero is

$$S_1(e^{j\omega}) = S_0(e^{j2\omega})H^*(e^{j\omega}).$$

Similarly the output of the second lowpass filter is

$$S_2(e^{j\omega}) = S_1(e^{j2\omega})H^*(e^{j\omega})$$

$$= S_0(e^{j4\omega})H^*(e^{j2\omega})H^*(e^{j\omega}),$$

and generally

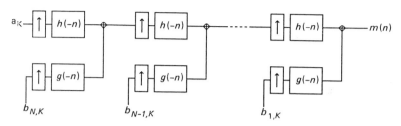

**Figure 4.6**
Inverse filterbank

$$S_n(e^{j\omega}) = S_0(e^{j2^n\omega}) \prod_{k=0}^{n-1} H^*(e^{j2^k\omega}),$$

$n = 1, 2, \ldots, N.$

Thus

$$S_n(e^{j2^{-n}\omega}) = S_0(e^{j\omega}) \prod_{k=1}^{n} H^*(e^{j2^{-k}\omega}),$$

and we can define the Fourier transform of a discrete scaling function as

$$\Phi_N(\omega) = \prod_{k=1}^{N} H^*(e^{j2^{-k}\omega}). \tag{7}$$

As $N$ increases, more and more samples of the scaling function are known, and in the limit the sampling grid will reach the continuum. The Fourier transform of a continuous-time scaling function can be defined as

$$\Phi(\omega) = \lim_{N} \Phi_N(\omega),$$

provided the product in equation 7 converges to a continuous square integrable function. In a similar fashion the Fourier transform of a discrete wavelet is defined as

$$\Psi_N(\omega) = G^*(e^{j\omega/2}) \prod_{k=2}^{N} H^*(e^{j2^{-k}\omega})$$

$$= G^*(e^{j\omega/2})\Phi_{N-1}(\omega/2), \tag{8}$$

from which, as $N \to \infty$, we obtain the Fourier transform of a continuous-time wavelet:

$\Psi(\omega) = G^*(e^{j\omega/2})\Phi(\omega).$

Note that discrete wavelets are all estimations of a unique continuous-time wavelet on different sampling grids. In the limit, however, they are copies of one and the same wavelet function $\psi(t)$ at various time scales: $\psi_{n,0}(t) = \psi(2^{-n}t)$, $n = 1, 2, \ldots$.

The synthesis parameters of a finite transform are directly extracted from the analysis filterbank. Indeed they are the output sequences $b_{n,k}$ of the bandpass filters plus the output of the rightmost lowpass filter. If we pick a sufficient number of stages $N$, the latter sequence will bring information only on the subsonic part of the signal, and it can be discarded. The musical signal $m(t)$ can be expanded as

$$m(t) = \sum_{n=1}^{N} \sum_{k=0}^{\infty} b_{n,k} \psi_{n,k}(t). \tag{9}$$

In an alternative to the inverse filter bank, table lookup local oscillators can be used to generate the set of elementary signals $\psi_{n,k}(t)$. A single table containing samples of $\psi(t)$ at a sufficiently high sampling rate can be shared by several step-plus-phase counters in which the step is a power of 2. The outputs of the oscillators are then scaled by their respective expansion coefficients and accumulated.

## Examples of Orthonormal Wavelet Bases

In the previous section I showed how a filterbank structure can be designed to compute wavelet expansions. Here I provide some useful examples of wavelets.

Although introduced independent of the wavelet theory, a well-known orthonormal wavelet basis is given by the *Haar system* (Haar 1910, Beauchamp 1975), for which

$$\psi(t) = \begin{cases} 1 & 0 \le t < 1/2 \\ -1 & 1/2 \le t < 1 \\ 0 & \text{otherwise} \end{cases}$$

is one cycle of square wave, with the Fourier transform

$$\Psi(\omega) = e^{-j(\omega + \pi)/2} \frac{\cos(\omega/2) - 1}{\omega/2},$$

as illustrated in figure 4.7. In the same figure few vectors forming the Haar basis are shown. The Haar wavelet $\psi(t/2)$ can be obtained as a linear combination of positive rectangular pulses that are translations of the prototype pulse (Haar scaling function):

$$\phi(t) = \begin{cases} 1 & 0 \le t < 1 \\ 0 & \text{otherwise} \end{cases},$$

In fact we have

$$\psi(t/2) = \phi(t) - \phi(t-1). \tag{11}$$

The Fourier transform of the Haar scaling function $\phi(t)$,

$$\Phi(\omega) = e^{-j\omega/2} \frac{\sin \omega/2}{\omega/2},$$

is a lowpass function, as shown in figure 4.7.

The scaled version $\phi(t/2)$ of the Haar scaling function is a rectangular pulse of twice the duration of $\phi(t)$, thus

$$\phi(t/2) = \phi(t) + \phi(t-1). \tag{12}$$

If we let

$$\psi(t/2) = 2 \sum_n g(n)\phi(t-n)$$

and

$$\phi(t/2) = 2 \sum_n h(n)\phi(t-n),$$

where, from equations 11 and 12, $g(0) = \frac{1}{2}, g(1) = -\frac{1}{2}, h(0) = \frac{1}{2}, h(1) = -\frac{1}{2}$, and $g(n) = h(n) = 0$ for all other $n$, we obtain the transfer functions of the Haar QMF pair:

$$H(z) = \frac{1+z}{2},$$

$$G(z) = \frac{1-z}{2}.$$

Incidentally note that to obtain causal filters computing the wavelet transform, we have to consider noncausal wavelet functions.

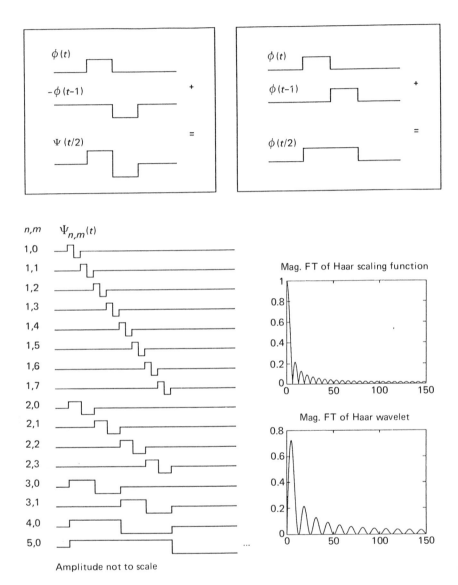

**Figure 4.7**
The Haar wavelet system

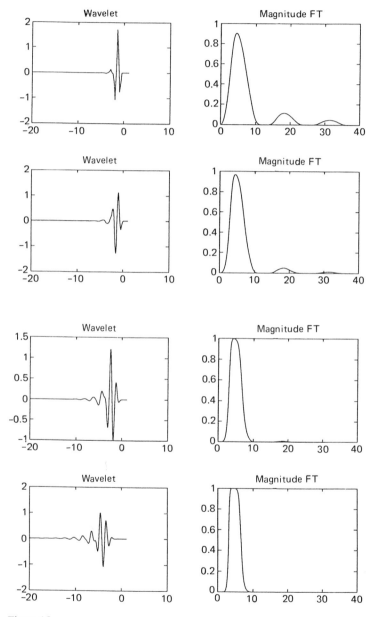

**Figure 4.8**
Wavelet sampler

Although well localized in time, the Haar basis functions have slowly decreasing Fourier transforms. In many sound analysis and synthesis applications, a tighter energy concentration in the frequency domain is desirable. Several techniques have been devised to design both finite and infinite impulse response quadrature mirror filter pairs, obtaining a large class of orthonormal wavelet bases (Evangelista 1989). A sampler of wavelets is given in figure 4.8, together with their magnitude Fourier transforms.

## Intuitive Facts About the Wavelet Expansion and Applications

The wavelet coefficient $b_{n,k}$ in equation 9 represents the frequency content of $m(t)$ in some octave frequency band indexed by $n$ and around time $2^n k$. Because for musical purposes we are interested in representing $m(t)$ in the finite frequency band 20 Hz to 20 KHz, only a finite number of filter sections are actually needed to analyze sounds. Intuitively a wavelet synthesis system consists of a graphic equalizer, each octave band being driven by a train of narrow pulses. The pitch of the inputs doubles with the octave, the lower band being driven by a slow train. The gain and the sign of each band can be dynamically controlled in synchrony with the input train. This is of course equivalent to controlling amplitudes and signs of the excitation pulses. The sequence of gains to synthesize a particular sound is exactly given by the analysis algorithm with no further processing. From equation 9 we can extract the $N$ subsignals (wavelet partials),

$$m_n(t) = \sum_{k=0}^{\infty} b_{n,k} \psi_{n,k}(t),$$

representing the contributions of $m(t)$ to $N$ octaves.

In figure 4.9 the wavelet transform of a segment of speech signal corresponding to a voiced "A" sound is shown. Figure 4.10 shows some of the subsignals obtained by partial wavelet resynthesis of the speech segment. Figure 4.11 compares a fragment of the original vowel with a partial reconstruction obtained by resynthesizing the maximum energy band only.

In many occasions we are interested in modifying the parameters obtained from the analysis. A class of time-varying filters can be easily implemented in the transform domain (Evangelista and Barnes 1990). Indeed by modifying the gains of our graphic equalizer in the time, we can create dynamic filtering of the original sound. Formally the impulse re-

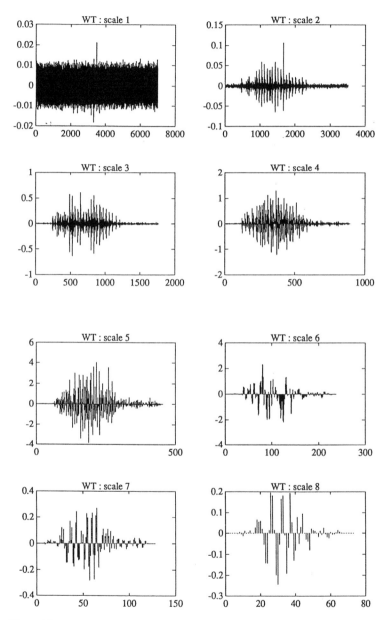

**Figure 4.9**
Wavelet coefficients of a speech segment (voiced "a"—male speaker)

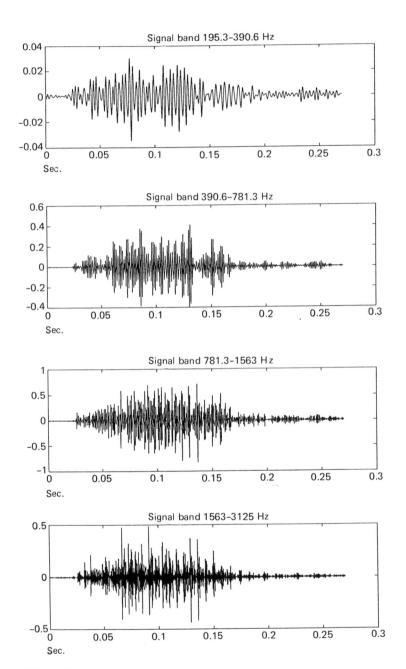

**Figure 4.10**
Time and frequency domain wavelet partials corresponding to some of the coefficients in
figure 4.9

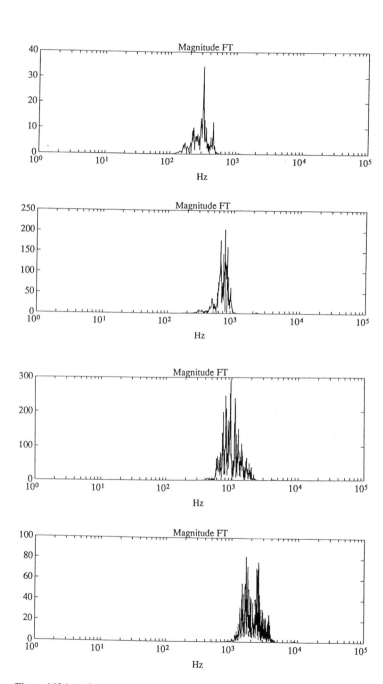

**Figure 4.10** (cont.)

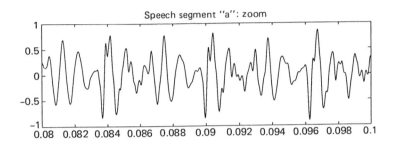

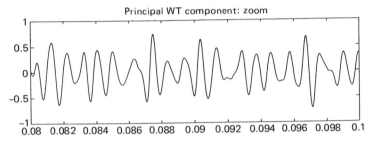

**Figure 4.11**
Principal component wavelet resynthesis and original speech fragment

sponses that can be realized by simply scaling the wavelet coefficients have
a diagonal representation:

$$h(t, \tau) = \Sigma_{n,k} h_{n,k} \psi_{n,k}(t) \psi_{n,k}(\tau).$$

Here again the index $k$ is related to time and the index $n$ to frequency band.
Due to the orthogonality of the wavelet functions, a generalized convolution
operation of $h(t, \tau)$ with a signal

$$m(t) = \Sigma_{m,l} b_{m,l} \psi_{m,l}(t)$$

gives the output

$$y(t) = \int h(t, \tau) m(\tau) \, d\tau = \Sigma_{n,k} h_{n,k} b_{n,k} \psi_{n,k}(t).$$

The maximum speed and minimum effective bandwidth of this class of
dynamic filters are controlled by the time and frequency uncertainty of the
wavelet. Good tradeoffs can be achieved by accurate design of the quadrature mirror filters generating the wavelet function.

The interesting fact about the wavelet transform is that the time resolution of the filtering operating varies with the frequency in octaves. Wavelet domain filtering seems to be more adapted to our perception of sounds than short-time Fourier transform domain methods. Subtractive synthesis techniques can be easily implemented in a wavelet system. In fact the wavelet coefficients of a white noise process are perfectly uncorrelated. One can simply obtain colored noise by enveloping the coefficients with gain sequences at various scales. The shape of these envelopes directly reflects the time evolution of the color. Formant synthesis can be realized with quasi-periodic wavelet coefficients (excitation). The choice of the wavelet should reflect characteristics of the vocal tract or resonances of the instrument. Formants can be shaped and changed in the time with the methods illustrated.

## Conclusions

The wavelet transform promises to be a powerful tool for the analysis, processing, and synthesis of signals. Its properties have not yet been fully explored, and many problems are still open. I believe that a lot of experimentation is needed to derive suitable algorithms for speech and sound production, and I hope that this simple tutorial can stimulate more ideas on the subject or initiate the nonspecialist reader to a fairly new concept.

## References

Bastiaans, M. J. 1981. "Gabor expansion of a signal into gaussian elementary signals." *Proceedings of IEEE* 68: 538–539.

Beauchamp, K. G. 1975. *Walsh Functions and Their Applications.* London: Academic Press.

Crochiere, R. E., and L. R. Rabiner. 1983. *Multirate Digital Signal Processing.* Englewood Cliffs: Prentice Hall.

Daubechies, I. 1988. "Orthonormal bases of compactly supported wavelets." *Communications on Pure and Applied Math.* XLI: 909–996.

Dolson, M. 1986. "The phase vocoder: a tutorial." *Computer Music Journal* 10(4): 14–27.

Evangelista, G. 1989. "Wavelet transforms and wave digital filters." To appear in the proceedings of the conference "Wavelets and some of their applications," Marseilles.

Evangelista, G., and C. W. Barnes. 1990. "Wavelet transforms and multirate filter banks" (manuscript in preparation).

Gabor, D. 1946. "Theory of communication." *Journal of Institute of Electrical Engineers* 93: 429–459.

Grossmann, A., and J. Morlet. 1984. "Decomposition of Hardy functions into square integrable wavelets of constant shape." *SIAM Journal of Mathematical Analysis* 15: 723–736.

Haar, A. 1910. "Zur Theorie der Orthogonalen Functionensysteme." *Math. Annal.* 69: 331–371.

Mallat, S. G. 1989. "A theory for multiresolution signal decomposition: the wavelet representation." *Transactions of IEEE PAMI* 11(7): 674–693.

Moorer, J. A. 1977. "Signal processing aspects of computer music: a survey." *Proceedings of the IEEE* 65(8): 1108–1137. Reprinted in J. Strawn, ed. *Digital Audio Signal Processing.* Los Altos: A-R Editions.

Roads, C. 1978. "Automated granular synthesis of sound." *Computer Music Journal* 2(2): 61–62. Revised version published as "Granular synthesis of sound," in C. Roads and J. Strawn, eds. 1985. *Foundations of Computer Music.* Cambridge, Massachusetts: MIT Press.

Vaidyanathan, P. P. 1987. "Theory and design of m-channel maximally decimated quadrature mirror filter with arbitrary m, having the perfect reconstruction property." *Proceedings of the IEEE ASSP* 35: 476–498.

# II GRANULAR REPRESENTATIONS OF MUSICAL SIGNALS

# Overview

## Giovanni De Poli

Granular synthesis is an innovative approach to the representation and generation of musical sounds. The basic idea is that a sound can be considered as a sequence, possibly with overlaps, of elementary acoustic elements called grains. Granular synthesis constructs complex and dynamic acoustic events starting from a large quantity of grains. The features of the grains and their temporal location determine the sound's timbre. We can see it as being similar to the cinema, where a rapid sequence of static images gives the impression of objects in movement.

The initial idea of granular synthesis dates back to Gabor's work (1946, 1947) aimed at pinpointing the physical and mathematical ideas needed to understand what a time-frequency spectrum is. Starting from similar developments in quantum mechanics, where we find partial mathematical similarity with time-frequency analysis, it is possible to consider sound as a sum of elementary gaussian functions that have been shifted in time and frequency. Gabor considers these elementary functions as *acoustical quanta*, the basic constituents of a sound.

In the scientific field these works have been rich in implications in the field of information theory and of signal processing. In particular they have been the starting point for studying time-frequency representations, although they were developed along slightly different lines. The idea of acoustic quanta was not followed up explicitly in this field.

In music, granular synthesis arises from the experiences of taped electronic music. In the beginning musicians had tools that did not allow a great variation of timbre, for example, fixed oscillators and filters. They obtained dynamic sounds by cutting tapes into short sections and the putting them together again. The rapid alternation of acoustic elements gave a certain variety to the sound. The source of the elements could be electronic or live recorded sounds that were sometimes electronically processed.

Xenakis (1971) developed this method in the field of analog electronic music. Starting from Gabor's method, Xenakis considers the grains as being music quanta and suggests a method of composition that is based on the organization of the grains by means of screen sequences, which specify the frequency and amplitude parameters of the grains at discrete points in time.

Roads (1978) implemented granular synthesis in the field of computer music where a greater accuracy of control of the grains is obtainable. He experimented with various types of grains and suggested a high-level organization of grains based on the concept of tendency masks (clouds) in the time-frequency plane. Recently other composers have adopted a variation of this technique, including Barry Truax (1988).

Other methods of synthesis, based on particular forms of elementary waveforms, have been proposed in computer music, especially as a way of realizing subtractive synthesis. The most important are VOSIM by Kaegi and Tempelaars (1978) and formant-wave function method of Rodet (1980). These methods can also be considered as particular types of granular synthesis. In this case the temporal position of the grains is directly related to the pitch of the sound, and their waveform determines the spectral envelope.

It can be pointed out that even sound synthesis from time-frequency representations can be realized in a granular manner, as shown in the chapters by Grossmann and Kronland-Martinet and Arfib in part I. Granular synthesis is in fact the other face of additive synthesis, and it allows the production of the same sounds in an alternative way.

These and other approaches can be unified by granular interpretation. Thus it is clear how different choice and organization strategies of the grain allow us to realize different synthesis techniques, from those based on time-frequency representations, to subtractive synthesis, from sonic texture production, to time-scale modification. In this light the grain can be considered as the primitive element of sound. It also follows that from an implementation point of view granular synthesis can constitute an important unifying factor.

From the point of view of the musician who uses these techniques, granular synthesis is all the more useful the more one understands the theoretical basis and practical consequences of choosing the various strategies. It is also important to have the available software tools that make its use easier and clearer, without having to go down to the lower levels of the grain parameters. From a compositional point of view, we can thus think of granular synthesis as a way of realizing various synthesis techniques.

It also possible to think of the grain as the basic element for the organization of the musical macrostructure. Along these lines compositional methods with an integrated approach of the various levels of musical structuring can be developed.

This part of the book aims to impart the cultural background of granular synthesis, coming from various fields of experience, to make musical uses of this approach easier. Granular synthesis is examined from two different points of view: In chapter 5 Roads illustrates the various types of granular synthesis, in particular a technique that uses an irregular (asynchronous) temporal distribution of the grains. He examines the musical implications and illustrates a compositional method based on the granular approach.

In chapter 6 DePoli and Piccialli try to bring methodologies and techniques of digital signal processing into a granular synthesis context. With this goal in mind they develop the case in which the grains are synchronized with the pitch period of the signal.

## References

Gabor, D. 1946. "Theory of communication." *Journal of the Institute of Electrical Engineers* Part III, 93: 429–457.

Gabor, D. 1947. "Acoustical quanta and the theory of hearing." *Nature* 159(1044): 591–594.

Kaegi, W., and S. Tempelaars. 1978. "VOSIM: a new sound synthesis system." *Journal of the Audio Engineering Society* 26(6): 418–424.

Roads, C. 1978. "Automated granular synthesis of sound", *Computer Music Journal* 2(2): 61–62. Revised version printed as "Granular synthesis of sounds." in C. Roads and J. Strawn, eds. 1985. *Foundations of Computer Music.* Cambridge, Massachusetts: MIT Press. pp. 145–159.

Rodet, X. 1980. "Time domain formant wave function synthesis." In J. G. Simon, ed. 1980. *Spoken Language Generation and Understanding.* Dordrecht: D. Reidel.

Truax, B., 1988. "Real-time granular synthesis with a digital signal processor." *Computer Music Journal* 12(2): 14–26.

Xenakis, I. 1971. *Formalized Music.* Bloomington: Indiana University Press.

# 5 Asynchronous Granular Synthesis

## Curtis Roads

Starting with Thaddeus Cahill's massive Telharmonium instrument (Cahill 1897, 1914, 1917, 1919, Rhea 1972), the flow of electrical current has brought forth a steady proliferation of musical tone qualities. By a common analogy to painting, electronic music synthesis has expanded the traditional acoustic palette of colors. In addition to the pure, saturated sound colors created by mathematical formulas, recording technology lets us integrate rich multicolored *concrète* (microphone recorded) textures into the musical palette (Schaeffer 1977).

Beginning in the 1950s, the electronic digital computer introduced a new set of possibilities. We might characterize these as expanding the kit of available brushes and other implements with which to apply and manipulate sound color (figure 5.1). These possibilities derive from the precision of digital circuits coupled with the automation and flexibility provided by software programs. Today's sound tools allow precise control at the extremes of auditory phenomena, from the level of elementary sonic grains to massive clouds of evolving sound spectra.

Musical possibilities have expanded far beyond the trinity of "melody, harmony, and rhythm" to the point that our composing universe is truly what Varèse called the domain of "organized sound" (Varèse 1971). In this vast domain of acoustical phenomena, machine assistance is not only welcome, it is a necessity. This is especially true of such computationally intensive techniques as *asynchronous granular synthesis* (AGS), where the artist's brush becomes like an extremely refined spray jet fed by an array of colored paints. In AGS each dot in the spray is a sonic grain, and the tone color of the grain is determined by both its waveform and frequency.

The rest of this chapter surveys methods of granular synthesis. It then focuses on the asynchronous approach, including an empirical study of the waveform, frequency band, duration, density, and spatial effects created by the technique.

One of the most interesting features of granular synthesis is that we can insert any waveform into a grain, including waveforms extracted from recorded (sampled) sounds. After a survey of techniques for time-granulation of sampled soundfiles, the final part of the chapter describes possibilities for time-granulation with asynchronous playback.

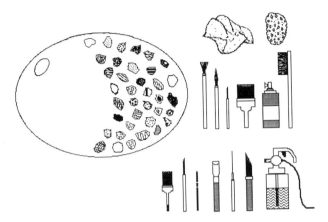

**Figure 5.1**
Although analog electronic music enlarged the musical palette, the digital computer
provides an expanded set of brushes and implements for manipulating sound color.

## Fundamentals of Granular Synthesis

A *grain of sound* is a brief acoustical event, with a duration at or near the
threshold of human auditory perception (typically several milliseconds). To
create a complex, time-variant sound, we combine thousands of grains over
time. Hence the grain serves as a kind of building block for sound objects.

The seed idea of a *quantum* or *granular* representation for sound was
sown in a pair of brilliant papers by the British physicist Dennis Gabor
(1946, 1947). In Gabor's conception any possible sound can be formed by
the appropriate combination of thousands of elementary sonic grains. The
grain is a particularly apt and flexible representation for musical sound
because it combines *time-domain* information (starting time, duration, envelope shape, waveform shape) with *frequency-domain* information (the
frequency of the waveform within the grain). This stands in opposition to
sample-based representations that do not capture frequency-domain information, and abstract Fourier methods, which account only for the frequency domain.

The flexibility of the granular representation has led to diverse proposals
for organizing the grains in time. We can divide these proposals into two
broad groups: those that start from model of traditional vocal/instrumental
sounds, and those that do not rely on an a priori analysis stage.

In the techniques based on a vocal/instrumental model, the sound in question is analyzed by a computer and dissected into its basic ingredients (the analysis data). By specifying the exact proportion of these ingredients, the sound can be resynthesized in a precise reconstruction. This entire process is called *analysis-synthesis* (or perhaps more aptly, *analysis-resynthesis*). In the granular approach to analysis-resynthesis, the grains act as feature detectors in the analysis and as a generating kernel function in the resynthesis. Pure analysis-resynthesis is not in itself musically significant because it merely replicates a sound that already exists. The technique becomes interesting only when the analysis data are transformed in musically compelling ways before resynthesis, to create variants of the original signal. See Wessel and Risset 1982 and chapter 1 by Risset for an overview of analysis-resynthesis techniques.

The subject of this chapter, asynchronous granular synthesis, does not necessarily start from a model of traditional vocal/instrumental sounds. Rather AGS generates a broad family of synthetic sounds, in particular, *sound clouds* made up of thousands of elementary particles scattered about the frequency-time space.

Because of the massive amount of data required to drive this technique, we use statistical controls to shape the clouds for musical purposes. If $n$ is the number of parameters per grain, and $d$ is the density of grains per second, it takes $n \times d$ parameter values to specify one second of sound. Because $d$ can exceed 1000, it is clear that a high-level unit of grain specification and organization is necessary to relieve the burden of manually stipulating the parameter values for each grain. A high-level specification greatly reduces the amount of data that the composer must supply to the synthesis engine.

### Theoretical Background

Gabor's original papers combined theoretical insights drawn from quantum physics with practical experiments (1946, 1947). According to Gabor's theory, a *quantum* (granular) representation could describe any sound. This hypothesis was verified mathematically by Bastiaans (1980, 1985).

Gabor actually constructed a sound granulator based on a sprocketed optical recording system adapted from a 16-mm film projector. He used this mechanism to make *time/rate-changing* experiments—changing the pitch of a sound without changing its duration, and vice-versa.

A granular representation for sound was suggested in the writings of the cybernetician Norbert Wiener (1964) and in those of information theorist Abraham Moles (1968). See Roads 1985 for a summary of their papers.

The composer Iannis Xenakis (1960, 1971) coined the term *grains of sound*. He was the first to explicate a compositional theory for sound grains. He began by adopting a lemma, "All sound, even continuous musical variation, is conceived as an assemblage of a large number of elementary sounds adequately disposed in time. In the attack, body, and decline of a complex sound, thousands of pure sounds appear in a more or less short interval of time $\Delta t$." The next section deals with the properties of the grains in more detail.

**Anatomy of a Grain**

A grain of sound lasts a very short time, which approaches the minimum perceivable event time for duration, frequency, and amplitude discrimination (Whitfield 1978). In practice the grain duration usually falls into the range of 5 to 50 ms, although Green (1971) has suggested that temporal auditory acuity (the ability of the ear to detect discrete events and discern their order) extends down to durations as short as 1 or 2 ms. Our experiments show this to be true. Grains less than about 2 ms in duration are heard as a click, but we can still change the waveform and frequency of the grains to vary the tone color of the click. Hence extremely short grains can also be musically useful. Short grains, however, tend to be costly from a computational standpoint because there is overhead associated with each grain, and it takes more short grains to fill a given timespan. For a more detailed discussion of grain duration, see the section on parametric effects in asynchronous granular synthesis.

Each grain has an amplitude envelope. In Gabor's original conception the envelope is a bell-shaped curve (figure 5.2A) generated by the gaussian method:

$$p(x) = \frac{1}{\sqrt{2\pi}} e^{-x^2/2} \, dx.$$

A variation on this is a quasi-gaussian curve (figure 5.2B) (Roads 1978). In analysis-synthesis a Hanning window (also called a *cosine bell* or *raised cosine*) may be convenient (figure 5.2C) because it is also used in conjunction with the fast Fourier transform (Oppenheim and Willsky 1983).

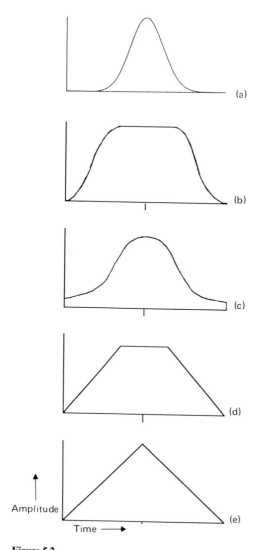

**Figure 5.2**
Grain envelopes. (A) Gaussian. (B) Quasi-gaussian. (C) Hanning. (D) Trapezoid. (E)
Triangle.

For real-time granular synthesis it may be necessary to use simple line-segment envelopes to save memory space and computation time (figure 5.2E, F) (Truax 1987, 1988) (Gabor [1946] also suggested line-segment envelopes for practical reasons.)

The grain envelope and duration can vary in a frequency-dependent way (shorter envelopes for high-frequency sounds); such a correlation is characteristic of the *wavelet transform* (chapter 2 and Kronland-Martinet 1988), which is a kind of granular technique. See the following section on Fourier/wavelet grids.

A musically important grain parameter is the waveform inside the grain. This parameter is significant because it can vary from grain to grain, which gives the granular representation unusual flexibility. For fixed-waveform grains the typical set of waveforms includes a sine wave and several other waves with increasing harmonic content up to a bandlimited pulse. Another possibility is to insert a time-varying waveform into the grain, such as a wave generated by frequency modulation or another mathematical technique (Jones and Parks 1988). As we will see later, the grain waveform can also be extracted from a recorded (sampled) sound.

Other parameters of the grain include the frequency of its waveform, its amplitude coefficient, and its spatial location (Roads 1978).

**The Grain Generator**

The grain generator can be designed as a simple digital synthesis "instrument." The most basic granular instrument is a sine wave oscillator controlled by an envelope generator with a gaussian curve (figure 5.3). An extension of this instrument would allow a choice between several waveforms or interpolation between several bandlimited waveforms.

As we will see later, we can also attach a bandpass filter to the output of the instrument to counteract some of the spectral effects caused by the grain envelope.

Because the instrument is simple, the complexity of the sound generated by granular synthesis derives from the massive amount of control data that is fed to it. These data take the form of values for each parameter (for example, frequency, amplitude, waveform, and so on) of each grain. The next section reviews several methods of organizing the grains into higher-level musical units and leads into the discussion of AGS.

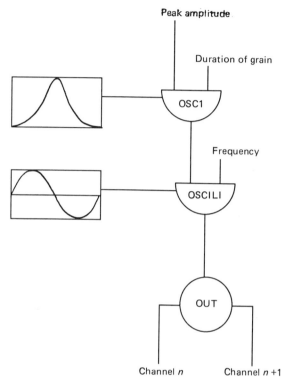

**Figure 5.3**
Simple granular synthesis instrument. Sine oscillator controlled by an envelope generator
with a gaussian curve.

## High-Level Granular Organizations

Existing granular synthesis methods can be classified into five types, depending on how they organize the grains:

• Fourier/wavelet grids and screens

• Pitch-synchronous overlapping streams

• Quasi-synchronous streams

• Asynchronous clouds

• Time-granulated sampled sound streams and clouds, with overlapped,
quasi-synchronous, or asynchronous playback

This section briefly surveys the first three methods, leaving the third and fourth to be covered in more detail in the central section of the chapter.

### Fourier/Wavelet Grids and Screens

Two related techniques, the *short-time Fourier tranform* (STFT) and the *wavelet transform*, analyze a time-domain sound signal along the axes of frequency and time. The goal of analysis is to associate each point in the analysis grid with a unit of time-frequency energy. This unit is the grain or wavelet.

The STFT is well known and can be computed using the fast Fourier transform (chapters 3 and 4). The "grain" in this case is a set of overlapping analysis windows within each of the $n$ channels of the Fourier analyzer. That is, we can view the grains as if they were aligned on a two-dimensional time/frequency grid, where the intervals between the grid are equal.

The wavelet transform (chapter 2) performs a similar operation, but the spacing of the analysis channels and the duration of the window (called the *analyzing wavelet*) are different from those of the STFT. In the STFT the spacing between the channels on the frequency axis is linear, whereas in the wavelet transform it is logarithmic. In the STFT the window duration is fixed, and in the wavelet transform it varies as a function of frequency. Specifically, in the wavelet transform, the channel frequency interval (bandwidth) $\Delta f/f$ is constant.

Both techniques permit analysis, transformation, and resynthesis, which make them potentially very powerful musical tools for the manipulation of sampled sounds. The first and most obvious transformations using Fourier/wavelet grids have involved time/rate changing, that is, shifting pitch while keeping the duration the same, and vice-versa.

Another grid-oriented method is based on Xenakis's (1960, 1971) concept of *screens*. A screen is an amplitude-frequency grid on which there are scattered grains. A synchronous sequence of screens constitutes the evolution of a complex sound. Rather than starting from an analyzed sound, as in Fourier/wavelet grids, proposals for screen-based synthesis use generative algorithms to fill the screen with grains. For example, one proposal suggested that the grain parameters could be derived from the interaction of cellular automata (Bowcott 1989).

### Pitch-Synchronous Granular Synthesis

*Pitch-synchronous granular synthesis* (PSGS) is an analysis-synthesis technique designed for the generation of pitched sounds with one or more

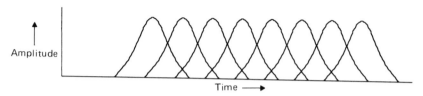

**Figure 5.4**
Overlapping grains in pitch-synchronous granular synthesis

formant regions in their spectra (chapter 6). The technique starts from a spectrum analysis of a sound. The analysis spectrum is divided into significant frequency/time areas, each area corresponding to a grain.

As a preparation for resynthesis, at each grain boundary along the frequency axis, a standard algorithm derives the coefficients for a filter. The impulse response of this filter corresponds to the frequency response of that region. At each grain boundary along the time axis, a pitch detection algorithm determines the fundamental pitch period.

In resynthesis a pulse train at the detected frequency drives a bank of parallel minimum-phase finite impulse response filters. The musical signal results from the excitation of the pulse train on the weighted sum of the impulse responses of all the filters. At each grain time frame the system emits a waveform that is overlapped with the previous grain to create a smoothly varying signal (figure 5.4).

An implementation of PSGS by De Poli and Piccialli features several transformations that can create variations of the original sound. A central point of their implementation is the use of data reduction techniques designed to save computation and memory space. See chapter 6 for details.

## Quasi-Synchronous Granular Synthesis

In *quasi-synchronous granular synthesis* (QSGS) sound is created by generating one or more streams of grains, one grain following another, with a variable delay period between the grains. Figure 5.5 shows a stream of five 20-ms grains, each with a quasi-gaussian envelope and a constant delay before the next grain. We say "quasi-synchronous" because the grains follow each other at more or less equal intervals.

When the interval between successive grains is equal, the overall envelope of a stream of grains forms a periodic function. Because the envelope is periodic, the signal generated by QSGS can be analyzed as a case of

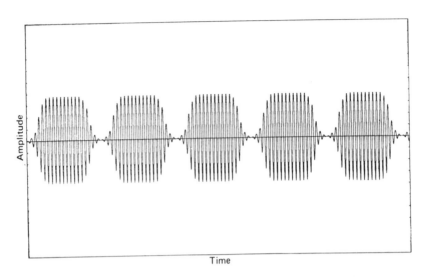

**Figure 5.5**
Stream of equispaced grains with constant delay

*amplitude modulation* (AM). AM occurs when the shape of one signal (the *modulator*) determines the amplitude of another signal (the *carrier*).

From a signal processing standpoint we observe that for each sinusoidal component in the carrier, the periodic envelope function contributes a series of *sidebands* to the final spectrum. (Sidebands are additional frequency components above and below the frequency of the carrier.) The sidebands are separated from the carrier by a distance corresponding to the inverse of the period of the envelope function. For the 20-ms grains shown in figure 5.5, the sidebands in the output spectrum are spaced at 50-Hz intervals. The shape of the grain envelope determines the precise amplitude of these sidebands.

The result created by the modulation effect of a periodic envelope is that of a *formant* surrounding the carrier frequency. That is, instead of a single line in the spectrum (denoting a single frequency), the spectrum looks like a sloping hill (denoting a group of frequencies around the carrier). QSGS in this sense similar to the formant synthesis methods *VOSIM* (Kaegi and Tempelaars 1978) and *formant-wave-function* (FWF) synthesis (Rodet 1980, Rodet, Potard, and Barrière 1984).

By combining several streams of quasi-synchronous grains in parallel (each stream creating its own formant around a separate frequency), the

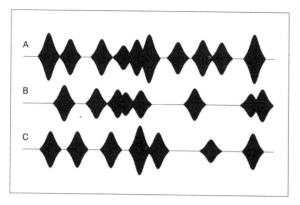

**Figure 5.6**
Graphical depiction of quasi-synchronous granular synthesis, showing three parallel
streams of grains with variable delay. The grains inside stream A are at one frequency, the
grains inside stream B are at another frequency, and the grains inside stream C are at a
third frequency.

signal can be made to simulate the resonances of the singing voice and some
acoustic instruments.

When the interval between the grains is irregular, perfect grain synchronization is forgone, along with its predictable side effects due to the periodic
envelope function. Sound is still created by one or more streams of grains,
but the onset time of each grain with respect to the next is randomized
(figure 5.6). This leads to a controllable thickening of the sound texture
through a "blurring" of the formant structure (Truax 1987, 1988).

In its simplest form the variable-delay method is similar to amplitude
modulation using low-frequency colored noise as a modulator. This is not,
in itself, particularly new or interesting. The granular representation, however, lets us take this technique far beyond simple noise-modulated AM.
In particular we can simultaneously vary several other parameters on a
grain-by-grain basis, such as grain waveform, amplitude, duration, and
spatial location. On a more global level we can also dynamically vary the
density of grains per second, which creates a variety of nonstandard effects.

## Asynchronous Granular Synthesis

In asynchronous granular synthesis (AGS) the concept of linear streams of
grains is abandoned. Instead the grains are scattered probabilistically over

a specified duration within regions inscribed on the frequency/time plane. These regions are called *clouds*—the units with which a composer works.

**Cloud Parameters**

The composer specifies a cloud in terms of the following parameters (figure 5.7):

1. Start time and duration of the cloud

2. Grain duration (usually from 5 to 50 ms, but can also vary above and below these bounds; see the discussion of grain duration)

3. Density of grains per second, with a maximum density that is implementation specific; density can vary over the duration of the cloud

4. Frequency band of the cloud; usually specified by two curves that form high- and low-frequency boundaries within which grains are scattered; alternatively the frequency of the grains in a cloud can be restricted to a specific set of pitches

5. Amplitude envelope of the cloud

6. Waveform(s) within the grains

7. Spatial dispersion of the cloud, where the number of output channels is implementation specific

The grain duration parameter 2 can be set to a constant (in milliseconds), or it can be automatically determined as either a function of the frequency of the grain, where higher-frequency grains have shorter envelopes, or a random factor that takes values between 10 and 100 ms. The next section explains the effects of different grain durations in more detail.

Parameter 3, grain density, specifies the number of grains per unit of time. For example, if the grain density is low, then only a few grains are scattered at random points within the cloud. If the grain density is high, grains overlap to create rich, complex spectra.

Parameter 6, waveform(s), is one of the most complicated and powerful cloud parameters. Briefly we can say that we can fill a cloud with grains having different waveforms. The next section deals with waveforms and other parameters in more detail.

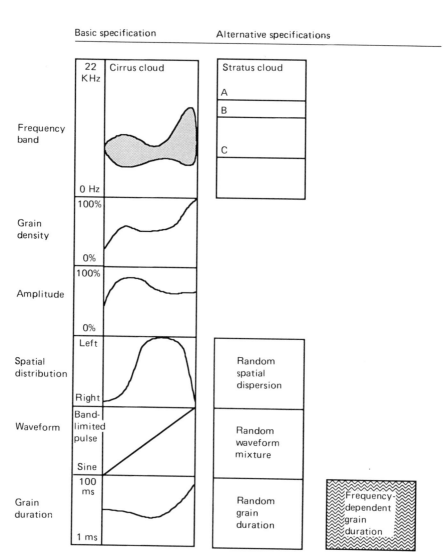

**Figure 5.7**
Graphical representation of the parameters of a cloud. Several parameters can be specified
in more than one way. (See also table 5.1.)

## Parametric Effects in Asynchronous Granular Synthesis

Research into sound synthesis is governed by aesthetic goals as much as by scientific curiosity. Well-known techniques like *frequency modulation* (FM) and *waveshaping* have elegant mathematical interpretations, but these are not always used in practice. For example, an inspection of patent claims reveals that Yamaha's implementations of FM (see, for example, Tomisawa 1981) differ significantly from Chowning's (1973) theory.

As both musicians and synthesizer manufacturers know, some of the most interesting techniques result from applied engineering practices, rather than formal theory. Once a digital music instrument has reached prototype form, manufacturers hire "sound designers" to voice program their instruments, a highly skilled task that some musicians also do for themselves. At this stage of experimentation musical intuition and taste are the primary guides.

Hence our experiments follow an empirical approach. This section reports on our study of the effects created by manipulating the grain duration, waveform, frequency, band, density, and spatial parameters of AGS. These parameters provide the characteristic "control handles" for the unique results possible with asynchronous granular synthesis.

Each parameter can create different types of effects, and each type implies a different specification. Table 5.1 shows some different types of specifi-

**Table 5.1**
Cloud Specifications

| Parameter | Specifications |
|---|---|
| Grain duration | Constant |
| | Random |
| | Frequency-dependent |
| Frequency band | Cumulus: upper and lower frequency bounds |
| | Stratus: a list of specific frequencies |
| Grain waveform | Monochrome: one waveform |
| | Polychrome: $n$ waveforms, random mixture |
| | Transchrome: transformation over $n$ waveforms |
| Density | Percentage of a maximum |
| Spatial distribution | Envelope across $n$ channels |
| | Random dispersion |

cations for each parameter. The rest of this section explains their effects in more detail.

**Grain Duration Effects**

For musical purposes we have implemented three classes of grain durations for clouds:

• Constant duration (the duration of every grain in the cloud is the same, a parameter that can be set by a composer)

• Random duration (the duration of a grain is random between two boundaries, typically 10 and 100 ms)

• Frequency-dependent duration (the duration of a grain is tied to its fundamental frequency period, as it is in synthesis with wavelets)

With respect to constant durations, early estimates of the optimum grain duration varied from 10 ms (Gabor 1946, 1947) to 60 ms (Moles 1968). In AGS the duration of the grains within a cloud has profound effects on the resulting audio signal. For the constant duration case we can demonstrate these effects with a series of figures.

Figure 5.8A shows a time-domain view of a two-second cloud filled with 40 sine-wave grains with the relatively long duration of 100 ms. The amplitude modulation effects caused by grain addition are clear. If the grain duration is $D_g$, the center frequency of the AM is $1/D_g$. Because $D_g$ is $\frac{1}{10}$ s, the AM that is heard is a kind of aperiodic, fluttering tremolo around 10 Hz. A frequency-domain plot of this waveform appears in figure 5.8B. In this case the waveform in the grains is set to a 500-Hz sine wave, so the spectrum appears as a narrow formant.

Acoustics principles tell us that the shorter the duration of a pulse, the greater its bandwidth. This is shown in figure 5.9, which compares the time functions of three elementary signals and their spectra.

As a general rule the total width of the frequency band $B$ is inversely proportional to the duration of the sound $D$:

$$B = 1/D_g.$$

As expected, the dramatic effect caused by lowering the grain duration to 1 ms is shown in figure 5.10. The time-domain view (figure 5.10A) shows a signal that is entirely positive in energy. This is by-product of the ratio of the grain duration to the fundamental frequency period of the grain wave-

(a)

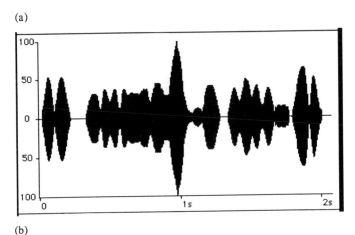

(b)

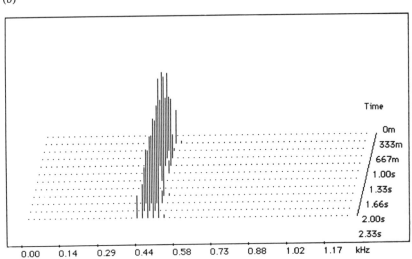

**Figure 5.8**
A cloud at a constant frequency of 500 Hz with 100-ms grains. (A) Time-domain view. (B)
Frequency-domain view, with time plotted from back to front.

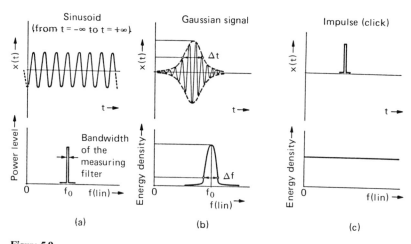

**Figure 5.9**
Time functions and spectra of three elementary signals (after Blauert 1983). (A) Sine wave of infinite duration. (B) Gaussian grain. Notice the formant effect. (C) Impulse.

form $D_g/P_f$. This rectification effect occurs whenever $D_g/P_f$ is less than 1. In the specific case of a 1 ms grain with a fundamental frequency of 500 Hz, the ratio is 0.001/0.002 second. The effects of grain duration are shown in table 5.2.

Common sense tells us that for a single grain, the duration must be at last equal to the frequency period to completely represent one period of that frequency. If we took this criterion as a standard, we would require grains to last no less than 50 ms (corresponding to the period of 20 Hz) to completely capture low-frequency signal energy. As it happens, however, much shorter grains can represent low-frequency signals, but the short grain duration introduces modulation products. Our experiments show that grains shorter than 5 ms tend to generate particulated clouds in which a sense of center pitch is still present, but is diffused by noise.

The modulation products caused by the grain envelope and their combination sometimes result in transient energy that extends above and below the center-frequency range. The low-frequency energy can lead to clicks and pops similar to those caused by direct current offset imbalances at splice points in audio editing. To attenuate these effects we can apply a bandpass filter to the signal, centered on the fundamental frequency period of the waveform within the grain.

(a)

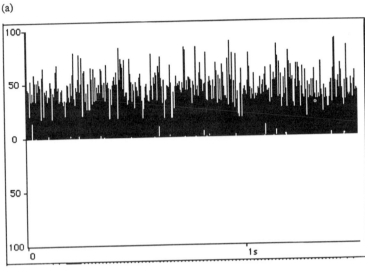

(b)

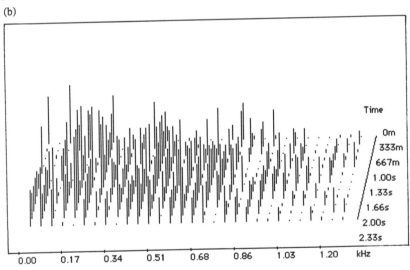

**Figure 5.10**
A cloud at a constant frequency of 500 Hz with 1-ms grains. The grain density of the cloud
made up of 1-ms grains is 100 times greater than the cloud shown in figure 5.8 made up of
100-ms grains. (A) Time-domain view. (B) Frequency-domain view, with time plotted from
back to front.

**Table 5.2**
Effects of Grain Duration

| Grain duration | Average Frequency of Envelope Modulation | Effect |
| --- | --- | --- |
| 200 $\mu$s | 5000 Hz | Noisy, particulate disintegration |
| 500 $\mu$s | 2000 Hz | |
| 1 ms | 1000 Hz | |
| 10 ms | 100 Hz | Fluttering, warbling, gurgling |
| 50 ms | 20 Hz | |
| 100 ms | 10 Hz | |
| 200 ms | 5 Hz | Aperiodic tremolo, jittering spatial position |

**Waveform Effects**

One of the most interesting features of granular synthesis is that we can insert any waveform into a grain. The waveform can vary on a grain-to-grain basis; this gives us the flexibility to create microanimated textures that can evolve directionally over time or simply scintillate from the effects of constantly changing grain waveforms.

The simplest grain waveforms are synthetic, of the fixed-waveform type. These range from a sine wave to a bandlimited waveform formed by the addition of $n$ sine waves, where $n$ is an implementation-specific number (figure 5.11). In our experiments we use ten synthetic waveforms created by adding 1 to 10 sine waves.

First, we specify the cloud's *color type*, of which there are three possibilities: *monochrome* (specify a single waveform), *polychrome* (specify two or more waveforms), and *transchrome* (the grain waveform evolves from one waveform to another over the duration of the cloud; specify two or more waveforms).

In the monochrome case we specify a single wavetable for the entire cloud. When we want to create clouds with a multicolored texture caused by interspersing many different waveforms, we specify two or more wavetables to create a polychrome cloud. Each grain is supplied with one of the specified wavetables on a random selection basis, which evenly distributes them within the cloud.

The transchrome cloud mutates from one waveform to another over the duration of the cloud. If we specify a list of $n$ waveforms, the cloud mutates from one to the next, through all $n$ over the duration of the cloud.

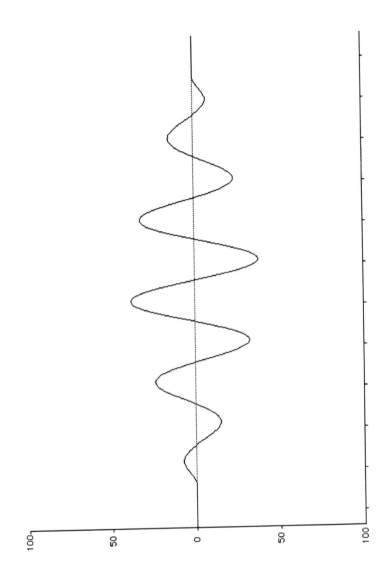

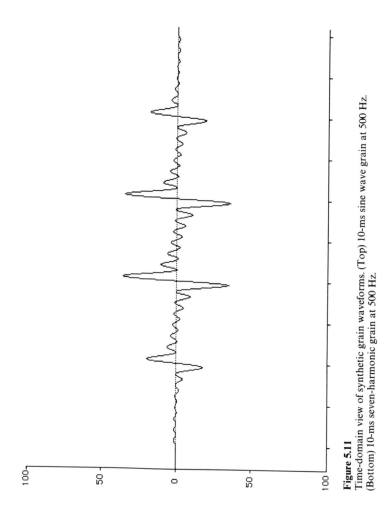

**Figure 5.11**
Time-domain view of synthetic grain waveforms. (Top) 10-ms sine wave grain at 500 Hz.
(Bottom) 10-ms seven-harmonic grain at 500 Hz.

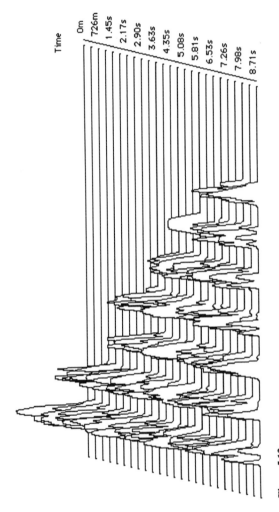

**Figure 5.12**
Spectral envelope of a transchrome cloud that mutates from sine wave waveform to bandlimited seven-harmonic additive waveform. Time is plotted from back to front.

Transchrome clouds mutate from one waveform to another in a statistical manner. Figure 5.12 shows the spectral effect that occurs in a transchrome cloud that mutates from a sine wave to a bandlimited additive waveform. The grain frequency is constant at 500 Hz.

The grain microstructure can be complicated by using a time-varying waveform, such as a signal generated by frequency modulation or another nonlinear technique (Jones and Parks 1988). But because the duration of the grain is usually so short, such techniques tend to result in noisy, distorted textures, unless the modulating frequencies and the amount of modulation are strictly controlled.

As a practical aside it is often necessary to use the standard 44.1- or 48-KHz sampling rates for software and hardware compatibility in recording, synthesis, and playback. These sampling rates provide little "frequency headroom," so we must be aware that when the fundamental frequency of a grain is high, and the waveform is complex, foldover can occur. (Foldover causes frequency components above half the sampling rate to reflect into the lower part of the spectrum.) To avoid this, we can constrain the choice of waveform, depending on the fundamental frequency, particularly in the region above half of the Nyquist frequency (11.025 or 14 KHz, depending on the sampling rate). Above these limits waveforms other than sine will cause foldover effects. A more elegant solution, of course, would be to use a much higher sampling frequency throughout the entire audio chain, which would eliminate concern about foldover.

The grain waveform can also be extracted from a sampled sound, either in real time or not. See the section on time-granulation.

**Frequency Band Effects**

The fundamental frequency of the grain waveform is determined by the band parameters. Within the upper and lower boundaries of the band, the grain generator scatters grains randomly. This creates complex timbral/harmonic effects when the band is beyond several semitones and the density is high.

To generate more pitch-controlled harmonic textures (which retain a statistical character), we can constrain the choice of fundamental frequency to a particular set of pitches within a scale. Hence we allow two classes of frequency specifications: *cumulus*, in which the frequencies of the grains fall at random within the upper and lower bounds of a single band specified

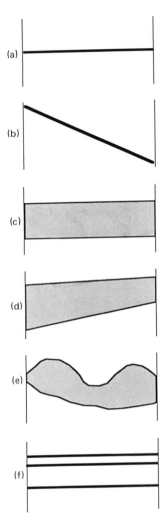

**Figure 5.13**
Different band specifications for a cloud. (A) Single-frequency band. (B) Glissando band.
(C) Constant wide band. (D) Variable wide band. (E) Continuously variable band.
(F) Stratus (harmonic) cloud, with several frequency bands.

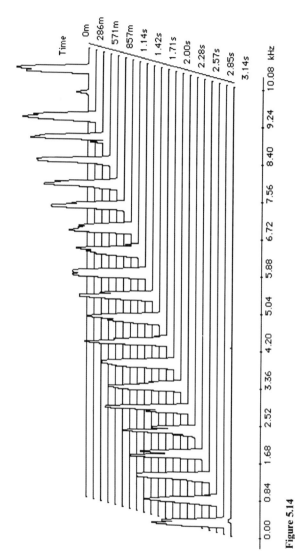

**Figure 5.14**
Spectral plot over the frequency range 0 to 10 KHz showing a glissando from 10 KHz to 20 Hz over a 3-second span. The grains last 20 ms; and the grain density is 150 grains per second. Time is plotted from back to front.

by the composer, and *stratus*, in which the frequencies of the grains are constrained to a set of specified pitches.

Figure. 5.13 shows examples of band specifications. Bands A through E are cumulus band specifications. In figure 5.13A the band centers on a single frequency, so the cloud sounds a single pitch. This frequency can change to create a glissando effect, shown in figure 5.13B. (See figure 5.14 for a frequency-domain view of a granular glissando.) Wnen the band is wider than a single pitch, as in figure 5.13C, the grains are scattered randomly between the upper and lower boundaries. When the initial and final bands are different, as in figure 5.13D, the shape of the band changes over time. In the most flexible case the band is shaped by two time-varying curves, as shown in figure 5.13E.

A stratus cloud contains more than one frequency specification. Figure 5.13F shows a cloud stratified into three frequency levels, forming a C-major triad. With sampled soundfiles we can achieve the harmonic effect of a stratus cloud by keeping a database of tones at all the pitches from a desired scale. A given cloud may draw from only a few of these soundfiles to create a harmonic impression, given sufficient grain density (see figures 5.23 and 5.24 later).

**Density Effects**

Although density can be defined simply as the number of grains per second, this measure becomes meaningless when the duration of the grains is variable. To clarify its meaning, we define several levels of density:

- Sparse: More than 50 percent of the duration of the cloud is silence.
- Filled: The cloud is filled in by sonic grains.
- Dense: The cloud is filled with a high degree of overlapping grains.

These are informal definitions. For example, when we say that a cloud is "filled in," there may still be several milliseconds of silence, but these gaps are so short that the ear hears the cloud as a continuous sound. In any case grain duration and density factors are directly related. A 100-ms grain "fills" five times more of the cloud than does a 20-ms grain, so we could say it is five times more dense.

Because the exact starting time of a grain is random in AGS, we cannot guarantee that, for example, fifty 20-ms grains will completely fill a one-second cloud. Some grains may overlap, leaving silences at other points in the cloud. To create what we hear as a filled cloud, a good rule of thumb is to set the density per second of the filled cloud to at least $2/D_g$. Hence for 20-ms grains it takes about 100 grains to "fill" a one-second cloud.

We can see the effects of increasing the grain density factor in figure 5.15. All the figures show a cloud with a duration of three seconds containing 20-ms grains at a constant frequency of 1 KHz. Figure 5.15A is a pointillistic cloud with a density of 5 grains per second. At a density of 25 grains per second, as shown in figure 5.15B, almost half of the cloud is silence. Even so, the rate of grains per second is fast enough to sustain the perception of a continuous but "gurgling" sound.

Tiny gaps in a cloud (less than about 50 ms) are heard not as silences but rather as momentary fluctuations of amplitude. We can still see tiny gaps in figures 5.15C (100 grains per second) and 5.15D (200 grains per second), at densities of 100 and 200 grains per second, respectively, but the 20-ms gaps are not perceived as silences.

Density and frequency band effects are also synergistic. In particular the musical effects of the band parameter differ, depending on the grain density. To obtain pointillistic effects, for example, where each grain is heard as a separate event, keep the grain density to less than $0.5/D_g$. Hence, for a grain duration of 20 ms, the density should be less than 25 grains per second (0.5/0.02).

By increasing the grain density, we intensify the sound, creating effects that depend on the bandwidth:

1. Narrow bands and high densities create pitched streams with formant spectra, like those of quasi-synchronous granular synthesis.

2. Medium bands (for example, intervals of several semitones) and high densities generate turgid colored noises.

3. Wide bands (for example, an octave or more) and high densities form massive *clouds* of sound.

As we have seen, we can also modify the bandwidth of the cloud by changing its grain duration parameter. See the section on grain duration effects.

### Spatial Effects

The distinctive characteristics of granular synthesis are enhanced by multichannel spatial distribution. That is, granular texture is articulated by scattering individual grains in different spatial locations.

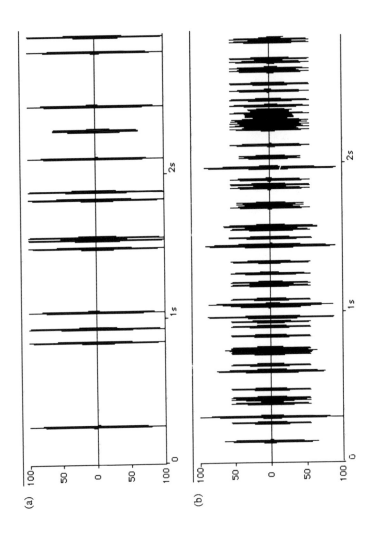

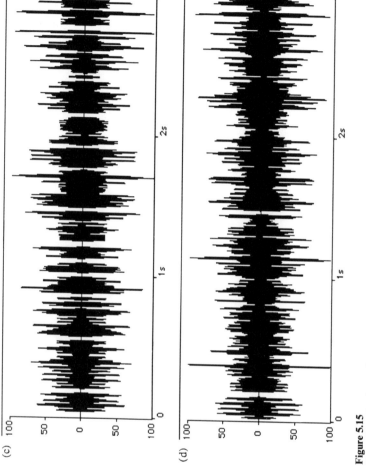

**Figure 5.15**
Time-domain views of grain density effects using 20 ms grains. (A) 5 grains per second. (B) 25 grains per second. (C) 100 grains per second. (D) 200 grains per second. The two visible gaps in D, at 0.17 s and 1.4 s, are about 20 ms in duration.

From a psychoacoustical point of view, the perception of the spatial position of a grain or series of grains is determined by both the physical properties of the signal and the *localization blur* introduced by the human auditory system (Blauert 1983). The presence of localization blur reflects the fact that a point source sound produces an auditory image that is spread out to a certain degree in space. For gaussian tonebursts the horizontal localization blur is in the range of 0.8° to 3.3°, depending on the frequency of the signals (Boerger 1965). The localization blur in the median plane (starting in front, then going up above the head and down to behind the head) is greater, or the order of 4° for white noise and becoming much greater (less accurate) for purer tones. (See Boerger 1965 for an in-depth study of the spatial properties of gaussian grains.)

Localization blur notwithstanding, we can specify the spatial distribution of the grains in one of two ways: as an envelope that pans across $n$ channels or as a random dispersion of grains among $n$ channels. Figure 5.16 shows a simple linear spatial envelope panning across two channels

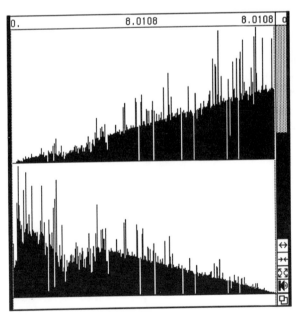

**Figure 5.16**
Spatial panning in a cloud. 1040 grains panning from right (bottom window) to left over the course of an 8-second cloud.

in an eight-second cloud. Random dispersions of grains are especially effective in the articulation of long grains at low densities.

## Time-Granulation of Sampled Sounds

A most powerful possibility offered by the granular representation is the *time granulation* of recorded (sampled) sounds. Time granulation minces a time-domain signal into grains and resynthesizes it with the grains in a new time order and microrhythm.

Three basic approaches to time granulation exist:

1. Time/rate changing effects

2. Continuous real-time granulation of a given input sound

3. Granulating a stored soundfile—such as a note played by an acoustic instrument, an animal sound, or a fragment of spoken text—and playing back the grains asynchronously

The next three sections explore these approaches in detail.

### Time/Rate Changing Effects by Granulation

One technique that has been used extensively in computer music is *time/rate changing*. This technique has two facets: On the one hand the duration of a sound can be stretched or shrunk (time compression/expansion), while the pitch of the sound remains unchanged. On the other hand the pitch of the sound can be transposed up or down (pitch shifting), while the duration remains constant. These two effects can be achieved, with varying degrees of success, by several strategies, including Fourier methods (such as the phase vocoder), the wavelet transform, linear predictive coding, granular techniques, "harmonizer" devices, and other decimation/interpolation schemes.

Gabor (1946) built one of the earliest electromechanical time/rate changers. (A German company, Springer, made a magnetic tape device based on the same principles in the early 1970s.) The basic principle of Gabor's device was the time-granulation or time-segmentation of recorded sounds. Contemporary digital methods can be explained by reference to the operation of these early devices.

In an electromechanical time/rate changer, a rotating head (the sampling head) spins across a recording (on film or tape) of a sound (figure 5.17). The

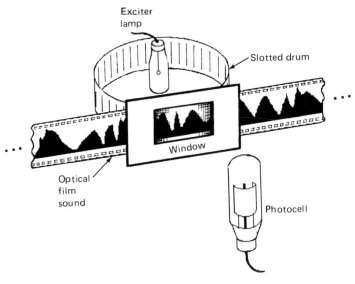

**Figure 5.17**
Gabor's "Kinematical Frequency Converter" (1946) was based on a modified 16-mm film projector with optical soundtrack. The film moves by an exciter bulb at a speed $v$, while a slotted drum rotates at speed $u$. A continuously graded window ensures that the light from each slot is transmitted through the film according to a gaussian curve. The photocell on the other side of the film collects fluctuations of light at the frequency $f_1 = [(v - u)/v]f_0$. If the output of the photocell is recorded onto a second film played back at the normal speed, any frequency on the original is shifted by a factor of $f_1$.

sampling head spins in the same direction that the tape is moving. Because the head comes in contact with the tape for only a short period, the effect is that of "sampling" the sound on the tape at regular intervals. Each of these sampled segments is a grain of sound, and the process of extracting segments from a continuous sound is a form of time granulation.

In Gabor's system the grains were reassembled into a continuous stream onto another recorder. When this second recording was played back, the result was a more or less continuous signal, but with a different time base. For example, if the rotating head spun very quickly, it sampled multiple copies (slightly staggered clones) of the original signal. When these samples were played back as a continuous signal, the effect of the multiple copies was to stretch out the duration of the resampled version. Note that the local frequency content, in particular the pitch, of the original signal is preserved in the resampled version. Shrinking the duration of the original signal was achieved by slowing down the rotation speed of the sampling head. This meant that the resampled recording contained a sequence of grains that formerly had been widely separated.

To effect a change in pitch without changing the duration of a sound, one needed only to change the playback rate of the original and use the time-scale modification just described to adjust its duration. For example, to halve the duration of a signal while preserving its pitch, use time granulation to extract half of the signal while maintaining the local frequency content (figure 5.18). To shift the pitch up an octave while maintaining the duration, clone one new grain for every existing grain and playback all the grains at double speed.

An early digital implementation of time/rate changing by time-granulation at the University of Illinois simulated the effect of rotating-head sampling (Otis, Grossmann, and Cuomo 1968). It also pointed out the flaws of this method in its most basic form. The main problem was that the waveforms at the beginning and end of a sampled grain may not match in level with preceding and successive resampled grains. This creates a discontinuity at the junction of the two grains, an effect shown in figure 5.19. Electro-mechanical time/rate changers and some digital implementations exhibit a periodic clicking sound caused by these transients.

More recent work, by Jones and Parks (1988), showed how a smoother, reconstruction of the signal could be achieved by using grain envelopes (or windows) that overlap slightly, creating a seamless crossfade between grains (as in figure 5.4). In their scheme the spacing between window starting location is not equal, but the overlap between windows is always in phase. Lent's method (1989) is an extension of the Jones and Parks technique that performs a preliminary pitch detection on the original sound to determine the duration and spacing of the Hanning windows used in time compression and expansion.

Apart from crossfading, digital time granulation operates in a manner similar to electromechanical time/rate changing devices. For example, to double the duration but not the pitch of the sampled signal, each grain is cloned so that two grains are heard for every one grain in the original. To halve the duration, every other grain is deleted before playback. This method works because the local frequency contant to the grains is preserved, whereas the time scale is altered by cloning (to stretch duration) or deleting (to shrink duration) grains.

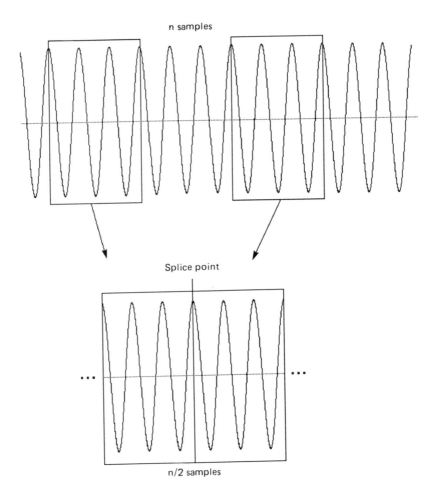

**Figure 5.18**
Resampled grains for time/rate changing. Shortening the duration while maintaining the local frequency content.

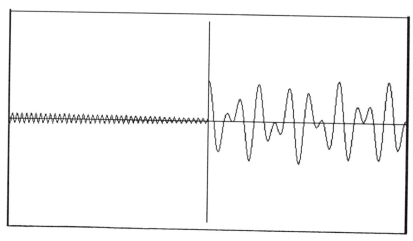

**Figure 5.19**
Discontinuities at grain junctions.

To shift the pitch of a sampled signal up an octave, but not change its duration, the playback sampling rate is doubled, and every grain is cloned to restore the duration to the original. To shift the pitch down an octave, but not change the duration, the playback sampling rate is halved, and every other grain is deleted to restore the duration to the original.

Of course we are not limited to octave shifts and duration halving and doubling. The frequency and time scales can be altered by arbitrary ratios by sample rate changing and grain cloning or deleting in corresponding ratios.

### Real-Time Granulation of Continuous Input Sound

Real-time granulation of continuous sound is usually accomplished with a high-speed digital signal processor that acts as a programmable *delay line* or *moving window* that can be tapped to furnish the various grains (figure 5.20). The effect of real-time granulation is to enrich the input sound with the spectral products of the granulation window and the mixture of the original and delayed sound. The goal is to distort the input sound in a controllable way.

Truax reports experiments in which the playback rate is varied by changing the speed at which the processor advances through the samples. The playback can vary from normal speed to a slowed rate in which a single sample is repeated over and over again.

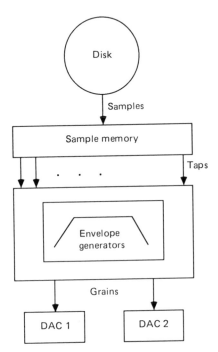

**Figure 5.20**
Real-time granulation with a DSP, as implemented by Truax. Sound samples recorded on disk are fed continuously into an 8-Kbyte sample buffer memory, which can be tapped at any point. The sample stream outputs from the buffer memory are enveloped and sent to one of two digital-to-analog converters in real time. The Digital Music Systems DMX-1000 signal processor used by Truax can generate up to 2000 10-ms grains per second from sampled sound files.

## Time-Granulation with Asynchronous Playback

When the sound to be granulated is stored in a file, we have the flexibility of extracting individual grains in any order: sequential, reversed, random, or an arbitrary succession. For example, we can extract a single large grain from a snare drum and clone a periodic sequence of hundreds of grains to create a single-stroke roll (figure 5.21). To avoid the repetitive quality of commercial drum machines and samplers, a variation on this method is to select grains from several strokes of a roll and to extract each grain from a different set of samples in the selected soundfile.

We can intermingle grains sampled from any instrument, of course, not just percussion instruments. For example, we can extract grains from

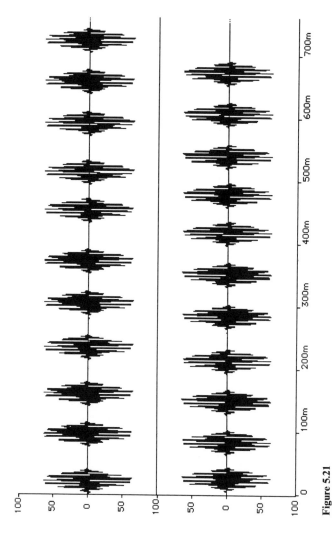

**Figure 5.21**
Time-domain plot of a two-channel time-sampled granular snare drum roll. The grains last 40 ms with a variable delay period between grains.

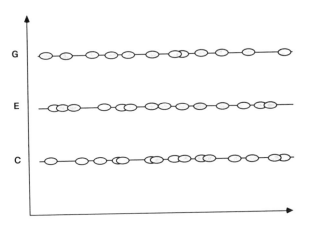

**Figure 5.22**
Time/frequency diagram of a harmonic cloud formed by time-sampled grains at the pitches C, E, and G

several soundfiles to create interwoven fabrics of sound. When the soundfiles consist of different notes of a scale played by an instrument, the result is a harmonic cloud, where the layers are stratified at particular pitches (figure 5.22).

An example of such a texture is shown in the musical example of figure 5.23. The first two seconds of the texture intermingle grains from three soundfiles. Each soundfile contains one of the pitches (CEG) played by an alto saxophone. At about 2.1 seconds the single pitch/grain C emerges from the cloud.

In figure 5.24 we see a diagram of the effect that occurs when two harmonic clouds overlap. The sound is a statistical evolution from the first cloud to the second.

An extension of these techniques is to extract the grains from several entirely different sources to create hybrid textures, such as mixing grains from a cello or voice with grains from a cymbal (figure 5.25). By controlling the distribution of the grains from different sources, it is possible to create clouds that evolve from one texture to another.

In any of these time granulation methods, grain duration is an important parameter. Sampled soundfiles often have intrinsic semantic qualities that are lost when the duration of the grain is very short. For soundfiles consisting of spoken text or other identifiable material that is to be preserved, longer duration grains (in excess of 50 ms) appear to work better.

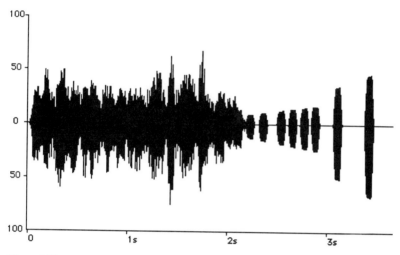

**Figure 5.23**
Time-domain view of a cloud of 100 ms grains extracted from three sampled alto saxophone soundfiles at the pitches C, E, and G. At about 2.1 s the pitch C emerges from the cloud.

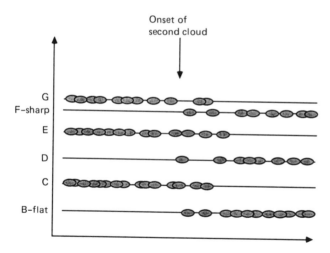

**Figure 5.24**
Time/frequency diagram of two harmonic clouds overlapping

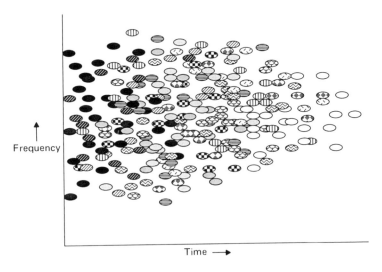

**Figure 5.25**
Graphical depiction of a cloud that intermingles grains from several different source soundfiles, with the mixture statistically evolving over time

## Implementation Notes

Early implementation and musical applications of asynchronous granular synthesis are described in Roads 1978 and 1985. Recently I have developed another implementation of AGS and time-granulation of sampled soundfiles as a suite of programs interfaced to a version of the Music 4C language, modified for granular synthesis. Music 4C (Gerrard 1989) is a C-language variant of the venerable Music IVBF language developed in the 1960s (Mathews and Miller 1965, Howe 1975).

The programs currently run on an Apple Macintosh II–family computer. They generate soundfiles that are compatible with professional sound recording, mixing, and editing systems, in our case the Studer Editech Dyaxis. This environment is adequate for experiments and musical work by a patient composer because the process of generating a short soundfile is carried out in software and can take several minutes. Of course a more ideal musical platform would integrate flexible graphical/performance interfaces and real-time operation in an open environment in which AGS is one synthesis option out of many.

## Conclusion

Granular synthesis is a family of techniques that are based on the manipulation of sonic grains. The quantum (Gabor 1946, 1947), gaussian elementary signal (Helstrom 1966, Bastiaans 1980), Hanning window (chapter 3), sliding window (Bastiaans 1985), wavelet (chapter 2), formant-wave-function (Rodet 1980), VOSIM pulse (Kaegi and Tempelaars 1978), and even the toneburst (Blauert 1983, Pierce 1990) can all be described as granular representations of musical signals.

Asynchronous granular synthesis sprays thousands of tiny sonic grains into cloudlike formations across the audio spectrum. The result is often a "particulated" sound complex that varies over time. In musical contexts these types of sounds can act as a foil to the smoother, more sterile sounds emitted by digital oscillators. Although AGS is driven by a large amount

**Figure 5.26**
Particle synthesis in computer graphics. This frame from *Star Trek II: The Wrath of Khan* shows the cratered moonlike planet on fire from explosion of the Genesis Device. The fire of the Genesis Device is modeled with particle synthesis. (© 1982 Paramount Pictures Corporation. All rights reserved.)

of control data, we can manipulate thousands of grains by setting just a few parameter specifications. One of the most interesting extensions of AGS granulates sampled sounds that are subsequently reassembled asynchronously to create especially rich textures.

Asynchronous granular synthesis adds several unique implements to the kit of the composer and suggests new ways of organizing musical structure—as clouds of evolving sound spectra. Indeed the granular representation seems ideal for representing statistical processes of timbral evolution. Time-varying combinations of clouds lead to dramatic effects such as evaporation, coalescence, and mutations created by crossfading overlapping clouds. A striking analogy exists between these processes and those created in the visual domain by *particle synthesis*. (For more information on this computer graphics synthesis technique, see Reeves 1983.) Particle synthesis has been used to create fire, water, clouds, fog, and grasslike textures (figure 5.26), which are analogous to some of the audio effects possible with AGS.

## Acknowledgments

I am grateful to Professor Aldo Piccialli and the University of Naples for the opportunity to serve as a visiting faculty member during the spring of 1988. The ideas behind parts of this chapter were clarified by discussions in Italy and the USA with Professor Piccialli, Dr. Sergio Cavaliere, and Professor Giovanni De Poli. I thank Professor Ivan Tcherepnin and the Department of Music at Harvard University for a visiting faculty appointment in electronic music composition in 1989, during which time part of this chapter was written. My thanks also to Iannis Xenakis for his comments on a draft of this chapter.

## References

Bastiaans, M. 1980. "Gabor's expansion of a signal into gaussian elementary signals." *Proceedings of the IEEE* 68: 538–539.

Bastiaans, M. 1985. "On the sliding-window representation of signals." *IEEE Transactions on Acoustics, Speech, and Signal Processing* ASSP-33(4): 868–873.

Blauert, J. 1983. *Spatial Hearing.* J. S. Allen, trans. Cambridge, Massachusetts: MIT Press.

Boerger, G. 1965. "Die Lokalisation von Gausstönen." [The localization of gaussian tones.] Doctoral dissertation. Berlin: Technische Universität, Berlin.

Bowcott, P. 1989. "Cellular automation as a means of high level compositional control of granular synthesis." In T. Wells and D. Butler, eds. *Proceedings of the 1989 International Computer Music Conference*. San Francisco: Computer Music Association, pp. 55–57.

Cahill, T. 1897. U. S. Patent 580,035.

Cahill, T. 1914. U. S. Patent 1,107,261.

Cahill, T. 1917. U. S. Patent 1,213,803 and 1,213,804.

Cahill, T. 1919. U. S. Patent 1,295,691.

Chowning, J. 1973. "The synthesis of complex audio spectra by means of frequency modulation." *Journal of the Audio Engineering Society* 21(7): 526–534. Reprinted in C. Roads and J. Strawn, eds. 1985. *Foundations of Computer Music*. Cambridge, Massachusetts: MIT Press, pp. 6–29.

De Poli G., and A. Piccialli. 1988. "Forme d'onda per la sintesi granulare sincronica." In D. Tommassini, ed. *Atti di VII Colloquio di Informatica Musicale*. Rome: Associazione Musica Verticale, pp. 70–75.

Gabor, D. 1946. "Theory of communication." *Journal of the Institute of Electrical Engineers* Part III, 93: 429–457.

Gabor, D. 1947. "Acoustical quanta and the theory of hearing." *Nature* 159(4044): 591–594.

Gerrard, G. 1989. "Music 4C—A Macintosh version of Music IVBF in C." Melbourne: University of Melbourne.

Green, D. 1971. "Temporal auditory acuity." *Psychological Review* 78(6): 540–551.

Helstrom, C. 1966. "An expansion of a signal in gaussian elementary signals." *IEEE Transactions on Information Theory* IT-12: 81–82.

Howe, H. S., Jr. 1975. *Electronic Music Synthesis*. New York: Norton.

Jones, D., and T. Parks. 1988. "Generation and combination of grains for music synthesis." *Computer Music Journal* 12(2): 27–34.

Kaegi, W., and S. Tempelaars. 1978. "VOSIM—a new sound synthesis system." *Journal of the Audio Engineering Society* 26(6): 418–426.

Kronland-Martinet, R. 1988. "The wavelet transform for the analysis, synthesis, and processing of speech and music sounds." *Computer Music Journal* 12(4): 11–20.

Lent, K. 1989. "An efficient method for pitch shifting digitally sampled sounds." *Computer Music Journal* 13(4): 65–71.

Mathews, M., and J. Miller. 1965. *Music IV Programmer's Manual*. Murray Hill: Bell Telephone Laboratories.

Moles, A. 1968. *Information Theory and Esthetic Perception*. Urbana: University of Illinois Press.

Oppenheim, A., and A. Willsky. 1983. *Signals and Systems*. Englewood Cliffs: Prentice-Hall.

Otis, A., G. Grossman, and J. Cuomo. 1968. "Four sound-processing programs for the Illiac II computer and D/A converter." Experimental Music Studios Technical Report Number 14. Urbana: University of Illinois.

Pierce, J. R. 1990. "Rate, place, and pitch with tonebursts." *Music Perception* 7(3): 205–212.

Reeves, W. 1983. "Particle systems—a technique for modeling a class of fuzzy objects." *ACM Transactions on Graphics* 2(2): 359–376.

Rhea, T. 1972. "The evolution of electronic musical instruments in the United States." Ph.D. dissertation. Nashville: Peabody College.

Risset, J.-C., and D. Wessel. 1982. "Exploration of timbre by analysis and synthesis." In D. Deutsch, ed. *The Psychology of Music*. Orlando: Academic.

Roads, C. 1978. "Automated granular synthesis of sound." *Computer Music Journal* 2(2): 61–62.

Roads, C. 1985. "Granular synthesis of sound." In C. Roads and J. Strawn, eds. *Fundations of Computer Music*. Cambridge, Massachusetts: MIT Press, pp. 145–159.

Rodet, X. 1980. "Time-domain formant-wave-function synthesis." In J. G. Simon, ed. *Spoken Language Generation and Understanding*. Dordrecht: D. Reidel. Reprinted in *Computer Music Journal* 8(3): 9–14, 1984.

Rodet, X., Y. Potard, and J.-B. Barrière. 1984. "The CHANT project: from synthesis of the singing voice to synthesis in general." *Computer Music Journal* 8(3): 15–31. Reprinted in C. Roads, ed. 1989. *The Music Machine*. Cambridge, Massachusetts.: MIT Press.

Schaeffer, P. 1977. *Traité des objets musicaux*. Second edition. Paris: Éditions du Seuil.

Tomisawa, N. 1981. "Tone production method for an electronic music instrument." U. S. Patent 4,249,447.

Truax, B. 1987. "Real-time granulation of sampled sound with the DMX-1000." In S. Tipei and J. Beauchamp, eds. *Proceedings of the 1987 International Computer Music Conference*. San Francisco: Computer Music Association. pp. 138–145.

Truax, B. 1988. "Real-time granular synthesis with a digital signal processing computer." *Computer Music Journal* 12(2): 14–26.

Varèse, E. 1971. "The liberation of sound." In C. Boretz and E. Cone, eds. 1971. *Perspectives on American Composers*. New York: Norton, pp. 26–34.

Whitfield, J. 1978. "The neural code." In E. Carterette and M. Friedman, eds. 1978. *Handbook of Perception*, Vol. IV, Hearing. Orlando: Academic.

Wiener, N. 1964. *I Am a Mathematician*. Cambridge, Massachusetts: MIT Press.

Xenakis, I. 1960. "Elements of stochastic music." *Gravensaner Blätter* 18: 84–105.

Xenakis, I. 1971. *Formalized Music*. Bloomington: Indiana University Press.

# 6 Pitch-Synchronous Granular Synthesis

**Giovanni De Poli and Aldo Piccialli**

Granular synthesis builds up dynamic sounds by means of overlapping time-sequential acoustic elements having short durations, called *grains* (chapter 5, Roads 1978, 1985, Truax 1986, 1987, 1988). The basic parameters of this technique are the waveform of the grain, its duration, and its starting time. The parameters can be determined by various criteria, at the base of which, for each one, there is a model of the sound production process (De Poli and Piccialli 1988a). In general, granular synthesis is not a single synthesis model but a way of realizing many different sound production models using waveforms that are locally defined. The choice of a particular model implies operational processes that have varying degrees of effectiveness in musical use.

What is a model? If we think of a particular class of sounds that feature a certain number of parameters that either specify the physical mechanism of sound production or the psychoacoustic mechanism of perception, then we can talk of acoustic synthesis based on a model (De Poli 1983). For example, vocal sounds feature a physical model based on resonance cavities that are excited by acoustic waveforms. The model concept can be extended to the production of more abstract sound macrostructures. We can still talk about parameters of the model, but now the choice stems from the musician on the basis of aesthetic considerations. This is what happens in granular synthesis.

Analysis and synthesis systems such as wavelets or the short-time Fourier transform (STFT) supply a local representation by means of waveforms or grains multiplied by coefficients that are independent from one another. This provides a theoretical foundation for granular synthesis. In general the interpretation of these coefficients is not always significant, from the musician's point of view. On the other hand, when the aim of the chosen interpretation is the separation of local spectral information from a time-domain signal, then such analysis systems can be very useful (Moorer 1978, Gordon and Strawn 1985, Dolson 1986).

Many other analysis and transformation techniques developed in the field of digital signal processing can also be used for granular synthesis. These analysis approaches allow us to obtain specific musical information, for example, pitch and formant structure. It is possible to adapt the grains so as to exploit these representations. The validity of granular synthesis in musical applications depends on the effectiveness of the chosen model in representing the required sounds and on the simplicity and efficiency of its implementation.

Performing sound synthesis means choosing a model and thus determining the parameters that produce the required sound. For efficient musical use, it is therefore necessary that the parameters be few and in relation with a conceptual model that musicians can naturally form by themselves. A good standard is the possibility of directly and separately controlling a few perceptually significant parameters.

From a practical point of view, it is not always important that the parameters of the model be specified by a deterministic algorithm; it is sufficient that they be set from a statistical point of view. This makes the synthesis model easier to control and often more powerful in musical applications. Therefore another aim of the model could be the separation of deterministic information from those of a stochastic nature. The latter can be represented by a much lower number of parameters compared with the deterministic representation (Serra and Smith 1989).

In our research we have faced the problem of developing a method for granular synthesis of pitched sounds. We developed a *source-filter* model as an example of the application of methods derived from digital signal processing to granular synthesis. It generalizes some techniques for synthesis (Kaegi and Tempelaars 1978, Rodet 1980, Bass and Goeddel 1981, Goeddel and Bass 1984, Lienard 1978, D'Alessandro and Lienard 1988) and time compression of sounds (Fairbanks et al. 1954, Roucos and Wilgus 1985, Makoul and El-Jaroudi 1986, Jones and Parks 1988). This model is significant over a wide range of musical sounds and allows an efficient implementation of granular synthesis.

## Granular Synthesis of Nonparametric Analysis Systems

Short-time Fourier analysis (Allen and Rabiner 1977, Rabiner and Schaefer 1978, Crochiere and Rabiner 1983, Nawab and Quatieri 1988) and, even more so, wavelet analysis (see chapter 2, as well as Grossmann and Morlet 1984, Kronland-Martinet et al. 1987, and Kronland-Marinet 1988) supply formal support for granular synthesis. Apart from Gabor's (1946, 1947) suggestion aimed at the representation of acoustic signals by means of grains, the idea of granular synthesis was formulated in the musical environment. Hence the main explanation of this approach can be found in the asethetic and cultural climate surrounding the development of computer music during the past two decades. Supplying granular synthesis with a theoretical base derived from digital signal processing could thus be useless, unless we want to supply the musician with the means of controlling the construction of macrostructures from granular microstructures or to modify natural sounds represented by the latter.

We now see how nonparametric analysis-synthesis methods have implementations with granular synthesis.

Many of these methods can be interpreted as banks of passband filters, called *analysis filters*, which divide the signal into various channels. The bandwidth of the various channels is small compared with the overall bandwidth of the original signal. Thus each channel can be sampled at a lower sampling rate, that is, the output of each channel can be *time decimated*. The decimation operation, or sampling rate compression, consists of taking a sample at each $L$ samples of the input signal, where $L$ is called *decimation factor*. In our case it allows us to reduce the redundancy introduced by the analysis process. In the STFT the channels all have the same bandwidth, and the decimation factors are equal. In the wavelet transform the bandwidths are related to the constant $Q = \Delta f / f$; therefore the decimation factors are different for the various channels.

During synthesis the process is reversed. The signal of each channel is brought back to the original sampling rate by inserting $L - 1$ zeros between one sample and the next. It is then fed through a bandpass filter, called the *synthesis filter*, which interpolates the signal. Summing the output of the various channels, we obtain the required signal. The decimation and interpolation operations are nonlinear; therefore they can introduce aliasing and imaging. The signal can be reconstructed by means of the suitable choice of analysis and synthesis filters and likewise for decimation factors.

Perfect reconstruction from analysis data without redundancy can be obtained using *quadrature mirror filters* (QMF), which eliminate, during synthesis, the aliasing introuduced in analysis. In the wavelet transform this is obtained by orthogonal wavelets (chapter 4), the implementation of which is a particular QMF (figure 6.1).

In musical applications the aim of such procedure is not to exactly reproduce the original signal, but to introduce musically interesting modifications.

In synthesis we can see that each channel consists of a synthesis filter that is excited by equispaced impulses having suitable amplitude and phase.

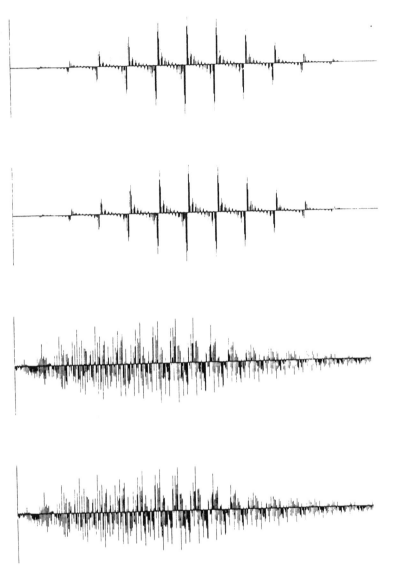

**Figure 6.1**
Sound reconstruction by orthogonal wavelet transform. The top image is the original synthetic sound, and the second one is its reconstruction. The third image is the original natural speech sound, and the bottom one is its reconstruction.

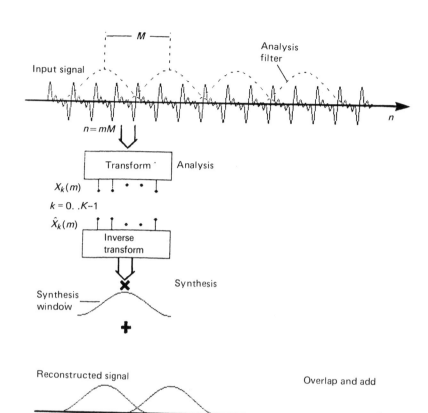

**Figure 6.2**
Interpretation of overlap and add synthesis as a form of granular synthesis

The output will be given by the convolution between the input and the impulse response of the filter; thus it consists of waveforms that are equispaced in time. If the synthesis filter is a finite-impulse-response (FIR) filter, as is normally the case, each channel output consists of a sequence of complex grains. We can thus see how we can define the parameters of granular synthesis starting from nonparametric analysis-synthesis.

The STFT has another interpretation that suggests a granular synthesis implementation. Interpreting it as a block Fourier transform, we see the STFT as a discrete Fourier transform (DFT) analysis of signal segments. The segments are obtained by multiplying the signal by a function, called the *analysis window*, which is time-shifted by a fixed number of samples. In synthesis, performing the inverse DFT, we still obtain short-time sections of the windowed signal. Overlapping and adding these sections, we synthesize the signal (figure 6.2). If the sum of all the shifted analysis windows is a constant, we obtain the original signal. This synthesis method is called *overlap and add* (OLA), and it builds a signal by means of the sum of a sequence of waveforms. The similarity with granular synthesis is evident. The method can be generalized by multiplying the signal sections, obtained by the inverse DFT, by a suitable synthesis window. This is called weighted overlap and add. With this technique it is unnecessary to set restrictions on the analysis windows. The final signal is still obtained by overlap and add of the modified sections (Crochiere 1980). These methods, which synthesize the signal starting from short-time segments of sound, can thus be defined as granular. STFT analysis, followed by possible transformation of the parameters, supplies the criterion for grain waveforms.

This model requires a very large amount of grains. At least one grain for each input signal is necessary for perfect reconstruction. A reduction can be obtained by eliminating grains whose amplitudes are not significant. For a more efficient solution a parametric model can be employed.

## The Pitch Synchronous Approach

To design a synthesis model, it is necessary to have good knowledge of the acoustic process that we intend to analyze or modify. The use of such a priori information (especially in computer music) allows us to design a model that is a close approximation of the process being examined. The choice of such a model for the production of synthetic sounds is then closely related to the psychoacoustic or musical significance of its parameters.

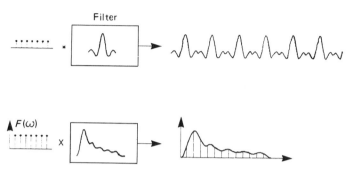

**Figure 6.3**
Interpretation of subtractive synthesis with a periodic pulse train as input signal. In the time domain (top) the convolution of the input signal with the impulse response produces a sequence, with possible overlap, of the impulse responses, one in correspondence with each input impulse. In the frequency domain (bottom) the product of the spectra gives rise to a line spectrum whose envelope is the magnitude of the frequency response of the filter.

The model suggested here, which covers a very significant class of musical sounds, is the classical source-filter model. It uses a quasi-periodic signal as the excitation of a time-varying linear filter that shapes the spectral envelope of the sound (that is, it is a form of subtractive synthesis). The fine structure of the excitation signal is realized by means of a quasi-periodic unit impulse train whose frequency varies according to the pitch of the sound (figure 6.3). The shaping filter is a (possibly linear phase) time-varying FIR filter. This model allows us to generate a wide range of musical sounds that are easily and naturally controllable. The time-varying properties result from updating both the excitation and the spectral envelope parameters. The latter are updated synchronously with the input impulses.

Selecting a pulse train as the input signal might seem to restrict musical sound synthesis because the shape of the quasi-periodic excitation function plays a noticeable role in affecting the "naturalness" of the sound. This problem is overcome, however, by including the spectral envelope of the excitation signal in the frequency response of the filter (figure 6.4).

Hence the source-filter model is a good form of representation, and we can estimate its parameters using linear predictive analysis (Markel and Grey 1976) and the homomorphic deconvolution (Oppenheim and Schafer 1975). If the synthesis model is time-invariant, the output signal is the convolution of the excitation signal $u(n)$ with the impulse response $g(n)$,

$$s(n) = u(n) * g(n) = \Sigma_i g(n - d_i),\tag{1}$$

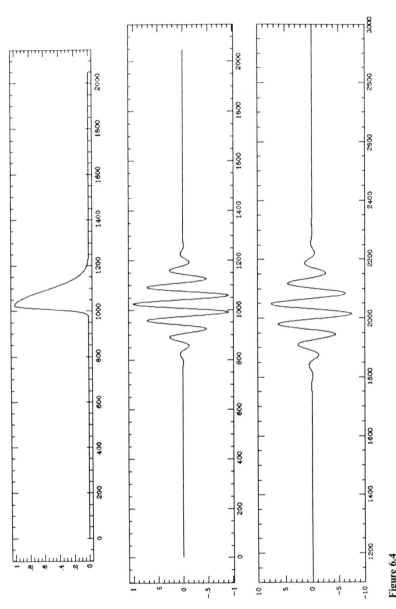

**Figure 6.4**
Representation in the time domain of the modification of the filter impulse response to use an impulse as input. (Top) Excitation function. (Middle) Impulse response. (Bottom) New impulse response obtained by convolution of the previous excitation function with the old impulse response.

where $u(n) = \Sigma_i \delta(n - d_i)$ is an unit impulse train, and $d_i$ is the temporal location of the $i$th grain. In the general case of a linear time-varying filter, the output signal is given by the convolution of the input signal with a time-varying impulse response $g(n, m)$, but its interpretation is far from simple. However, in the case of a quasi-stationary (time-invariant over short-time) system, a fairly realistic hypothesis for many sound structures, the output signal can still be put into a form that retains much of the simplicity and ease of interpretation of equation 1, namely,

$$s(n) = \Sigma_m e(m)g(n, m) = \Sigma_i g_i(n - d_i), \tag{2}$$

where $g_i$ is the impulse response of an FIR filter with $g_i(k) = 0$ for $k < 0$ and $k > N_i$. The waveforms $g_i$ can be different and the instants $d_i$ distributed in a more or less regular pattern.

We can immediately interpret the input-output equation 2 from the granular synthesis point of view. In fact we can identify the $i$th grain with the response $g_i(k)$ of the FIR filter and the grain's temporal location with the instant $d_i$. The problem of determining the waveform of a grain is thus traced back to the design of a FIR filter.

A few suggestions can be made regarding the implementation of this model. In music the dynamic development of the spectrum is very important. Therefore it is advisable to consider this fact when designing the model and the filters. The direct form structure consists of using a single filter, the frequency response of which globally approximates the required spectral envelope. If the filter is static, design by standard methods suffices. In the time-varying case a new design should be made for every small variation of the spectrum. Obviously this is not a generally satisfactory solution from a computational standpoint. We can lessen the computational burden by singling out a few spectral envelopes and creating dynamic variations by means of interpolation among these envelopes. In this case the number of designs and grains to be stored is small. Furthermore a repertoire of spectral envelopes, thus timbres, is created. On the other hand physical and perceptual considerations suggest that we consider the overall development of the sound as consisting of various separate and simpler developments. This is the case, for example, when the resonator consists of various cavities that can vary independently and when the combination of various effects over time creates the final result. Furthermore such a separation can make control of the model easier and more natural. Thus it is advisable to realize the model using a structure consisting of various filters connected in series (cascade) or in parallel (Holmes 1983). In our case this means FIR filters with an impulse excitation in a parallel configuration, for reasons of computational efficiency. This results in a structure consisting of a parallel FIR filter bank excited by an impulse train having an impulse at each pitch period:

$$r(n) = \Sigma_i \Sigma_j h_{ij}(n - d_i). \tag{3}$$

It can be noticed that a sum of grains $h_{ij}$ results for each instant $d_i$. In fact equation 3 corresponds to equation 2, if we define $g_i$ as

$$g_i(n) = \Sigma_j h_{ij}(n). \tag{4}$$

To make control easier, it is often convenient to stipulate that each grain is used for controlling a certain frequency area. In this case the grain should have its energy localized both in time and frequency, as in the original suggestion by Gabor. Thus the grains are located on the time-frequency plane, and $f_{ij}$ is the reference frequency of the grain.

With respect to short-time Fourier transform and wavelet transform, in which the grains are defined in a grid that is independent from the sound (figures 6.5 and 6.6), here instead the grid depends directly on the sound

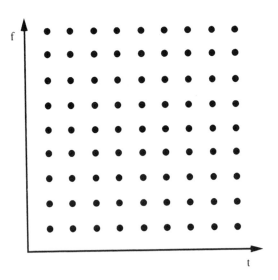

**Figure 6.5**
Short-time Fourier transform analysis/synthesis grid

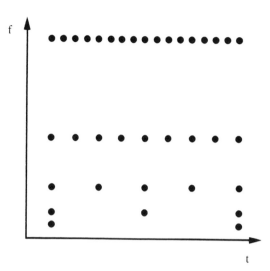

**Figure 6.6**
Wavelet transform analysis/synthesis grid

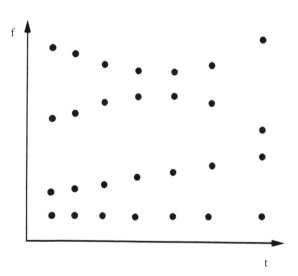

**Figure 6.7**
Pitch-synchronous synthesis grid. The grains are synchronized in correspondence with the beginning of each pitch period of the sound. In this example the period duration is increasing.

(figure 6.7). On the other hand the shape of the grain, and thus the width and shape of the spectrum, is generally different both in the various parallel branches and in time. The grains can therefore be placed where necessary with the appropriate shape. Thus a much smaller number of grains is necessary. Furthermore the temporal aspect is easily separated from the spectral one, which in the previously mentioned representations merges in magnitude and phase. Moreover natural control of the synthesis results, and the design of the grain waveform becomes easier.

## Choosing the Waveform for the Grains

In our model the spectral envelope of the sound is determined by the Fourier transform of the grain, whereas the pitch articulations are determined by the temporal location of the grain.

The problem of choosing a grain waveform is traced back to the design of the FIR filter, given the desired frequency response. Often we are content to only specify the desired frequency response magnitude; in so doing we simplify the solution of the problem without compromising much on the audio plane. In particular cases it can be useful to perform a final phase correction with an allpass filter.

### Direct Form Structure of the Filter

In the direct form structure we have to approximate the overall spectral envelope of the sound. Standard FIR filter design techniques can be used, adapted to the particular case. Among various filter design techniques, the ones that supplied the best results in our case are the window method and the optimum approximation with minimization of relative error in the Chebyshev norm.

The window method is used when we deal with an (often infinite) impulse response having the desired spectral envelope, for example, when we analyze the signal by *linear predictive coding* (LPC) or by *homomorphic deconvolution* using the cepstrum. It is possible to obtain an FIR filter multiplying the impulse response by a suitable window. In our application the spectra are often continuous functions with continuous derivatives; in this case a rectangular window suffices. If we do not have the impulse response coefficients, we can still obtain an approximation of them by sampling the frequency response and then computing the inverse DFT on an adequate number of points to reduce aliasing to a minimum.

This model is quite versatile. In fact the user, which in our case is almost always a musician not intimately familiar with the mathematical theory of Fourier analysis, can directly draw the desired spectral frequency shape (for example, by means of an interactive graphic editor program) and automatically obtain the required impulse response.

It is advisable that the filters, and thus the waveforms, be as short as possible so that the number of overlapping grains is reduced to a minimum, for increased computing efficiency. The window method is excellent from the computational and versatility point of view; however, it produces a filter that is optimum from the standpoint of the minimum square norm, which does not match perception well. Among the various optimization criteria, the most suitable for our aim is the minimax minimization of the relative error. This criterion has the favorable perceptual feature that it also minimizes the difference between the desired and the approximated spectra, expressed in decibels. Linear phase and minimum phase filters can be designed using this method. It is also possible to define upper and lower bounds in some bands, constraining the approximation (Grenez 1983). Figure 6.8 shows the linear phase approximation of the vowel /a/.

The linear phase requirement is important when there are various filters in parallel, so as to avoid unwanted cancellations in the spectrum. In

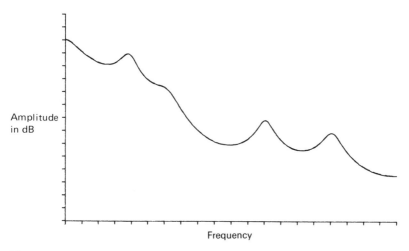

**Figure 6.8**
Optimum design of a grain by linear phase approximation of the spectral envelope of a vowel /a/

the direct structure we can use minimum phase filters, obtaining shorter filters with an equivalent approximation, but losing the symmetry of the waveform.

**Parallel Structure**

In the parallel structure each grain sequence separately controls a part of the spectrum. Sometimes it is convenient to use one grain to produce the general lowpass shape of the spectrum and the others to control the local spectrum details.

It is possible to design the specific waveform at each instant, using similar techniques to those of the direct case. Nevertheless various different waveforms are necessary for each period. Therefore it is wise to try and reduce them, picking out certain operations or transformations that allow us to obtain all the waveforms that are necessary in an approximated manner (Jarske et al. 1988; DePoli and Piccialli 1988a, 1989). These transformations can be applied both to prototypes and to the various waveforms progressively transformed. In this manner only a few prototype waveforms have to be created, and then by means of suitable transformations it is possible to obtain the required waveform. For example, it is well known that a bandpass impulse response can be obtained by modulation of lowpass prototypes. Thus the prototype waveforms will typically be impulse responses of the lowpass filters with relevant features depending on the model. These waveforms can be designed by using the same methods as the direct form structures. Moreover standard waveforms can be used for this application, such as the decreasing exponential, gaussian, or other windows used in the analysis of signals (Harris 1978, Nuttal 1981, 1983, Streit 1984, Mathews et al. 1985). Other waveforms which proved to be useful are the Maxflat filters (Hermann 1971, Kaiser 1973) and the linear phase approximation of the one-pole impulse response.

**Waveform Transformations**

Let $p(n)$ and $q(n)$ be two waveforms and $P(f)$ and $Q(f)$ their Fourier transforms. The first transformation, which we call *amplitude transformation*, consists of changing the filter gain, multiplying the waveform by a constant

$$r(n) = G[a, p(n)] = a \cdot p(n). \tag{5}$$

The resulting spectrum will be multiplied by the same constant, $R(f) = a \cdot P(f)$. This transformation is often used in combination with other transformations. Furthermore it is used to change the amplitude normalization of the waveform. Indeed, in the implementation the samples are stored with normalized values so that they can best exploit a limited memory space and have the maximum possible dynamics.

We call the following expression *additive transformation*:

$$r(n) = A[p(n), q(n)] = p(n) + q(n). \tag{6}$$

The spectrum of $r(n)$ is given by $R(f) = P(f) + Q(f)$. If $p(n)$ and $q(n)$ are zero phase, $r(n)$ will also be zero phase, and the addition of spectra is a real operation. Thus disturbing interferences and cancellations in the spectrum are avoided. A combination of this transformation with the preceding one gives the *weighted additive transformation*, defined by

$$r(n) = W[p(n), q(n), a1, a2] = a1 \cdot p(n) + a2 \cdot q(n), \tag{7}$$

where $a1, a2$ are constants. We used this kind of transformation to modify various parts of the shape of a formant. For example, the added grain can control the skirt of the transition band. Another application is designing a grain for each different spectral region and then combining the resulting waveforms using this transformation (figure 6.9). In this way we have a simple control mechanism for complex grains with easier musical usage. Our experience suggests that zero phase prototype waveforms are preferred.

The *multiplicative transformation* is given by

$$r(n) = M[p(n), q(n)] = p(n) \cdot q(n). \tag{8}$$

The spectrum of $r(n)$ is the convolution of $P(f)$ with $Q(f)$. We now examine some important specific cases. Let $p(n)$ be the impulse response of a lowpass prototype and $q(n)$ the complex exponential function, then $r(n)$ will be a bandpass version of $p(n)$. Considering the real signal and a generic phase $\Phi$ of the exponential, we obtain

$$r(n) = p(n) \cdot \cos(2\pi f_c n + \Phi), \tag{9}$$

where $f_c$ is the normalized center frequency of the bandpass region. This operation corresponds to a frequency translation of the prototype spectrum. It allows an accurate control of formant frequency (figure 6.10).

(a)

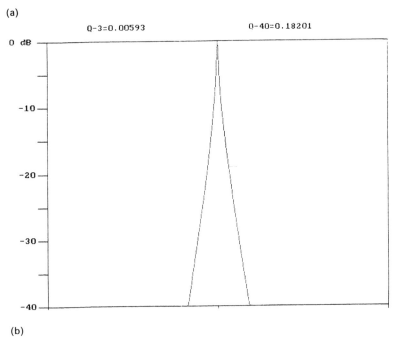

(b)

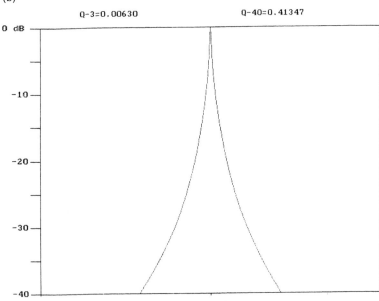

(c)

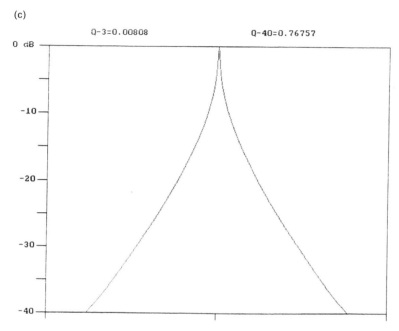

**Figure 6.9**
Examples of weighted additive transformation, which changes the skirt of the transition band. (A) Spectrum of the first prototype. (B) Spectrum of the second prototype. (C) Spectrum of the grain obtained by a weighted additive transformation of the two previous prototypes.

Other choices of $q(n)$ are possible (figure 6.11). But it is advisable to use waveforms where the energy is localized in a few regions of the spectrum, to have a natural idea of the resulting spectrum. In any case they must not be highpass in the frequency domain, to avoid foldover.

The *time scale transformation* is defined by

$$r(n) = S[p(n), b] = b \cdot p(b \cdot n). \tag{10}$$

The spectrum is given by $R(f) = P(f/b)$. Therefore a reduction of the time scale determines an inverse widening of the frequency scale. An important application is to control the bandwidth of a lowpass prototype. In this case $b$ will be equal to the ratio between the desired bandwidth and the original bandwidth of the prototype (figure 6.12). If the prototype waveform is stored in a table, the time scale change can be obtained by reading the table scanned with a step value $b$. Thus it is advisable to have more detailed tables containing various intermediate values. Often a more efficient im-

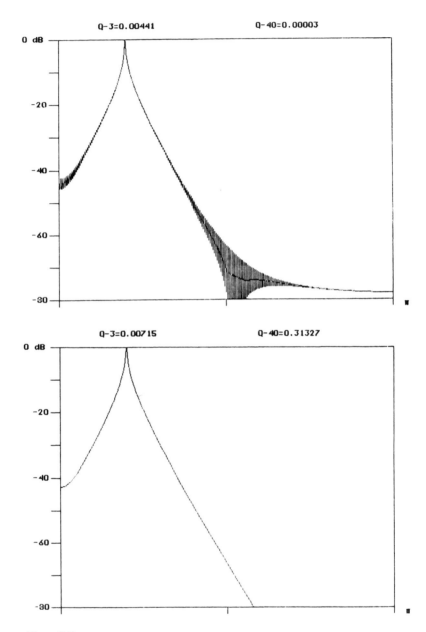

**Figure 6.10**
Examples of multiplicative transformation. A window applied to a grain improves the
frequency response. (Top) Spectrum of the original waveform. (Bottom) Spectrum of the
windowed waveform.

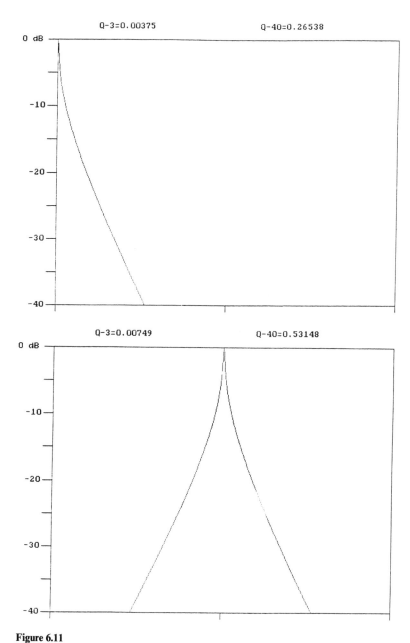

**Figure 6.11**
Multiplicative transformation applied for frequency translation. (Top) Spectrum of the
original prototype. (Bottom) Spectrum of the frequency translated prototype by means of a
multiplication of the original waveform by a cosine of suitable frequency.

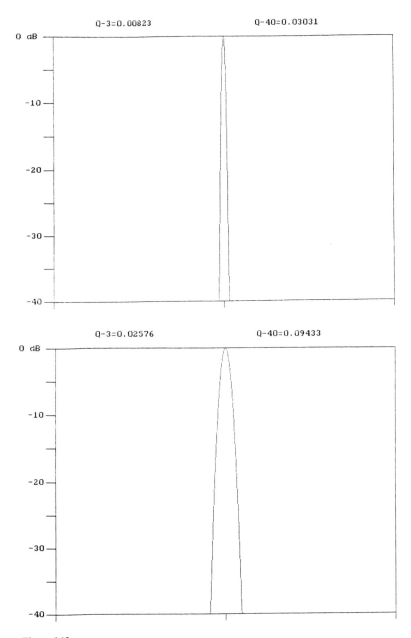

**Figure 6.12**
Time scale transformation. (Top) Spectrum of the prototype. (Bottom) Increase of the bandwidth obtained by compression of the time scale.

plementation can be obtained by grouping the products of waveform by their constants that appear in the transformation. When the multiplicative (by a cosine) transformation is applied to a time-scaled prototype, we can easily control dynamically the bandwidth and center frequency of the formants. If the time-scaled waveform corresponds to a bandpass signal, we modify both the bandwidth and the center frequency. Their ratio remains constant, so we have a *constant-Q* synthesis property, analogous to wavelet synthesis.

Besides these transformation, which have a precise interpretation in digital signal processing theory, we propose some useful nonlinear transformations. Time-scale distortion and nonlinear amplitude distortion are given by

$$r(n) = N[p(n), q(n), c] = p[c \cdot q(n)], \tag{11}$$

where in the first case $q(n)$ is the function expressing the time-scale distortion of $p(n)$, and in the second case $p(n)$ is the nonlinear amplitude distorting function applied to $q(n)$. Factor $c$ acts as a "modulation index" and allows complex variations of the grain spectrum. Small distortions of this type allow an efficient control of fine details of the sound spectrum (figure 6.13). Note that in the implementation of this transformation, the functions are normally stored in tables, and linear interpolation is used to compute values at noninteger abscissae.

Among various possibilities we found that distorting the time scale of the shifting cosine before using it in the multiplicative transformation was particularly interesting from a musical standpoint. This creates a phase-modulated sinusoidal signal, enveloped by a grain waveform

$$r(n) = p(n) \cdot \cos[2\pi f_c n + c \cdot \Phi(n)]. \tag{12}$$

The control of the modulation index and of the time scale of the modulating function allows a continuous and smooth control of the generated signal's spectrum shape (figure 6.14).

## Implementation of a Formant Synthesis System

Many musical instruments, as well as the voice, can be modeled as a resonance cavity excited by an acoustic waveform. An efficient implementation of such a system can be realized by means of our model, using the

(a)

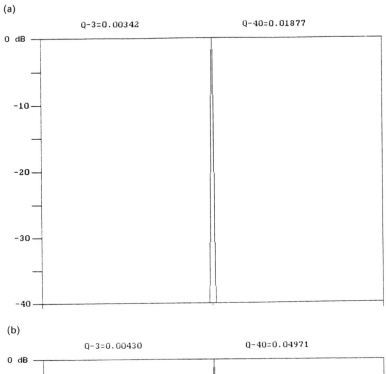

(b)

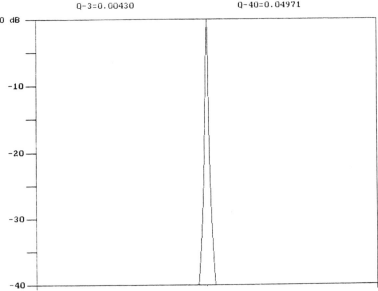

(c)

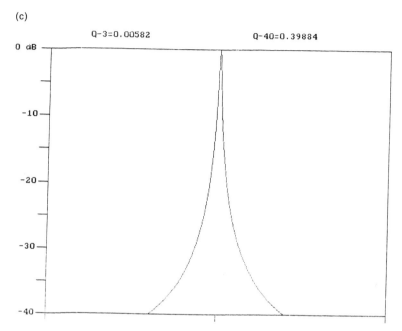

Figure 6.13
Transformation by time-scale distortion. (A) Spectrum of the prototype. (B) Spectrum of the transformed waveform obtained by scanning the prototype table using a sampling increment that is slightly linearly increasing. (C) Same transformation, but with a wider variation of the sampling increment.

parallel structure. In the case of a formant spectrum, if each feature (apart from the pitch frequency) can be traced back to prototype lowpass filter features, the problem is reduced to the pitch-synchronous temporal control of bandwidth, central frequency, amplitude, and shape of each formant (figure 6.15).

As previously seen, we can control these parameters by a suitable choice of the prototype and of the transformations. For example, the bandwidth can be controlled by time-scale transformation and the center frequency by multiplicative transformation (figure 6.16). Many tranformations can be used to control the shape of the formant. For example, consider the typical case of a formant with independent control of the central area compared with the skirts. The grain can be obtained from the sum of the two bandpass-type grains, as in figure 6.9. The parameters to be specified will be prototype waveform, relative amplitude, center frequency, and the band of each component grain. Another example could be a formant, the shape

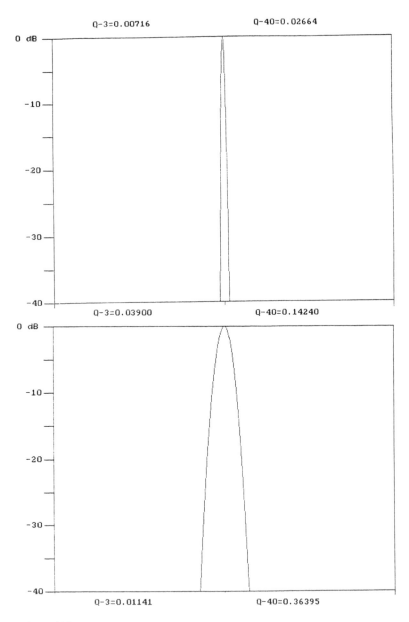

**Figure 6.14**
Transformation by phase distortion. (Top) Spectrum of a bandpass grain obtained by multiplying a low-pass prototype by a cosine. (Bottom) Bandwidth increase obtained phase modulating the shifting cosine before the multiplication.

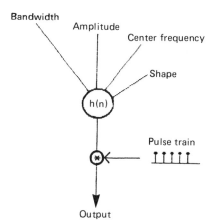

**Figure 6.15**
Formant control parameters

of which is controlled by means of phase modulation of the shifting cosine, as in figure 6.14. In this case our parameters will be the prototype waveform, center frequency, bandwidth, modulation index, and modulating waveform.

Apart from varying the parameters of the transformations, it is also possible to vary the types of transformations used. We suggest two implementations for synthesis, starting from equation 3. The first (figure 6.17) calculates the total impulse response at time $d_i$,

$$g_i(k) = \Sigma_j h_{ij}(k),\tag{13}$$

and then the convolution is performed, which consists of summing the grains that are properly time-shifted:

$$s(n) = \Sigma_i g_i(n - d_i).\tag{14}$$

In the latter implementation (figure 6.18) we perform convolution for each formant independently, and afterward we obtain the output as a sum of partial results:

$$y_j(n) = \Sigma_i h_{ij}(n - d_i),\tag{15}$$

$$s(n) = \Sigma_j y_j(n).\tag{16}$$

Obviously the two implementations do not differ in the manner of controlling the structure of the waveform. The former has fewer operations, but is less versatile than the latter.

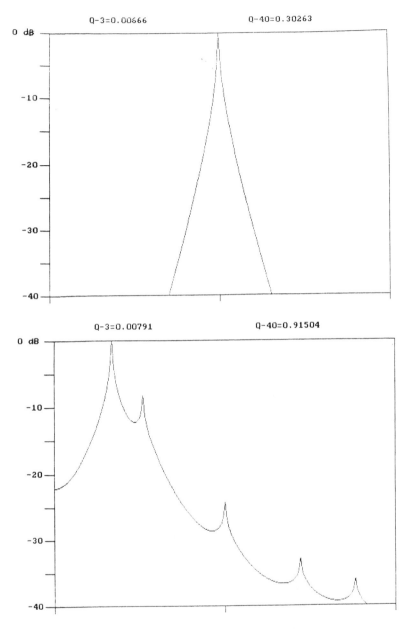

**Figure 6.16**
Example of formant synthesis. (Top) Spectrum of a simple formant. (Bottom) Spectrum of a vowel obtained by adding five formants derived from the same prototype.

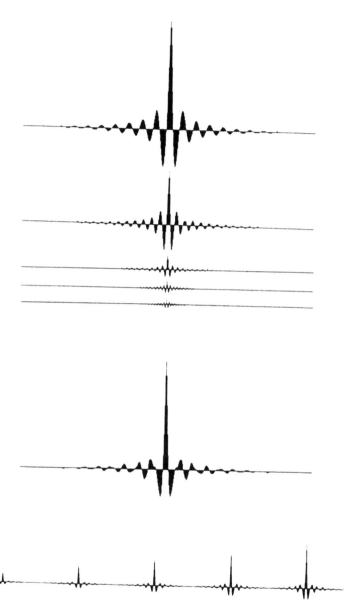

**Figure 6.17**
Total impulse response and convolution with a pulse train. (Top) The five signals are the
grain waveforms corresponding to the five formants of figure 6.16. (Middle) Total impulse
response obtained by the sum of the previous five waveforms. (Bottom) Convolution of the
total impulse response with a pulse train.

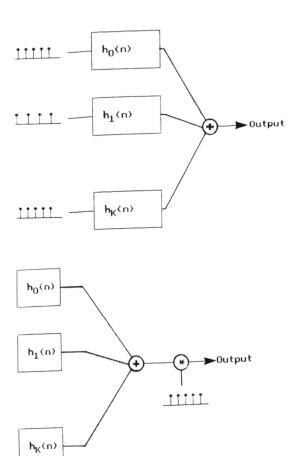

**Figure 6.18**
Comparison of two implementations of a formant synthesizer. (Top) Convolution is
performed for each formant independently, and then the partial results are summed.
(Bottom) Total impulse response is computed before convolution is performed.

The frequency of the excitation impulses determines the pitch of the resulting sound. Therefore, apart from matching the melody, it must be carefully controlled in transitions. This pitch frequency, in the case of natural sounds, is not to be interpreted in a deterministic manner but as a mean value of a random process. Random variations around the mean value, which can vary in time, allow as to perceive the spectral envelope and the fusion of the sound components.

In pitch-synchronous granular synthesis the excitation impulses are only a time reference of the impulse response, with reference to the previous one, and are not physically existent. Therefore the impulses can be fixed at intermediate instants between two effective signal samples. If we defined the prototype waveforms using oversampled tables, during synthesis it is sufficient just to move the point of reference, which will no longer coincide with a sampling instant. This procedure is similar to what happens in the table look-up oscillator (Mathews 1969), where it is unnecessary that a period begin exactly at a sampling instant.

From the musician's point of view, it could be useful to imagine that the control parameters follow certain continuous traces. Therefore, during the

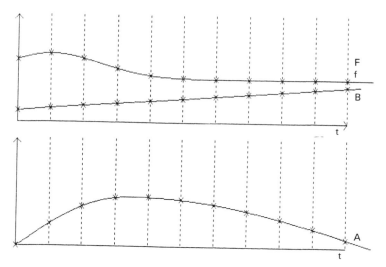

**Figure 6.19**
Example of how the parameters of the grains, producing a formant, can be derived from analysis data. The continuous traces are the output of an analysis channel. In correspondence of each pitch impulse, the values of the parameters are obtained. (Top) Center frequency and bandwidth. (Bottom) Amplitude.

realization, in correspondence with each pitch impulse, the values of the parameters are calculated or read from tables. A possible variation of the macrostructure in granular synthesis can be obtained by directly acting on these traces through editing, for example, varying the time scale of the sound's articulation or moving the center frequencies of the formants. An example might be useful to clarify this idea: Let's consider the case of formant structure. In figure 6.19 we can see the trajectories of an analysis channel, from which we can derive the development over time of the parameters.

The best results are obtained when these transformations are coordinated with the microstructures of the sound to be transformed. The random variations will also have to be reformulated so as to counter relative staticness (or excess variation) caused by a widening (or shortening) of the stationary section.

## Conclusions

In this chapter some principles and realizations of a pitch-synchronous granular synthesis system using prototype waveforms are investigated. When this waveform satisfies some well-known conditions, granular synthesis coincides with wavelet synthesis. Thus musicians have at their disposal a rigorous analysis framework that allows the reproduction of any natural sound, with transformations that increase its power in musical applications.

Nevertheless more compact sound representation are required in the musical practice; in particular control of the parameters must correspond to the physical phenomena of sound production and to musical perception. One such representation can be realized in granular synthesis using the wave transformation techniques described in this chapter. From this point of view granular synthesis could constitute a unifying approach for various theoretical and practical experiences developed in digital signal processing and sound synthesis.

## References

Allen, J. B., and L. R. Rabiner. 1987. "A unified theory of short-time spectrum analysis and synthesis." *Proceeding of the IEEE* 65(11): 1558–1564.

Bass, S. C., and T. W. Goeddel. 1981. "The efficient digital implementation of subtractive music synthesis." *IEEE Micro* 1(3): 24–37.

Crochiere, R. E. 1980. "A weighted overlap-add method of Fourier analysis-synthesis." *IEEE Transactions on Acoustics, Speech and Signal Processing* 28(1): 99–102.

D'Alessandro, C., and J. S. Lienard. 1988. "Decomposition of the speech signal into short-time waveforms using spectral segmentation." *Proceedings of ICASSP 88.* New York: IEEE, pp. 351–354.

De Poli, G. 1983. "A tutorial on digital sound synthesis techniques." *Computer Music Journal* 7(4): 8–26. Reprinted in C. Roads, ed. 1989. *The Music Machine.* Cambridge, Massachusetts: MIT Press, pp. 429–448.

De Poli, G., G. Longo, and G. Mian. 1986. "An effective software tool for digital filter design." *Proceedings of the IASTED International Symposiun.* pp. 237–242.

De Poli, G., and A. Piccialli. 1988a. "Forme d' onda per la sintesi granulare sincrona." Rome: Associazione di Musica Verticale, pp. 70–75.

De Poli, G., and A. Piccialli. 1988b. "Dynamic control of FIR filters for sound synthesis." *Proceedings of EUSIPCO 88.* pp. 559–562.

De Poli, G., and A. Piccialli. 1989. "Waveform transformation techniques for sound synthesis." *Proceedings of the International Congress on Acoustics,* Belgrade.

Dolson, M. B. 1986. "The phase-vocoder: a tutorial." *Computer Music Journal* 10(1): 14–27.

Fairbanks, G., W. L. Everitt, and R. P. Jaeger. 1954. "Method for time or frequency compression-expansion of speech." *IRE Transactions on Audio* (2)1: 7–12.

Gabor, D. 1946. "Theory of communication." *Journal of the Institute of Electrical Engineers* Part III 93: 429–457.

Gabor, D. 1947. "Acoustical quanta and the theory of hearing." *Nature* 159(1044): 591–594.

Goeddel, T. W., and S. C. Bass. 1984. "High quality synthesis of musical voices in discrete time." *IEEE Transactions on Acoustics Speech and Signal Processing* 32(3): 623–633.

Gordon, J. W., and J. Strawn. 1985. "An introduction to the phase vocoder." In J. Strawn, ed. *Digital Audio Signal Processing: An Anthology.* Madison, Wisconsin: A-R Editions.

Grenez, F. 1983. "Design of linear or minimum-phase FIR filters by constrained Chebyshev approximation." *Signal Processing* 5: 325–332.

Grossmann, A., and J. Morlet. 1984. "Decomposition of Hardy functions into square integrable wavelet of constant shape." *SIAM Journal on Mathematical Analysis* 15: 723–736.

Harris, F. J. 1978. "On the use of window for harmonic analysis with discrete Fourier transform." *Proceedings of the IEEE* 66(1): 51–85.

Hermann, O. 1971. "On the approximation problem in nonrecursive digital filter design." *IEEE Transactions on Circuit Theory* 18(3): 411–413.

Holmes, J. 1983. "Formant Synthesizers: Cascade or Parallel?" *Speech Communication* 2: 251–273.

Kaegi, W., and S. Tempelaars. 1978. "VOSIM: A new sound synthesis system." *Journal of the Audio Engineering Society* 26(6): 418–424.

Kaiser, J. F. 1973. "Design subroutine (MXFLAT) for symmetric FIR low pass digital filters, with maximally flat pass and stop bands." *Programs for Digital Signal Processing.* New York: IEEE Press, 5.3.1–6.

Kronland-Martinet, R., R. J. Morlet, and A. Grossmann. 1987. "Analysis of sounds patterns through wavelet transforms." *International Journal of Patterns Recognition and Artifical Intelligence* 1(2): 97–126.

Kronland-Martinet, R. 1988. The wavelet transform for the analysis, synthesis and processing of speech and music sounds." *Computer Music Journal* 12(4): 11–20.

Jones, D. L., and T. Parks. 1988. "Generation and combination of grains for music synthesis." *Computer Music Journal* 12(2): 27–34.

Jarske, P., Y. Neuvo, and S. K. Mitra. 1988. "A simple approach to the design of linear phase FIR filters with variable characteristics." *Signal Processing* 14(3): 313–326.

Lienard, J. 1987. "Speech analysis and reconstruction using short-time elementary waveform." *Proceedings of ICASSP 87*. New York: IEEE, pp. 948–951.

Mathews, J. D., J. K. Breakall, and G. K. Karawas. 1985. "The discrete prolate spheroidal filter as a digital signal processing tool." *IEEE Transactions on Acoustics, Speech and Signal Processing* 33(6): 1471–1478.

Mathews, M. V. 1969. *The Technology of Computer Music*. Cambridge, Massachusetts: MIT Press.

Markel, J. D. and A. H. Grey. 1976. *Linear Prediction of Speech*. Berlin: Springer-Verlag.

Moorer, J. A. 1978. "The use of the phase vocoder in computer music applications." *Journal of Audio Engineering Society* 26(1/2): 42–45.

Moorer, J. A. 1979. "The use of linear prediction of speech in computer music applications." *Journal of Audio Engineering Society* 27(3): 134–140.

Makoul, J., A. El-Jaroudi. 1986. "Time scale modification in medium to low rate speech coding." *Proceedings of ICASSP 86*. New York: IEEE, pp. 1705–1708.

Nawab, S. H., and T. F. Quatieri. 1988. "Short-time Fourier transforms." In J. Lim and A. Oppenheim, eds. *Advanced Topics in Signal Processing*. Englewood Cliffs: Prentice-Hall.

Neuvo, Y., C. Dong, and S. K. Mitra. 1984. "Interpolated finite impulse response filters." *IEEE Transactions on Acoustics, Speech, and Signal Processing* 32(3): 563–570.

Nuttal, A. H. 1981. "Some windows with very good sidelobe behavior." *IEEE Transactions on Acoustics, Speech and Signal Processing* 29(1): 84–91.

Nuttal, A. H. 1983. "A two-parameter class of Bessel weighting for spectral analysis for array processing." *IEEE Transactions on Acoustics, Speech and Signal Processing* 31(5): 1309–1312.

Oppenheim, A. V., and R. W. Schafer, 1975. *Digital Signal Processing*. Englewood Cliffs: Prentice-Hill.

Portnoff, M. R. 1980. "Representation of digital signals and systems based on the short-time Fourier transform." *IEEE Transactions on Acoustics, Speech and Signal Processing* 28(2): 55–69.

Portnoff, M. R. 1981. "Time-scale modification of speech based on short-time Fourier analysis." *IEEE Transactions on Acoustics, Speech and Signal Processing* 29(3): 374–390.

Rabiner, L. R., and R. W. Schafer. 1978. *Digital Processing of Speech Signals*. Englewood Cliffs: Prentice-Hall.

Roads, C. 1978. "Automated granular synthesis of sound." *Computer Music Journal* 2(2): 61–62. Revised version printed as "Granular synthesis of sound," in C. Roads and J. Strawn, eds. 1985. *Foundations of Computer Music*. Cambridge, Massachusetts: MIT Press. pp. 145–159.

Roads, C. 1985. "Granular synthesis of sound: past research and future prospects." *Atti del VI Colloquio di Informatica Musicale*. Naples.

Rodet, X. 1980. "Time domain formant wave function synthesis." In J. G. Simon, ed. *Spoken Language Generation and Understanding*. Dordrecht: D. Reidel.

Roucos, S., and A. M. Wilgus. 1985. "High-quality time scale modification for speech." *Proc. ICASSP 85*. New York: IEEE, pp. 493–496.

Serra, X., and J. O. Smith. 1989. "Spectral modeling synthesis." *Proceedings of the 1989 International Computer Music Conference*. San Francisco: Computer Music Association, pp. 281–284.

Streit, R. L. 1984. "A two-parameter family of weights for nonrecursive digital filters and antennas." *IEEE Transactions on Acoustics, Speech and Signal Processing* 32(1): 108–118.

Truax, B. 1986. Real-time granular synthesis with the DMX-1000." In P. Berg, ed. *Proceedings of the 1986 International Computer Music Conference*. San Francisco: Computer Music Association, pp. 231–235.

Truax, B. 1987. "Real-time granulation of sampled sound with the DMX-1000." In J. Beauchamp, ed. *Proceedings of the 1987 International Computer Music Conference*. San Francisco: Computer Music Association, pp. 138–145.

Truax, B. 1988. "Real-time granular synthesis with a digital signal processor." *Computer Music Journal* 12(2): 14–26.

# III PHYSICAL MODEL REPRESENTATIONS OF MUSICAL SIGNALS

# Overview

**Giovanni De Poli**

The dynamic behavior of a mechanically produced sound is determined by the physical structure of the instrument that created it. The musician acts on this structure by means of suitable external action. The sounds produced by a certain structure show uniformity and coherence of dynamic behavior. This part of the book considers the physical mechanism of sound production as the object of the representation. In so doing, among other things, we highlight the uniformity of the dynamic behavior of the whole class of signals generated by the same production model.

As a comparison to a physical model representation, the methods of nonparametric time-frequency representation (such as Fourier analysis) are substantially neutral with respect to the represented sound. That is, the nonparametric representation does not highlight any particular feature of the sound, and this is reflected in the types of transforms that can be applied to signals with this representation.

To obtain a physical representation, we usually proceed in two steps: The first consists of finding a mathematical model that describes the essential aspects of the sound-producing mechanism, generally by using continuous variables. Once the various parts of the model have been established, possibly having strong internal cohesion and with a well-located interaction with the outside, we can use two approaches for developing the model: The first is the black box, in which we limit ourselves to describe the functional input-output relations, without worrying about the internal structure. The second approach is the white box, in which instead we make more accurate hypotheses on the internal structure, and the description arises from the laws of physics that govern its temporal development. For example, in the first case the resonator can be described by a transfer function, whereas in the second case it can be described by a sequence of elementary masses connected by springs and friction.

The second step in the model's development consists of "discretization" in time and space of the continuous model so as to obtain a simulation model. Both steps introduce an approximation that is to be estimated case by case. The presence of nonlinearity makes it very difficult to develop analysis techniques that allow us to estimate the parameters of the model.

It could be useful to compare physical model synthesis with other synthesis techniques from the point of view of how to obtain complex dynamic behavior starting from simple elements. Additive synthesis and granular synthesis reach this aim by means of overlapping and temporal sequencing of elementary acoustic elements. Another approach consists of linear and nonlinear transformation of simple waveforms, for example, by means of filtering and modulation, respectively. In this case we have one or more blocks that produce the input signals fed to a transformation block. A third method produces sounds as a product of the interaction, possibly nonlinear, of many elementary elements. The latter is the physical model synthesis approach, in which the blocks are the digital correspondent of moving mechanical parts.

The use of physical models to produce sounds and their implementation, at first analog and then digital, were initially developed for research in the field of acoustics of musical instruments. By means of simulation, we can understand certain acoustic phenomena better, and we can check hypotheses on physical mechanisms that produce sounds. Decades of research in this field have produced substantial know-how on many specific mechanical-acoustical phenomena and on certain general points. This scientific culture is not widespread in the field of computer music, however, due to partly to the fact that it is not always directly usable. The strong emphasis on physics tends to overlook certain aspects that are very important for musical usage. These include realizations that do not take into account the amount of calculation nor the interaction in real time with the user.

A most significant contribution to computer music from musical acoustics was given by McIntyre, Schumacher, and Woodhouse (1983), who, by studying the physical mechanisms of sound production of the various instruments, managed to formulate a unified approach to the description of oscillations in musical instruments. This work is the basis of the renewed interest for sound synthesis using physical models, highlighting the importance of the nonlinear interaction between exciter and resonator.

One aim of computer music is to produce sounds that are musically interesting. Some current work models general sound-producing mechanisms. In so doing, an exact reference to one specific instrument is abandoned. Nonetheless dynamic instrumental behavior is maintained, which is physically based and thus cognitively characterized.

Another research trend uses this approach not only for sound synthesis but also for other musical activities like performance and composition. For example, if the user is to have a physically based interaction with the synthesis device, as occurs with the traditional mechanical instrument, then we must build an appropriate controller for the musician to manipulate. Finally, some are trying to develop composition methodologies that take these results into account.

It can be argued that often behind the use of physical models we find the quest for realism and naturalness, which is not always musically desirable. It would be as limiting as figurative painting in the field of visual arts. On the other hand we can notice that even with a physical model it is easy to obtain unnatural behaviors, by means of few variations of the parameters. Moreover, the acquired experience is useful in creating new sounds and new methods of signal organization.

By examining the history of the musical use of physical models, we can see that after the pioneering work by Hiller and Ruiz (1971), which was aimed at simulting vibrating structues, such an approach was not followed up for some time. It was taken up again by Cadoz (ACROE, Grenoble) and collaborators, who developed all the above-mentioned lines. Smith and his collaborators at Stanford are working to develop models of instruments with the aim of formulating new synthesis techniques. They are particularly interested in efficient algorithms, (Smith 1986, Garnett 1987), whereas Adrien and his collaborators at IRCAM (Paris) are busy on a modular approach to instrument simulation and in interactions with the user. Several other centers, including the Laboratory of Acoustics (University of Paris VI), University of California (San Diego), and the Centro di Sonologia Computazionale (Padua) are working in this field.

In chapter 7 Florens and Cadoz discuss the various approaches that can be followed, also stopping to point out the direction of their research.

In chapter 8 Adrien presents the modal synthesis technique in detail, both as a method for building modular models and as a reference point that makes it easier to use by musicians. (See also Adrien and Rodet 1985, Adrien et al. 1988.)

Chapter 9 presents the physical model representation from a different point of view. In the field of voice research, the source-filter model has had widespread success. It can be considered as a simple physical model built by the black-box approach. The articulatory model is also used in research, which is instead developed by the white-box approach. In his chapter Sundberg presents the musical side of these studies that discuss the synthesis of singing. These are presented in particular from the user's point of view, a user who adapts the models to obtain sounds that are musically interesting. Thus both criteria for the choice and development of synthesis models and their problems of control for obtaining musically expressive results are discussed.

## References

Adrien, J. M., and X. Rodet. 1985. "Physical models of instruments: a modular approach." In B. Truax, ed *Proceedings of the 1985 International Computer Music Conference.* San Francisco: Computer Music Association, pp. 85–89.

Adrien, J. M., R. Caussé, and E. Ducasse. 1988. "Dynamic modeling of stringed and wind instruments: sound synthesis by physical models." In C. Lischka and J. Fritsch, eds. *Proceedings of the 1988 International Computer Music Conference.* San Francisco: Computer Music Association, pp. 265–271.

Cadoz, C., A. Luciani, and J. Florens. 1984. "Responsive input devices and sound synthesis by simulation of sound mechanism: the Cordis system." *Computer Music Journal* 8(3): 60–73.

Cadoz, C. 1988. "Instrumental gesture and musical composition." In C. Lischka and J. Fritsch, eds. *Proceedings of the 1988 International Computer Music Conference.* San Francisco: Computer Music Association, pp. 1–12.

Garnett, G. 1987. "Modelling piano sound using waveguide digital filtering techniques." In J. Beauchamp, ed. *Proceedings of the 1987 International Computer Music Conference.* San Francisco: Computer Music Association, pp. 89–95.

Hiller, L., and P. Ruiz. 1971. "Synthesizing musical sounds by solving the wave equation for vibrating objects." *Journal of the Audio Engineering Society* 19(6): 462–470.

McIntyre, M. E., R. T. Schumacher, and J. Woodhouse. 1983. "On the oscillations of musical instruments." *Journal of the Acoustical Society of America* 74(5): 1325–1345.

Smith, J. O. 1986. "Efficient simulation of the reed-bore and bow-string mechanism." In P. Berg, ed. *Proceedings of the 1986 International Computer Music Conference.* San Francisco: Computer Music Association, pp. 275–280.

# 7 The Physical Model: Modeling and Simulating the Instrumental Universe

## Jean-Loup Florens and Claude Cadoz

In this chapter we are concerned with the simulation and modeling of objects in the physical world. As a rule the objects are those known empirically or from general knowledge. They are material in the sense that we can manipulate them physically. However, among these objects we select those that either directly or in combination display instrumental qualities that is, the ability to produce varied and controllable sound phenomena.

We extend the idea of instrumental quality to those objects that appeal to our tactile-kinesthetic, visual, and auditory senses. This is because the multisensory aspect of the instrumental approach seems fundamental in itself, but also because a similar approach can be imagined for that other creative field to which the computer may be linked, namely, animated imaging. There is no question here of confusing the demands of these two arts. Nonetheless both require an "instrument," and they are both arts that work on events in time. They can thus highlight each other, and we might even consider their interrelation.

The modeling approach we are to embark on simultaneously takes into account three fundamental and complementary aspects: These are perceptual pertinence (which is purely auditory in the case of music), instrumental experimentability, and the constructability of the simulated object by means of a dialog with the creative tool.

Our first modeling system was the CORDIS system (Cadoz 1979, 1984), at first given over exclusively to music. Then the ANIMA system was added to it (Luciani 1985), which more especially developed visual movement aspects. CORDIS and ANIMA have a strong conceptual basis in common. This is shown in the general approach to modeling the universe of instrumental objects according to the multisensory approach described previously.

The CORDIS-ANIMA system of modeling stems from a number of basic principles. It has given rise to a series of implementations in progressively evolving contexts of complexity and performance. Such implementations, as outlines of the proposed creative tool, have enabled numerous experiments and consequently both a more essential formalization of the principles and a wider range of applications.

## CORDIS-ANIMA

A model must consider that which is manipulable, deformable, and animated by movements. Our model is made up entirely of three primitive element categories: *point masses, pure springs,* and *microdampers,* which, when combined in sufficient number, should enable the reproduction of a spatial continuum in the same way that samples, at 44,100 per second, reproduce the temporal continuum of the sound signal.

These elements are both physical and functional. They refer to simple physical objects, but each of them is an idealization, for there is no mass that is really a point, no spring without inertia or friction, and no damper without elasticity or inertia.

No abstract model can truly be the object of a thorough machine representation: To simulate an isolated spring, we need an algorithm, but also input and output "organs" that respectively accept a force and measure its resistance. To simulate a mass, we need a means to communicate movement to it and to observe it. These organs introduce delocalized and indissociable combinations of the three preceding functions. Moreover the machine can only simulate by calculating the output data from the input data in a finite time. The temporal inertia of the calculation prohibits simulation of zero mechanical inertia. We have made abstractions of these limits in our model.

This point of departure derives from classical linear mechanics. For each component we consider a mathematical expression that describes its behavior: the fundamental law of dynamics for a point mass, $F(t) = M \times \Gamma(t)$, from which we can predict its movement if its inertia $M$ and the force that is applied at each moment are known. For the spring, $F(t) = -K \times \Delta X(t)$, which gives, in passing by its stiffness constant $K$, the value of the force that it resists when we apply an elongation $\Delta X$ to it. For the damper, $F(t) = -Z \times V(t)$, where $Z$ is the friction coefficient and $V(t)$ the displacement speed.

Thus in this initial examination each object is analyzed as a more or less complex combination of small masses, springs, and dampers discretely distributed over its entire surface. A major simplification therefore resides in the fact that the expressions are constructed from real one-dimensional variables. Figure 7.1 shows the structures that can be modeled. Figure 7.1A represents a set of independent axes that point masses can move along. They define many independent one-dimensional spaces that can

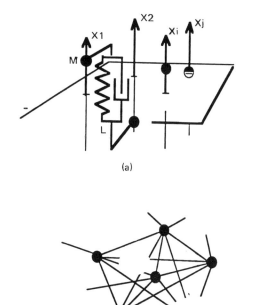

**Figure 7.1**
Sound-producing objects modeled as a combination of small masses, springs, and dampers.
(A) Point masses on independent axes. (B) General form of a sound-producing object
portrayed as a network.

only accommodate a single particle. We call a particle a *material element*.
The springs and dampers are then the *link elements* between the particles
themselves. In figure 7.1A they are also represented vertically to clearly
show that they are active compared with the difference in positions and
speeds on each axis. The distance between each axis is of no significance.

A more synthetic graphic representation (figure 7.1B) avoids showing
each particle's movement; this enables us to characterize the general form
of all buildable structures. We have a classical network that can be portrayed on a plane surface. We could also represent this in a two- or
three-dimensional perspective if needed, depending on its topology. Strictly
speaking, a graphic or physical representation of a genuine concrete area
cannot exist. All deformations and movements consist of a set of motions
correlated by the link elements and material elements. Moreover there are

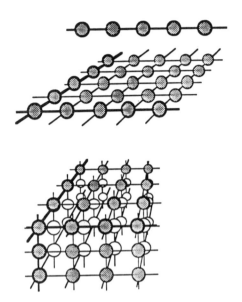

**Figure 7.2**
Topology of networks. One-dimensional (top), two-dimensional (middle), and three-dimensional (bottom) forms.

two types of dimensions to our object (or our area). These are the deformation and propagation dimensions. The first correspond to the preceding vertical axes and the second to the dimensions in figure 7.2. The two are independent. It follows that it is quite possible to reproduce propagation, fixed points, excitation points, vibratory modes, and emission points.

The topology of the network demonstrates that linear structures are not the only ones possible. A membrane or a volume can be built by structuring the links between the point masses in a particular way. The best description of this is provided with the help figure 7.2. In this case there are three independent propagation dimensions. Couplings can be introduced by means of carefully placed link modules.

We have here an initial universe of possible objects, albeit limited, for we can only build structures in one block. There can be multiple blocks, but there is no interaction between them, for the objects do not collide with each other. To represent an instrument's vibrating structure, we must realize that an instrument is generally composed of several parts. The bow, hammers, bass drumstick, and the plectrum excite a vibrating structure when they come into contact with it and are then detached from it. A link exists, but it is not permanent. It is conditioned by a number of factors connected to the behavior of the objects.

## A Fourth Basic Element: The Conditional Link

We thus introduce a fourth type of basic element: the *conditional link*. Built from a spring and a parallel damper, its intervention is conditioned by the values of the material elements that it links together. The modificaton conditioned in this manner consists of a change in the stiffness and friction constants, depending on the circumstances. The conditional link is a sort of system within the CORDIS system itself. Before we describe this sub-system, we introduce a representation of the whole, in terms of functional blocks.

**CORDIS Functional Blocks**   This representation facilitates the realiza-tion of algorithms imagined as a combination of modular blocks. Each block produces output data from input data.

Two elements exchange their energy and information by means of an intrinsically bidirectional link: For example, where a string is attached to a soundboard, two dual mechanical variables (for example force and dis-placement) circulate. We cannot tell which of the objects imposes its dis-placement or its force on the other in a unilateral way. This bidirectionality is not representable by means of calculation modules; any bidirectional link must be considered as a couple of unidirectional links oriented in opposite directions. For a given "connection" two dual solutions exist that are equivalent from the standpoint of the behavior of the whole. In one of them the forces produced by the first object make up its output and are "con-sumed" by the second, while the displacements produced by the second are consumed by the first. In the other solution the situation of forces and displacements is reversed.

When the system is structured into a network, we can state the following: The material elements are the nodes, and the link elements are the arcs of the network. It is possible to put two link elements in parallel, but not in series. It is also possible to attach several link elements, whose other extremities are distributed onto different masses, but attaching several masses to the same extremity of a link element is prohibited. The connection mode can thus be described by limiting the inputs and outputs in the first way for material elements and in dual manner for the link elements. The

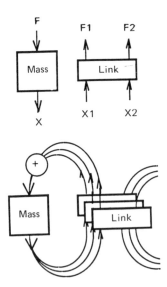

**Figure 7.3**
CORDIS functional blocks: mass, link, and connected masses and links.

construction rules we recommend impose taking force inputs and position outputs for material elements and symmetry for link elements. When several link elements are connected to the same mass, the force applied thereon is the result of all the forces produced by these elements, and the position is calculated as a function of the mass distributed to each of their inputs (figure 7.3).

We can now completely specify the function of each of the primitive elements and associate them with a descriptive diagram (see figure 7.5). These functions and their combination rules, as well as the corresponding diagram, constitute the vocabulary, grammar, and symbols of what will appear as an object description language.

### Conditional Links: Formal Definition

Now we can define conditional links more formally. As their name indicates, they belong to the link element category, and so they have two position inputs and two force outputs. They combine the spring friction functions, represented by a single equation,

$$F_1 = -F_2 = -K \cdot (X_1 - X_2) - Z \cdot (V_1 - V_2),$$

where $F_1$, $F_2$, $X_1$, $X_2$, $V_1$, and $V_2$ are the variables for time, force, displacement, and speed on the respective extremities of $K$ and $Z$, which are respectively the stiffness and friction constants. The calculation also includes some intermediate variables. Their utility will be clear once we have completed our description of this subsystem. In particular there is a length for the spring, when at rest, which can be modified for some applications. We designate this by the variable $L_A$, the elongation being $L = X_1 - X_2$; the length at each moment is thus $L_R = L - L_A$.

We also introduce $V$, the relative speed of the extremities at each moment. The preceding formula therefore becomes

$$F_1 = -K \cdot L_R - Z \cdot V.$$

The conditional modification principle is as follows: When two constituents are likely to come into a conditional relation, we begin by linking them by a conditional link. The modification is affected by, among others, a change in the $K$ and $Z$ constants, the simplest case being their cancellation, which "cuts out" the relation. However, the most general form stipulates that a particular value is affected by $K$ and $Z$ among others in a predefined set.

Three characteristics of a conditional link are link state, state change conditions, and dispositions caused by a change of state.

The link is continually characterized by a *link state* that is referenced by an index variable and a certain number of conditions relative to the input variables. *State change conditions* are expressed in the following general manner:

CONDITION ARGUMENT, VARIABLE ARGUMENT,

(PARAMETER).

The condition types are applicable to all the variales $X_1$, $X_2$, $L$, $L_R$, $V$, and they are

AUG (the variable increases)

DIM (the variable decreases)

CHS (the variable changes sign)

SUP, *parameter* (the variable is greater than *parameter*)

INF, *parameter* (the variable is less than *parameter*)

There is also an *external condition* or CDX that enables a change of state to be commanded by an event that is exterior to the object.

Each defined state is associated with a set of conditions that ensure a change in state. They are

IN STATE, *STATE INDEX*

IF, *CONDITION*, PASS INTO STATE *STATE INDEX*

IF, CONDITION, PASS INTO STATE *STATE INDEX*

and so on. The condition list is unlimited. Different conditions can lead to the same state. Several conditions can be verified that do not lead to the same state; in this case the last one encountered takes priority. Finally, if no conditions can be verified, there is no change of state.

When state change occurs, certain *dispositions* are taken that characterise the link in this state:

$LA$ ($LA$ takes the values of $L$ when the state changes)

$LRN$ ($LR$ is forced to 0 as long as the state remains unchanged)

$VN$ ($V$ is forced to 0 as long as the state remains unchanged)

$CHK, P$ ($P$ is taken as a new value for the spring stiffness constant)

$CHZ, P$ ($P$ is taken as a new value for the friction constant)

We can summarize the functioning of this device by a state automaton, shown in figure 7.4.

The conditional link system lets us model a large number of impermanent and nonlinear relations between two mechanical objects. We can then

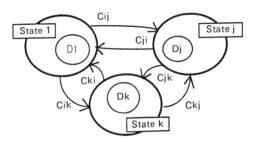

**Figure 7.4**
State automaton representing a conditional link

separate the object into two basic components: the exciter and the vibrating structure. In this way we have been able to produce highly varied and parameterized models of percussion, plucking actions, and bow-type frictions. There is no obstacle to using conditional links to model internal nonlinearities of the vibrating structure.

**Complementary Elements**

Another category of nonlinearities is introduced by developing another type of module that is more functional than physical. These are the *parameter control modules* (stiffness or friction coefficients) of a link element. They are defined by the position of a material element, conditionally calibrated and centered by the parameters associated with the module. An example is the servo-control of spring stiffness in the position of one of the masses that the spring is connected to. This simple artifice lets us control membrane tension, for example.

To conclude this description, we add four other useful elements of the CORDIS system: *Infinite mass* is homogeneous to an elementary mass. This receives all the force applied to it, but produces a constant position, represented by an arbitrary fixed point. *Gravity* is homogeneous to a link element. It applies constant force to its mass, whatever its movements. *Gestural inputs* are homogeneous to material elements or to link elements. They represent, inside the system, the intervention of the operator, who is modeled in terms of his extremities, just like a material or link element. *Listening point* modules are homogeneous to link elements with one extremity. They decide which particular material element movement makes up the sound signal to be heard.

**CORDIS Version I**

The first CORDIS modeling system can be entirely characterized by the construction language that we summarize in describing the function, parameters, and the two associated symbolic representations (pictorial and functional block) of each basic element (figure 7.5). The diagrams provide a physical description, and the blocks give a more functional description.

**Algorithmic Translation**

Each of the previously described functional blocks gives rise to an algorithm. All of them have the same structure: They are defined by a calcula-

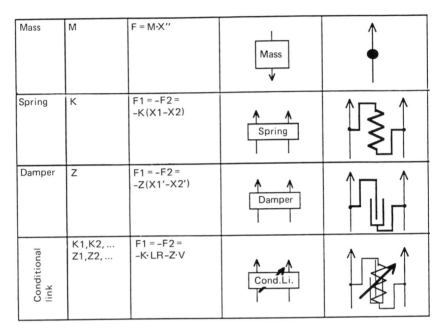

**Figure 7.5**
Functional, parametric, and two symbolic representations of the first CORDIS modeling system

tion, linked to parameters, have inputs, and generate outputs. In this way there is total isomorphy between the model components' laws of combination and those of the algorithms.

Essentially, three types of functionality are needed: data transfers, algebraic calculations (sums, products, and so on), and conditional tests. We will limit our comments to the most significant point, which is the digital equivalent of the three basic element functions: mass, spring, and damper. The prime condition for a digital algorithm is that we can establish a correspondence between continuous variables and their discrete implementation.

Sampling under Shannon conditions solves the problem. Any variable of position $X(t)$ or force $F(t)$ is replaced by a discrete variable $X(n)$ or $F(n)$, where $n$ represents the sampling moment. From this we adopt a simple approximation for representation of derived functions. By convention the internal time unit is taken as equal to the sampling period, which enables us to suppress a certain number of awkward denominators. Thus for speed $V(n)$ at moment $n$, we consider

$$V(n) = X(n) - X(n - 1),$$

and for acceleration

$$\Gamma(n) = V(n) - V(n - 1),$$

hence

$$\Gamma(n) = X(n) - 2 \cdot X(n - 1) + X(n - 2).$$

This enables us to define the algorithms in the following way: The mass position is calculated at moment $n$ as a function of the force applied,

$$X(n) = F(n) \cdot W + 2 \cdot X(n - 1) - X(n - 2),$$

where $W = 1/M$, inverse of the mass. It will be seen that the algorithm must include two memory elements to store the two preceding positions.

The spring calculates forces $F_1$ and $F_2$ from extreme positions:

$$F_2(n) = A \cdot (X_1(n) - X_2(n)) + C,$$

$$F_1(n) = -F_2(n),$$

where $A = K$, the stiffness constant, and $C = K \cdot L$, where $L$ is the spring length at rest.

For the damper,

$$F_2(n) = B \cdot (X_1(n) - X_1(n - 1) - X_2(n) + X_2(n - 1)),$$

$$F_1(n) = -F_2(n),$$

where $B = Z$, the friction constant.

In the conditional links the spring and damper algorithms are superimposed, and the conditions are processed from a test of the $X(n)$ variables, which, as a function of their result, change the calculation parameters $A$, $B$, or $C$.

As soon as they had been debugged, these algorithms were "encapsulated" into procedures, avoiding the need for mathematical knowledge by the user. A CORDIS programming language was developed, whose vocabulary and syntax can be imagined from the preceding symbolic representations.

## Implementations of CORDIS

Our first implementations of the CORDIS system were run on very small machines (of the LSI-11 type from Digital Equipment Corporation). They enabled us to simulate a number of elementary objects, such as strings or membranes that were struck, plucked, rubbed, and so forth. However, the sampling frequencies were low (1000 Hz in the best of cases). This let us apply a gestural input in real time, but not generate a sound output. We had to store sound in mass memory before listening with a suitable sample frequency. So we built a special processor whose hardwired and micro-programmed operators correspond to these algorithms. We thus built the first real-time sound synthesis system for physical models.

This CORDIS system enabled an initial investigation and opened a large number of perspectives. Nevertheless it had major limitations, which justified the far-reaching developments that we have since carried out.

**Limits to the First Version of CORDIS**   The main limitation of the system was the overly large atomicity of its components. Although the components could easily be linked to simple representations, the effort required to move from elementary to complex structures, considered according to their overall mechanical, instrumental, and acoustic behavior, was not equally easy. Atomicity is necessary for some parts of a structure, for example, a close study of the excitation process, but we also had to manipulate macroscopic vibrating structures, if only in strings, where the number of atomic elements was substantial. In addition, for these parts the micro-structure contains all the objectively necessary information, but provides only indirect information about the vibratory or modal properties, for example. We were thus led to a more sophisticated approach to modularity. We kept the notions of material elements, link elements, and conditional links, but applied them to modules whose size was adapted to their macro-level functions.

Following the same order of ideas, the exclusively one-dimensional definition of elements, and especially the inhomogeneity of propagation and deformation dimensions, is artificial if we consider the exciter or the gesture's dimensions itself. Let us show some simple examples, such as the percussion of a membrane. We want to change its timbre and thus its impact point position. The overall gesture (including the gesture and the displacement) develops in two dimensions. Dimension homogeneity appeared as vital and was even clearer when the model was enlarged to that of objects distinguished by their shapes, deformations, and visual displacements. The ANIMA system tackled these problems more fundamentally.

## ANIMA

ANIMA (Luciani 1985) introduced two- and three-dimensional elements. The consequences were felt essentially in the "spring" module. In a two-or three-dimensional space, if we can project onto the axes the forces that exert on the elements that link it, we cannot project the spring itself and substitute for it three one-dimensional springs acting separately according to each of the dimensions. Although the spring, in isolation, is mechanically linear, its action in a multidimensional space is not. In ANIMA, insofar as the objects concerned are surfaces or volumes that have nonvibratory movements or displacements, the manipulation of more macroscopic elements was felt to be important. Finally, the first implementations of ANIMA were also an opportunity to develop improved dialog devices for the creation phase of the object itself. The alphanumeric mode of the first version of CORDIS was replaced in ANIMA by a graphic mode that enabled all the objects to be described by positioning and symbolically linking the graphic representations of the mechanical constituents on a display screen.

## Macrostructural Instrument Modeling and Simulation

To go beyond the limits inherent in the "atomic" modularity of the first CORDIS-ANIMA modeling system, we approached the structural analysis of the instruments at a more macroscopic level. This analysis is based on the identification of the material constituents necessary to establish a gestural relation to the sound. Moreover, we studied more typical instrumental object categories. These were plucked or struck vibrating bodies corresponding to a first category of excitation modes, frictioned vibrating bodies (continuous vibration maintenance), and stochastic excitation (of the maracas type). For each of these implemented cases, we sought to simplify the models and to optimize the algorithms, to the detriment of a partial and temporary abandon of general modularity. The system used for all this research is a configuration of several interconnected processors given over respectively to acquisition, processing, and emission of the input/output signals, to general control (a supervisor), and to simulation in real time. The latter is achieved by an array processor (an FPS AP120 with 12 MFLOPS of theoretical power). Finally, a recently perfected gestural device composed of 16 force-feedback keys enables an elaborate instrumental gesture to be applied in real time.

### Macrostructural Instrument Analysis

An instrument, or more generally a sound body, necessarily includes one part (or several parts) oscillating at acoustic frequencies. This *vibrating structure* (SV) is distinguished from the other parts of the object to which it is attached by a small number of points. It can in its turn be divided into an *oscillator*, the center of the basis vibration, and a *radiating part*. The latter, whose property is to ensure an efficient aerial radiation, modifies the acoustic properties of the basic vibration.

Because no linear system can produce energy in a frequency zone where it receives none, if we admit that the vibrating structure is a linear structure, a special component must be situated between the gesture (devoid of energy in the acoustic frequencies) and the system. The *exciter* function, in an instrument, enables gestures to be exerted in a rich, varied manner that is adapted to human morphology, but the exciter also introduces nonlinearity.

In the most general case the nominal chain of exciter/oscillator/radiating part can be present in various forms. For a given instrument some links can be reduced, even absent (for example, hand percussion on a membrane). But there may also be a multiplicity, either of the complete chain or some elements, for example, several strings, a single bow, or a single soundboard for bowed string instruments. We now tackle the simulation and modeling problems that arise essentially in the vibrating structure, the exciter, its link with the vibrating structure (SV), and the instrumental gesture.

### Vibrating Structure Models and Simulations

The nature of the vibrating structure environment is the first SV classification criterion. There are aerial SVs, such as tube cavities whose environment (the air) is necessarily homogeneous and always identical. Their specificity stems from their form and dynamic properties (reflectivity, among others) from the edge of the cavity. There are also solid structures; a solid environment leaves room for diversity in the choice of material and also in the deformation wave modes. Three-dimensional varieties are not used because of the high propagation speeds of pressure waves. Some one- or two-dimensional bodies cover the acoustic spectrum with little bulk, thanks to low-speed controllable flexion waves.

Elasticity forces can arise from two origins in the case of flexion (bending) waves. In bells, tubes, chimes, and gongs, the rigidity of the material produces these forces, which in this case are purely local. For membranes and strings they mainly result from an orthogonal tension to displacement. In this case, apart from the obvious interest in regulating the feedback constant by means of the tension forces, local constraints and deformations are extremely low during the vibration cycle. (Only very weak stiffness and viscosity flexion deformations intervene. Moreover, because the movements are generally of low amplitude, the curvatures due to flexion remain very low.) Because of all this the visco-elastic characteristics of the material do not intervene so preponderantly as with the purely elastic feedback forces. String deadening can thus be extremely low, regardless of the kind of material used, because the strings are not coupled with the air environment, and this is independent of the type of material used. It is therefore clear from this summary classification that using strings enables a much more developed function specialization than with any other type of vibrating structure, for the string in itself only fulfills the inertia function of the oscillator.

There are also hybrid vibrating structures that bring different vibratory materials into play (tubular bells) or that are made up a great number of similar coupled vibrating elements (coupling the strings to the soundboard of a piano). The radiating elements of the external aerial environment itself always react a little on the vibrating structure. Common sound sources can also be classified in the preceding categories: air cavities represent the human voice, a drop of water, and so forth.

It should be noted that the presence of an oscillator is not necessary to produce a sound. Totally aperiodic devices can produce sustained sounds, where a highly damped radiation element makes up the oscillator. This is the case with sirens (the cavity is limited by a horn, or is inexistent) or highly damped relaxation systems.

**General Characteristics of Vibrating Structures**  Vibrating structures are centers of low-amplitude elastic deformation. Except in special cases, a linear model describes them satisfactorily. Oscillation frequencies are about 20 times those of gestural frequencies. The "wealth" of the SV, that is, its state order is high, which generally confers to it a large number of its own frequencies that can occupy a wide spectrum. In contrast, the coupling signal order that enables emission as well as control, is generally low.

We now introduce three different approaches to modeling vibrating structures. The first stems from the initial CORDIS model, the second is the so-called method of "delay lines," and the third is "simulation by modes," developed in special simulations that we have previously referred to (Florens, Luciani, and Cadoz 1986) and that Adrien (1989 and chapter 8) deals with in detail.

## CORDIS-type Modeling

We begin with a comparative analysis of three simple models of the the vibrating string. The first is an undamped homogeneous string with distributed masses, fixed at both extremities, described by a vibrating string equation. The second is an undamped *homogeneous string of beads*—a spatially discrete version of the preceding model. For each segment of the model with distributed elements, a material point of the same mass and a spring with the same elasticity is substituted. The total mass and elasticity of the structure is therefore conserved in the transformation. The third model is obtained by making a discrete time version from the second, following the plan used in CORDIS. The temporal and spatial discretization diagram thus obtained is usual: This is the five-point *explicit cross*. Within the framework of the CORDIS system, only the relation between models 2 and 3 is meaningful because the references are always to localized elements. However, we have included the continuous (or distributed) model as an implicit point of reference. This enables us to show the limits of spatial discretization and to clearly situate "pure delay methods."

At each of these steps an extra parameter is introduced: the discrete spatial step $L_e$ for model 2 and the discrete temporal step $T_e$ for model 3. The definitions and relations between the parameters of the three models are grouped together in figure 7.6. Note that $T = (M \cdot E)^{1/2}$ represents (in the first model) the propagation time, that is, the fundamental half period. This parameter is a common structural characteristic to all three models, but in cases 2 and 3 the same equality with the fundamental period is not strictly verified. We should also introduce $H = T/T_e$.

We are now going to make a comparative qualtiy assessment of these models. A functional comparison is possible to the extent that temporal and spatial relations exist between the definition areas in the different cases.

| | | Continuous | Localized elements | Localized and discrete elements |
|---|---|---|---|---|
| Local or linear constraints | Mass | M/L | (M/L).Le | (M/L).(Le/Te) |
| | Elasticity | E/L | (E/L).Le | (E/L).(Le/Te) |
| Global constants | Mass | M | M | M/Te |
| | Elasticity | E | E | E/Te |
| | Length | L | Q = L/Le | Q = L/Le |
| | Time | t | t | n = t/Te |
| | Structural coordinate | x | q = x/Le | q |
| Model parameters | Structural spatial step → Le = L/Q | | | Le |
| | Temporal step → Te | | | Te |

**Figure 7.6**
Comparison of the three modeling systems: continuous, localized elements, and localized and discrete elements.

This can only be understood as a finite number of points in the structure when it is being sampled.

**Properties of the String Models**  If we examine the spectrum of natural frequences (figure 7.7), we can observe that the localized constants model comprises $Q$ modes whose frequency spectrum is compressed compared with the harmonic spectrum of the continuous model. This occurs on the level of the high-order partials. Also the discrete time model (model 3) tends to compensate for the discrete spatial effect, in that the spectrum is less compressed than before. However, to retain the behavioral stability of this last model, $H$ must remain greater than or equal to $Q$: The sampling period cannot then exceed a certain value that depends on the parameters of the continuous model.

**Algorithmic Modularity**  Modularity is the property of the simulation system that enables simulatible models to be constructed from elements by

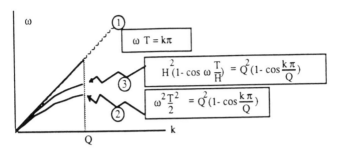

**Figure 7.7**
Spectrum of natural frequencies for the three modeling systems: (1) continuous, (2) localized
elements, (3) localized and discrete elements

assembly operations. This property supposes that the algorithm/model
transformation is isomorphic to the model assembly laws and also to the
algorithms:

$\text{Algo}(\text{Assem}(a, b)) = \text{Assem}_{\text{algo}}(\text{Algo}(a), \text{Algo}(b)).$

Model 3 represents the one used in the CORDIS system to simulate an
object described by model 2. Their comparison shows that the property of
algorithmic modularity cannot be thoroughly verified. The perturbation of
$\omega$ (a partial's $\omega$ pulse) due to temporal discretization can be evaluated from
the preceding relations. It leads to an increase in frequencies, expressed as

$\Delta\omega/\omega \approx \omega^2 T^2/(24 \cdot H^2) = \omega^2 T_e^2/24.$

This relation shows no constants dependent on the model. In fact it applies
to the general case of undamped vibrating structures. If we increase the
sampling frequency, we can reduce the error and simultaneously improve
the compatibility of the temporal discretization with the assembly operations. Thus to guarantee a margin of error lower than 5 percent (0.07 octave)
on all the partials, we must use a sampling frequency that is about three
times that of the Shannon frequency.

   The modularity property that we describe here is quite primitive when
placed in the context of physical instrument making. The construction of
a vibrating structure is based not only on the assembly of the macroscopic
parts but on the choice of material (wood, metal, air, and so on) and shape
(length, in the case of strings). It is only mass assembly of structured
microcells that reveals the character of their common functional properties.

The two examples that follow do not claim to describe the real objects in fine detail, but do show the existence of such relations.

**Example 1: A Combination of Different Dampers**   The "mesh" of the preceding undamped string model has two types of damping forces introduced into it: One is proportional to the relative speed of the two consecutive masses and the other to the absolute speed of each mass (figure 7.8). This model represents the effects of the internal viscosity of the structure ($\zeta_1$) and that of the viscosity due to the external environment ($\zeta_2$). The constant distribution propagation equation takes the form

$$y''_{x^2} = \mu \cdot \varepsilon \cdot y''_{t^2} + \zeta_2 \cdot \varepsilon \cdot y'_t - \zeta_1 y'''_{x^2 t}.$$

The final term (internal viscosity) is shown by a coefficient in $k^2$ in the damping factor of the $k$th partial, while the viscosity of the environment introduces a term that is independent of the order of the partial. Friction distribution is thus a microscopic structural characteristic that affects the overall behavior of the structure.

**Example 2: Stiffness Effect in Flexion in a String**   The coupling of two parallel chaplets, point by point following the mesh diagram of figure 7.8, produces at its utmost limit a bar model (evidencing a given stiffness in flexion) (figure 7.9). All parameters of the material making up this bar are then regulated by the geometry and the parameters of the mesh.

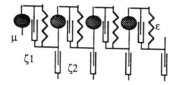

**Figure 7.8**
Mesh diagram of the damped string model

**Figure 7.9**
Model of a bar

In a general manner the visco-elastic behavior of the homogeneous and continuous matter can be described by a small number of mass-spring-damper meshes. The usual model is that of a finite set of relations between the constraint $\sigma$ and deformation $\varepsilon$ tensors (Bramberger 1981, Germain 1973): $\sigma = \lambda \cdot \varepsilon$.

Passage to the limit toward a homogeneous continuous representation requires the introduction of invariants (density) defined by the mesh space occupation principles. Continuous matter is obtained when at constant density the mesh dimensions become zero. It is, however, possible to preserve a significant size of the mesh (nonzero), in which case a wider variety of mesh structures remains pertinent. The following example (figure 7.10) illustrates this in a simple way: a "string of beads" or chaplet with alternate masses. The mesh is made up of two (different) masses linked by springs (Roseau 1984). We can show that this structure, at its ultimate limit, behaves exactly like a string of beads with identical masses. The two-mass mesh is thus only of interest when its dimensions are significant.

The properties evoked do not pertain to systems made from localized macroscopic elements. It appears nevertheless important in the long run to include this type of approach in our simulation system. This means that assembly operations can be effected at microscopic level, for example, to build a network mesh from standard base elements of mass, spring, and friction. The use of microscopic-level construction elements implies on the one hand that the time constants attached to these elements will be of a different order of magnitude than those of any object resulting from assembly and on the other hand that special assembly operations exist to build the macroscopic elements from precedents by periodization, that is, contributing little information compared with microscopic struuctures.

Extensions of this modularity principle on an algorithmic level pose no

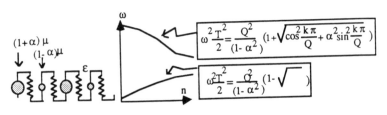

**Figure 7.10**
Two-mass mesh and spectrum of natural frequencies of a "string-of-beads" or chaplet structure

problems in the case of the CORDIS-type method, but it implies a large increase in calculation power. The direct method necessarily processes the model in a spatially discrete form, and thus introduces a systematic error of which the preceding models 1 and 2 provide a summary evaluation:

$$\Delta\omega/\omega \approx -\omega^2 T^2/(24Q^2) = -\omega^2 \cdot \tau^2/24,$$

where $\omega$ is the frequency of a partial, and $\tau$ is the time constant of the smallest element of the localized element structure. If a low "spatial discretization" error is desired—of around 5 percent, that is, 0.07 octave—this leads to using the elements that have a time constant of a magnitude of 0.3 times the Shannon period, evaluated as before. This defines the maximum "size" of the cells of the microscopic level that are compatible with an acceptable representation of the continuous model and in consequence the *multiplicity factor* of the microscopic level (around three after the criterion chose). An increase in the number of elements is necessary to approach the continuous model. The factor introduced characterizes this increase in a general manner.

**The Pure Delay Methods**

Pure delay methods appear as a particular case of the preceding one. We noted that the spatial and temporal discretization effects were inverses, and if we consider the relations indicated in figure 7.2, it is clear that when $Q = H$, the two effects exactly compensate for each other. The spectrum of frequencies proper to the discrete model is harmonic, but obviously always limited to $Q$ components. On a more microscopic level this condition signifies that the network elementary cell has a frequency equal to the sampling period ($\mu\varepsilon = T_e^2$), and therefore it appears in the discrete time field in exactly the same fashion as a pure delay cell (of delay $T_e$). The algorithm is simplified in this case because the product of the linear elasticity and mass coefficients becomes equal to 1 (see column 3 of figure 7.6). It can be easily shown that this simplification leads to a recursive filter with one or two pure delays.

This method is advantageous for two reasons: on the one hand because of the simplified form of the algorithm that only contains a small number of arithmetical operations and, on the other hand, because it works at the limit of the usual Shannon condition (corresponding to maximal use of the transmission band of the processing machine). It is particularly efficient and often used to simulate strings, with or without explicit reference to a given physical model, (Mcintyre and Woodhouse 1978, 1979) or in synthesis by Karplus and Strong (1982), Smith (1986), and Adrien (1989).

The main drawback to the basic algorithm is the impossibility of continually adjusting the resonance frequencies, for these vary necessarily by a step of $1/T_e$. Smith avoids the difficulty by completing the pure delay module with a special phase-shifter filter that allows an extra adjustable delay between 0 and $T_e$. The dispersion introduced by this filter appears acceptable (Smith 1985). The introduction in the simulation of a modulation of a physical parameter, like the tension or length of a string over a wide frequency range, enables us to act simultaneously on the number of cells and on the parameters of the correction filter.

Some simulation methods of material allowing wave propagation (two- or three-dimensional) also use this principle (the "TLM method"). The algorithm is not economical, however, for at each network node the reflection and transmission coefficients have to be recomputed (Johns 1971, Mohaghegh-Montazeri 1980).

**Pure Delay Methods and Modularity**   The pure delay method is only adapted to processing special cases. The basic algorithm introduces few parameters compared with its order of complexity. Even the field of strings is far from covered, for the basic algorithm excludes dispersiveness, whose origins can be multiple in this type of structure. It is clear that this method does not have the requisite properties to make up a modular system, although its effective aspects could be used within the context of a more general modular system.

**Simulation by Modes**

In our specialized simulations (Florens, Luciani, and Cadoz 1986) we have used a new method, based on the decomposition of the model into its own modes. For a linear model with a finite number of localized masses, there exists a functional equivalent made up of the same number of *elementary oscillators* (mass-spring-damper cell). Their elongation vector is linked to the point displacement vector by an invertible linear transformation. The simulation uses as many *elementary oscillators* as there are modes. The inputs to the oscillators are the result of the product of external forces to the different points of the model. An inverse operation on output provides the positions and speeds in these same points.

**Properties of Modal Systems**  Modal systems do not meet the criterion of algorithmic modularity discussed previously. The modal representation has these advantages, however:

• First of all, the decomposition into modes conserves a physical sense, for it is a structure of mass-spring-friction elements linked to the external coupling points via a conservative mechanism without inertia. Functionally it can be integrated into a modular system (such as CORDIS) (figure 7.11). It can be of dipolar (one link point), quadripolar, or $N$ dipolar form.

• The algorithm exists in the form of a set of noncoupled identical modules. This form is particularly adapted to implementation on an array processor or a multiprocessor. Among other things it enables algorithms for different objects to be grouped in the same module of vectorized program.

• There is no direct relation between the structural complexity of the model and that of the algorithm. In contrast to the preceding methods, the processing of a continuous model no longer requires a structural discretization; rather it only requires a simple reduction to a finished set of its system of modes (high frequencies with little significance are suppressed).

• Temporal discretization effects are evaluated independently from the complexity of the object to be simulated; the problem is dealt with on the level of the elementary modal oscillator. The discrete schema of $\{mx'' + zx' + kx = f\}$ is

$$X(n + 1) = AX(n) + BX(n - 1) + CF(n)$$

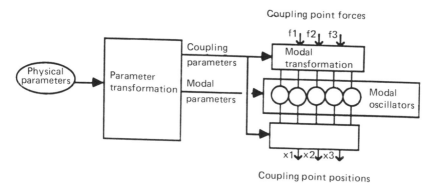

**Figure 7.11**
Modal simulation derived from physical parameters. This shows damper and frequency constants (modal parameters) and coupling parameters being fed to the modal system.

with

$$x(nT_e) = X(n)$$

and

$$f(nT_e) = F(n).$$

It follows that

$$A = 2 \cdot \exp(-z \cdot T_e/2m) \cdot \cos(T_e(k/m - z^2/4m^2)^{1/2}),$$

$$B = -\exp(-z \cdot T_e/m).$$

If $k \neq 0$, then $C = (1 - A - B)/k$.

If $k = 0$ (damped inertia), then $C = (1 - \exp(-z \cdot T_e/m)) \cdot T_e/z$.

If $k = 0$ and $z = 0$ (pure inertia), then $C = T_e^2/m$.

• As the structural information of the model "transforms itself" into parametric information, some structural variations are simulatible, like that of the position of coupling points (excitation or vibration).

• Finally, a relation exists between the modal constitution of a vibrating structure and its acoustic properties. Direct mode control enables us to adjust the simulation parameters as a function of purely acoustic criteria and occasionally to partially compensate for the restrictions that are necessarily introduced compared with a given physical instrument. In this way we can adjust the frequencies of the partials while conserving the coupling parameters that determine the excitation point on a string. The simulation may lose some structural coherence, but it gains in creating more interesting acoustic effects.

There are, however, some difficulties with this method. Developing algorithms from structural data is more complex than in the case of the direct method; we must either know or calculate the modal model. Moreover when simulating physical parameters, the demands of modulation require an *in line* calculation of the modal parameters.

**Algorithm Construction for Modal Synthesis**  As the structure of the algorithm is independent from the simulated physical structure, its construction is limited to the calculation of the modal parameters. This calculation may result from an earlier mathematical analysis, but in the case where the structures (with a finite number of elements) are inaccessible to mathematical analysis, it may be processed digitally.

The model is a network of material points linked together by springs that are dampened linearly. The displacements of each point are presumed to be parallel and one-dimensional. The dynamic of the network is thus described by an equation of the type

$$MX'' + ZX' + KX = F,$$

which links the displacement vector of all the $X$ points to the vector of the external forces $F$.

By setting $U = (X, X')$, we obtain the ordinary state equation $U' = AU + BF$. The modes are then obtained by diagonalization of $A$ that in general presents $N$ pairs of conjugated eigenvalues (Lang 1987). The method can be applied to make a modular simulation system, for example, the assembly of objects with localized constants. A compiler can translate the structural information into coefficients in matrix $A$. (See Lascaux 1986 for more on digital diagonalization methods.)

**Parameter Control During Simulation of Modal Systems**   The notion of parameter has a precise meaning in the case of linear physical models. In simulation by modes, parametric control means transforming the signal representing the evolution of a physical parameter into a control signal for an algorithm. This transformation should take place at the same time as the processing specific to the simulation. Although the form of the simulation algorithm is simple and does not vary, it is completely different for the parameter transformation algorithm. If the model is accessible to mathematical calculation, explicit formulation of mode parameters as a function of the physical parameters can simplify the transformation algorithm. As a general rule each parameter modification requires digital diagonalization. It should be noted, however, that algorithmic parameters are divided into two categories: the damper and frequency constants relative to each mode and the coupling coefficients determining their weight (see figure 7.11). The former characterize the isolated object, the latter their interaction points with the exterior. Exclusive modification of the coupling points done dynamically remains a simple operation because the complete matrix of coupling coefficients is, in this case, calculated once and for all. Nevertheless, to use this property, the invariance of the modal structure must be imposed beforehand, which means limiting the range of the physical parameters.

The processing of microscopic models or those with nonlocalized elements is quite conceivable in simulation by modes. The only difficulty is the growth in the order of the system if a digital diagonalization method is used for a discrete, high-order representation of the object. The effect on the calculation cost is zero, as only the pertinent modes are taken into account.

**Conclusion on the Three Methods**

Among the three possible methods, that is, the CORDIS method, modal synthesis, and pure delays, only the first two seem suitable to constitute a modular simulation system. We can summarize the following essential points:

• The modal method is superior compared with the complexity of the model (the number of masses). It introduces no errors, and the simulation algorithm is more economical, for it depends little on this complexity.

• The variability of physical parameters is superior in the CORDIS method. However, the modal method allows more direct access to acoustic parameters.

• Rapid and in-depth modification of the simulated structure is economical in the CORDIS method, but very difficult or even impossible in the modal method.

It should be noted in conclusion that a hybrid of the two methods is possible for the simulation of the same object. The complementarity of these two methods therefore enables a large variety of models and simulation conditions, including the critical case of real time.

## Simulations and Models of the Excitation Mechanism and of Parametric Control

The fundamental nonlinearity referred to earlier is rarely attributable to a specific constituent. In particular it appears that no element fixed to the vibrating structure can give rise to nonlinearity. Sliding or nonpermanent contact is therefore a necessity, at least in the case of solid vibrating structures.

Besides this the entire mechanical chain transmitting the gestural movement up to the vibrating structure can include various constituents in complex shapes whose specific knowledge is meaningful only in the technical sphere of instrument making. This is why, for example, the driver mechanisms for piano hammers exist in various shapes and configurations. Hence we are more interested in local functional properties than in a fine structural characterization. We will refer to mechanical functions as idealized constituents that enable us to avoid the difficulty of mechanics, that is, the interdependence of functional motions and the spatial localization of components.

The gestural effect on the vibrating structure may be of two different kinds:

1. *Parametric coupling*—In taut structures (strings or membranes), or in closed tubes, an orthogonal coupling to the vibration direction modulates the tension and hence the frequencies. In the piano the felt of the damper should be considered as an extension of the vibrating structure because the distance from the felt to the string controls the sound absorption. In these two cases the interaction with the vibrating structure is parametric. The mechanical energy communicated by this channel to the vibrating structure is low and in general is not significant.

2. *Excitation*—Coupling takes place following a deformation direction of the vibrating structure, which allows it to communicate mechanical energy. The excitation can be temporary, as in percussion or plucking, or sustained, as in the majority of wind instruments, the violin, or the human voice. A rarer third category in classical instruments is stochastic excitation, found in maracas, which puts into play a chaotic system capable of producing a wide spectrum excitation signal. In this type of system the reaction of the vibrating structure on the exciter can be neglected, whereas in sustained excitation like bowing friction it is essential.

In the specialized simulations achieved in 1986 and 1988, we tried to scan the range of the different excitation modes. The calculation power of the vibrating structure remained limited (in the number of modes; the limit is around 25 modes at $F_e = 15\,\text{kHz}$). The modeling and simulation techniques used did not rely on any a priori modularity concept, and the modules for the mechanical functions of the different exciters were made as occasions demanded. We recall that in all these simulations the mechanical functions of the exciter were modeled and translated into algorithms independent of the vibrating structure, using parts that were more directly linked to the gestural interfaces. In this way we managed to save a relative overall algorithmic modularity in all cases. The limit to this modularity (still with reference to CORDIS) can be found at two opposite poles: (a) by the use of less atomic models based on the concepts of mechanical functions rather than on the structural decomposition into normalized elements and (2) by a global implementation of the algorithms on the array processor.

**Exciter Categories**    The exciter examples that follow are those used in the simulations. For each of them we describe the basic model and the type of algorithm used as well as the user context. Most of them describe an algorithmic form of the type input position/output force similar to the (conditional) link modules in CORDIS.

The *elastic buffer* is a simple, common, nonlinear function that we used directly as an excitation function or as an element of the exciter mechanism that did not interact directly with the vibrating structure. It is characterized by force/position relation $f = F(\Delta x)$ (figure 7.12). Three algorithmic methods were used:

1. In CORDIS the elastic buffer is realized by a conditional link module in procedural form: if $Dx < 0$, then $f = 0$, else $f = kDx$.

2. $F$ can be stored in a table in computer memory.

3. $F$ can be expressed in the form $f = k/2(\Delta x + |\Delta x|)$.

Method 3 can be useful in vectorization. Moreover the absolute-value operator that consists of masking one bit for some formats can be easily hardwired.

*An example of an elastic buffer involves the simulation of a maracas.* The maracas model is a rectangular box manipulated by a force feedback key. Inside there are 16 balls that move along an axis without interacting among themselves. We sought a compromise between simulation simplicity and realism of effect. The balls are modeled as inert material points with one degree of freedom. The box was modeled as a linear system, with one degree

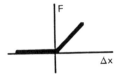

**Figure 7.12**
Graph of the force-versus-position relation $f = F(\Delta x)$

(a)

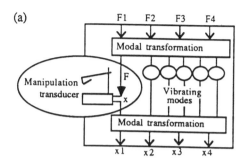

(b)

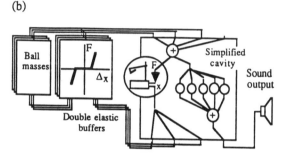

**Figure 7.13**
Maracas simulation. (A) Modal representation of a four-point coupling maracas cavity. The inertia mode is replaced by the external manipulation device. (B) Maracas simulation.

of freedom following the same axis, with five vibratory modes and an extra mode. The extra mode takes into account the "slow" functions of inertia and manipulability of the cavity (figure 7.13A). The ball and box models are linked by two elastic buffer–type functions, each corresponding to the interaction with one of the sides of the box. In this system the reaction of the vibratory modes of the cavity on the elastic buffer can be suppressed. The overall functional diagram resulting from this simplification is represented in figure 7.13B. The elastic buffer thus no longer intervenes as a nonlinear excitation function directly from the vibrating structure, but as a component of a chaotic system producing a wideband exciter signal applied to the input of the latter system.

*A damped elastic buffer* may sometimes be necessary. In this case the three preceding algorithmic methods are applicable: (1) The procedural method: If $\Delta x < 0$, then $f = 0$, else $f = k\Delta x + z\Delta v$. In methods two and three an auxiliary function $\varphi(\Delta x)$ takes on two values, 0 and 1, and is a substitute to some extent for the test of method 1. The function $\varphi$ can then be stored in a table (method 2) or evaluated in the form

$$\varphi(\Delta x) = 2/s(abs(\Delta x) - abs(\Delta x - s) + s) \qquad \text{(method 3)}.$$

The force of interaction is calculated in the form

$$f = (k\Delta x + z\Delta v) \cdot \varphi(\Delta x).$$

Note the parabolic form of the elastic characteristic obtained in proximity to $\Delta x = 0$.

An example of a damped elastic buffer involves simulation of a simple Celesta-type instrument. The vibrating structure is composed of 16 elementary independent oscillators. Each one is excited by percussion mass. A 16-key force feedback keyboard coupled to the real-time simulation process takes charge of driving these simulated hammers. The drive mechanism in its simplest form presents no nonlinearity. If we had strictly followed the Celesta model (Bouasse 1927), we would have had to use two extra elastic buffers: one to limit the stroke of the key and the other to uncouple the movements of the harmmer from that of the key. These elements were replaced by simple elastic links.

In plucking action plectrum interaction with an obstacle having the thickness of a string can be modeled from an interaction function similar to that of the elastic buffer we have already introduced. Parameter $e$ represents string thickness. In practice the internal elasticity of the plectrum and its inertia make the obstacle/plectrum interaction into a bistable system. The addition of these properties to the preceding function leads to a mass/elastic interaction model that represents these properties well (figure 7.14A). It should be noted, however, that the plectrum time constant is low and quantitatively not significant. This results in major simplifications in the model. The overall object obtained should be considered as an interaction function that is different from the preceding ones because of its memory. The time constant chosen is very low, of the same order as the sampling period. Additional damping can be done by following the same technique as in the case of percussion.

The algorithmic realization can be of the procedural type, with a conditional link in CORDIS with $t = T_e$ or using a nonlinear recursive system

(a)

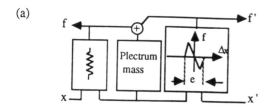

(b)

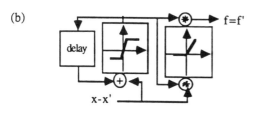

**Figure 7.14**
Plucking simulation. (A) Structural model. (B) Simplified functional model, where $e = 0$ and $m = 0$.

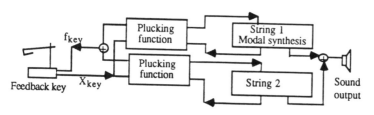

**Figure 7.15**
Plucked string simulation with a force-feedback key

with adjustable delay. The nonlinear functions, of which one is of the elastic buffer type, are calculated from the absolute-value operator as before (figure 7.14B).

The model described was used in a simulation of plucked strings. Two independent strings placed near each other can be plucked by the same plectrum that is moved perpendicularly in their common direction. The plectrum can be manipulated by means of a force feedback key. The interconnection diagram of the different simulation modules is shown in figure 7.15. The plucking module was implemented in the form of an algorithm using conditional trapping (method 1). The modules corresponding to each of the strings are processed in parallel, but the number of strings remains limited to two. Another version using the piecewise linear function technique was implemented in the form of a vector module in which the number of strings could be increased. However, the first module remains more economical for the case in point (two elements).

*Bow friction* is the last exciter category to be discussed. The simulation of a bowed string carried out in 1985 (Florens, Luciani, and Cadoz 1986) totally dissociates the simulation of the vibrating structure from that of the bow interaction. Hence the same module could be applied to any other form of vibrating structure. The simulation we effected is, moreover, only limited to the case of the string by the choice of certain parameters.

There are numerous models of friction. We confined ourselves to characterizing friction by a relation linking the transverse force to the relative bow/string speed. Its graph is shown in figure 7.16. This is a rough approximation of the model proposed by Bouasse (1926),

$$f = kN/(1 + a\Delta v),$$

in which $N$ represents the force of pressure from the bow onto the string. We included the following means of control in our simulation. The operator manipulates the extremity of a guided rod that can be moved over a distance of approximately 50 cm; the force of vertical pressure exerted acts directly on the $N$ coefficient in the calculation of $f$. In addition the horizontal translation speed of the manipulated point is detected and controls, in the same calculation, the "bow speed" parameter. Friction is described by a piecewise linear function. As before, its calculation uses the absolute-value operator and can thus be vectorized. Despite the simplicity of the model, this simulation enables very fine and subtle gestural control of the bowed string process.

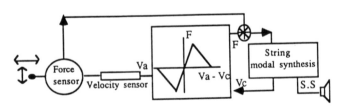

**Figure 7.16**
Simulation of a bowed string. The graph shows friction.

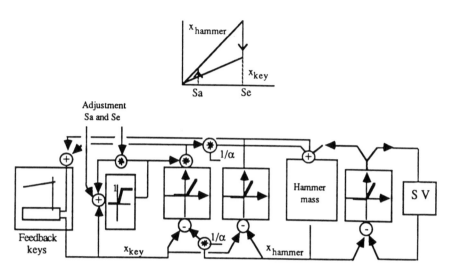

**Figure 7.17**
Keyboard instrument simulation with an escapement mechanism

**Modeling a Complex Excitation Mechanism: Escapement**   We wanted to perfect the keyboard instrument described previously by the introduction of an escapement mechanism. The hammer and the nonlinear interaction module with the vibrating structure remains unchanged, as does the return spring that fixes the position of the hammer's equilibrium. A functional diagram of the simulation algorithm is represented in figure 7.17. When the key is pressed, the hammer is driven at high speed by means of the elastic buffer $BE1$. The coefficient $\alpha$ ($\gg 1$) regulates the speeds' ratio. Beyond a certain position the driver force disappears and can only reappear when the key returns to its rest position. This is because of a two-state automaton. The latter's threshold trigger levels can be adjusted (release threshold and compensation threshold) as well as its rapidity (the slope of the $\phi$ function). Because of the elastic buffer $BE2$, the hammer cannot pass "underneath" the key, which would cause a shock when compensation occurred. The cycle representing the movement of the hammer as a function of the key, at zero speed, is represented. It shows clearly the effect of the different parameters.

### The Choice of Algorithms in the Models

The different mechanical functions encountered when designing the excitation mechanism, whether on the level of immediate interaction with the vibrating structure or in the other parts, belong to one of the three following categories:

1. Simple nonlinear interaction:

$$f = F(x, v) \quad \text{or} \quad f(n) = F(x(n), v(n))$$

2. Nonlinear interaction with memory (as in a plucked string):

$$e' = E(e, \Delta x) \qquad e(n) = E(x(n), v(n), e(n-1))$$

$$f = F(e, \Delta x) \qquad f(n) = F(x(n), v(n), e(n))$$

3. Material elements (material points, inertia, oscillator):

$$x'' = Ax' + Bx + Cf$$

or $x(n+1) = \mathbf{A}x(n) + \mathbf{B}x(n-1) + \mathbf{C}f(n)$

Mechanical functions of types 1 and 2 are similar to the conditional links. These functions enable efficient control of transitory states by the introduction of continuity. In addition their calculation, from a general standpoint, can be reduced to a function of the form

$$y(x) = \sum_i |x - a_i| + bx + c$$

that is better adapted to an array processor.

**Discrete Methods**　　For each of these functions we have provided an explicit discrete representation. The algorithm of the overall mechanism is constructed naturally from these constituents in the same way as in CORDIS by alternate assembly of material elements/link elements.

The discretization is accurate in the case of simple nonlinear interaction functions without memory (type 1). The centered discretization schema from acceleration is satisfactory in most cases. This is not the case for speed. Type 1 modules use speed ($v(n)$). This term, calculated locally by the Euler method, makes the algorithm unstable for low time constant values. We can improve the method without altering the modularity if we penalize the calculation of the material elements. The arrangement used is $Vn = (\chi_n - \chi_{n-1})/T_e$, where $\chi_n$ is an estimator for $X_{n+1/2}$ calculated on the material module level. $V_n$, that is also calculated on this level, is transmitted to the link module in addition to $X_n$. To calculate $\chi_n$, different methods are possible, based on the linear nature of the "material" module. In contrast no extra constraint appears concerning the nature of the link elements. The penalization boils down to doubling the calculation frequency on elements where we take speed into account.

We can show simply that the method combining mechanical elements defined in the CORDIS system, applied to a set of basic elements defined by continuous equations (i.e., time is not discrete), or by calculation procedures, enables us to define the overall system resulting from the assembly in an analog form. We obtain a global procedure that enables us to evaluate the derivative of the state vector. Application of an explicit discretization method is then possible and does not therefore alter the modularity. The cost in terms of calculation is high: it is multiplied by four in the case of the Runge-Kutta classical method, compared to present-day algorithms.

**Coupling to the Vibrating structure: Optimizing the Calculation Frequency**

It is advantageous in terms of calculation cost and rounded approximation errors to use a calculation frequency adapted to the time constants of the instrument (Reynaud 1978). On the one hand there are those used in the gestural transmission mechanism (excitation and parametric control) and, on the other, those of the vibrating structure. Both are different, so it is normal to process each of the parts at a specific frequency. Let us make clear the calculation frequency choice criteria:

• The calculation frequency has a bearing on the accuracy and the stability of the algorithm.

• The discrete representations of the observation signals (outputs) and commands (inputs) must satisfy the Shannon condition.

• Another criterion results from the causal nature of the simulation processing. We may wish to consider an algorithm as an exact model of the simulation process. The discrete time model obtained from the algorithm differs from the simulated model by the "execution context," which includes a pure delay of one or several extra temporal steps in the simulated model. This can be verified if the time constants resulting from the coupling of this process with an outside system are large compared to the temporal step selected.

These different criteria applied to practical cases have led us, in the case of the vibrating structure, to calculation frequencies of between 12 and 40 kHz and around 200 Hz to 1500 Hz for the gestural control mechanism.

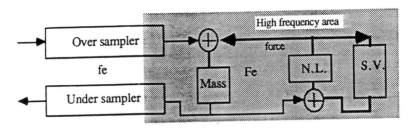

**Figure 7.18**
Percussion simulation with two processing frequencies

For percussion (figure 7.18) we obtain an exact discrete model with two frequencies by extending the set of processed elements at high frequency to the hammer/vibrating structure interaction (marked N.L.) and to the mass of the hammer.

The exactitude of the model is due to the dissociation of the contact states of the hammer with the vibrating structure and with the drive mechanism. In other types of exciters this property is not verified, but the method remains valid because the inertia of the exciter device fulfills the function of the antialiasing filters, which are associated with sampling frequency conversion in signal processing systems. It should be remarked that the addition of such filters is needless and even harmful in our model.

This method has been used in keyboard instrument simulation and in a simplified manner in simulating a bowed and plucked string. The maracas was totally simulated at high frequency.

**Conclusions on the Excitation Mechanism**

The general methods of the CORDIS system have been used to represent and simulate excitation mechanisms. On the model level this means decomposition into material elements (inertia) and link elements. The global algorithm results from the assembly of the elementary algorithms.

However, we processed conditional links in the form of continuous iteraction functions. This was done for several reasons: First, the algorithmic form leads simply to the evaluation of linear piecewise functions and thus avoids conditional trapping, which is difficult to implement in an array processor. Second, the continuity introduced limits the effects of temporal discretization in the elastic buffers. Last, the time constants associated with the conditional link state transitions become adjustable.

## Implementation of the Simulation Algorithms

In these simulations we saw that up to the development of the algorithm, we were able to maintain certain modularity principles with a view to extending the methods introduced to a modular system. The ultimate step, that is, the production of the optimized code from the algorithmic data, remains nevertheless delicate because of the type of machine (array processor) used to attain the necessary calculating power. In the following sections we specify, again in reference to the simulations effected, the impact of problems stemming from code production on modularity. Finally, we describe the execution and synchronization context of the simulation algorithms.

### Simulation Program Organization

The array processor used (FPS AP120) is of the pipeline type. Its optimal use is obtained on repetitive algorithms whose elements are uncoupled, that is, they present no causal links. (Stone 1987, pp. 102–176). We therefore endeavor by different methods to make such a form appear, if not in the overall algorithm then at least in some or all of its parts. The simulation program is thus made up of a set of "vectorized" modules, each corresponding to a type of repetitive structure found in the algorithm. It should be pointed out that each of these modules requires an initialization phase for the pipeline when the machine is underutilized. We must therefore try to reduce their number or avoid the inconvenience by overlay techniques (Stone 1987, p. 125).

CORDIS-type simulation systems and modal synthesis lends itself well to vectorization: A vectorized module can be associated to each basic element of the model. The construction of a program for a given simulation boils down to calling up these modules. Another technique consists of using the possible multiplicity of certain high-level elements that can be encountered in a given situation. In the case of the simulation of the Celesta, we used the repetivity of the elementary instrument corresponding to each key. This method is very effective, and the average load of the machine is 82 percent compared with 40 percent to 60 percent in the other simulations, but it excludes all modularity, as the vectorized modules remain specific to the processed model. Automatic generation of vectorized code would be an alternative to the latter limitation. We are reticent to look in this direction, however, for the existing systems are not much more efficient than what can be expected from "manual" vectorization by basic elements.

## Execution Context

We describe here the configuration and the overall execution context of the simulation processes in the representative case of the keyboard instrument built in 1988. Apart from the array processor used for high-frequency processing, the configuration includes a machine designed to interface with the gestural transducer (the keyboard) as well as an auxiliary simulation processor given over more specially to processing the excitation mechanism. A general-purpose machine (Digital Equipment Corporation VAX-11/730) is used for global control of the simulation and program upload on the different machines. To do this, a low data rate communication network links the VAX to the different specialized machines. A second network that is more especially meant for rapid data transfers, such as algorithmic parameters, or for bulk data files, or even the simulation programs, also links the VAX computer to the different machines. Finally, there is a third network designed for coupling the simulation processes to the different machines: It links the specialized processors and interfaces that take part in the real-time simulation. The different processes of simulation are synchronized by their I/O streams on the samplers situated on the interfaces, which are themselves synchronized to a single clock. The interfaces include the output sound converter and the converters for the force feedback keyboard.

We use the double frequency sampling principle, and the two frequencies are in an integer ratio that can vary between 8 to 128. The array processor executes the algorithms concerned with the vibrating structure, the nonlinear interaction, and the inertia of the hammer. The slow simulation processor processes the movement transfer mechanism between the keyboard and the hammer. However, the execution of the two coupled simulation processes in parallel, which justifies their implementation on two distinct machines, introduces a pure delay of one temporal step (at low frequencies) compared with a sequential execution context. The choice of this frequency takes this effect into account. The sequential execution of the two processes, if done on two machines, avoids the difficulty mentioned previously, but entails an extra transfer between two clock steps that thus doubles the processors' synchronization frequency. The existence of multiple independent elements in the model, which is the general case in keyboard instruments, enables total occupation of the two processors by interleaved execution of these elements. The latter method is useful when the number of elements increases.

## Conclusion

It is impossible to circumscribe all the theoretical and technical problems that arise in modelizing and simulating instrumental objects in a short space. For example, it would have been interesting to introduce the synthesis elements that we have derived from two complementary approaches (the advanced modularity and generality of CORDIS—and specialization and performance under restricted modularity in our recent experiments), but we must limit this to a few brief remarks.

One of the first positive aspects of this investigation has been the emergence of stronger principles for modularity. While retaining, from the initial versions of CORDIS-ANIMA, the network form of composite objects and the material/link distinction for elements, we have introduced the idea of a *macro-module* that is compatible with the basic logic combination. We have also thoroughly reconsidered this logic of combination (Cadoz 1986), which, although it retains its physical significance, is more general in that if no longer attaches itself to the nature of interlinked elements but rather to their links (connections), which can be multiple for a single component.

This new framework is promising because we can even incorporate research on optimization. There is no ideal solution ideally adapted to a given material context, either in a model or in its algorithmic translation. For each real situation, specific solutions enable some degree of performance to be obtained, but to the detriment of generality. Modeling and simulation are thus founded in a permanent dualism between generality and a precise performance. For this reason, the macro-module concept, which is entirely compatible with the combinatory logic of the CORDIS system, gives rise to research into algorithms that are better adapted to the desired functions and limits of the system.

These specialized studies have had another positive dimension that is perhaps more essential on the theoretical level, because they were undertaken within the previous global conceptual framework that was set up in our initial general approach.

The first step was the investigation of specific physical devices so as to target simulation efficiency above all. This naturally oriented the system around practical "islands" like instrumental objects and even more limited categories within instruments. The practical impact of this consists in integrating this specialization into the construction language of objects that can be simulated (an instrument-making system). For example, it appears that structuring the instrument into two layers of vibrating structure and control mechanism, will be an incentive to make up an adequately specified tool for both.

Nonetheless, over and above these purely formal aspects, limiting the field of modeled objects to instrumental ones, has led to a much more thorough theoretical investigation of a physical type. This, guided by the original objective of optimization, is leading toward deeper functional characterizations.

This article has tried to demonstrate that modeling and simulation must not be confused. In fact, the two appear in two different domains. Simulation in itself is a system that is first material and then conceptual and formal. However, over and above the "simulation of the physical," a "physics of simulation" is beginning to take shape. The latter, by extension, highlights the characterization and knowledge of the objects from which it originated. Because of this, we can dig deeper into the nature of what is instrumental in instruments and thus sketch out a "physical theory of musical instrumentality." Physical knowledge (more accurate than general physics) that is specific to the representation of instruments is of value.

This theory constitutes the truly objective opposite (to the subjective desires of the musician) needed in the dialectic for the creation of musical material. It is the computer, in its capabilities for representation that leads us to it.

## References

Adrien, J.-M. 1989. "Simulation numérique de systèmes vibrants complexes. Application à la synthèse sonore par modelisation physique." Doctoral thesis. Paris: Université Paris VI.

Belevitch, V. 1962. "Summary of the history of circuit theory." *Proceedings of the IRE* 50(5): 848–855.

Benade, A. 1976. *Fundamentals of Musical Acoustics*. New York: Oxford University Press.

Bouasse, H. 1926. *Cordes et Membranes*. Paris: Delagrave. New edition 1987 published by Blanchard.

Bouasse, H. 1927. *Verges, Plaques, Cloches, et Carillons*. Paris: Delagrave. New edition 1987 published by Blanchard.

Boutillon, X. 1988. "Model for piano hammers: experimental determination and digital simulation." *Journal of the Acoustical Society of America* 83(2): 746–754.

Bramberger, Y. 1981. *Mecanique de l'ingénieur, Milieux déformables.* Paris: Hermann.

Burris, C., and T. Parks. 1970. "Time-domain design of recursive digital filters." *IEEE Transactions on Acoustics, Speech and Signal Processing* A-18: 137–141.

Cadoz, C. 1979. "Synthèse sonore par simulation de mécanismes vibratoires." Thèse de troisieme cycle. Grenoble: I.N.P.G.

Cadoz, C. 1986. "Langage pour la definition et la simulation d'objets instrumentaux." Grenoble: ACROE.

Cadoz, C., and J.-L. Florens. 1978. "Fondements d'une démarche de recherche informatique/ musique." *Revue d'Acoustique* 45: 86.

Cadoz, C., A. Luciani, and J.-L. Florens. 1984. "Responsive input devices and sound synthesis by simulation of instrumental mechanisms: the Cordis system." *Computer Music Journal* 8(3): 60–73. Reprinted in C. Roads, ed. 1989. *The Music Machine.* Cambridge, Massachusetts: MIT Press, pp. 495–508.

Chafe, C. 1985. "Bowed string synthesis and its control from a physical model." Report STAN-M-32. Stanford: Department of Music, Stanford University.

Cremer, L. 1974. "Bow pressure influence on the self-excited vibrations of a string during contact." *Acustica* 30(3): 119–136.

Crochiere, R., and L. Rabiner. 1983. *Multirate Signal Processing.* Englewood Cliffs: Prentice-Hall.

Florens, J.-L., A. Luciani, and C. Cadoz. 1986. "Optimized real-time simulation of objects for musical synthesis and animated images synthesis." In P. Berg, ed. *Proceedings of the 1986 International Computer Music Conference.* San Francisco: Computer Music Association.

Foulard, G. 1977. *Commande et Régulation par Calculateur Numerique.* Paris: Eyrolles.

Gear, C. W. 1971. *Numerical Initial Value Problems in Ordinary Differential Equations.* Englewood Cliffs: Prentice-Hall.

Germain, P. 1973. *Cours de mécanique des milieux continus.* Paris: Masson.

Gough, C. 1981. "The acoustics of strings instruments studied by string resonances." *Catgut Acoustical Society Newsletter* 35: 22.

Gough, C. 1981. "The theory of string resonances on musical instruments." *Acustica* 49(2): 124–141.

Jaffe, D., and J. Smith. 1989. "Extensions of the Karplus-Strong plucked string algorithm." *Computer Music Journal* 7(2): 56–69. Reprinted in C. Roads, ed. 1989. *The Music Machine.* Cambridge, Massachusetts: MIT Press, pp. 481–494.

Johns, P. 1971. "Numerical solution of two-dimensional scattering problems using a transmission line matrix." *Proceedings of the IEEE* 118(9): 1203–1208.

Karplus, K., and A. Strong. 1982. "Digital synthesis of plucked string and drum timbres." *Computer Music Journal* 7(2): 43–55. Reprinted in C. Roads, ed. 1989. *The Music Machine.* Cambridge, Massachusetts: MIT Press, pp. 467–480.

Lang, S. 1987. *Linear Algebra.* New York: Springer-Verlag.

Lascaux, T. 1986. *Analyse numérique matricielle appliquée à l'art de l'ingénieur.* Paris: Masson.

Lawergren, B. 1980. "On the motion of bowed violin strings." *Acustica* 44(3): 194–220.

Luciani, A. 1985. "Un outil informatique de création d'images animées: modèles d'objets, langage, controle gestuel en temps réel. Le système ANIMA." Doctor of Engineering thesis. Grenoble: Institut National Polytechnique de Grenoble.

Macintyre, M., and J. Woodhouse. 1978. "The acoustics of stringed musical instruments." *Interdisciplinary Science Review* 3(2): 157–173.

Macintyre, M., and J. Woodhouse. 1979. "On the fundamentals of bowed string dynamics." *Acustica* 43(2): 93–108.

Marchouk, G. 1977. *Méthodes de calcul numérique.* Moscow: Editions MIR.

Mathews, M., and J. Kohut. 1973. "Electronic simulation of violin resonances." *Journal of the Acoustical Society of America* 53: 1620–1626.

Merlier, B. 1983. "Modélisation de la propagation acoustique en trois dimensions par la méthode T. L. M." Internal document. Grenoble: Institut National Polytechnique de Grenoble.

Mohaghegh-Montazeri. 1980. "Simulation pars les lignes de transmission, de la propagation des micro-ondes." Thesis. Grenoble: Institut National Polytechnique de Grenoble.

Oppenheim, A., and R. Schafer. 1975. *Digital Signal Processing.* Englewood Cliffs: Prentice-Hall.

Parks, T., and MacClellan. 1972. "A program for linear phase finite impulse response (FIR) digital filters." *IEEE Transactions on Audio and Electroacoustics* AU-20: 195–199.

Rabiner, L., and B. Gold. 1975. *Theory and Applications of Digital Signal Processing.* Englewood Cliffs: Prentice-Hall.

Reynaud, J. C. 1978. "IMAG3—un système de simulation et optimisation de circuits électroniques." Thesis. Grenoble: Institut National Polytechnique de Grenoble.

Roseau, M. 1984. *Vibrations des systèmes mécaniques.* Paris: Masson.

Schafer, R., and L. Rabiner. 1973. "A digital signal processing approach to interpolation." *Proceedings of the IEEE* 61: 692–702.

Smith, J. 1985. "A new approach to digital reverberation using closed waveguide networks." In B. Truax, ed. *Proceedings of the 1985 International Computer Music Conference.* San Francisco: Computer Music Association.

Smith, J. 1986. "Efficient simulation of the reed-bore and bow-string mechanisms." In P. Berg, ed. *Proceedings of the 1986 International Computer Music Conference.* San Francisco: Computer Music Association.

Stone, H. 1987. *High Performance Computer Architecture.* Reading, Massachusetts: Addison-Wesley.

# 8 The Missing Link: Modal Synthesis

Jean-Marie Adrien

Digital sound synthesis basically consists of the generation of numerical samples associated, through a digital-to-analog conversion, with acoustical signals. Because of the richness of natural sounds, it is necessary to use specific tools, or synthesis methods, to generate complex and structured signals from simple input data. These methods involve computation algorithms and control facilities and can be represented by the general scheme shown in figure 8.1.

To evaluate a synthesis method implies that one evaluate the control facilities provided, the computation algorithm, and the resulting sounds, according to the goals of the simulation. If we restrict ourselves to musical purposes, some general objective criteria in terms of control are, for example, the significance of the control parameters for a user, the relation between the variations of these parameters and the resulting variations of the sounds, and the ability of the control devices to operate in a real-time situation.

The objective evaluation of sound involves a psychophysiological investigation that, in the ideal case, is developed in conjunction with the synthesis tools because it justifies and suggests the approximations and simplifications that can be done in the algorithm. (Benade 1976, Cocholle 1973, Erickson 1975, Grey 1975, Gribensky 1951, Helmholtz 1954, Hall 1980, Leipp 1984, McAdams 1983, McAdams and Bregman 1979, Moore 1978, Pierce 1984, Risset and Wessel 1982, Wessel 1978). In the absence of these psychophysiological methods, results and approximations can be directly evaluated by ear.

The synthesis algorithm has to be evaluated in relation to the control devices and the sound results provided. It involves essentially a representation of sound phenomena that is basic to the simulation method and whose characteristics are determinate in terms of control and efficiency and, more specifically, in terms of computing costs, robustness, and flexibility.

In any case the formal representation of sound phenomena is well adapted to specific control devices and sound results: every synthesis method thus permits typical applications (Bennett 1981, Baisnée 1985, Chowning 1973, 1981, Chowning and Bristow 1986, Karplus and Strong 1983, Jaffe and Smith 1983, Mathews 1969, Risset 1969, Roads 1978, 1979, Potard, Baisnée, and Barrière 1986, Rodet 1984, Rodet et al. 1984). Inversely, specific applications often suggest the use of a particular synthesis

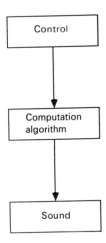

**Figure 8.1**
General scheme for "traditional" digital sound synthesis techniques

method. Sound synthesis methods can, in this respect, be compared with traditional instruments: Musicians can use various methods that are easily recognizable and efficient for limited applications, as are traditional orchestral instruments. It is thus difficult to give a definitive classification of the different sound synthesis tools, by we can review in more detail some aspects of classical synthesis methods to emphasize the specific features of the modal synthesis technique.

## Additive Techniques

Additive synthesis represents an important pole within classical sound synthesis methods (Risset 1969). For this technique each sound results from the addition of the components provided by its Fourier analysis. The basic representation is the Fourier formalism, and the computational algorithm reduces to the addition of sinusoids, whose amplitudes and frequencies are under the user's control. Thus simple controls—frequency amplitude—correspond to a complex structured signal. One can expect with this method good control of the spectral features of sound within the assumptions of periodicity resulting from the Fourier representation. But this method may be inadequate for quasi-periodic or transient sounds or for situations in which the number and the evolution of the components is too important. The richness of the produced sound is directly proportional to and limited by the complexity of the control. This method had, and still has, a significant impact on computer music because the Fourier formalism is so fundamental to acoustics and even more because it is closely related to our pitch-dominant musical culture.

## Resonator/Exciter Techniques

Another technique derived from the numerous studies on voice synthesis considers sound as the result of the filtering of a simple time-domain excitation signal by a set of second-order parallel filters (Bennett 1981, Potard, Baisnée, and Barrière 1986, Rodet 1984, Rodet et al. 1984). The representation formalism, which was inspired by the vocal system's structure, involves a *resonator* and an *exciter*. Sound is not modeled directly, as in the previous method, but through an intermediate model of the cause that produces it, providing the sound automatically with some of the causal device's structural features and thus reducing the complexity of the control data. In this technique spectral control is still very efficient, although it is indirect through the combination of parallel second-order elements. The excitation signal is made by hand and in most cases consists of impulses or noise.

The transient features of the sounds correspond to the transitory responses of the filters to the excitation signals. This approach is efficient in cases where the natural excitation is either very simple—impulses—or very complex—noise—but may be poorly adapted for cases where the excitation depends on coupling phenomena between resonant and exciting structures.

## Physical Model Techniques

Physical model synthesis techniques concentrate mainly on the causal systems that are at the origin of natural sound phenomena (chapter 7; see also Hiller and Ruiz 1971, Cadoz 1979, Cadoz, Florens, and Luciani 1984, Adrien and Rodet 1985, Adrien, Caussé, and Rodet 1987, Adrien, Caussé, and Ducasse 1988, Adrien 1988, McIntyre, Schumacher, and Woodhouse 1983). They associate sound with the vibrations of the structures producing it. The modeling simulates the propagation of the vibration information resulting from various excitations along resonant structures. Every musical instrument involves a set of vibrating structures, mechanical or acoustic, controlled by the instrumentalist and exciting the surrounding air. It is thus possible to represent a general sound-producing instrument as a collection of vibrating structures, responding to external demands, interacting together and feeding the radiated field. Sound synthesis by physical models consists of the digital simulation of the vibrations of these structures. The modeling techniques require both the characterization of the vibrational features of the structures and the description of the coupling interactions. The synthesis results from the time-step integration of the differential equations associated with the coupled structures responding to external driving forces or air flows.

The essential quantitative difference between physical modeling and the other methods is that the spatial properties of the causal devices are included in physical modeling, whereas traditional methods ignore the spatial specifications of sound and reduce the acoustic phenomena to the out-of-space vibrations of a single point. Because of this multidimensional approach, physical modeling techniques allow the simulation of interactions, both linear or nonlinear, between exciting and resonant structures. As a result they provide the computed sounds with significant information that is immediately perceptible by our ears. These idiosyncracies, which are generally bound to rapid variations in the sound and especially to transient phenomena reveal the inner properties of the vibrating structures, the excitation mode, and furthermore the global physical gesture that is responsible for this vibration. It is thus possible to achieve a realistic synthesis of transient and sustained sounds, and to obtain proper articulations between sounds resulting in convincing musical phrases.

These techniques give access to the simulated vibrating objects. The input and output data belong to the physical space. This allows us to simulate highly structured idiomatic instrumental behavior by applying the corresponding instrumental control. On the other hand it also provides multichannel, physically significant sound outputs that can be used to improve traditional spatial distribution of sound. Thus the general scheme associated with traditional sound synthesis techniques can be replaced, in the case of physical modeling techniques, by the scheme shown in figure 8.2.

In a real-time context (Cadoz, Florens, and Luciani 1984) it is possible to derive the digital "driving forces" from sensors and to use these signals as input data for the simulation algorithms. Furthermore the simulation

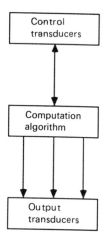

**Figure 8.2**
General scheme for physical model synthesis

programs can return the instantaneous reacting force applied by the structure to the excitation. Thus it is possible to build a transducer that is sensitive to input forces and that displays in real-time the corresponding reacting forces from the simulated structure, which restores the control relationship between the instrumentalist and the modeled instrument.

The simulation of interacting resonant and exciting structures does not provide, in the general case, specific sound outputs in the one-dimensional sense but rather surfaces, point velocities, or pressures that are, in the case of the real structure, at the origin of the radiated three-dimensional acoustic field. This suggests the use of special sound distribution devices that will provide the radiated acoustic field with the correct directional features.

In the general case the behavior of a vibrating structure can be described at a given point by a pair of conjugate dynamic variables. The first of these variables represents the external excitation applied at a point on the structure. This can be either a force, in the case of a mechanical structure, or an air flow, in the case of an acoustic system. The second variable represents the resulting instantaneous vibrating state of the structure at this point. This can be either the point velocity, in the case of a mechanical structure, or, in the case of an acoustic system, the local pressure. These two variables, for a continuous structure, are related by a wave equation involving space and time derivatives. The ratio of these two variables, the *point impedance* or *admittance*, characterizes the response of the structure to an external excitation. In other words it provides an image of the structure seen from the considered input point.

For digital simulation it is possible to make discrete both the space and time dimensions and thus to associate to a continuous structure represented by a set of $N$ points along the structure. The wave equation relating the dynamic variables associated with the structure reduces then to a system of $N$ coupled differential equations relating the $2N$ variables associated with the chosen points. In the general case the $N$ variables representing the excitations external to the structure are either zero or known input data, making it possible to integrate the differential equation system and to determine at each time step the $N$ variables representing the vibrating state of the structure. This general numerical solution, however, has significant drawbacks for musical purposes.

The discrete representation of the structure, which is equivalent to a mass and spring description, does not give any significant insight into the spectral properties of the structure, relevant for musical aims. For example, the mechanical change that has to affect a given set of masses and springs to produce a given timbral change is not obvious, even to mechanical engineers. Besides, no continuous dynamic modification of the structures is possible within the representation. For example, it is not possible to simulate the continuous lengthening of a string by the simple addition of mass elements to the string. Another drawback is that the structures and the models are, in this representation, very specifically associated. Thus any new structure will require new modeling involving expensive and time-consuming work.

Other formulations involving *progressive waves* have been developed in previous work (Karplus and Strong 1983, Jaffe and Smith 1983, Adrien and Rodet 1985, Adrien, Caussé, and Rodet 1987, Adrien, Caussé, and Ducasse 1988). In these models the vibrating state of a simple resonant structure is expressed as the sum of the contributions of two progressive waves. These models are very cheap in computing time, but are adapted only for particular physical structures, such as simple strings or acoustic tubes. Besides, the progressive wave approach consists of the propagation by hand of waves along delay lines. This poses many practical implementation problems. The drawbacks of this approach are summarized in Adrien 1988.

Physical model synthesis techniques are very efficient for the simulation of transitory phenomena, but they describe sound phenomena mostly in the time-domain, providing thus a poor spectral control. They have not been developed in the last three decades as much as other traditional techniques mainly due to the computing costs involved, the lack of experience in the field of digital simulation of complex structures and overall the lack of modularity and flexibility resulting from the involvement of physical laws for musical purposes.

## Theory of Modal Synthesis

Any sound-producing object can be represented as a collection of vibrating substructures characterized by modal data. These respond to external excitations and to interaction forces or air flows. Typical substructures are, for example, violin bridges or bodies, bows, acoustic tubes, chimneys or bells, timpani membranes. Interactions can be the bow/string or the hammer/membrane excitations, and so on. Thus the simulation algorithms consist essentially of the representation of the substructures and the simulations of their interactions.

### Modal Data

The modal data associated with a substructure consist of the frequencies and damping coefficients of the structure's resonant modes and of a set of coordinates representing the vibration mode's shapes (Navier 1826, Denk 1954, Turner and Clough 1956, Hurty and Rubinstein 1964, Guyan 1965, Craig and Bampton 1968, Hou 1969, Imbert 1984, Hurty, Collins, and Hart 1971, Skudrzyck 1971, Morse and Ingard 1986). A vibrating mode is a particular motion such that every point of the structure vibrates at the same frequency. This constraint restricts, for a given structure, the possible frequencies and the possible shapes of the corresponding motion. These frequencies, and the associated motion shapes or mode's shapes, are thus discrete and characterize the dynamic properties of the structure. With regard to our purposes, an important feature of this characterization is that any instantaneous motion of a structure, including block translations, can be expressed as the sum of the contributions of its modes.

Usually a given mode does not exist alone but rather contributes to a more general vibration pattern. A general external force applied at a given point on a structure excites the structure's modes. In other words the exciting force is displayed, or projected, over the structure's modes. Every

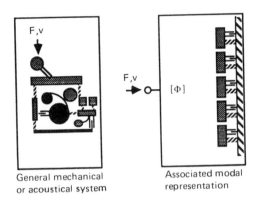

General mechanical            Associated modal
or acoustical system         representation

**Figure 8.3**
A modal scheme associated with a complex vibrating structure. The vibrating modes of the
structure can be represented as a set of parallel independent resonators, responding to the
external force $F$ and contributing to the resulting velocity $v$.

mode then responds to this excitation independently from the other modes
as a simple mass-and-spring system. The resulting velocities of all the
modes can be combined to compute the velocity of the excitation point. A
general structure can thus the represented, in the modal formalism, as the
set of parallel resonators of figure 8.3.

Theoretically the series of vibrating modes that can be associated with
a continuous structure is infinite, which corresponds to an infinite number
of degrees of freedom for the structure. The number of modes accounted
for in a practical situation is limited: this can be understood as a spatial
partitioning of the structure or a reduction of its degrees of freedom. This
means a reduction in the number of the associated coordinates. A given
instantaneous motion is then characterized by a set, or a vector, of $N$
instantaneous coordinates, associated with the $N$ chosen points displayed
over the structure. These coordinates and points are bound together in
such a way that the resulting geometrical and mechanical features are close
to the continuous structure's characteristics. The set of $N$ points is equivalent to the corresponding modal data consisting of $N$ resonant frequencies
and damping coefficients $v_i$, $\xi_i$ and a mode's shape $N \times N$ matrix $[\Phi^i_k]$. A
given vibration mode, which is associated with a particular elementary
motion of the structure, can be described by the corresponding relative
displacements of the $N$ points and thus by a particular vector noted $\{\Phi^i\}$
for the $i$th mode. The $N$ columns of the mode's shape matrix $[\Phi^i_k]$ are
formed with the coordinates of the vectors $\{\Phi^i\}$ for $i = 1, \ldots, N$.

For simple vibrating structures the modal data can be determined by a direct analytic computation. For example, in the case of a nondissipative string, partitioned in $N$ points and thus provided with $N$ vibration modes, the mode's frequencies $v_i$ are quasi-harmonics of the fundamental and follow

$$v_i = \frac{ic}{2L} \left[ \frac{\sin\left(\dfrac{i\pi}{2(N+1)}\right)}{\dfrac{i\pi}{2(N+1)}} \right],$$

which tends to the harmonic series for large $N$, and where $i$ is the harmonic number, $L$ the length of the string, and $c$ the velocity of transverse waves along the string.

Any motion of the string is characterized by the corresponding deflections of the $N$ points of the string. The mode's shapes can be expressed as vectors in this basis. In our case the $k$th coordinate of the $i$th mode is

$$\Phi^i_k = \sin\left(\frac{ik\pi}{N+1}\right),$$

showing that the mode's shapes are portions of sinusoids.

These expressions can be obtained from the differential equation system associated with the motion of the $N$ points of the string. Any instantaneous shape of the string submitted to an external force can be expressed as a combination of these elementary sinusoidally shaped modes. Proportional damping can be introduced so that the modes' shapes remain unchanged. Such losses can be associated with damping phenomena which are constant or proportional to the square of the frequency (Moore 1978).

For complex vibrating structures the determination of the modal characteristics by direct analytical computation becomes impossible and thus requires experimental measurement tools. The last decade has seen the development of powerful and reliable experimental analysis tools for the aircraft and car industries. Thus modal analysis tools are nowadays cheap and efficient. They include excitation and pickup devices and signal processing software for Fourier transforms and polynomial extraction of modal data. The modal analysis consists essentially of the measurement of transfer functions at chosen points displayed on the structure, and the determination, on the basis of these measurements, of the modes' frequencies, damping and contributions at these points, $v_i \xi_i [\Phi^i_k]$.

These techniques, and the corresponding experimental and theoretical knowledge, can be used directly for our purposes. For example, it is possible to compile substructures together and to deduce from the modal data of the separated substructures the data of the assembled set. This compilation, known as *modal synthesis* in industry, is mainly used for predictive purposes.

In the case of acoustic systems, the modes can be seen as the elementary deflections of acoustic potential at chosen points for a given resonance frequency. As in the case of mechanical structures, simple systems can be investigated by direct analytical computation. In the case of a partitioned cylindrical tube with an open end, assuming plane waves and an adiabatic regime, it is possible to obtain, from the equation of propagation, the expression of the resonant frequencies,

$$
v_i = (2i + 1)\frac{c}{4L}\,\frac{\sin\left[\dfrac{(2i + 1)\pi}{4N}\right]}{\dfrac{(2i + 1)\pi}{4N}}.
$$

In this case the coordinates of the normal modes in the basis associated with the acoustic potential deviations of the $N$ points of the tube are

$$
\Phi_k^i = \cos\left[\frac{(2i + 1)(k + 1/2)\pi}{2N}\right].
$$

It is possible to determine in the same manner the modal data associated with conical elements and simple bells. The acoustic systems encountered in usual instruments can in most cases be reduced to a set of tubes with simple geometrical specifications. This can compensate for the lack of standard analysis tools equivalent to the modal analysis devices for mechanical structures. It is possible to deduce the modal data from the measurement of the geometrical specifications and from the elementary component's modal data.

The modal representation provides the group of vibrating structures with extensibility and continuity features that are important for our purposes. The practical extensibility of this group is provided by the available experimental tools that allow quick measurements and modeling. Any new structure can be included and stored in the environment, without requiring the time-consuming and costly work involved by other numerical modeling techniques. The finite element modeling of a complex natural mechanical structure may require several weeks of work for a skilled mechanical engineer, which is certainly prohibitive in a musical context. A modal analysis requires only a couple of days.

The continuity results from the homogeneity of the modal formalism. Extremely different structures can be associated with the same pattern $v_i \xi_i [\Phi^i_k]$ of modal data, allowing continuous interpolations between distinct existing structures via nonexisting hybrid structures. This provides the algorithm with a welcome robustness in a musical context. Any kind of arbitrary modal data $v_i \xi_i [\Phi^i_k]$ corresponding to a physically unrealistic structure will produce sound if excited.

Finally, the modal formalism permits the implementation of an extensible database of modal features. The database provides an environment for the simulation programs. A group of structures can be presented as a collection of points corresponding to existing structures, with interpolation between these points.

**Dynamic Behavior**

As we have explained, any structure's deflection shape can be expressed as the sum of the contributions of the mode's deflections. Thus computing the deflection of each point of a structure or the deflection of each mode is equivalent. The main reason for realizing the computation on the basis of modes is that all vibrating structures can be described by the same dynamic equations, thus providing the algorithm with flexibility and modularity. These dynamic equations describe the response of the substructure to an excitation applied at a given point. They thus permit, in conjunction with equations describing the excitations, the computation of the substructure's motion and the resulting sound.

In the case of a mechanical structure partitioned into $N$ points, if $\Phi^i_k$ is the $k$th component of the $i$th mass-normalized mode; $F^{\text{ext}}_{j,t+1}$ the instantaneous external force applied to the $j$th point of the structure; $\Delta t$ the time-step; and $\omega_i$, $\xi_i$, and $\varphi_i$ respectively the pulsation, the damping coefficient, and the instantaneous deflection associated to the $i$th mode; then the instantaneous generalized velocity of the $k$th point of the structure resulting from the application of the $P$ external forces $F^{\text{ext}}$ is

$$\dot{y}_{k,t+1} = \sum_{i=1}^{N} \Phi^i_k \frac{\displaystyle\sum_{j=1}^{P} \Phi^i_j F^{\text{ext}}_{j,t+1} + \frac{\dot{\varphi}_{i,t}}{\Delta t} - \omega_i^2 \varphi_{i,t}}{\dfrac{1}{\Delta t} + 2\omega_i \xi_i + \omega_i^2 \Delta t}. \tag{1}$$

In the case of an acoustic system, the pressure of the $k$th point is obtained by deriving the acoustic potential at that point. The external forces are replaced by external flows $U^{\text{ext}}_{j,t+1}$ and the equation involves the density of air $\rho_o$.

$$p_{k,t+1} = \rho_o \dot{y}_{k,t+1} = \sum_{i=0}^{N_i} \Phi_k^i \frac{\displaystyle\sum_{j=0}^{P} \Phi_j^i F^{\text{ext}}_{j,t+1} + \frac{\dot{\varphi}_{i,t}}{\Delta t} - \omega_i^2 \varphi_{i,t}}{\displaystyle\frac{1}{\Delta t} + 2\omega_i \xi_i + \omega_i^2 \Delta t}. \tag{2}$$

These expressions can be understood as double projections. The pressure or velocity of the $k$th point results from the sum of the $N$ modes' contributions, each of which depends on the corresponding projections of the external excitations in the modal basis, via a finite difference integration. Note that in this representation, the velocities or pressure of different points of the structure are coupled at each time step, and they appear as a linear combination of forces or flows added with a source term depending on the past modal dynamic variables.

In the case where all the instantaneous external excitations are known, these equations permit the determination of the velocities of the modes, and the velocity of any point on the structure, although only the velocities of particular points—like the excitation or observation points—are of interest in most cases. In the general case, however, only the external excitations corresponding to control or driving data are known, and the other instantaneous forces or flows have to be determined. It is thus necessary to introduce additional coupling or interaction equations.

## External Demands

Substructures have to be assembled to form a complex sound-producing instrument. In traditional instruments substructures play specific roles, such as radiating the produced sound or exciting the radiating substructures. But in most cases they can be represented as interacting vibrating and translating systems. Thus the model's substructures are submitted either to external driving or internal coupling demands.

### Driving Data

External driving demands are force, air flows, pressures, or displacements that are applied to the substructures and represent the action of the instrumentalist. These data consist of instantaneous known variables to the equations that describe the vibrations of the structure. These data are stored in a driving parameter file and can be displayed by sensors. For a given instrument a given objects's inclusion in or exclusion from the modeling has significant consequences in terms of control and efficiency and thus in both the technical and the musical point of view.

For example, in the case of a finger/string interaction, it seems appropriate to include a mechanical model for the finger. In this case the mechanical substructure representing the finger is submitted to the reaction force of the string and the external driving forces from the instrumentalist. These driving forces are simpler and more significant than the actual coupling forces between the fingertip and the string because they are closely related to instrumental technique. The coupling forces are applied at a lower structure's level and depend on the driving forces, the mechanical characteristics of the finger, and the vibrating state of the string. It may be necessary in some situations to include in the model the parts of the instrumentalist's body that play a mechanical role in the sound production.

In the case of a hammer/string interaction, a mechanical hammer model provides an efficient and simple control, whereas the approximate analytical solutions representing the hammer/string excitation force, which have to be used in the absence of a hammer model, may produce poor results.

It is important to apply the input data at the appropriate level of the model. This is important for technical reasons because low-level control data are not known a priori, and analytical solutions at these levels are in most cases oversimplified. For musical reasons high-level control data may be more directly related to musical gestures, independent of mechanical artifacts. In any case there is no absolute reason to set the input level of the simulation programs at the corresponding level of the natural instrument. Every model has to be evaluated on its own in this respect.

**Interactions between Substructures**

The possible interactions between substructures are less numerous than the substructures themselves, but they are hardly representable within a general form. In many case the interaction introduces a highly nonlinear equation and specific test conditions involving the dynamic variables of the substructures at the point of excitation. This equation, added to the linear equations associated with the substructures, permits the determination of all the unknown dynamic variables at each time step. Complex situations, including various nonlinearities and shifts between distinct regimes, are computed by a finite difference integration of that equation system.

In the case of the bow/string interaction, for example, the coupled structures are both presumed to be linear, and they are represented by equations similar to equation 1. The interaction involves two distinct aspects: sticking and sliding contact. In the sticking, the velocities of the string and of the bow at the contact point are simply equated, and the forces are applied following Newton's principle of action and reaction. In the sliding, the interaction forces and velocities are related by a nonlinear equation.

$$
\text{Sticking} \begin{bmatrix} v_{t+1}^b = v_{t+1}^s \\ F_{y,t+1}^{s \to b} = -F_{y,t+1}^{b \to s} \end{bmatrix}
$$

$$
\text{Sliding} \begin{bmatrix} F_{y,t+1}^{s \to b} = -\dfrac{\Delta \mu \, \| F_{z,t+1}^{s \to b} \|}{\dfrac{v_{t+1}^b - v_{t+1}^s}{\alpha} + 1} \\[6mm] F_{y,t+1}^{s \to b} = -F_{y,t+1}^{b \to s} \end{bmatrix}
$$

(3)

In these expessions $F^{s \to b}$ and $F^{b \to s}$ are the interacting forces from the string to the bow-hair and from the bow-hair to the string, $v^s$ and $v^b$ are the velocities of the string and of the bow-hair at the contact point, $\alpha$ and $\Delta \mu$ are constants characterizing the bow. It appears clearly in these expressions that the bow/string interaction supposes a given geometry of the interacting structures that may restrict the possible applications of this interaction: The sliding force $F_y^{s \to b}$ in the direction $Oy$ of bowing is proportional to the $F_z^{s \to b}$ force representing the *bow pressure*. The equivalent bow pressure that should be considered, for example, in the case where the string is replaced by a membrane, is not obvious. This difficulty corresponds, however, to a physical reality: The bowing process, as other interaction processes basic to musical instruments, is optimized for the corresponding mechanical structures or acoustic system and is not adapted to any arbitrary structure.

The reed/air column interaction is another example of nonlinear interaction. In that case the coupled structures are the reed, described by equation 1, and the acoustic tube, associated with equation 2. The coupling equation involves the flow entering the bore $U_o^{\text{ext}}$, the pressure difference between the mouth and the bore $[P_m - P_o]$, the position of the reed $\xi$, the Backus constant $B$, and the additional flow $S_o \dot{\xi}$ due to the displacement of the reed.

The interaction involves in that case, as in the previous one, a shift between two regimes:

Opened reed $\quad [U_{o,t+1}^{\text{ext}} = B\|p_{m,t+1} - p_{o,t+1}\|^{2/3}\xi_{t+1}^{4/3} + S_o\dot{\xi}_{t+1}$

Closed reed $\quad \begin{bmatrix} U_{o,t+1}^{\text{ext}} = 0 \\ \xi_{t+1} = 0 \end{bmatrix}$ (4)

Because the velocities or pressure of different points of the structure are coupled at each step by the equations 1 and 2, it may thus be necessary to linearize equations 3 and 4 to simplify the resulting coupled equation systems. This linearization does not appear to affect the sound significantly if the (nonlinear) shifts are preserved.

These two interaction examples are in close correspondence with the behavior of natural instruments. Certain other types of interactions, like hammering or plucking, are more general and hence more robust. This is because they require no specific geometrical and mechanical features for the structures they apply to, so they can produce sound in a very wide range of situations. This means, for example, that they can be more easily used in structure interpolations.

Another type of external demand that can be fed into a structure is an arbitrary and physically insignificant signal—any sampled sound signal, noise, or impulse. In this case the structure behaves like a complicated filter, and the synthesis process is close to traditional filter synthesis techniques, except that in this case the filter involves spatial specifications.

Work remains to be done on the study of interaction processes, in conjunction with structure interpolations, toward greater generality in their formulation.

## Examples of Complex Structures

This section presents several examples of complex structures that have been analyzed by modal techniques. The examples include a plucked violin string, modeled as a mechanical structure, and an acoustic system.

### Mechanical Structure: Plucked Violin String

To illustrate briefly a practical application of the modal synthesis technique, we describe a mechanical model of a plucked violin string. The coupled mechanical structures are a violin body, four strings, a finger, and a bridge. Each structure is characterized by an equation of the form of equation 1, involving modal features and dynamic variables at coupling or excitation points.

The bridge and the finger models have four degrees of freedom. Their modal characterization can be obtained, in the case of the bridge, through an adaptation of Reinicke's (1973) work to our purposes (Adrien 1988). In the case of the finger, we obtain a modal characterization by considering the simplest two-mass model (Adrien and Rodet 1985). The string's modal data can be deduced directly from analytical computation. It involves two independent directions of polarization for each string. The modal features of the body can be measured experimentally (Marshall 1984).

The interaction forces are $F_u$, $F_v$ at the foot of the bridge, $F_{ch}{}^{iy}$, $F_{ch}{}^{iz}$ $i = 1, \ldots, 4$, forces applied by the string on the upper part of the bridge for the two polarization, $F_{pl}{}^{ly}$, $F_{pl}{}^{lz}$, reactions of the string $l$ to the finger, and $F^y{}_{pil}$, $F^z{}_{pil}$ the external driving forces applied on the finger.

These twelve forces, and the twelve velocities of their application points, have to be determined out of the twelve equations of the form of equation 1 associated with the structure, and the coupling equations that reduce, in this case, to simple sticking contact conditions. It is possible to eliminate, for example, all the velocities from these equations. The system reduces to the form shown in figure 8.4.

In figure 8.4 $\psi_{cor}$, $\psi_{ch}$, $\psi_{iy,z}$, $\psi_{pl}$ are the modal coefficients associated respectively with the body, the bridge, the $i$th string and finger, and $S$ the source terms of equation 1. The equation in figure 8.4 shows the top level of the structure's model consisting of all the access forces applied to the substructures. It permits the computation of all the interaction forces, which in turn produce the instantaneous point and mode velocities.

The *control matrix* involved in this equation has a form closely associated with the actual setup of the substructures. The removal of the finger from the string $l$ produces the removal of the two last columns and rows. The control matrix has to be updated at any important change of the mechanical structure. The sliding (glissando) movement of the finger along the string, for example, will affect the control matrix. It is thus important for computation costs to reduce the size of this matrix by compiling together substructures whose separation is not important. For example, in our case the compilation of the bridge with the body would reduce the control matrix to a $10 \times 10$ matrix, removing the two rows and columns corresponding to the bridge/body interaction. The compilation of the four

$$
\begin{pmatrix}
(\psi^{00}_{ch}+\psi^{00}_{cor}) & (\psi^{01}_{ch}+\psi^{01}_{cor}) & (\psi^{02}_{ch}) & (\psi^{03}_{ch}) & (\psi^{04}_{ch}) & (\psi^{05}_{ch}) & (\psi^{06}_{ch}) & (\psi^{07}_{ch}) & (\psi^{08}_{ch}) & (\psi^{09}_{ch}) & 0 & 0 \\
(\psi^{10}_{ch}+\psi^{10}_{cor}) & (\psi^{11}_{ch}+\psi^{11}_{cor}) & & & & & & & & (\psi^{19}_{ch}) & 0 & 0 \\
(\psi^{20}_{ch}) & & (\psi^{22}_{ch}+\psi^{11}_{1y}) & & & & (\psi^{ij}_{ch}) & & & (\psi^{29}_{ch}) & (\psi^{10}_{1y}) & 0 \\
(\psi^{30}_{ch}) & & & (\psi^{33}_{ch}+\psi^{11}_{1z}) & & & & & & (\psi^{39}_{ch}) & 0 & (\psi^{10}_{1z}) \\
(\psi^{40}_{ch}) & & & & (\psi^{44}_{ch}+\psi_{2y}) & & & & & (\psi^{49}_{ch}) & 0 & 0 \\
(\psi^{50}_{ch}) & & & & & (\psi^{55}_{ch}+\psi_{2z}) & & & & (\psi^{59}_{ch}) & 0 & 0 \\
(\psi^{60}_{ch}) & & (\psi^{ij}_{ch}) & & & & (\psi^{66}_{ch}+\psi_{3y}) & & & (\psi^{69}_{ch}) & 0 & 0 \\
(\psi^{70}_{ch}) & & & & & & & (\psi^{77}_{ch}+\psi_{3z}) & & (\psi^{79}_{ch}) & 0 & 0 \\
(\psi^{80}_{ch}) & & & & & & & & (\psi^{88}_{ch}+\psi_{4y}) & (\psi^{89}_{ch}) & 0 & 0 \\
(\psi^{90}_{ch}) & (\psi^{91}_{ch}) & (\psi^{92}_{ch}) & (\psi^{93}_{ch}) & (\psi^{94}_{ch}) & (\psi^{95}_{ch}) & (\psi^{96}_{ch}) & (\psi^{97}_{ch}) & (\psi^{98}_{ch}) & (\psi^{99}_{ch}+\psi_{4z}) & 0 & 0 \\
0 & 0 & (\psi^{01}_{1y}) & 0 & 0 & 0 & 0 & 0 & 0 & 0 & (\psi^{22}_{pl}+\psi^{00}_{1y}) & (\psi^{32}_{pl}) \\
0 & 0 & 0 & (\psi^{01}_{1z}) & 0 & 0 & 0 & 0 & 0 & 0 & (\psi^{23}_{pl}) & (\psi^{33}_{pl}+\psi^{00}_{1z})
\end{pmatrix}
\begin{pmatrix}
F_u \\ F_v \\ F^{1y}_{ch} \\ F^{1z}_{ch} \\ F^{2y}_{ch} \\ F^{2z}_{ch} \\ F^{3y}_{ch} \\ F^{3z}_{ch} \\ F^{4y}_{ch} \\ F^{4z}_{ch} \\ F^{1y}_{pl} \\ F^{1z}_{pl}
\end{pmatrix}
=
\begin{pmatrix}
S^{(1)}_{cor}-S^{(1)}_{ch} \\
S^{(2)}_{cor}-S^{(2)}_{ch} \\
S^{(2)}_{1y}-S^{(3)}_{ch} \\
S^{(2)}_{1z}-S^{(4)}_{ch} \\
S_{2y}-S^{(5)}_{ch} \\
S_{2z}-S^{(6)}_{ch} \\
S_{3y}-S^{(7)}_{ch} \\
S_{3z}-S^{(8)}_{ch} \\
S_{4y}-S^{(9)}_{ch} \\
S_{4z}-S^{(10)}_{ch} \\
S^{(1)}_{1y}-S^{(3)}_{pl}-(\psi^{20}_{pl})F^{y}_{pil}-(\psi^{21}_{pl})F^{z}_{pil} \\
S^{(1)}_{1z}-S^{(4)}_{pl}-(\psi^{30}_{pl})F^{y}_{pil}-(\psi^{31}_{pl})F^{z}_{pil}
\end{pmatrix}
$$

**Figure 8.4**
Matrix equation describing the mechanics of a plucked violin string

strings with this latter structure would result in a $2 \times 2$ control matrix, significantly reducing the computing costs involved and allowing real-time applications on affordable computers.

## Acoustic System: Conical Tube and Mouthpiece

To illustrate the case of a typical acoustic system, we can consider a conical tube with a simple reed mouthpiece and five holes. Six equations of the form of equation 2 can be associated with the cone, and one to each hole. Equations of the forms of equations 1 and 4 can be associated with the reed. Real reeds have more specific dynamic properties with, for example, varying mass and stiffness (Thompson 1979, Meynial 1987). Mass and stiffness variations can be obtained with the corresponding variations of the modal parameters in equation 1 by adapting, for example, Ducasse's work (Adrien, Caussé, and Ducasse 1988) to the modal formalism.

The interaction relations between the acoustic substructures involving flow conservation are equivalent to the sticking contact of the previous case. It is possible to eliminate all pressures to get a system relating the instantaneous flows $U_i^{ext} i = 0, \ldots, 5$, to the source terms of equation 2, as shown in the equation in figure 8.5.

The equation in figure 8.5 involves (as in the previous example) a control matrix that is closely related to the setup of the structures. Inversion of the control matrix provides the instantaneous interaction flows. It is possible to deduce from these flows the values of the pressures and the instantaneous displacement of the reed. Once again it seems interesting to compile the acoustic substructures together to reduce the size of the control matrix.

$$
\begin{pmatrix}
(\psi_{tp}^{00} + \Xi_{anc}) & & & & & \\
& (\psi_{tp}^{11} + \psi_{t1}) & & (\psi_{tp}^{ij}) & & \\
& & (\psi_{tp}^{22} + \psi_{t2}) & & & \\
& & & (\psi_{tp}^{33} + \psi_{t3}) & & \\
& & & & (\psi_{tp}^{44} + \psi_{t4}) & \\
& (\psi_{tp}^{ij}) & & & & (\psi_{tp}^{55} + \psi_{t5})
\end{pmatrix}
\begin{pmatrix}
U_0^{Ext} \\
U_1^{Ext} \\
U_2^{Ext} \\
U_3^{Ext} \\
U_4^{Ext} \\
U_5^{Ext}
\end{pmatrix}
=
\begin{pmatrix}
S_{Anc}\text{-}S_{tp}^{(0)} \\
S_{t1}\text{-}S_{tp}^{(1)} \\
S_{t2}\text{-}S_{tp}^{(2)} \\
S_{t3}\text{-}S_{tp}^{(3)} \\
S_{t4}\text{-}S_{tp}^{(4)} \\
S_{t5}\text{-}S_{tp}^{(5)}
\end{pmatrix}
$$

**Figure 8.5**
Matrix equation describing the acoustic properties of a conical tube with a mouthpiece

## Simulating the Radiated Acoustic Field

After the model is designed, the next problem is to decide which possible output signals we should listen to. The simulation algorithms provide many possible points on the structure at which to tap for sound output. Hence it seems inadequate, at least in principle, to mix various radiated signals to an ordinary stereo loudspeaker. The computer velocity or pressure information dispersed over the entire sound-radiating structure is at the origin of the radiation phenomena, and in theory this can create a better synthesis of the acoustic field. Moreover the sound-radiation differences between loudspeakers and natural instruments may be disturbing in performance situations where traditional instruments and loudspeakers are played simultaneously, especially for people who practice daily with traditional instruments. This is not, however, the usual case. Today a large majority of listeners experience music almost exclusively over loudspeakers, and they have few occasions to hear the natural acoustic fields of traditional instruments.

But even restricted to research matters, this issue poses many interesting practical and theoretical problems. Here again we can borrow techniques from industrial noise-reduction applications and apply them to our musical situation. The modal formalism seems to be a good starting point, in the sense that radiation patterns can be assoicated with the vibrating modes.

For example, when studying synthesis algorithms and radiation characteristics of stringed instruments, it is useful to eliminate the loudspeaker problem by using a natural instrument's body as a transducer. The bridge, the strings, and the exciters are simulated as usual, and the instrument's body is replaced with a (non)vibrating structure of infinite impedance to avoid any redundancy with the violin-transducer. Reciprocally, and for the same nonredundancy reason, the strings of the violin-tranducer are damped out. The sound outputs of the simulated model attached to the violin-transducer are the input forces at the feet of the bridge. This stereo output is played after an analog-to-digital conversion stage through an ordinary two-channel amplifier and B&K 4810 shakers into a cheap violin. Adapted stems allow the transmission of the excitation force from the shakers to the feet of the bridge mounted on the violin-transducer. For reference purposes we can also pick up natural force signals with piezo-electric ceramic transducers wedged between the bridge and the body of a driving violin (figure 8.6).

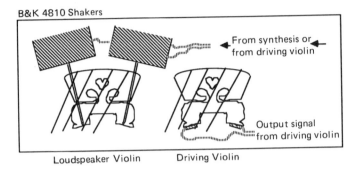

B&K 4810 Shakers

From synthesis or from driving violin

Output signal from driving violin

Loudspeaker Violin      Driving Violin

**Figure 8.6**
Output transducer for violin synthesis. The "loudspeaker- violin" transducer is excited by simulated force signals transmitted through an amplifier and B&K 4810 shakers. The corresponding signal is picked up by a piezoceramic transducer on the driving violin.

## Numerical Results

We can generate graphical displays of the simulated structures during the excitation. These displays are good tools for algorithm development and for a better understanding of complex vibration phenomena. The relation between the structure's motion and the transitory aspects of the sounds appear clearly, especially in the case of strings.

We can see in figures 8.7 and 8.8 the velocity distributions along a string with two transverse dimensions and a bridge. In this example the instrument's body is replaced by a structure with infinite input impedance. This does not, however, significantly affect the main motion features at the level of the strings. In these plots the horizontal axis corresponds to the direction $Ox$ of the string. Thus the contact point of the string with the bridge and with the bow are included between the two ends of the string corresponding to the right and the left ends of the plot. The vertical axis is the instantaneous velocity distribution along the string. The depth dimension is associated with time and results from the superimposition of the velocity distribution plots for 200 samples. Hence it shows the propagation in time of the velocity information generated at the bowing point, along with its reflection and transmission at the bridge and at the ends of the strings.

The velocities of figure 8.7A, B are respectively the velocities along the string for the $Oy$ and $Oz$ directions (direction of bowing and direction of the bow pressure) for 6.25 ms after the first contact between the bow and

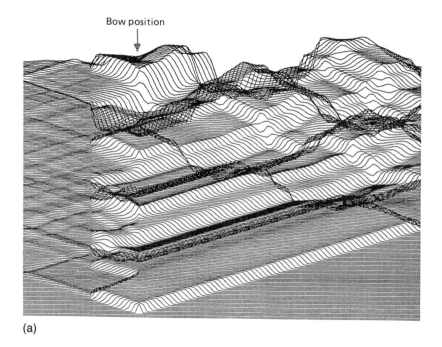

(a)

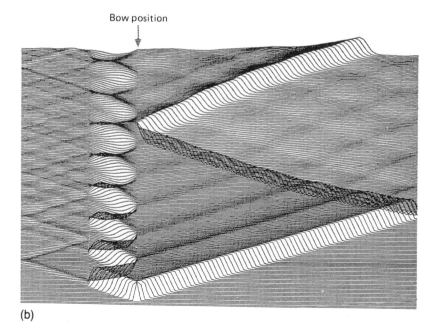

(b)

**Figure 8.7**
Velocity plots for a string model. (A) Velocity distributions for the $Oy$ dimension along the string at the moment of the bow-string contact. (B) Velocity distributions for the $Oz$ dimension along the string at the moment of the bow-string contact.

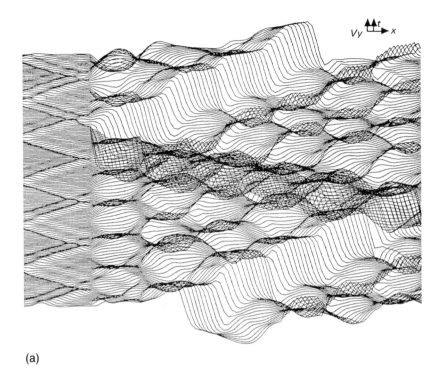

(a)

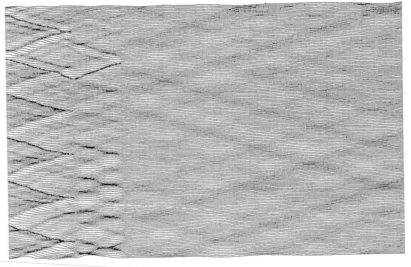

(b)

**Figure 8.8**
Velocity plots for a string model. (A) Velocity distributions for the $Oy$ dimension along the string 110 ms after the moment of the bow-string contact. (B) Velocity distributions for the $Oz$ dimension along the string 110 ms after the moment of the bow-string contact.

the string. This contact generates a pair of velocity steps of each dimension, respectively $V_y = 0.5$ m/s and $V_z = 1.0$ m/s, which propagate toward the right end of the string and toward the bridge. The steps are quasi-perfectly reflected at the right end and are both reflected and transmitted at the bridge. The evolution of the two dimensions is identical as long as the bow sticks to the string. The release of the string is apparent for the $Oy$ dimension in figure 8.7A some 43 samples after the beginning of the sequence. The bow later sticks again, sample 76, and the periodic stick/slide motion builds up.

In the $Oz$ direction, on the contrary, no steps are generated after the initial pair of steps, which are progressively damped. The remaining signal for the $Oz$ dimension is plotted—with a double scale for clarity—in figure 8.8B, 110 ms after the first contact. This results from the damping of the initial pair of steps, which added with velocities produced at the bridge by the coupling of the two dimensions. At the same time the situation for the bowing direction $Oy$ has evolved toward a periodic Helmholtz motion added with secondary waves (figure 8.8A). A more complete analysis of the transient is given in Adrien 1988.

For sound synthesis purposes the introduction of the vertical $Oz$ dimension in the modeling seems important because it provides realistic staccato and martelé attacks that are difficult to obtain otherwise. Figure 8.9 shows a membrane (percussion model) struck at two points. This illustrates, somewhat paradoxically, the *phrasing* possibilities of the models. An important point concerning transient phenomena in membranes is that a given excitation takes account of the past information present in the structures that result from a previous excitation. This is even more obvious in the case where two excitations are simultaneous. The membrane modeled in figure 8.9 has a tension of 100 N/m, a surface mass of 0.1 kg/m$^2$, and a radius of 0.18 m. The 496 modes are included between 208.32 Hz and 6190.9 Hz. The time gap between the plots is $5\Delta t$ (32 kHz).

Finally, figure 8.10 shows a very simple example of conical bore excited by a reed. In this example the mass and stiffness variations of the reed are neglected. We emphasize the nonlinear aspect of the interaction and the importance of the dynamic properties of the exciting structure. The clarinet is blown with a driving pressure increasing from zero to 3000 Pa in 10 ms. The length of the bore is 1 m, and its extreme radii are 0.75 cm and 5 cm. The reed parameters are: oscillating mass $3.10^{-3}$ g, stiffness 545 N/m, surface $3.34.10^{-4}$ m$^2$, reed equilibrium position 6 mm away from the lay.

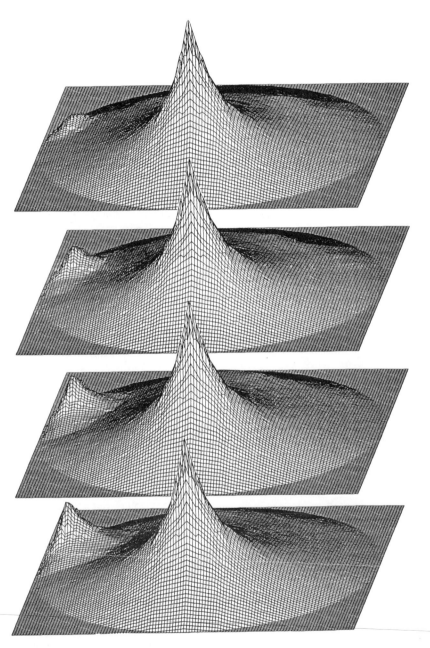

**Figure 8.9**
Rolled membrane excited simultaneously at two points

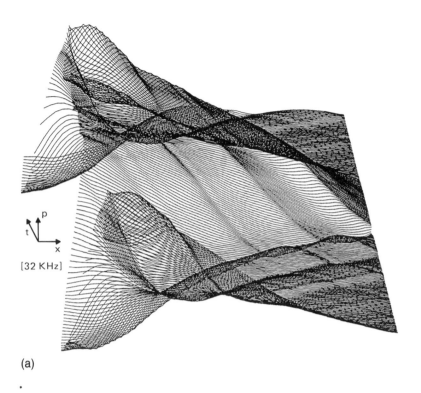

p
t
x
[32 KHz]

(a)

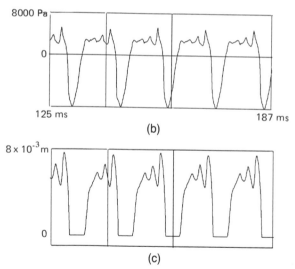

8000 Pa

0

125 ms                    187 ms

(b)

8 x 10⁻³ m

0

(c)

**Figure 8.10**
Plots of simple conical bore model. (A) Acoustic pressure distribution for a conical bore.
Horizontal axis: bore length, left-side mouthpiece and right-side bell. Vertical axis: acoustic
pressure. (B) Acoustic pressure versus time at the mouthpiece. (C) Reed displacement versus
time.

We have shown in figure 8.10B the pressure distributions along the bore for 300 time steps (32 kHz sampling rate), starting 156 ms after the attack and the trajectory of the reed. The horizontal axis of this three-dimensional view is the direction of the bore. The mouthpiece is on the left side of the plot, and the bell at the right side. The vertical axis is the acoustic pressure. As a result of the conicity and the inner losses, the acoustic pressure is logically more important at the left side of the bore than at the right side. The acoustic pressure on the side of the mouthpiece plotted versus time can also be seen in figure 8.10B. The vertical lines on this plot indicate the time window of figure 8.10A. The displacement of the reed is plotted in figure 8.10C. The oscillations of the reed superimposed on the oscillations produced by the bore can be seen in either figure 8.10B or C.

## Conclusion

To model the dynamics of interacting vibrating structures in instrumental performance, we use a modal formalism in conjunction with the simulation of nonlinear and linear interactions. This space- and time-domain approach lets us simulate phenomena that are difficult to realize with more traditional sound synthesis techniques. As examples of these phenomena, consider transient or sustained sounds that result from deterministic coupling interactions between exciting and resonating objects, or successive excitations of the same set of resonators resulting in a macroscopic phrase. These phenomena are fundamental to musical language.

The modal synthesis techniques also permits an additivelike control of the spectral properties of the structures. This flexible control allows specific applications of physical models to overcome the usual limits of these models in terms of generality, modularity, and robustness.

A link between additive/filter synthesis and physical modeling techniques is important for several practical reasons: It permits a continuous shift between typical filter synthesis and physical modeling applications, thus significantly enlarging the possibilities of these techniques. It makes physical modeling techniques easier to learn for musicians who are used to thinking and hearing with additive/filter techniques. It should also allow researchers to adapt models, user interfaces, and other tools from additive/filter synthesis enviroments to physical models.

As we have shown, musical research can greatly benefit by keeping in touch with highly developed industrial techniques for the multidimensional characterization of vibrating structures and for the design of vibration/ radiated field interfaces. In the future these techniques are sure to be profitable for audio synthesis applications.

## References

Adrien, J.-M. 1988. "Etude de structures complexes vibrantes, application à la synthèse par modèles physiques." Ph.D. dissertation. Paris: Université de Paris VI.

Adrien, J.-M., and X. Rodet. 1985. "Physical models of instruments, a modular approach, application to strings." In B. Truax, ed. *Proceedings of the 1985 International Computer Music Conference.* San Francisco: Computer Music Association.

Adrien, J.-M., R. Caussé, and X. Rodet. 1987. "Sound synthesis by physical models, application to strings." In J. Beauchamp and J. Melby, eds. *Proceedings of the 1987 International Computer Music Conference.* San Francisco: Computer Music Association.

Adrien, J.-M. Caussé, and E. Ducasse. 1988. "Sound synthesis by physical models, application to strings." In *Proceedings of the 1988 Audio Engineering Society Convention. Paris.* New York: Audio Engineering Society.

Baisnée, P. F. 1985 "Chant manual." Internal report. Paris: IRCAM.

Benade, A. 1976. *Fundamentals of Musical Acoustics.* New York: Oxford University Press.

Bennett, G. 1981. "Singing synthesis in electronic music." In J. Sundberg, ed. *Research Aspects of Singing.* Stockholm: Royal Swedish Academy of Music, pp. 34–50.

Cadoz, C. 1979. "Synthèse sonore par simulation de mécanismes vibratoires, application aux sons musicaux." *Mémoire de Thèse de Doctorat.* Grenoble: Institut National Polytechnique de Grenoble.

Cadoz, C., J.-L. Florens, and A. Luciani. 1984. "Responsive input devices and sound synthesis by simulation of instrumental mechanisms: the Cordis system." *Computer Music Journal* 8(3): 60–73.

Chowning, J. 1973. "The synthesis of complex audio spectra by means of frequency modulation." *Journal of the Audio Engineering Society* 21: 526–534. Reprinted in C. Roads and J. Strawn, eds. *Foundations of Computer Music.* Cambridge, Massachusetts: MIT Press, pp. 6–29.

Chowning, J. 1981. "Computer synthesis of the singing voice." In *Proceedings of the Melbourne 1981 International Conference on Music and Technology.* Melbourne: La Trobe University.

Chowning, J., and D. Bristow. 1986. *FM Theory and Applications.* Tokyo: Yamaha Music Foundation.

Cocholle, R. 1973. *Le Bruit, Third edition. Que Sais-je?* Number 855. Paris: Presses Universitaires de France.

Craig, J., and M. Bampton. 1968. "Coupling of sub-structures for dynamic analysis." National Aeronautics and Space Administration. NASA CR 27 81. February 1977.

Denk, P. H. 1954. "A matrix method of structural analysis." *Proceedings of the Second National Congress of Applied Mechanics.* American Society of Mechanical Engineers.

Erickson, R. 1975. *Sound Structure in Music.* Berkeley: University of California Press.

Grey, J. 1975. "An exploration of musical timbre." Department of Music Report STAN-M-2. Stanford: Stanford University.

Gribensky, A. 1951. *L'Audition. Que sais-je?* Number 484. Paris: Presses Universitaires de France.

Guyan, R. J. 1965. "Reduction of stiffness and mass matrices." *AIAA Journal* 3: 380.

Helmholtz, H. 1954. *On the Sensation of Tone.* Translation of the 1877 edition. New York: Dover.

Hall, D. 1980. *Musical Acoustics.* Belmont, California: Wadsworth Publishing.

Hiller, L., and P. Ruiz. 1971. "Synthesizing musical sounds by solving the wave equation for vibrating objects." *Journal of the Audio Engineering Society* 19(6): 462–470.

Hou, S. 1969. "Review of modal synthesis techniques and a new approach." *Shock and Vibration Bulletin, US Naval Laboratories Proceedings* 40(4): 25–39.

Hurty, W., J. Collins, and G. Hart. 1971. "Dynamic analysis of large structures by modal synthesis techniques." *Computers and Structures* 1.

Hurty, W., and M. Rubinstein. 1964. *Dynamics of Structures.* Englewood Cliffs: Prentice-Hall.

Imbert, J. F. 1984. *Analyse des Structures par Eléments Finis.* Toulouse: Cepadues Editions.

Jaffe, D., and J. Smith. 1983. "Extensions of the Karplus-Strong plucked string algorithm." *Computer Music Journal* 7(2): 43–55. Reprinted in C. Roads, ed. 1989. *The Music Machine.* Cambridge, Massachusetts: MIT Press, pp. 481–494.

Karplus, K., and A. Strong. 1983. "Digital synthesis of plucked string and drum timbres." *Computer Music Journal* 7(2): 43–55. Reprinted in C. Roads, ed. 1989. *The Music Machine.* Cambridge. Massachusetts: MIT Press, pp. 467–481.

Leipp, E. 1984. *Acoustique et Musique.* Second edition. Paris: Masson.

Marshall, K. D. 1984. "Modal analysis of a violin." *Journal of the Acoustical Society of America* 77(2).

Mathews, M. 1969. *The Technology of Computer Music.* Cambridge, Massachusetts: MIT Press.

McAdams, S. 1983. "Les fondements de l'acoustique" In M. Battier and G. Charbonneau, eds. *Musique et Ordinateur.* Les Ulis: Centre Expérimental du Spectacle, Université de Paris Sud, pp. 67–91.

McAdams, S., and Bregman. 1979. "Hearing musical streams." *Computer Music Journal* 3(4): 26–43, 60, 63. Reprinted in C. Roads and J. Strawn, eds. 1985. *Foundations of Computer Music.* Cambridge, Massachusetts: MIT Press, pp. 658–698. Translated as "L'audition des flux musicaux." In *Institut de Pédagogie Musicale et Chorégraphique, La Villette, Paris, décembre 1987.* pp. 97–118.

McIntyre, M. E., R. Schumacher, and J. Woodhouse. 1983. "On the oscillations of musical instruments." *Journal of the Acoustical Society of America* 74(5).

Meynial, X. 1987. "Systèmes micro intervalles pour instruments à vent à trous latéraux, oscillations d'une anche simple couplée à un résonateur de forme simple." Doctoral thesis. Le Mans: Université du Mans.

Moore, F. R. 1978. "An introduction of the mathematics of digital singal processing." *Computer Music Journal* 2(1): 38–47 and 2(2): 38–60. Reprinted in J. Strawn, ed. 1985. *Digital Audio Signal Processing: An Anthology.* Madison: A-R Editions, pp. 1–67.

Morse, P., and U. Ingard. 1986. *Theoretical Acoustics.* Princeton: Princeton University Press.

Navier, H. M. C. 1826. *Résumé des leçons de la résistance des corps solides.* Paris.

Pierce, J. 1984. *Le son Musical, Musique, Acoustique et Informatique.* Paris: Pour la Science, diffusion Belin.

Potard, Y., P. F. Baisnée, and J.-B. Barrière. 1986. "Experimenting with models of resonance produced by a new technique for the analysis of impulsive sounds." In P. Berg, ed. *Proceedings of the 1986 International Computer Music Conference*. San Francisco: Computer Music Association, pp. 269–274.

Reinicke W. 1973. "Die Uebertragungseigenshaften des Streichinstrumentensteges." Ph.D dissertation. Berlin: Berlin Technical University.

Risset, J.-C., and D. Wessel. 1982. "Exploration of timbre by analysis and synthesis." In D. Deutsch, ed. *The Psychology of Music*. Orlando: Academic Press, pp. 26–57.

Risset, J.-C. 1969. "An introductory catalog of computer synthesized sounds." Murray Hill: Bell Telephone Laboratories.

Roads, C. 1978. "Automated granular synthesis of sound." *Computer Music Journal* 2(2): 61–62. Revised version published as "Granular synthesis of sound," in C. Roads and J. Strawn, eds. 1985. *Foundations of Computer Music*. Cambridge, Massachusetts: MIT Press, pp. 145–159.

Roads, C. 1979. "A Tutorial on nonlinear distortion or waveshaping synthesis." *Computer Music Journal* 3(2): 29–34. Reprinted in C. Roads and J. Strawn, eds. 1985. Foundations of Computer Music. Cambridge, Massachusetts: MIT Press, pp. 83–94.

Rodet, X. 1984. "Time domain formant-wave-function synthesis." *Computer Music Journal* 8(3): 15–31.

Rodet, X., Y. Potard, and J.-B. Barrière. 1984. "The Chant project: from synthesis of the singing voice to synthesis in general." *Computer Music Journal* 8(3): 15–31. Reprnted in C. Roads, eds. 1989. *The Music Machine*. Cambridge, Massachusetts: MIT Press, pp. 449–466.

Skudrzyck, E. 1971. *The Foundations of Acoustics*. New York: Springer-Verlag.

Thompson, S. C. 1979. "The effect of the reed resonance on woodwind tone production." *Journal of the Acoustical Society of America* 66(5).

Turner, H., and R. Clough. 1956. "Stiffness and deflection analysis of complex structues." *Journal of the Aeronautical Society* 20.

Wessel, D. 1978. "Low-dimensional control of musical timbre." Rapport de Recherche IRCAM 12. Paris: IRCAM.

# 9 Synthesizing Singing

Johan Sundberg

Models (sometimes called physical models) have been found extremely helpful in scientific work. Indeed, the idea of *analysis by synthesis*, which has proven so productive in speech research, is ultimately based on the availability of some kind of a model. The ideal in this method is simple: One analyzes an object by synthesizing it. The method is particularly advantageous in research on complicated signals such as speech and music performance (Carlson et al. 1989).

Models have also been found useful in artistic research. Composers have sometimes found the limited sound generation possibilities of models useful for compositional work.

This article presents a model developed for singing synthesis at the Department for Speech Communication and Music Acoustics at KTH, Stockholm. It was originally constructed as an analog synthesizer that was played from a keyboard. It was later modified to be computer controlled.

The vowel synthesis produced by this device sounded quite natural (Sundberg 1978, 1989a). This fact had an unexpected consequence. When played by hand for performing various *vocalises*, that is, singing etudes with the text containing sustained vowels only, the performance sounded so flat and neutral that a listener felt almost offended. The naturalness of the synthesis suggested a living singer behind the performance. However, this "performer's" absence of a desire to communicate anything in particular gave a most displeasing impression. Because of the naturalness of the sound, the listener expected the performance to be not only vocally impressive but also musically convincing.

This suggested the possibility of using this model for a purpose that was both scientific and artistic. Expressive effects in music performance could be analyzed scientifically by applying an analysis-by-synthesis strategy. When an interface was constructed so that the synthesizer could be controlled and played by a computer, the machine could be used for synthesizing expressive effects adding to the musical acceptability of the performance. Thus the model could be used also for research regarding expression in music performance.

This paper first discusses models in more general terms. Then, the KTH model generating singing synthesis is presented. The synthesis of vowels and consonants as well as of certain expressive effects is then described.

## Models

What is a model? Let us first contemplate the different purposes that a model may serve, and also what different kinds of models of the human voice exist.

Models of the human singing voice can be constructed and used for many different purposes, and the way a model is constructed sets the limits for its applicability. One purpose of a model is to serve as a *synthesis machine*, that is, the goal is merely to generate sounds similar to those in singing. For this purpose, any appropriate computer program would do. The construction of such a model may be prompted by compositional needs, of course, but also by scientific needs, for example, for assessing the perceptual significance of an acoustic characteristic that has been found in analysis of sung tones.

However, a model built for synthesis purposes only cannot be used for answering questions regarding voice production, for example, how the vocal tract shape determines vowel quality. Such questions typically require a different type of synthesis model in which there is some functional analogy between the model and the actual thing modeled. For instance, if the relevant question is how the vocal tract works and how it influences the acoustic characteristics of speech sounds, the vocal tract must, of course, be represented in the model.

Let us consider, for example, the research model Gunnar Fant presented 30 years ago (Fant 1960). It was built mainly in order to test the acoustic theory of speech production. The model represented the vocal tract in terms of an electric line analog (figure 9.1). The model consisted of a series of 45 cascaded electric circuits, in which both an inductance and a capacitance could be varied in steps. Each circuit corresponded to a length section of a tube resonator, and each combination of inductance and capacitance in a circuit corresponded to a specific cross-sectional area of the corresponding length section of the tube modeled. The point with this model was that, as predicted by theory, its frequency curve, or its electrical transfer function, was the same as that of the acoustic system modeled. Thus by generating vowel sounds that had the same acoustic properties as real vowel sounds the model acoustically corroborated Fant's theory of voice production.

This model could also be used for many other purposes. It turned out to be an excellent tool for investigating the relationships between vocal

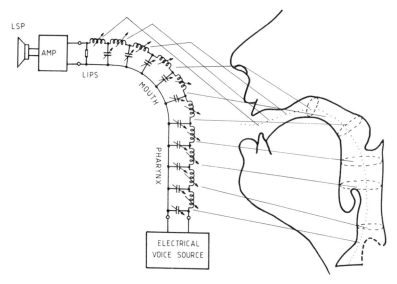

**Figure 9.1**
Fant's (1960) classic electric line analog of the voice. Each section of the vocal tract
corresponds to a LC (inductance/capacitance) circuit, and the entire vocal tract is modeled
by a cascaded series of such circuits. By varying L and C different cross-sectional areas can
be modeled. An amplifier (AMP) and a loudspeaker (LSP) offer the possibility to listen to
the sound.

tract shape and vocal tract resonance frequencies, that is, formant frequencies. Moreover, the model could be extended so as to explain how the
formant frequencies depend on the shape of the vocal tract.

Fant's electric line analog could not answer detailed physiologic questions on vowel production, such as what the acoustic consequences are of
a change of the jaw opening, simply because the jaw opening was not
represented in his model. If the relationships between an articulatory
parameter such as the jaw, the lips, the tongue shape, or the larynx is the
primary issue, in *articulatory model* comprising these structures is obviously
required.

Such articulatory models have been built (Lindblom and Sundberg
1971; Mermelstein, 1973). As illustrated in figure 9.2, the input is a tracing
of the midsagittal profile of the vocal tract that shows a specific positioning
of the various articulators, such as the lips, the lower jaw, or the tongue.
This tracing is then converted to an area function showing how the vocal
tract cross-sectional area varies along the vocal tract length axis. These

# ARTICULATORY MODEL

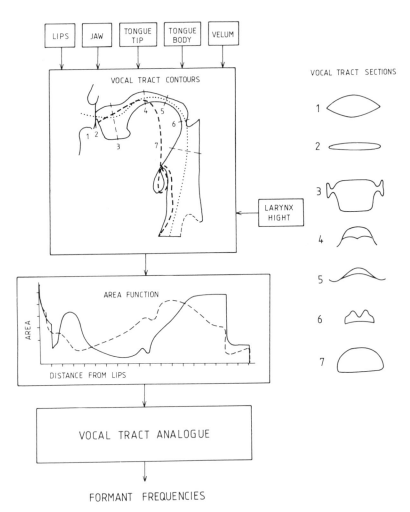

**Figure 9.2**
Schematic illustration of an articulatory model. The lateral x-ray tracing of the vocal tract is transformed into a series of vocal tract sections, so that the cross-sectional area can be estimated. The varying cross-sectional area is plotted as a function of the distance to the lips in the area function, which is realized in the vocal tract analog. This analog may be of the type shown in figure 9.1.

area functions are then implemented on an electric line analog or a computerized cousin of it, so that the formant frequencies can be determined. It this kind of model it is possible to determine the relationship between tongue shape and formant frequencies.

In a recent expansion of our articulatory model Lindblom and I have included also the tongue tip, which allowed us to analyze the articulation also of stop consonants. The vocal tract configuration for such consonants comprise a very abrupt change in vocal tract cross-sectional area. Large steps are difficult to model on a computer model of the vocal tract, because the mathematical equations needed for an accurate description of such area changes are complicated. Therefore, we shifted from a digital to an acoustic model of the vocal tract. It consists of Plexiglas plates, each 0.5 cm thick and with a hole in the center. A number of piles of such plates is available with 16 different sizes of the center hole. Using these plates, any vocal tract configuration could be faithfully modeled and the formant frequencies could be determined by acoustic sweep tone measurements. Thus we ended up with a model which, though serving its purposes, could not be used for generation of even one vowel sound.

There are advantages and drawbacks with all models. An articulatory model is physiologically analogous to the human voice organ and therefore allows manipulations that are physiologically realistic. It is possible on such a model to move the jaw, raise the larynx, or protrude the lips, perhaps even beyond the limits of a real singer. On the other hand, these models often need much computer power and so have a slow turnaround time.

To summarize, a number of different models exist of the voice organ. In one way or another any of these models would be capable of producing synthetic singing. However, their properties vary depending on the purpose for which they were being constructed, and therefore their usefulness for generating synthetic singing also varies.

**General versus Dedicated Models**

Let us now disregard the case that the model is being built for research purposes, and focus on models used for synthesis purposes only. It was mentioned that the purpose is decisive to the way in which a model is constructed. But the way in which a model is constructed also affects how easy it is to use for synthesis. From the user's point of view, a particularly important aspect is to what extent the model offers flexibility and fidelity. The advantage of flexibility seems obvious and needs no explication. The advantage of fidelity, on the other hand, may be worth commenting on, particularly as flexibility and fidelity are often conflicting properties.

It is easy to lose the vowel quality of a synthesized sound, even in cases where the typical spectral characteristics of human vowels are accurately replicated (Sundberg 1989b). Hypothetically, anything can destroy the naturalness if it does not faithfully reproduce the salient sound characteristics of the human voice organ.

This implies that the more flexible a singing voice model is, the higher the risk is that it will produce sounds which do not sound human. Locating the problem may not always be simple. For this reason it may sometimes be easier to work with high fidelity models than with high flexibility models. In any event, efficient use of flexible singing voice models requires a thorough acquaintance with voice acoustics and physiology.

Here I have mainly been considering naturalness. Still I realize that naturalness is by no means always a typical demand on synthesized singing. On the contrary, lack of naturalness may be what the composer needs in a given musical context. Still, according to what has been demonstrated so far, it seems that naturalness is far more difficult to obtain than unnaturalness.

## The KTH Model MUSSE

The KTH model MUSSE (Music and Singing Synthesis Equipment) has been developed over many years at the Department for Speech Communication and Music Acoustics, KTH. The first results, obtained by playing the keyboard and using one vowel setting at a time, were presented about a decade ago (Larsson 1977; Sundberg 1978). When the interface was constructed the synthesizer could be controlled by the computer. This offered opportunities for experimenting with synthesis of sung consonants. In 1984 Jan Gauffin and I made the first attempts in this direction, and we were later joined by Jan Zera during his stay as a guest researcher from the Warsaw Academy of Music (Sundberg 1987a; Zera, Gauffin, and Sundberg 1984).

The system works reasonably well in the situations in which it has been tried. A development of a modern digital version is under way. The synthesis recipes presented later are tentative in character, and some of them will, we hope, be improved in the future.

## Equipment

The synthesis is realized on a formant synthesizer controlled by a Data General ECLIPSE minicomputer (Larsson 1977). Figure 9.3 gives an overview of the setup. The input is written on a music staff on the computer screen by means of a notation editor NOTIN, written by Johan Liljencrants. This notation is converted into a quasiphonetic code specifying vowel, pitch name, octave number, and duration. By editing this code, consonants, diphthongs, and so forth, as well as signs for phrase boundaries, chord changes, and other factors can be inserted.

The quasiphonetic code is processed by the RULSYS program, developed by Carlsson and Granström (1975). It is a musical cousin of their

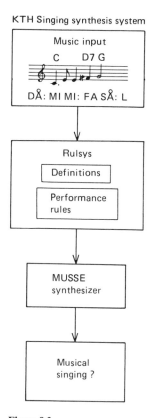

**Figure 9.3**
Block schema of the KTH singing synthesis system

text-to-speech conversion system. The system contains a set of definitions, assigning to each symbol phonetic features, such as front vowel, rounded, consonant, vocalic, voiced, and so on, as shown in figure 9.3. The definitions also attribute formant frequencies, bandwidths, source amplitude, constants for control signal filtering, and other parameters.

The system also contains contains a set of ordered, context-dependent rules. The format of a rule is quite simple: the basic form is "Every note possessing the characteristics. A, B, C, ... should be assigned the characteristics of D, E, F, ... provided that it is preceded by G, H, I, ... and followed by J, K, L, ...." The context conditions are optional.

The rules process each note in the sequence given in the input notation. Yet there are means to fetch values from tones far back and ahead in the sequence of note symbols. For instance, the system offers the possibility of letting the duration of a note depend on the pitch of the last note in the phrase. On the other hand, we do not make use of lexicons or any other straightforward means to deal with exceptions in our music system.

The output of the RULSYS program serves as the control signals for the MUSSE synthesizer. The MUSSE synthesizer, shown in figure 9.4, consists of a source oscillator generating a sawtooth signal with variable DC offset, as illustrated in figure 9.5. It allows variation of the pulse amplitude at the expense of the closed phase. The spectrum envelope slopes off at a rate of no more than 6 dB/octave, for reasons of noise reduction.

When the vocal intensity is increased, the higher overtones of the human voice gain more in amplitude than the lower overtones (Sundberg 1987b). In varying the overall amplitude of the synthetic source, a physiologic volume control circuit is used in order to generate a corresponding effect. Thus a 10 dB level change at 500 Hz is accompanied by a 15 dB level change at 3 KHz. This arrangement is quite important; when not included, crescendos sound merely like a reduction of microphone distance and vice versa.

This source signal is fed to five cascaded formant circuits with variable frequencies and, for the three lowest formants, also variable bandwidths. The manually controlled bandwidths of the two highest formants are set at 150 Hz. A higher-pole correction is provided in terms of a resonance circuit at 4,500 Hz with a wide bandwidth. The advantage with the cascaded arrangement of the formant circuits is that the amplitudes of the formants are automatically tuned according to the acoustic theory of voice production. This promotes natural-sounding vowels and consonants.

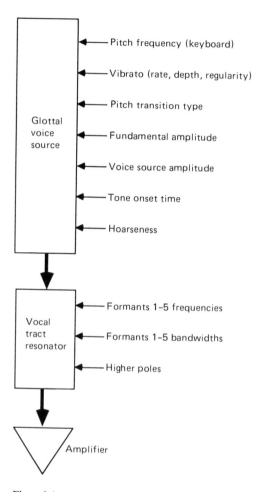

**Figure 9.4**
Block schema of the MUSSE singing synthesizer

**Figure 9.5**
Source waveform used in the MUSSE synthesizer, consisting of a sawtooth signal with a variable DC offset. This offset differs between the waveforms shown by the solid and dashed contours.

All consonants are produced with these means, except for the fricatives. For these, two computer-controlled noise generators are used, one at glottal end of the formant chain, and one at the lip end.

**Rules of Vowels and Consonants**

The basic strategy is to use target (locus) values for formant frequencies and bandwidths and for the source parameters. Thus the formants, bandwidths, and other parameters are changed between preset target values at a rate that can be varied. Some of the target values are modified by context-dependent rules, modelling coarticulation depending on the mentioned features. The transitions are smoothed by means of programmable filters. The characteristics of this smoothing are illustrated in figure 9.6.

Certain problems appeared with an unexpected clarity when the synthesis equipment was ready. One was the *timing of pitch change*. Intuitively, it may appear reasonable that the pitch is maintained throughout the tone and then changed. However, it can also be argued that the new note should start on its target pitch. The two cases are illustrated in figure 9.7. Informal listening tests have demonstrated that the former case sounds clearly

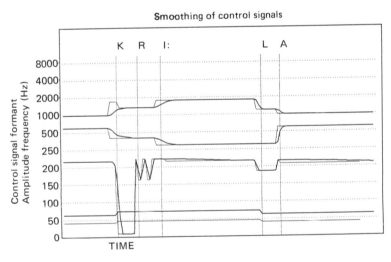

**Figure 9.6**
Smoothing of formant frequency changes. The thin and heavy contours show the control signals before and after smoothing, respectively. The text at the top is a phonetic transcription of the text; the colon sign (:) represents a long vowel. The dots on the horizontal lines represent 10 msec intervals.

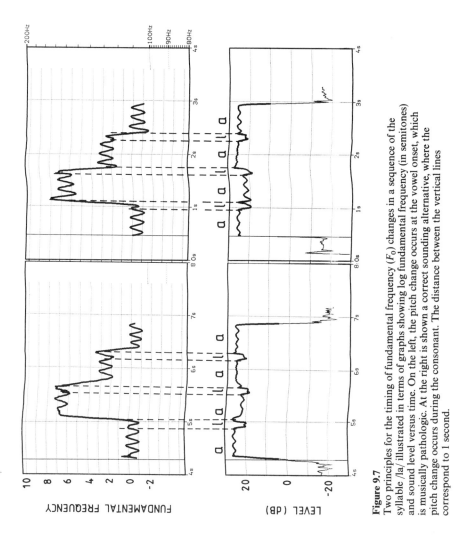

**Figure 9.7**
Two principles for the timing of fundamental frequency ($F_0$) changes in a sequence of the syllable /la/ illustrated in terms of graphs showing log fundamental frequency (in semitones) and sound level versus time. On the left, the pitch change occurs at the vowel onset, which is musically pathologic. At the right is shown a correct sounding alternative, where the pitch change occurs during the consonant. The distance between the vertical lines correspond to 1 second.

pathologic while the latter sounds correct. Thus, the general principle seems to be that the singer executes the pitch change at the end of the old note and not in the beginning of a new note.

*Duration of vowels and consonants.* In many languages, stress is signalled by syllable duration, so that vowels in stressed syllable are long, and in composition of songs, stressed syllables are often placed on metrically stressed positions within the bar, and vice versa. It seems necessary to mark stress also in singing nonsense texts. If a melody is performed using the syllable /la:/ for all notes, and all the /l/ sounds are 150 msec long, the result is musically poor. It is considerably improved if a different set of formant frequencies corresponding to the vowel [a] are used for all vowels in metrically unstressed position, that is for all "short" syllables. Another improvement is to lengthen consonants following such "short" vowels by 20% of the duration of the preceding vowel (figure 9.8).

*Syllable/note coordination.* If each note is sung on one syllable and the consonants need to be of various lengths depending on the the metrical position, the timing of syllables in relation to the notes is crucial.

One possibility is to subtract the duration of the consonant from the vowel following it. However, this solution does not correctly represent the musical rhythmic pattern. Another possibility is to subtract the durations of the consonants from the vowel preceding it, so that each note starts with a vowel as shown in figure 9.9. In this case the note is assigned not a complete

**Figure 9.8**
Principles for timing of consonants and vowels. The text is a sequence of the syllable /la:/, the colon sign representing long vowel. In the upper row all vowels are long and all consonants have the same duration except for the shortest note. In the lower row the long vowel /a:/ is used in stressed positions while the short vowel /a/ is used in unstressed positions; also, the principle is applied that short vowels are followed by long consonants and vice versa and the duration of a consonant is subtracted from the preceding vowel.

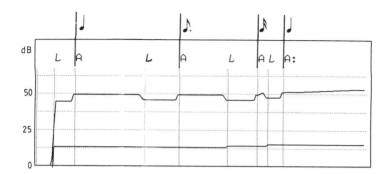

**Figure 9.9**
Synchronization of syllables and tones. Vowel and consonant durations are in accordance
with the lower row of figure 9.8; consonants are subtracted from the preceding vowel, so
that each note starts with a vowel.

syllable, but rather two complementary parts of two adjacent syllables.
This alternative clearly gives the correct representation of the rhythmic
pattern. Thus it seems that words are chopped into syllables according to
different principles in singing and orthography. On the other hand, orthography is different from speech; in verse reading consonants seem to be distributed in the same way as in singing (G. Fant personal communication).

*Marcato.* In music as in other types of human communication it is
necessary to emphasize certain events. In general, emphasis seems to result
from increases in the rate of change of sound parameters. Figure 9.10 shows
the voice pitch frequency behavior of a singer performing a vocalise, that
is, a song with no consonants in the text. We see that in downward pitch
changes the singer overshoots the target frequency and then returns up to
it. This generates a clear *marcato,* or emphasis effect. The effect is enhanced
if each note is marked also by a rapid increase and decrease of the amplitude
as shown in figure 9.11.

*Timbral legato.* It seems that for the purpose of musical expression good
musicians make use of all the means for acoustic variation that the instrument offers. In the human voice, these means are rich, to say the least. Thus
the formant frequencies of each vowel can be used for musical expression.
If the formant frequencies for all vowels but one are taken from the same
singer, the tone sung with the alien formant frequencies sounds emphasized.
If it is a structurally prominent note, the result is musically convincing,
otherwise it sounds clearly pathologic.

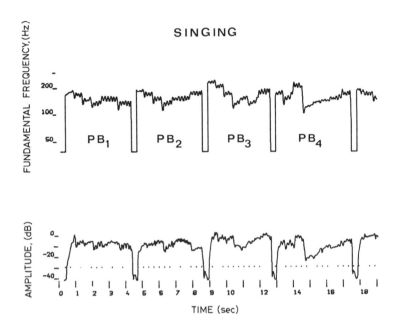

**Figure 9.10**
Fundamental frequency (upper curve) and sound level (lower curve) of a professional baritone singer performing an excerpt of a song. Markings of note boundaries by fundamental frequency overshoots can be observed in descending intervals.

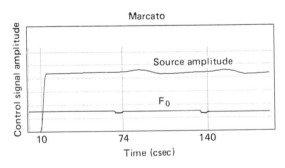

**Figure 9.11**
Synthesized marcato in a part of a descending scale sung on a sustained vowel. The effect was generated by fundamental frequency ($F_0$) overshoots combined with quick increases and decreases of the voice source amplitude on each tone. The frequency curve is shown before smoothing. The horizontal dotted lines represent a sound level difference of 12.5 dB.

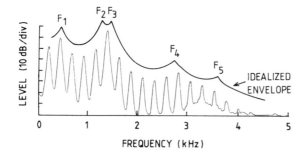

**Figure 9.12**
A spectrum and its envelope of a vowel where the frequencies of formants number 2 and 3 ($F_2$ and $F_3$) are tuned to the vicinity of spectrum partial number 6. As a consequence, the amplitude of this partial is considerably enhanced.

*Let the formants sing*! Obviously, a computer-controlled singing synthesizer can control pitch and formant frequencies much more quickly and accurately than human singers. One way of exploiting this possibility is to tune formants to partials.

From the theory of vowel production we know that the vocal tract resonances, or the formants, enhance those spectrum partials that are closest to them in frequency. If two formants both approach the frequency of a spectrum partial, the amplitude of that partial becomes very strong, as in figure 9.12. In such cases the partial may be perceived as an individual tone with a clearly identifiable pitch.

Of course, it is easy to play around with the formants in a systematic way, so as to play melodies on the harmonic spectrum partials, as shown in figure 9.13. As long as the fundamental frequency of the spectrum is kept constant, we have only the series of the natural harmonics to play with, just like a trumpet without valves.

But it is also possible to change the fundamental frequency of the drone. If it is moved one fifth up or one fifth down one gets access to a set of tones representing the complete diatonic scale. Hence all melodies can be played that use the tones of the diatonic scale.

Some singers use this special kind of singing already. The so-called Harmonic Choir, working in New York and Paris is one example (Hykes 1987). The so-called Tibetan chant is another example (Smith, Stevens, and Tomlinson 1967).

MULTIPLE PITCH SINGING

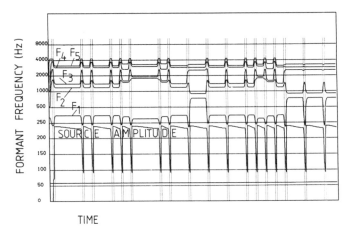

**Figure 9.13**
Patterns for formant frequencies $1-5$ $(F_1-F_5)$ for playing a melody by enhancing overtones of a drone tone of constant fundamental frequency and slightly modulated voice source amplitude. $F_2$ and $F_3$ are used for enhancing partials between 1 and 2 KHz, but for enhancing a partial below 1 KHz a clustering of $F_1$ and $F_2$ is used.

## Rules for Musical Expression

In addition to the rules for synthesizing vowels and consonants, we have also implemented some rules for musical expression that were originally developed for synthesized performance of instrumental music. These rules have been developed over a long period of time and have been reported in several publications (Sundberg 1983, 1988; Sundberg and Frydén 1985; Sundberg, Friberg, and Frydén 1989; Thompson, Sundberg, and Frydén 1989). They have also been applied successfully, with minor modifications, to contemporary keyboard music (Friberg et al. 1988).

In traditional harmonic music, there is no equality among chords. Some chords are "remarkable," and others are not. It seems that musicians are required to mark the remarkableness of musical events, such as chords. We have derived a measure that we call *harmonic charge* for quantizing the remarkableness of chords within a given tonality framework. The harmonic charge for a set of chords is shown in figure 9.14.

The harmonic charge is a weighted sum of the chord notes' *melodic charge* shown in the same figure. It represents the remarkableness of the

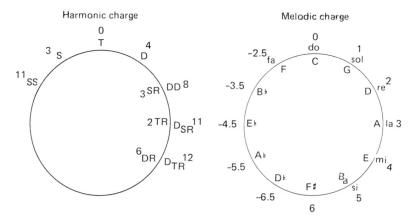

**Figure 9.14**
Harmonic charge for a set of chords (left): T = tonic, D = dominant, S = subdominant,
R = relative, DD = double dominant, SS = double subdominant, and melodic charge for
the diatonic scale tones (right).

scale tones as related to the root of the chord over which they appear; when calculating the harmonic charge, the tonic is used as the reference. The melodic charge corresponds to the positions along the circle of fifths, using the root of the reference chord as "12 o'clock"; the scale tone's on the subdominant side are more charged than the corresponding ones on the dominant side.

The harmonic charge shows a relationship with listeners' estimations of the remarkableness of chords according to independent experiments carried out by Carol Krumhansl at the Cornell University (Krumhansl 1987; Sundberg and Frydén 1987). In these experiments Krumhansl first played a cadence to establish a sense of tonality and then a "probe chord." The subjects' task was to rate how well the probe chord served as a continuation of the cadence. The correlation between harmonic charge and these ratings is shown in figure 9.15.

In our program performance, changes in harmonic charge in a harmonic progression generates crescendos/decrescendos. The technicalities are as follows. The harmonic charge is coverted into an amplitude increment typically amounting to 3 dB for the chord shift C major to A major. This amplitude increment is added to the first tone appearing over each chord. Then the amplitudes of the intermediate tones are linearly interpolated on a dB scale. Excessively slow crescendos are avoided by letting the amplitude

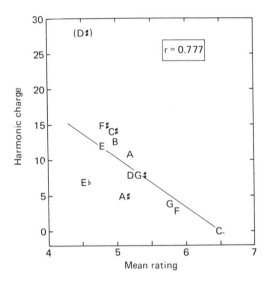

**Figure 9.15**
Relation between harmonic charge and mean probe chord ratings obtained in experiments
where subjects rated how well different chords served as a continuation of a preceding,
tonality defining cadence, according to Krumhansl (1987). Symbols represent the root of
major chords. The correlation coefficient $r$ for a linear regression analysis is shown in the
frame.

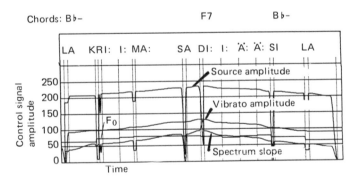

**Figure 9.16**
Effect on some performance parameters of the harmonic charge rules. The harmonic charge
of the chords, given in the top line, are 0, 4, and 0. On the sound level scale a difference of
25 dB corresponds to 100 units. The text is given in a phonetic transcription, where the
colon sign (:) represents long vowel. These performance rules affect the voice source
amplitude, the depth of the vibrato undulations of fundamental frequency and the spectrum
tilt.

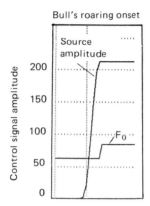

**Figure 9.17**
Patterns for voice source amplitude and fundamental frequency $F_0$ (before smoothing) in the "bull's roaring onset"; $F_0$ starts 11 semitones below the target which it reaches after about 300 msec (after $F_0$ smoothing), while the voice source amplitude increases from zero to the target during the initial 40 msec of the tone. The interval between adjacent dots on the time scale corresponds to 10 msec, and 25 dB corresponds to 100 units along the control signal amplitude scale.

remain constant until about 2 seconds before the next chord appears. The result is crescendos toward chords having a higher harmonic charge than the preceding chord, and decrescendos toward chords having a lower harmonic charge than the preceding chord, as shown in figure 9.16.

In addition, the amplitude of the vibrato undulations and, as mentioned, the slope of the source spectrum vary with the source amplitude. Also, the notes are slightly lengthened and shortened in proportion to the sound level increase so that, for example, a crescendo is accompanied by a slight, gradual decrease in tempo.

Another rule for musical expression is applied to high notes appearing after a pause. In these cases the fundamental frequency sweeps quickly one octave up to the target frequency during the tone onset. (Figure 9.17). In the laboratory this effect is called the "bull's roaring onset."

**Rules for Choral Synthesis**

Together with my laboratory colleagues Sten Ternström and Anders Friberg, I have also attempted to synthesize choral sounds (Ternström Fribery, and Sundberg 1988). As yet, we have refrained from synthesizing consonants; after all, consonants are often rather hard to perceive clearly even when many real choirs perform!

The origin of the chorus is assumed to be a random variation in the amplitude of the spectrum partials. Presumably it arises as a consequence of a finite fundamental frequency agreement between the choral singers. Initially, several attempts were spent trying to read one digitally stored waveform simultaneously at slightly differing speeds. However, we invariably encountered artifacts in terms of very salient and disturbing beat patterns. A great improvement occurred when we stored two waveforms and read those at independently irregular speeds.

The piece contained six different vowels. Real versions of these vowel sounds were collected from eight choral singers and were analyzed with regard to formant frequencies. Using these formant values each of the eight singers' vowels were synthesized on the MUSSE singing synthesizer, and one period of each of these waveforms was stored in a Casio digital sampler synthesizer. In this way a total of $6 \times 8 = 48$ vowel waveforms were stored on the sampler. A small fundamental frequency discrepancy, ranging from 16 cents for the bass part to 4 cents in the soprano part was introduced between the two voices in each part. A random function built into the sampler was used which, however, was very far from realistic. Finally digital reverberation was added, which is highly important for creating the typical choral sound.

Thus the choir consisted of eight choral singers, all synthesized by the MUSSE singing synthesizer and performing as a choir according to the recipe just demonstrated. The orchestra was synthesized by two synthesizers. All three synthesizers were controlled from an Apple Macintosh II computer, in which the performance rules mentioned before were implemented.

## Conclusion

Analysis by synthesis is an excellent strategy for developing a description of the important features of very complicated systems. However, in a sense it can only provide relative evidence and can never prove that the description tried is the best possible. For instance, we would not like to assert that our recipe for synthesizing singing is the best possible. We do propose that, at least with the quality obtained in the examples, singing can be synthesized by means of a rule system of ordered, context-dependent rules that operate on the music and the phonetic text.

## Acknowledgments

This is a revised version of the auther's presentation at the International Workshop on Models of Singing Voice and Musical Sounds, Sorrento, October 1988. Sound examples demonstrating most of these effects have been published on a compact disc (Mathews and Pierce, 1989). This project was supported by the National Bank of Sweden Tercentenary Foundation and, as regards the choral synthesis, also by the Rector's office at KTH.

## References

Carlson, R., A. Friberg, L. Frydén, B. Granström and J. Sundberg. 1989. "Speech and music performance: parallels and contrasts." *Contemporary Music Review* 4: 389–402.

Carlsson, R., and B. Granström. 1975. "A phonetically oriented programming language for rule description of speech." In G. Fant, ed. 1975. *Speech Communication II*, Stockholm: Almqvist and Wiksell. pp. 245–253.

Fant, G. 1960. *Acoustic Theory of Speech Production.* The Hague: s-Gravenhage.

Friberg, A., L. Frydén, L.-G. Bodin, and J. Sundberg. 1988. "Performance rules for computer." In D. Tommassini, ed. 1988. *Atti di VII Colloquio di Informatica Musicale.* Rome: Musica Verticale. pp. 92–96.

Hykes, D. 1987. "Harmonic singing and the Harmonic Choir." *Journal of the Acoustical Society of America* 82(S1): 68.

Krumhansl, L. 1987. "Tonal and harmonic hierarchies." In J. Sundberg, ed. 1987. *Harmony and Tonality.* Pub. No. 54. Stockholm: Royal Swedish Academy of Music. pp. 13–32.

Larsson, B. 1977. "Music and singing synthesis equipment (MUSSE)." *Speech Transmission Laboratory Quarterly Progress and Status Report* 1/1977: 38–40.

Lindblom, B. and J. Sundberg. 1971. "Acoustical consequences of lip, tongue, jaw, and larynx movement." *Journal of the Acoustical Society of America* 50: 1166–1179.

Mathews, M., and J. Pierce. 1989. *Current Directions in Computer Music Research* (with sound examples on a compact disc.) Cambridge, Massachusetts: MIT Press.

Mermelstein, P. 1973. "Articulatory model for the study of speech production." *Journal of the Acoustical Society of America* 53: 1070–1082.

Smith, H., K. Stevens, and R. Tomlinson. 1967. "On an unusual mode of chanting by certain Tibetan Lamas." *Journal of the Acoustical Society of America* 41: 1262–64.

Sundberg, J. 1978. "Synthesis of singing." *Swedish Journal of Musicology* 60(1): 107–112.

Sundberg, J. 1983. "Musical performance: a synthesis-by-rule approach." *Computer Music Journal* 7(1): 37–43. With sound examples. Reprinted in C. Roads, ed. 1989. *The Music Machine.* Cambridge, Massachusetts: MIT Press. pp. 693–699.

Sundberg, J. 1987a. "Synthesis of singing." In C. Acreman, I. Ortosecco and F. Razzi, eds. 1987. *Musica e Tecnologia: Industria e Cultura per lo Sviluppo del Mezzogiorno.* Quaderni di Musica/Realta 14, Proceedings of Associazione Informatica Musicale Italiana Milano: Edizioni Unicopli. pp. 145–161.

Sundberg, J. 1987b. *The Science of the Singing Voice.* DeKalb: Northern Illinois University Press.

Sundberg, J. 1988. "Computer synthesis of music performance." In J. Sloboda, ed. 1988. *Generative Processes in Music.* Oxford: Clarendon Press. pp. 52–69.

Sundberg, J. 1989a. "Synthesis of singing by rule." In M. Mathews and J. Pierce, eds. *Current Directions in Computer Music Research.* Cambridge, Massachusetts: MIT Press.

Sundberg, J. 1989b. "Lundamöte."

Sundberg J., and L. Frydén. 1985. "Teaching a computer to play melodies musically." In *Analytica—Studies in the Description and Analysis of Music in honor of Ingmar Bengtsson.* Publication No 47. Stockholm: Royal Swedish Academy of Music.

Sundberg, J., and L. Frydén. 1987. "Melodic charge and music performance." In J. Sundberg, ed. 1987. *Harmony and Tonality.* Stockholm, Royal Swedish Academy of Music, Publ. Nr 54. pp. 53–58.

Sundberg, J., A. Friberg, and L. Frydén. 1989. "Rules for automated performance of ensemble music." *Contemporary Music Review* 3: 89–109.

Ternström, S., A. Friberg, and J. Sundberg. 1988. "Monteverdi's Vespers. A case study in music." *Speech Transmission Laboratory Quarterly Progress and Status Report* 2-3/1988. pp. 93–105.

Thompson, W., J. Sundberg, and L. Frydén. 1989. "The use of rules for expression in performance of music." *Psychology of music* 17: 63–82.

Zera, J, J. Gauffin, and J. Sundberg. 1984. "Synthesis of selected VCV-syllables in singing." *Speech Transmission Laboratory Quarterly Progress and Status Report* 2-3/1984. pp. 119–126.

# IV ARCHITECTURES AND OBJECT REPRESENTATIONS OF MUSICAL SIGNALS

# Overview

## Curtis Roads

A hardware and software architecture is the core of a computer music system. It can open up new possibilities for music-making, or it can constrain musical expression. It shapes the way the musician must conceive of and realize a musical idea, and therefore it cannot be neglected.

The articles in this part are directly concerned with the substrate technologies of computer music system. The first paper, by Guy E. Garnett, is a survey of music representations that weaves a coherent view through a latticework of philosophical theories and available technologies. The author compares score, synthesis, and signal processing languages in an effort to find the most important features. The goal of the survey is a representational foundation for the next generation of music workstations. Because of the importance of time in musical performance, the study places particular emphasis on models of time and temporal knowledge.

Carla Scaletti and Kurt Hebel's KYMA is a hardware and software music system based on an elegant concept: *sound objects*—a general representation for music that can equally incorporate data (such as sound files or lists of notes) as well as procedures for generating sound (including arbitrary musical transformations). Of course the term "sound object" or "object sonore" is not new; it derives from Pierre Schaeffer (1977) and dates back to the 1940s. Like Schaeffer's object sonore, the Scaletti-Hebel sound object paradigm is flexible enough to represent any sound, not only those sounds that can be represented in standard music notation and produced on traditional music instruments.

The Scaletti-Hebel approach resembles the work of William Buxton and his Toronto colleagues over a decade ago (Buxton et al. 1978) in that it turns an innovative representation scheme into a practical system. The result is one of the most interesting musical workstations yet developed, complete with its own signal processing engine, and coded in the Smalltalk language.

Many sound synthesis techniques developed in the past two decades, such as frequency modulation (Chowning 1973) and waveshaping (LeBrun 1979, Arfib 1979), were designed to make efficient use of limited computational resources. Although these techniques can be used to emulate traditional instruments, there is usually an audible degree of approximation involved.

In contrast, some of the techniques discussed in this book, such as wavelet transforms and granular analysis-synthesis, permit exact reconstruction of a given sound signal. Physical model synthesis, discussed in part III of this book, provides a much closer approximation to the behavior of a instrument than, for example, waveshaping. This is because there is a tighter correspondence between the synthesis algorithm and the physics of the instrument. Not surprisingly, techniques such as analysis-synthesis and physical modeling require much larger amounts of computational power.

Fortunately, new architectures for digital processing are emerging to meet this need. Sergio Caveliere's contribution to this part is survey and tutorial on architectures for signal processing. He discusses the internal design of individual processors (including recent floating-point DSP chips) and parallel designs that interconnect many processors for simultaneous operation. Presently several different approaches to parallel processing compete with one another. The author compares the features of data flow, systolic array, wavefront array, and connectionist architectures and explains their benefits and liabilities in audio signal processing applications.

## References

Arfib, D. 1979. "Digital synthesis of complex spectra by means of multiplication of non-linear distorted sine waves." *Journal of the Audio Engineering Society* 27(10): 757–779.

Buxton, W., W. Reeves, R. Baecker, and L. Mezei. 1978. "The use of hierarchy and instance in a data structure for computer music." *Computer Music Journal* 2(4): 10–20. Revised and updated version in C. Roads and J. Strawn, eds. 1985. *Foundations of Computer Music*. Cambridge, Massachusetts: MIT Press. pp. 443–466.

Chowning, J. 1973. "The synthesis of complex audio spectra by means of frequency modulation." *Journal of the Audio Engineering Society* 21(7): 526–534. Reprinted in C. Roads and J. Strawn, eds. 1985. *Foundations of Computer Music*. Cambridge, Massachusetts: MIT Press. pp. 6–29.

LeBrun, M. 1979. "Digital waveshaping synthesis." *Journal of the Audio Engineering Society* 27(4): 250–266.

Schaeffer, P. 1977. *Traité des Objets Musicaux*. Second edition. Paris: Editions de Seuil.

# 10 Music, Signals, and Representations: A Survey

Guy E. Garnett

This paper gives an overview of signals and implementations of signals from a musician's perspective. In particular, the notion of a *music signal* is defined that is useful in many musical contexts. General models of computation are presented as a background for a discussion of implementations of signals. The semantics of programs are discussed with particular emphasis on functional programming, object-oriented programming, and logic programming. Since time is of crucial importance to music, the paper also examines various models of time and temporal knowledge. It then discusses existing models of signals and present descriptions of existing programs by way of examples. The survey is not meant to be exhaustive but merely to exemplify the various types of systems currently in use. The final section of the paper is a proposed signal model, based on many of the ideas covered in the rest of the survey.

## Signals

The notion of information is indeed clear enough, nowadays, when properly relativized. It is central to the theory of communication. It makes sense relative to one or another preassigned matrix of alternatives—one or another checklist. You have to say in advance what features are going to count. (Quine 1970)

A *signal* is a representation of information. It should not be confused with the information itself, nor should it be confused with the medium that carries it. The particular kinds of signals I am concerned with here will be called music signals to distinguish them from both the concept of "signal" as used in information theory and the concept of "signal" prevalent in engineering theory, though there are many similarities with the latter. For the purposes of this paper, music signals are defined specifically as representations of information from the physical domain of music and not including representations of information belonging to the perceptual or cognitive domains of music. The differences between these domains are discussed in more detail later. As I will show, music signals, as defined, differ from the common engineering concept of "signal' in that they are more inclusive. In the main, the engineering concept of "signal" includes only functions of time. Music signals will be seen to include some other related concepts as well.

The distinctions between the physical, perceptual, and cognitive domains of music are simply this: the *physical* domain of music is primarily that which we perceive through our senses, the auditory phenomenon itself. The most common example of this domain is the variation in air pressure associated with performed (or recorded) music. The *perceptual* domain is more the psychoacoustic percept itself; it is not so much the air pressure variations themselves but what our ear makes of them. An example here might be the fact that we hear periodic and quasi-periodic waveforms in a certain frequency range as having a pitch. Finally, the *cognitive* domain of music has to do with how we make sense of these perceptions, the syntactic and semantic structures we "make" of the music. For example, the way certain dispositions of pitches form or relate to a conception of tonality. It is the cognitive domain that most differentiates the specifically musical from the other fields of auditory study. This definition of a music signal is designed so that it includes, among other things, acoustic waveforms but excludes such things as notated scores.

In this paper, I am concerned mainly with music signals that can be manipulated in digital computing systems. These are called *digital music signals*, digital representations of physical-domain music information. The following section discusses in more detail the kinds and natures of these signals.

## Music Signals

Music signals can be divided into three classes: acoustic, analytic, and parametric signals. I will discuss musical applications of each of these kinds of signals.

### Acoustic Music Signals

Acoustic music signals are strictly concerned with the variation of air pressure over time, whether the variation is caused by an instrument such as a violin or flute, or whether it is caused by electronic devices such as oscillators, amplifiers, loudspeakers, digital-to-analog converters (DACs), or any number of electronic means of sound production. One of the most prevalent and most significant acoustic music signals is the acoustic waveform (often called the *time-domain waveform* in the literature). The information here (or, at least, the information we want to select) is a pattern of in air pressure; the air itself serves as a medium or communication channel to convey that information from one place to another.

This same acoustic information can be (to a sufficient degree of accuracy) represented in other ways: by a continuous variation in electrical voltage; by a continuous variation of displacement of a speaker cone or ear membrane; by a continuous variation of an electromagnetic field (radio, for example); by a sequence of digitally represented magnitudes proportional to the acoustic pressure or proportional to the electrical voltage. What each of these has in common is variation of some quantity over time. Thus, acoustic information can be represented by (possibly multivalued) functions of time.

It should be noted that a digitized version of a sound pressure waveform does not represent the sound pressure waveform, it only represents the acoustic information content of that waveform. Furthermore it represents only that portion of the total information that has been "selected" by the analog-to-digital converters (ADCs), namely, only the variations that fall within a particular amplitude and frequency range and only to within certain levels of quantization. This is what Quine, in the previous quote, meant by information making sense relative to some preassigned matrix of alternatives. We must choose what aspect of the information is significant. For example, we may decide that we only need to represent a certain bandwidth (say, 0 KHz to 22.05 KHz) and only some range of amplitude variation, and only the variations at a particular point in space. Information theory (Shannon and Weaver 1949) can help us determine how many symbols (or how many bits) we need and at what rate we need them in order to accurately characterize this information. But it cannot tell us what information is important in the first place.

### Analytic Music Signals

Another class of music signals are those directly derivable from acoustic signals by means of more-or-less standard mathematical techniques; thus they are most often used in digital form. These signals will be termed *analytic*. This use of the word "analytic" should not be confused with the concept of an analytic function, a function that is differentiable at every point. My meaning here is also different from the use of the term "analytic" to describe a signal "in which the frequency response is zero for negative frequencies" (Rabiner and Gold 1975). The meaning I have in mind here derives primiarily from two sources. One source is the common language concept of analyzing some complex into its constituent parts, such as when an acoustic signal is "analyzed" to reveal its frequency components. The other concept involved derives from the philosopher Kant, mainly by way of Frege. In this sense, all the truths of mathematics and logic are said to be analytic truths (it is distinguished from empirically derived "truth" which is said to be "synthetic"). By this definition, an analytic music signal is one that is derived from another music signal mathematically or logically.

The literature of signal processing theory often does not consider representations of analytic information to be signals at all. However, in practical computer programs this analytic information is often represented similarly or identically to the acoustic information. Therefore I feel justified in including representations of such information in the class of music signals.

Some standard analytic music signals (in this special sense) are the *Fourier transform* of an acoustic signal (Rabiner and Gold 1975, pp. 24–25), the *Wigner distribution* (Claasen and Mecklenbraüker 1980), the *autocorrelation* of an acoustic signal (Rabiner and Gold 1975, p. 401), and the *wavelet transforms* (see chapters 2 and 4). Ascertaining the mathematical properties of such signals is the primary work of signal processing theory. Most of these transformations are "information-preserving" transformations; hence these analytic signals denote the same information as their acoustic counterparts, and they can be characterized as different representations of the same information. Indeed, it is usually possible to move back and forth between a digital acoustic signal and a corresponding analytic signal with little or no loss of information. Nonetheless, the connotative differences between the two classes of signals are usually of great significance.

Most analytic music signals are not functions of time—or, at most, they may be functions of time and another variable. The Wigner distribution, for example, is a function of time and frequency. But as I will illustrate later, in most musical applications, analytic music signals are almost always closely associated with time.

## Parametric Music Signals

Parametric music signals are associated with models of musical sound production and the parameters that are needed to instantiate and drive the models. In a discussion of speech, Rabiner and Schafer (1978) describe a similar concept: "Parametric representations ... are concerned with representing the speech signal as the output of a model for speech production" (p. 6). Similarly, parametric signals are the input to a parameterized model for musical sound production. Thus a simple bandpass filter can be a model of an acoustic resonator; the parametric signals associated with it are the various, possibly time-varying, coefficients and internal states needed to drive the model. For another example, a common model of speech production is a linear time-varying filter, with the appropriate time-varying parameters, driven by a pulse generator with its own set of time-varying parameters. The translation between acoustic signals and information-equivalent parametric signals is currently the subject of much research. This field is known as *parameter estimation* or *system identification* and is mostly dominated by research on speech (see for example Flanagan 1972). Most of these signals are functions mapping time into model parameters.

### Summary of Music Signals

Thus the signals I am concerned with here are broad ranging. Table 10.1 should help make this division of the music signals clear. Although many music signals can be classified as functions of time, a significant number cannot. But even those that cannot be thus classified are nevertheless derived from functions of time or translatable into functions of time. For this reason, time must play a large and important part in any representation of music signals. The other needs of representations for music signals are discussed next, while the importance of time and temporal representations are discussed in greater detail in a separate section later in this paper.

**Table 10.1**
Music Signals

| Domain | Acoustic | Analytic | Parametric |
|--------|----------|----------|------------|
| Origin | Time-pressure waveforms | Derived from time-pressure waveforms | Derived from models of sound production |
| Examples | Sounds, electrical sound signals (from a microphone), digital sound signals (from an ADC), sampled sounds | Fourier transforms, autocorrelations | Control signals, model parameters, synthesizer parameters, LPC coefficients |

## Representation of Music Signals

Nothing is ever represented either shorn of or in the fullness of its properties. A picture never merely represents X, but rather represents X as a man or represents X to be a mountain. (Goodman 1976)

This section presents a brief overview of the general requirements for representing music signals in computers. Since the field of representation is vast and cannot be thoroughly covered here, the present goal is merely to supply a context for later discussion of specific examples.

Representation in computer systems can be conceived of as lying along a continuum from the most specific and local to the most general and global. The most specific end of this spectrum contains representations of the most primitive data elements or the most machine-specific elements. This includes numeric representations and ASCII code, as well as things like machine addresses and ports. The other extreme of this continuum encompasses representations of cognitive data, including knowledge, ideas, and relationships. Representations that are relatively close to the former are often termed *data structures* or *data representations*. Representations closer to the latter are more often termed *knowledge representations*. Figure 10.1 shows this schematically. Most signals, so far as they have been implemented in computers, usually have been implemented at close to the data structure level. But a few more recent implementations, a few of which are discussed later, attempt to embody also some of our knowledge about signals and thus are closer to knowledge representation as such.

The basic issue involved here is balancing the tradeoff between efficiency and ease of use. A simple data representation can be implemented very efficiently. A complicated knowledge representation, if it can be imple-

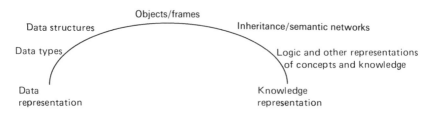

**Figure 10.1**
Data versus knowledge representations

mented at all, usually takes up more machine resources. Another way to look at this issue is as a tradeoff between machine efficiency and human efficiency. In the past it was almost always necessary to favor machine efficiency just to get anything done; but in the future it will be possible to favor human efficiency and still solve the tremendous computational problems associated with music signals. The next section describes some of these problems for typical uses of music signals and points out the advantages of knowledge-oriented representations rather than the more traditional, data-oriented representations.

## Problems and Uses of Music Signals

Much of this section of the paper owes a large debt to a discussion group that has recently formed in the San Francisco Bay area. Participants in this group are musicians, engineers, and computer scientists. In particular, Stephen Pope and Lounette Dyer have greatly influenced my discussion here. The goal of this group is more or less to determine the basic requirements for a music representation, not music signal representation, and to come up with a specification defining these requirements along with, if possible, specifications for an implementation satisfying these requirements. While this is more general than defining a specification for music signals in programs, many of the needs are the same as are many of the uses to which the representations will be put.

The first thing to note are the difficulties music signals share with representations of signals for engineering applications. These computational problems can be divided into three principal areas. A large portion of the work of computer science and engineering is devoted to solving these problems so I will not cover them in detail here (see also Moorer 1977). The three problem areas are the need for high-bandwidth computation and throughput; the need for high-volume data storage; and the need for short response time.

Although these computation problems are not unique to music signals, any representation of music signals has to take them into account in order to do useful work. I now present the difficult representation areas that are specific to music signals. (For a discussion of many of these issues from a music composition view, see Loy 1989.) Later I discuss computational models that are helpful for dealing with these computational problems.

Music representations can be divided into categories as follows:

1. Complex specifications

2. Indefinite or imprecise specification

3. Complex relationships and referencing

4. Multilevel uses

5. Complex time relationships

*Complex specifications* are required in many music applications. For example, in synthesizing sound a composer or performer must specify an acoustic signal precisely to a very fine level of detail. Depending on the particular technique involved, this may require specifying parametric signals for envelope shapes, amplitude values, frequency trajectories, filter coefficients, and other parameters.

*Indefinite* or *imprecise specifications* typically occur during the creation phase of a work. In order to not get bogged down in minutiae, or in order to leave exact specification up to performers (as in improvised or partially improvised music), a composer might specify aspects of the final piece of music in a relatively vague form. Later performance or more detailed composition session is then required to fill in the details precisely. For example, a composer in the act of composition may specify simply "use some flute-like sounds here" and only later determine whether to get those sounds from a sampled flute, to synthesize them directly, or to realize them in some other ways.

*Complex relationships and referencing* refers to the need to specify things in relation to other things. For example, a sound in a section of music may be specified as derived from a sampled sound (an acoustic signal) by way of one or more analytic signals. The original sound could be subjected to a Fourier transform, the resulting analytic signal could be reshaped by multiplication in the frequency domain, then this result could finally be inverse Fourier transformed to yield the desired sound. A representation should keep track of not only the original, intermediate, and resulting signals, but it should also keep track of the operations involved in generating the final result.

The need to support *multilevel uses* was implicit in the preceding examples. It is necessary for users to have access, possibly even simultaneously, to different levels of the representation, from a low-level detailed specification of a time-domain waveform, to a high-level conceptual specification. For example, at a relatively high level a user may want to specify "play an

A minor scale here," but at a lower level may need to say "multiply these samples by a ramp to eliminate that discontinuity." Often users must be able to activate multiple levels simultaneously such as in "increase the amplitude parameter as this ascending A minor scale is played."

The issue of representing complex *time relationships* is fundamental to music signals. Details of time representations will be taken up in a later section, but for now the key point is that in music the temporal domain is more elaborately structured than is typical in engineering applications. The signal processing field, for example, is mostly concerned with signals during a continuous period of time and with how those signals change over such a period. Music is equally concerned with these relationships, but it is also concerned with relations of discontiguous periods of time and with hierarchical, or even more complicated, relationships among these different periods of time. These musical time relations are so important to music signals that they will be discussed in a separate section of this paper later.

A further requirement for signals in music applications, and probably too for engineering applications, is just beginning to emerge. Due primarily to the proliferation of networks, and such quasi-networks as MIDI (Musical Instrument Digital Interface, discussed later), the music domain is becoming more heterogeneous than in the past. A single piece of music may rely on many different kinds of signals, many kinds of processing, and many kinds of hardware. The underlying model must therefore be broad enough and flexible enough to encompass this diversity. It should be possible to use the same basic representation across different hardware and software implementations in a mixed, network environment.

To summarize, in terms of the computation problems, music signals are similar to signals in other engineering applications. However, important differences between engineering applications and music signals—particularly in time representation, types of specification required, and levels of use—have been pointed out.

I will therefore argue that for a signal implementation to be adequate for such musical uses, it must be combined with a more comprehensive knowledge representation scheme. Specifically, it must represent temporal knowledge and relations; it must provide support for solving the previously discussed computation and music-specific problems.

In a later section I survey some representations that partially meet these requirements. I do not know of any representations that solve all of these problems. The final section of this paper sketches a proposed model that incorporates many of the features of the other models presented and moves closer to satisfying the remaining musical requirements, especially in the area of time represention, though it does not yet solve all the problems we have mentioned. Before I do that, however, I present an overview of the principal computational models that serve as the foundation for all of the representations surveyed in this paper.

## Computation Models

So far we have separated the problems involved in representing music signals into computation problems and music-specific problems. Each of these has significant impact on the design of a signal representation. For example, the need for high-bandwidth computation leads to a consideration of efficient models of computational dynamics (program flow); the music-specific requirements lead to concern with models of computational semantics. This section addresses these computation problems.

### Dynamics and Semantics

Underlying every programming language is a model of a computing system that its programs control. Some models are pure abstractions, some are represented by hardware, and others by compiling or interpretive programs. (Backus 1978, p. 147)

I divide models of computation into two classes representing two conceptual levels of computation: models of *computational dynamics*, and models of *computational semantics*. The *dynamics* models refer to a particular underlying operational flow of data and instructions, implicitly defining a machine type, whereas *semantic* models are models of program meaning. A given semantic type can usually be implemented on top of any of the dynamics types, though some are more suitable than others, and a particular dynamics model could be simulated on hardware of a different type entirely. Informally, we might say that semantic models deal with how a user wants to think of the program, and dynamics models deal with how a machine might actually run.

### Models of Computational Dynamics

Models of computational dynamics can be classified based on the concepts of *stream* and *block*. At its most basic, a stream refers to elements in series, a block refers to elements in parallel. The models can be further divided according to whether the instruction flow is *simple* (one instruction or one processing element at a time) or *compound* (multiple instructions or multiple processing elements simultaneously). Thus there are four conceptual classes of models which I call *simple stream, compound stream, simple block, and compound block.*

An independent consideration in the compound models is coordination among the *processing elements*, or processors. Fundamentally, each processing element must be given the right data at the right time. In the simple-instruction-flow models, simple stream and simple block, this is relatively easy; only one processing element exists, so it is not hard to keep track of what data to give it at any time. However, in the compound-instruction-flow models (compound stream and compound block), many processors can operate simultaneously, so there is the possibility of the input to one processor requiring the output of one or more other processors. Thus interdependent processors must be coordinated in some manner.

We must also determine whether the processors are synchronous or asynchronous. In a *synchronous* system, all processors execute instructions in synchrony with the same clock. One technique often used in real-time music processing is to have all of the processors locked to the sample clock, the clock that drives the DACs. This is usually called *sample-locked.* A different use of this is mentioned later in the discussion of hierarchical waveguide networks.

In an *asynchronous* system, the processors are free to execute at their own rate. Of the two types, the asynchronous is by far the more complicated to coordinate. One much-discussed coordination technique is *dataflow* (Dennis 1980) wherein a processor (or a computation block) executes whenever it has data for its inputs. A different technique can be thought of as deriving from object-oriented programming: A processor executes whenever it receives a message; this I term *messageflow* (see the Actors model presented by Agha and Hewitt [1987]). Table 10.2 lists the four classes and depicts their relationships.

Figure 10.2 depicts these different types of computation models graphically. The circles each represent a datum, the triangles, squares, and diamond represent arbitrary operations. The top shows one datum going through one operation and resulting in one datum. The next shows three data going through one operation simultaneously, resulting in three new data. The third (labeled "compound stream") depicts three data passing through three different operations at different times. The final diagram

**Table 10.2**
Computational Models

| Instruction | Data | Name |
|---|---|---|
| Simple (one at a time) | Stream | Simple stream |
| | Block | Simple block |
| Compound (many at once) | Stream | Compound stream |
| | Block | Compound block |

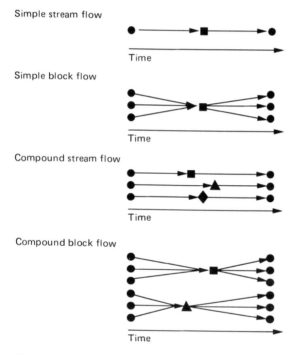

**Figure 10.2**
Computational dynamics model (see text)

shows two blocks of three data each being independently processed by different operations. The next four sections discuss these four types in turn.

**Simple Stream**    This is the standard von Neumann serial-machine model. A central store of memory contains data and programs, and a single processor operators on that data. Typically, data are moved to a work area (register) one datum at a time (through the von Neumann bottleneck); the processor acts on it and returns any results back to the store. Though the data in memory can be accessed at random, it is the manner in which computation occurs that is the more important characteristic of this model. The data are given to the processing element one at a time in a stream. Even when an operation requires more than one operand, such as a binary multiply operation, first one and then the other operand is moved. The simple stream model is also called a *single-instruction-single-data* (*SISD*) model. The simple stream has been the primary processing model for general digital computation.

**Simple Block**    This model is exemplified by a machine that operates on multiple data simultaneously but with only a single instruction at a time. A block of data enters the machine and the single operation is applied to every element in parallel. This kind of computation is often implemented with a *pipeline* where each stage of the computation (such as operation fetch, operation decode, data fetch) occurs simultaneously. But implementation details at this level of granularity need not concern us here; the computation appears at a higher level as a single operation on a block of data. This model is also referred to as a *single-instruction-multiple-data* (SIMD) computation. It provides a good speedup of data flow with minimal added complexity of coordination. The simple block model is particularly efficient when the computation consists of a simple series of operations, each of which can be performed on a large block of data. Thus this model is most suitable for *array processing* (vector arithmetic) and therefore is quite appropriate for many signal processing tasks. It is the conceptual model underlying many array processors and supercomputers.

**Compound Stream**    In this model there are many computation elements capable of independent operations. Though compound-stream computation consists of multiple instruction streams, each individual computation element operates on a single datum at a time.

**Compound Block**    In the compound-block model each processor operates on an entire block of data simultaneously. This can be thought of as multiple array processors operating in parallel.

Compound models are often categorized as *multiple-instruction-multiple-data* (MIMD) models, with no further distinction between them. The difference is in granularity. In the compound-stream model, each processor is itself relatively simple; it handles only a single datum at a time. In the compound-block model, each processor is complex and can handle blocks of data; and there are many processors in the system as a whole. Because of the difference in the granularity of data operated upon, I maintain a distinction between compound-stream and compound-block models. As mentioned previously, both of these compound models require some mechanism for handling coordination among the different processors.

Any of these models of computational dynamics can serve as a foundation for music signals. The simple-stream and simple-block models are simpler conceptually and usually are more economical as well. However, they are often not efficient enough to handle the high-volume computation needed for operations on music signals. Thus the compound models are being explored. Compound models bring greater computation bandwidth but at a cost of greater complexity, both in the system design and in their use. The following section discusses semantic models that help to simplify use of these more complex dynamics models.

### Models of Computational Semantics

Semantic models come in many varieties, but the ones that are most interesting from a signal processing or music view are the *procedural* (also called *imperative*), the *object-oriented*, and the *functional* models. Relational logic semantics have been used in many fields but have not been much exploited in signal processing or music, though they can provide an important tool especially for dealing with time. For this reason, I present in a later section some work from relational models of time and at the end of the paper I present a sketch of a model of music signals that provides a foundation for such a representation of time.

Table 10.3 lists the models of semantics considered along with the closely related dynamics model for each type.

**Procedural Semantics**    Procedural models of computation are still the standard. They are embodied in programming languages such as Fortran,

**Table 10.3**
Semantics Models and Related Dynamics Models

| Semantics Model | Related Dynamics Model |
| --- | --- |
| Procedural | Simple stream |
| Object-Oriented | Compound stream or compound block |
| Functional | Simple block or compound block |

C, Pascal, and many others. They typically imply a simple-stream dynamics model, with assignment operations, local and global variables, and explicit control flow. To effect a computation, the user writes a sequence of commands explicitly specifying operations to be performed on data in memory.

The standard signal processing textbooks and the standard music computation languages still utilize this model almost exclusively. The problems, especially for data intensive computation, are well known; Backus (1978) discusses them at length.

**Object-oriented Semantics** Object-oriented models are becoming more popular. They are used in such languages as Smalltalk, and in extensions to more standard languages such as $C_{++}$, the Common Lisp Object System (CLOS), and others. Though not everyone agrees on what an object-oriented programming language must include, they usually include abstract data types, inheritance, encapsulation, and communication via messages.

The first two of these features are extremely important for knowledge representation as well as for code development and maintenance, that is, for the general programming environment. The key ideas are simple. An *abstract data type* is a specification of an interface to data. The interface determines only what the data does, but not how it does it. Because only the interface is specified, not the data structures, the data structures themselves are themselves are only abstract. *Inheritance* is the ability to create objects with new characteristics based on previously created objects. If I create an abstract data type called **Event** with attribute called **time**, I could create another abstract data type simply by specifying that the new type inherits all the functionality, all the interface, from the existing **Event** type. Once this is accomplished it is possible for the new type to add additional behavior or protocols, such as handling new but related kinds of interaction. The new type is also called a *subclass* of the existing type. Byte (1986),

Meyer (1988), and Shriver and Wegner (1987) discuss these aspects of object-oriented programming.

For computational models, however, the most important aspects of object-oriented programming are *localization of data* (associated with encapsulation) and communication via *messages* (Goguen and Meseguer 1987). Localization of data simply means each object, from a conceptual view, has its own local memory that it alone is capable of accessing. In order to alter or even read that memory another object must send a message, which can be thought of as a kind of request, to the first object. Thus, encapsulation supports the abstract data type.

These two concepts together, localization and communication via messages, support a compound (stream or block) computational model. Since an operation is handled (locally) by a particular object, it would be natural to have each object implemented as a separate processor with messages passing between them. Even so, most object-oriented languages to date have been implemented on simple-stream machines.

Most current object-oriented systems, such as Smalltalk, are *synchronous*—a message is sent to an object and the sending object must wait for a reply—and therefore most suited to simple-stream or simple-block computations, recent work points out the efficacy of an asynchronous model as well (see the Actors model in Agha and Hewitt 1987). The basic idea here is that after sending a message, the sending object continues on with what it was doing instead of waiting for a reply as it would in the synchronous case. An entirely asynchronous model helps eliminate many of the difficulties associated with coordination of multiple processes discussed previously.

**Functional Semantics**   Of the models presented here, the functional programming paradigm most directly addresses the bandwidth, storage, and response time problems we have discussed since it promises to eliminate the processing bottleneck associated with procedural models (Backus 1978). The fundamental principles of functional programming are that all operations consist of functions that can be applied to data (hence it is also referred to as *applicative programming*). Functions return data (that is, the operations are mappings from the domain of data objects into itself). Functional programming uses primitive *functional forms* in order to define new functions in terms of existing ones and to specify ways of combining functions algebraically. The applicative style implies an absence of both variables and assignment operations. A good short introduction to these ideas can be found in Harrison and Khoshnevisan (1985). Some of the most interesting newer signal processing systems, such as those in Dannenberg, MacAvinney, and Rubine (1986) and Kopec (1985b) which I describe later utilize this model.

Another way to think of the functional programming approach is to contrast it to the previously discussed computational dynamics models. In the simple-steam model, data flows in a serial stream one datum at a time; in the simple-block model, data flows in large chunks at a time, but still, it flows. In the applicative model, data stays put and is "acted on" by a function.

Since I later present several representations that use a functional model, I here describe a simple algebra and notation from Backus (1978) in some detail to provide a common notation for the later examples. A functional programming system contains the following components:

1. A set of objects, $O$
2. A set of functions $F$, where $F$ is a mapping of $O$ into $O$
3. The *application* operation, denoted by ":"
4. A set of *functional forms* $FF$
5. A set of definitions $D$ (defining some functions in $F$).

$O$ is a domain of objects, such as the set of integers or the set of real numbers. The functions in $F$ are defined as mappings from this domain into itself. Backus uses the notation

$$f: \langle x, y, z \rangle$$

to mean there is a function $f$ applied to the objects $x$, $y$, and $z$.

Functional forms are a small set of "combining forms" out of which new functions can be defined. The set of functional forms listed by Backus includes: composition, construction, condition, constant, insert, apply-to-all, and binary-to-unary. For example, the composition operator "∘" can be used to define a function representing the mathematical composition of two other functions $f$ and $g$. If $h$ is defined as the composition of $f$ with $g$,

$$h \equiv f \circ g,$$

then $h(x)$ is the same as

$$f(g(x)).$$

This discussion has only explained the most basic aspects of functional programming. For the uses to which I put it later in the paper, this is sufficient.

**Logical models**   Fundamentally, logic programming languages "are rigorously based on *deduction* in some well-understood logical system" (Goguen and Meseguer 1987, p. 418). Though there is growing interest and success in devising a logic that encompasses both object-oriented and functional programming. I use the term "logic programming" to refer only to the relational-logic programming languages such as Prolog.

The underlying model in these languages is usually a first-order predicate calculus implemented by Horn clauses. A Horn clause is basically an assertion. The fundamental computation of a logic program is to make deductions from the assertions of the system. There is still much debate over whether logic, especially first-order logic, can provide an adequate base for knowledge representation. An interesting discussion of the pros and cons of logical representations of knowledge is given by David Israel (1983) in a special knowledge representation issue of *IEEE Computer* (McCalla and Cercone 1983).

Logic-based programming languages have not yet been used extensively in either music or signal processing. However, as discussed later, logical models are being used extensively in the database and knowledgebase fields and they are particularly useful in the area of representing time and time relations. Since it is mostly in that context that I use these models, I leave further discussion until the section on logical models of time.

These are the semantic models on which most signal representations are built. In the following section I discuss models of time that are of particular importance for music-signal applications. After that, I discuss example signal representations in light of the computation models and time models presented.

## Models of Time

Time is a fundamental aspect of all music signals. Even analytic signals, which do not always have time as their explicit domain, are still temporal in nature since they are transforms of (or can be transformed to) an explicitly temporal signal. Thus, the Fourier transform of a time-domain signal, (which is a mapping from radian frequencies into magnitudes) represents the frequency content of that time-domain signal (the signal that it is the transform of) at a particular time or during a particular interval of time. It is thus important to understand something about modeling this time domain.

In the rest of this section I survey the following models of time for use in music and signal processing:

1. *Implicit time* includes times that are defined only by their position in a sequence and is therefore also referred to as *stream time*. Often there is an implied regularity in the succession of events in the sequence. Implicit time is divided later into two categories: static streams and dynamic streams.

2. *Calendar time* includes any time referenced to some particular calendar or clock.

3. *Music time* consists of either of the above two kinds of time as well as temporal concepts particular to music. It thus includes times that are to some degree unspecified or imprecise.

4. *Logical time* has much in common with the other time models, but it is the particular model that seeks to support varieties of reasoning about time.

Aspects of each of these temporal models and their significance for music signals are discussed next.

**Implicit Time**

Implicit time is a general class of time models that is also called stream time. Implicit time models the flow of time as events in a sequence. One particular location in the sequence is distinguished from the rest and is called the stream's *now pointer*. There are two distinct types of stream time that are primarily distinguished by the behavior of the now pointer.

The first of these models I call *dynamic-stream time* (figure 10.3). In this case the now pointer is constantly and automatically keeping up with the

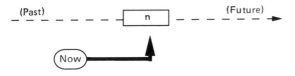

**Figure 10.3**
Dynamic stream. Only "now" exists.

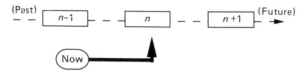

**Figure 10.4**
Static stream. All past and future states exist.

perpetually moving, but historyless, "now" of the external world; the stream is constantly disappearing into the past and being created or extended from the future. This is the case, for example, in many real-time systems, such as MIDI described later, where events occur "now" without explicit reference to any particular clock or calendar.

The second kind of implicit time I call *static-stream time* (figure 10.4). In this case the entire stream already exists. The now pointer is, usually under program control, free to move along the stream from beginning to end; it is even possible to add data to the end of such a static stream—principally, because there is a well-defined end.

The representation of a digital signal as an array of samples is an example of the static-stream model of time. In much of the digital signal processing literature it is further assumed that time is uniform and moves in discrete pulses. In this case, there is also usually a reference to a global value that specifies the relation between the assumed pulse size and some unit of an external real-world clock time (seconds, minutes, and so on). This global value is referred to as the *sampling rate*. (This global reference to a unit of an external clock does not change implicit time into calendar time. For one thing the reference is only to a unit of an external clock and not to particular times on that clock. For another, each event in the sequence is not individually referenced; each event's time is still implicitly defined by its position in the sequence of events.)

Another typical static stream is that used to access files (or other external storage devices). The basic operation is "fetch the next event/object." The time associated with, for example, a particular sample from a file of digitized audio, is entirely implicit in its position in the stream of samples. Because of the possibility of space-efficient implementations, static-stream–based time is particularly important for dealing with the large amounts of data needed to store digital audio signals.

## Calendar Time

The general concept of calendar time is of any time that is explicitly referenced to some particular calendar or clock. Thus it can refer to times in the past, present, or future with equal ease. An important type of calendar time is called *real time*. Real time is here taken to refer to any system of time that must synchronize in some manner with the current, perpetually moving "now" of an external (or idealized) real-world clock.

Because the real-time model can refer to any real-world clock, the particular granularity of the clock is not a decisive factor. In some of the literature, it is assumed that a real-time system implies a fine temporal granularity on the human perceptual scale. But this is difficult to quantify because each application many use a different scale. Thus we have real-time systems that operate in the millisecond or microsecond range, such as robot-controlled manufacturing systems, and real-time systems that operate in the daily or monthly range, such as many business accounting systems. Similarly, in music we have real-time systems operating in the millisecond range, such as MIDI, and real-time systems operating in the microsecond range or less, such as common audio CD players.

In the literature on real-time programming a distinction is often made between *hard real time* in which time constraints are absolute and where a failure to meet the constraints is catastrophic (as in many music-performance applications), and *soft real time* in which time constraints have no set boundary but results are more useful the closer to actual time they are available (such as in word-processing, or music composition applications).

Another important distinction is that between real time, as embodied in an ideal external clock, and *computer time*. Computer time is time as realized by "a discrete approximation to real-time [sic] implemented on machines by a variety of hardware and software methods" (Shaw 1989). This distinction between real time and computer time is often significant in music and signal processing applications because of the extremely fine granularity of time needed in such applications and the susceptibility of the applications to catastrophic failure if the computer time approximation is inadequate.

Another useful distinction is that made between the time an event is scheduled (sometimes called *transaction time*) and the time the event is supposed to occur (*valid time* or *logical time*). Shaw also presents a discussion that takes into account the passage of real time during the execution of a computer program (which effects the relationship between transaction time and valid time), and explains the distinctions between real time and computer time. This is of particular significance for many music systems where the time needed to compute and schedule an event must be taken into account so that transaction time does not come after valid time.

**Music Time**

Three senses of music time are important here. Events can have temporal relationships that are either (1) not specified (that is, not even implicitly); (2) only relatively specified; (3) specified contingently. These kinds of temporal relationships come about in particular during performing and composing music. For example, type 1 occurs when, during the compositional process, a composer has a particular musical idea without yet knowing where in a piece it will eventually go.

Type 2 occurs most frequently. For example, common music notation (CMN) specifies events both relative to one another and relative to particular (and often highly variable) tempi. The entire musical notion of beats and meter is a relative temporal specification.

Finally, type 3 occurs often (but not only) in recent computer-generated pieces and performances of pieces. For example, an event might be specified as occurring only if certain conditions are met during a particular performance. Though in its most obvious sense this seems to imply an improvised performance, it need not. Even a fully "composed" score, in the traditional sense, has many constraints left up to performance. One such constraint might be, "when playing this in a large reverberant hall, take the tempo somewhat slower so as to keep the shortest notes distinguishable." In this case, the time of occurrence of some events in the piece is contingent on some external, and even extramusical, conditions being met.

**Logical Time**

The final kind of time to be considered is logical time (Segev and Shoshani 1987). Most of the previously discussed kinds of time can be modeled by one or another variety of logical time. Devising and implementing models of logical time and temporal knowledge is an important area of contemporary database and knowledge representation theory (Bolour et al. 1982, Dutta 1989).

Allen (1983) presents some important characteristics of temporal representations in general that are useful in music implementations.

The representation should allow significant imprecision. Much temporal knowledge is strictly relative.
The representation should allow uncertainly of information.
The representation should allow one to vary the grain of reasoning.
The model should support persistence.

It is easy to see that much of this is common with music time as just described. By "varying the grain of reasoning," Allen means it should be possible to represent days or years, seconds, nanoseconds, and so on. This too is a significant need for music signals: It is important to be able to represent music signals that govern, for example, the amplitude levels over a range of beats at the musical phrase level, and it is also important to be able to represent amplitude levels over the course of a single note such as in an envelope. "Persistence" is the notion that things do not change unless something happens to change them. While this may at first glance not seem susceptible of a musical interpretation, it has applicability in everything from simply sustaining a note to the musical notions of ostinato and other concepts that embody some form of repetition. For example, the injunction to, "Repeat this section of sampled data until I release the key," requires a conception of time that is open ended; the object (or event) persists until something happens to stop it.

I next introduce two models currently in use that attempt to capture logical knowledge of time. The first is *state-based time*; a good presentation of this and its logic is McDermott (1982). The second important model is *interval-based time*. Allen (1983) presents this view with a definition of principles in Allen and Hayes 1985. A third model that in some ways subsumes elements of both the state-based and interval-based models is presented in Segev and Shoshani 1987. This third model, because it deals specifically with temporal data very similar to music signals, is particularly important. It will be presented in some detail as it provides a foundation for music signals that supports reasoning as well as efficient computation.

**State-based Time**    In the state-based representation, time is modeled as a potentially infinite collection of states. Each of these states represents "an instantaneous snapshot of the universe" (McDermott 1982, p. 105). On the other hand, state-based temporal logic seems to provide a natural way of dealing with the problems of representing persistence.

The main problems with this are (1) inefficiency—it is necessary to maintain a large number of successive states to represent a single changing entity; (2) entities are defined only "indirectly as facts that are true over a consecutive set of states" (Dutta 1989).

**Interval-based Time**   In the interval-based model, time is represented by events having nonzero duration. Allen (1983) and Dutta (1989) present some of the arguments for interval-based time and against state-based time. Allen and Hayes (1985) present an axiomatization of interval time based on the single primitive MEET. Two time intervals MEET when "there is no time between the two intervals, and no time that the intervals share" (p. 528). His ontology consists of TIMES, which "correspond to our intuitive notion of when some event occurs." MEET is thus a "primitive relationship between times."

The authors are able to show the "complete set of possible relationships between intervals in terms of MEETS." For example, the relation "comes before" can be defined in terms of MEETS as follows.

An interval $i$ comes before an interval $j$ if there is some interval $k$ such that $i$ MEETS $k$ and $k$ MEETS $j$.

Thus, the interval model seems to be sufficient for representing all of the logically possible qualitative, temporal relationships between two events.

## Example Signal Systems

So far I have presented many abstract models. The next sections discuss particular implementations and their relationships to the models already developed. While some fall fairly neatly into one particular model, in other cases the underlying model seems to be heterogeneous. This heterogeneity is true also of most programming languages, so it is not surprising that implementations of signals would share the same trait. For presentation purposes, I group the different examples based on the particular model that is most prominent or characteristic. The exposition starts with simple-stream models, which all use procedural semantics. It then presents some block-diagram simulators, each of which uses a different underlying computational dynamics model. Next follow three examples that use primarily functional programming semantics. This is followed by a model from database research. In the final section I sketch a signal model that incorporates elements of object-oriented, functional, and logical semantics, as well as a logical model of time relations. It is hoped that this example will eventually prove useful for developing a representation of music signals.

### Simple-Stream Systems

Simple-stream systems are most common. They are primarily data representations with little or no attempt to represent any higher levels of knowledge or even to make a computational model explicit. They usually assume a procedural computational semantic and a simple-stream dynamic. Examples include MIDI, general signal processing software, and Music V. Each of these is discussed in turn.

**MIDI** MIDI, the Musical Instrument Digital Interface, is more of a communications protocol than a representation of either signals or music. Its inclusion here is due mainly to its enormous popularity and ubiquitous use in digital synthesizers and music software that supports these. Since "[w]hat MIDI communicates is ... indications about pressed keys and switches, turned knobs and pedals—in other words—human gestural control information" (Loy 1985, p. 9), it can be thought of as a rather ill-defined system for handling at least parametric signals; in this case, the parameters are those of a keyboard-based digital synthesizer. Basic MIDI defines nontimed events (all events occur "now"—that is, when received) for "commands." This includes representations for things such as "key *n* has been pressed (or released)." This fits into a simple dynamic-stream model of time as described above. MIDI also includes an explicit representation of control signals (misnamed "continuous controller"—it is discrete and potentially even sporadic) in which the values of the "signal" are available in a dynamic stream. This is typically used to control microtonal variations in frequency (called *pitchbend*) or to control the amplitude of a modulating waveform in a frequency modulation synthesis model.

Even for the limited uses for which it was designed (control of keyboard-based digital synthesizers) MIDI seems almost hopelessly inadequate and has been much decried in the technical literature (see, for example, Moore 1988). "The limitations include limited bandwidth between devices, limited frequency and time resolution, limited access to synthesizer parameters, ... and lack of bidirectionality in communication" (Loy 1985, p. 8). MIDI does not support any computational model explicitly; it is a simple stream of data. It is most often manipulated from within procedural, von Neumann-style programs, such as C and Pascal.

**General Signal Processing**   Probably the simplest implementation of a digital signal is a sequence of values indexed by positive integers; a tremendous amount of software to do general purpose signal processing has been written this way and it is the most prevalent implementation found in text books on signal processing. Typically, the implementation consists of an array of integer, floating point, or complex numbers in a procedural language such as Fortran or C. Operations on the signal consist of iterative procedures making use of language primitives such as array accessors (**SIGNAL[I]**, for example, to retrieve the Ith value of the array **SIGNAL**) and mathematical operations (the usual assortment of $+$, $-$, $*$, and $/$). This is a simple-stream computational model with implicit time and procedural semantics. An example is the standard implementation of a fast Fourier transform as given by Rabiner and Gold (1975, p. 367). The data is stored in an array and the routine accesses elements of the array and operates on them successively. This version is called *in-place* because the same storage is used for the input and the output.

While the drawbacks of this representation may be obvious—lack of flexibility, lack of high-level structure, lack of explicit temporal operations and temporal knowledge, and so on—the advantages are often considered to outweigh them: it is simple, ubiquitous (therefore, a de facto standard), and efficient; it maps simply and directly onto hardware processor and memory configurations.

**Music V**   Music V culminates a series of programs developed by Max Mathews (1969) that have been of great importance to the field of computer music. These programs provide basic support for digital synthesis of music out of real time. They have an underlying structure that separates a synthesis specification into two parts: an *orchestra* (meaning the synthesis algorithms themselves), and *score* (meaning the parameter lists that feed the orchestra models). These two parts provide an elementary parametric-signal model (figure 10.5). The score part also provides a simple implementation of music time in the concept of a beat with tempo specifications hence, Music V can model a form of relative time. Basically, Music V and its many derivatives (for a recent one see Jaffe and Boynton 1989) use music signals in the following ways:

• As stored functions to be sampled for envelopes and as stored functions to be periodically sampled by digital "oscillators" to generate periodic time-domain waveforms (wavetable synthesis).

**Figure 10.5**
Music V score and orchestra

• As potentially multiple static streams of samples (one stream to each simulated or real channel) written to a storage device and from there played back through DACs to produce the continuous-time acoustic waveform, a dynamic stream.

• As lists of parameters and update values for those parameters to control the various functional blocks of the synthesis model.

These systems use simple stream data flow along with procedural semantics. Typically, at some point in the code, there is a "sample loop" (which is sometimes implicit) that is repeated for each sample of sound to be generated.

A great many predefined subroutines are available for simulating such electronic audio components as oscillators, envelope generators, and noise generators; these are called *unit generators*. The book by Dodge and Jerse (1985) gives an overview of the techniques and uses of these programs (see pp. 75–77 on the Music IV, IVBF, and Music V programs.) The concept of unit generators as in the Music V–type programs is very similar to the concept of functional blocks as used in the block-diagram models discussed next.

**Block-Diagram Models**

It used to be common for engineers to design hardware on paper by diagramming, using circles, triangles, or rectangles, low-level functional units, such as adders and multipliers. These geometric shapes were called *blocks* and were connected together by lines representing wires or connectors and showing the signal path through the functional blocks. Such a diagram was called a *block diagram*. Later, computers were used to simulate these computations and the functional units that make them up. Languages that support such simulations are called *block simulation* languages.

Three examples of block simulation languages (BLODI, HWN, and

BLOSIM) illustrate the features of these languages. Each of these is based on a different model of computational dynamics.

The first example is called BLODI, short for block diagram (Kelly, Lochbaum, and Vyssotsky 1961). BLODI is a stream-oriented block-diagram compiler. It can be thought of as a simple, stateless machine implemented with simple-stream dynamics. At each tick of the (program) clock a new datum enters the computation loop, passes through each computation unit, and pops out on the output stream. BLODI was implemented in a procedural language.

Hierarchical waveguide networks (HWN) (Garnett and Mont-Reynaud 1988) were developed for modeling the acoustics of musical instruments. They consist of two elements: *branches* that represent an acoustic medium (a waveguide), and *junctions* that represent the interconnection or interface between branches. The junctions correspond roughly to the functional blocks in a block simulators, the branches correspond to wires but introduce an element of delay. In a HWN all of the junctions operate simultaneously on the current inputs from their branches. In a simple, static network, there are just three sequential steps each of which can be executed simultaneously on all computation units: (1) all junctions read and scale their inputs; (2) all junctions sum their scaled inputs; (3) all junctions write the difference between the sum and the $n$th input to the $n$th output. Thus, it can be looked on as a sequence of three simple-block computations in a sequence.

In contrast to BLODI and HWN, each computation block in BLOSIM, short for block simulator (Messerschmitt 1984), is designed to operate on a group of data at the same time (the block thus represents a data block as well as a computation block). Since each block is also independent in theory, BLOSIM is suited to implementation on a compound-block dynamics model. Each block reads its (multiple) inputs and writes a block of data to a buffer. In theory therefore, BLOSIM could be implemented on multiple array-processor machines; each computation block would be handled by a separate machine operating on its own array of input data in parallel. So in this case there are two levels of parallelism available—one at the block simulation level and one at the data array level.

**Three Functional Models**

In this section I present three models that use functional semantics. Two of the models, GROOVE and Arctic, were developed with music applications in mind. The third model, SRL, was developed for general-purpose signal processing.

## GROOVE

One of the advantages gained by treating control signals as functions of time is that they may then be operated on mathematically. It is easy to image relatively complex control signals which are really only the sums, differences, products, etc., of several simple functions of time. (Mathews and Moore 1970)

It is interesting that the computer music engineers Mathews and Moore designed what is basically a functional-programming semantics for their real-time performance system more than eight years before functional programming was popularized by the computer scientist Backus. It is even more surprising that so much of what was accomplished in this program has been virtually ignored by the commercial music industry, to everyone's loss.

At the heart of the GROOVE system is an extremely general and flexible concept of digital signal. Digital signals are simply static or dynamic streams, the former are stored on disk, with time remaining implicit within the signal but relative to an external, interactively defined sampling rate; thus it incorporates a kind of music time: the speed of sampling the signals is itself a signal, and can be edited in real time. The authors call this knob-controlled program time.

Another important concept in GROOVE is that "[i]n the composing mode...a human being is in the feedback loop" (p. 715). It is possible for the musician to manipulate and generate signals in real time and hear the results while creating them. It is also interesting to note the authors' awareness of different kinds of time, such as "control of program time needs to be quite different for composing than for editing" (p. 716).

Though the actual hardware used was primitive by today's standards ("An analog-to-digital converter plus multiplexor allows sampling up to 20 voltages in about 10 μs per voltage." Inputs come from "rotary potentio-meters... which may be turned by the operator in real-time [sic]" [p. 716]) the flexibility achieved seems tremendous compared to current synthe-sizers. The following is an example of another mode of interaction with the system. In this case, the user types statements on a (text) keyboard. This simple text-based language exemplifies the functional semantics used:

Some examples of typical statements are
T6. T2 + 480,

T1. T1,

T13: $-F1 * (K3 - 2000)$,

T28: $4095/(1 + U1(F1 + U2(T1 + K2)))$.

The left-hand side of this statement is one of T1, T2, ..., T40, which specifies one of the disk functions.... The right-hand side of the statement is any arithmetic expression made up of the four standard arithmetic operators ($+$, $-$, $*$, and $/$), any number of balanced parentheses, and the following operands:

T1–T40, which refer to the current value of a disk function,

K1–K7, which refer to the current value of some real-time input device, such as a knob or keyboard, and

F1–F40, which refer to the current value of a periodic function.

In addition, the right-hand expression may include a notation of the form U1 ($\langle X \rangle$), when U1 refers to the first of 95 possible user supplied arithmetic functions, and $\langle X \rangle$ is any allowable arithmetic expression. The period means "Replace the value of the specified disk function with the value of the expression, but do *not* change the permanent record of this disk function...."

The colon both assigns the expression value to the disk function and *does* change the permanent record. (Mathews and Moore 1970, p. 718)

The Arctic language takes a similar approach to real-time control. A different emphasis is found in the system described next. Its concerns are more oriented to static-stream music signals and analytic music signals.

**Signal Representation Language**    The Signal Representation Language (SRL) of Kopec (1985a) is one of the most interesting programming environments for signal processing. Kopec presents a signal abstraction that is powerful, flexible, and highly useful. For Kopec, signals are mathematical objects and so his signal abstraction attempts to embody what he thinks of as the significant mathematical properties. Thus, his "set of requirements for signals is motivated by three elementary observations about the mathematics of discrete-time signals and the notations commonly used to describe them" (Kopec 1985a, p. 242). His three observations are:

1. Signals are constant values whose mathematical properties are not subject to change.

2. Two signals are equal if they have the same domain and their values are equal at each point of their domain.

3. A class of signals is often defined by giving an expression for the value of the prototypical sample of the prototypical signal of the class. (Kopec 1985b, p. 922)

From observation 1, a signal in SRL is immutable. This means that all operations on signals result in the creation of a new signal rather than in the modification of an existing signal. Kopec points out the similarity of signals in this respect with ordinary implementations of numbers and characters rather than with ordinary arrays whose values may be changed at any time. This is both conceptually and pragmatically a very useful concept. It "contributes to an applicative style of programming" (Kopec 1985b, p. 930). However, there is a drawback in that there is at least a potential for inefficiency in storage—when a signal is very large and only a small modification to it is desired, it is not always practical to create an entire new signal for the modified version.

It may be true as in observation 2 above that, mathematically, two functions are considered identical if and only if they have the same domain and their values are equal at every point. But this only takes in the *extensional* identity of a function, in the logical sense. In signal processing and music processing languages, however, it is useful or even necessary to take into account, at least on occasion, how the signals are created, and thus their *intensional* properties.

SRL uses functional semantics with a static-stream-based model of time; the latter is evidenced by SRL's access function **signal-fetch** which returns the *n*th value of the signal. Provision is made for block access of the entire range of the signal by means of the **with-signal-values** Lisp form. SRL thus supports both simple-stream and simple-block computation.

Because it does not explicitly allow access to just a portion of the signal, without creating a new signal that includes just that portion, SRL excludes what might be called "stream-of-blocks" computations. In a stream-of-blocks computation, a block processor accesses successive or overlapping portions of a complete signal as blocks and then processes them in a simple-block or compound-block fashion. This formulation of stream-of-blocks computations owes much to discussions with Bernard Mont-Reynaud. As in Meyers 1986 it would thus be useful to add access to an arbitrary portion of the signal as well.

A simple example of SRL is the following, taken from Kopec 1985b:

```
(defsigtype     sine-wave
    :a-kind-of      basic-signal
    :parameters  (omega   phi    length)
    :finder      signal-sine-wave
    :init  (setq-my  dimensions  length)
    :fetch  ((n)  (sin  (+  (*   omega   n)
                    phi))))
```

This would be instantiated by evaluating the expression:

(signal sine-wave omega phi length)

The real value of SRL is not its computation dynamics, nor its quasi-functional semantics, but its exploitation of abstract data types. The work of Scaletti and Hebel (Chapter 11) extends this work by extending the class of available abstractions.

What is missing in SRL, from a musical point of view, is a more fully developed model for time, (and of course this is not a failing of SRL, since it was not designed with music in mind). It defines only implicit, static-stream time. It is also not feasible in SRL to handle real time or any dynamic streams adequately. Kopec states that inquiry operations on what I have called dynamic streams (and, I presume, real-time signals) are useless because the size of a stream is not always known in advance (see Kopec 1985a, p. 248). Although this is obviously true, it points up the narrowness of Kopec's definition of a signal (at least, compared with my musically motivated one) rather than any inadequacy of the stream model itself. Lack of random access is a liability of all real-time systems.

**Arctic**   Arctic is described by Dannenberg, MacAvinney, and Rubine (1986). It is a functional language with an ontology of *higher-order functions*. The *higher-order functions* are functions whose range consists of functions of time. These higher-order functions (Dannenberg calls them *prototypes*) operate on the domain of (real) numbers. The typical prototype takes three arguments: a starting time, a duration factor, and a termination argument; each of these can be supplied with a default value. It is argued (p. 68) that "the reason for higher-order functions is that they give us the ability to model responses at higher levels of abstraction." An important result of the combination of higher-order functions and the applicative semantics of Arctic is the ability to manipulate prototypes prior to instantiating them. A potential drawback is the lack of an explicit representation of preexisting instances—such as static-stream music signals. In Arctic, a static-stream music signal is apparently represented only as an arbitrary "input" to the system. From this it can be seen that Arctic and SRL are essentially complementary. The former emphasizes dynamic streams, the latter emphasizes static streams.

Arctic "is based on a nonsequential model in which behavior in the time domain is specified explicitly. This model describes possible system responses to real-time conditions and provides a means for manipulating and composing responses" (p. 67).

Arctic provides a unit-step prototype (**unit**), a ramp prototype (**ramp**), and a sinewave prototype (**sin**) as primitive objects. It also provides the following primitive operations that I divide into operations on the temporal components of prototypes, operations on the value components of prototypes, and aggregation operations on prototypes as a whole (though Arctic makes no such distinction, it is a useful aid in conceptualizing the operations).

First, the operations on times: stretch (denoted by " $\sim$ "), and shift (denoted by " $@$ "). Stretch alters the duration factor, shift alters the starting time. Second, the operations on "values" of the prototypes. These are $+$, $-$, $*$, $/$, and the relational operators $=$, $<$. Third, the aggregation operations are: collect (denoted by square brackets "[ ]" surrounding prototypes that are separated by semicolons ";"), and sequence (denoted by square brackets "[ ]" surrounding prototypes that are separated by vertical bars "|"). Collect allows the grouping of prototypes in parallel; sequence allows grouping in series. These can be thought of as similar to Backus's "sequence" of objects ($\langle x_1, \ldots, x_n, \rangle$).

Dannenberg presents a notation for Arctic that brings out its procedural aspects. For example, to sum a **ramp** prototype and a **sin** prototype they write

**value** $x$;
$x := $ **ramp** $+$ **sin**(2.0);

This obscures the applicative nature of many operations in Arctic and returns it to a more procedural style (complete with this quasi-assignment statement). This seems to contradict some of the intentions of Arctic's designers. In order to keep its functional aspects explicit, I will present Arctic in the Backus-like notation that has been described above.

$O$ is the set of prototype functions: **unit**, **ramp**, **sin**, and others that can be built from them.

$F$ is the set of primitive operations such as: $\sim$, $@$, $+$, $*$, $-$, $/$, collect and sequence. The first two of these operations, stretch and shift, take additional numeric arguments.

$FF$ the set of functional forms, is apparently not explicitly defined in Arctic. Some new functions may be defined in terms of the primitive members of

$F$, but only in a procedural style. However, we could take all of the functional forms described by Backus and define them in Arctic.

The only notational difficulty is that the time operators, shift and stretch, take arguments that are not themselves in the domain of prototypes but are simple real numbers. I will denote this by parenthesizing the arguments this way $\sim(3.2)$ to denote the shift function with an argument of 3.2 (seconds). Thus, if $p_0, \ldots, p_n \in O$, we can say

$\sim(3.2): p_0$

meaning "apply the shift operation, with an argument of 3.2, to the prototype object $p_o$." To multiply a prototype by a **ramp** prototype, we can write

$*: \langle \mathbf{ramp}, p_0 \rangle$

This simply multiplies the ramp and the given prototype together.

Another notational issue comes up here: Dannenberg uses the expression **ramp * 90** to mean the amplitude of the ramp prototype is scaled by 90. This notation is very similar to that of GROOVE. Here, it is really just a shorthand for something like **ramp * unit(90)** which means the ramp prototype is multiplied by a unit-step function and the unit step function is instantiated with an amplitude of 90.

Arctic does not explicitly provide the full complement of functional forms described by Backus. Rather, it uses a notation that makes it look much more like procedural programming. That is, new functions can be defined in terms of existing functions by means of quasi-variables. Thus, in their example on page 73, a functon **Random** for generating random notes is defined this way:

```
Random (in N) causes [
  if N > 0
    then [Note(irnd(50 + 30))|
      Random(N − 1)]
    else zero ~ 0];
```

This departs from the flavor of applicative programming, which would presumably define this using functional forms.

As we have seen, Arctic is a functional programming system using prototypes. It explicitly represents only real-time models of time (computer time and clock-time), but could possibly be adapted to account for other musical times as well. It does not directly support reasoning about time or incorporation of its fundamental relations into a musical knowledge base. It is most suitable for compound-stream computations due to its emphasis on the dynamic-stream aspect of real-time control. It does not seem well suited to block computation unless it is done out of real time. As defined, it seems most suited to parametric signals, and thus synthesizer control, but might be adapted for static streams and analytic music signals.

**Time Sequences: A Database Model**   Segev and Shoshani (1987) present interesting model for handling temporal concepts that are closely related to music signals. I explain this in some detail because it forms one of the primary bases for the signal model presented at the end of this paper. The authors deals specifically with temporal data from "applications in scientific and statistical databases (SSDBs), where physical experiments, measurements, simulations, and collected statistics are usually in the time domain ... [and where] in most cases the concept of a 'current version' does not even exist" (p. 454). They are "interested in capturing the semantics of ordered sequences of data values in the time domain, as well as operators over them" (p. 454).

Basically, they define temporal data values as a triplet $\langle s, t, a \rangle$ where $s$ is a unique identifier denoting some object and is called a *surrogate*, $t$ represents the time, and $a$ is the value of the attribute at that time. If the data has no time associated with it, its time is considered to be "now" and can be omitted. This property is useful for signals with a dynamic-stream model.

"[F]or a given surrogate the temporal data values are totally ordered in time; that is they form an ordered sequence" (p. 455). This sequence is called a *time sequence* (TS). "Since all the temporal values in a TS have the same surrogate value, they can be represented as $\langle s, (t, a)^* \rangle$, that is a sequence of pairs $(t, a)$ for a given surrogate." (The "*" means one or more items.) To give a musical example, if the sequence of data values represents a sampled flute sound, the surrogate might be "flute." Then the data values $(t, a)^*$ would be the time and sample value for each element of the sequence Of course, in such a case, the time values are uniformly spaced and it is not necessary to explicitly store a time value for each sample. Segev and Shoshani handle this by defining four properties of TSs that would allow the system to infer the times in such a sequence. These four types are mentioned below.

They also define a time sequence collection (TSC) as a collection of TSs for objects that have the same attributes. This collection can be denoted by a triplet of classes $\langle S, T, A \rangle$. The identifier for a *composite class* uses more than one surrogate; thus, a composite class can denote a relationship between surrogates. This relational property is significant for the music signal model outlined at the end of this paper.

When $S$ is not a single element it is denoted by $\bar{S}$ or $(S, S)$. A TSC with a composite surrogate can also be represented as $((S, S), T, A)$ where $(S, S)$ stands for two surrogates and $A$ corresponds to some relationship between them. For example, if we take the "flute" TS and a similar "oboe" TS, we might specify a relation between these as $\langle$("flute", "oboe"), $T, A\rangle$ where $T$ is the set of times and $A$ is a relational attribute that exists between the "flute" and the "oboe." It might be that this represents all the time and value pairs where both the flute and the oboe are nonzero, or we might use it to represent a sample-wise sum of the flute and oboe values.

Similarly, where $T$ is a compound element there is more than one time sequence associated with the objects and attributes and when $A$ is composite, denoted $(S, T, \bar{A})$ "several attributes occur (or are measured) at precisely the same time points .... An important special case is in representing non-temporal data as the degenerate TSC $(S, \bar{A})$, where all the non-temporal attributes can be treated together in a single TSC" (p. 457).

Temporal data have four properties that assist in operations on them and in designing efficient implementations.

1. *Time granularity* can be either ordinal or related to a calendar. Ordinal is what I have termed implicit stream time—time is determined by place in an ordinal series. Calender time is as described above. For music purposes, we might also wish for various relative times beat $n$, two thirds of beat $m$, and so on.

2. *Life span* refers to the duration of a TS.

3. *Regularity* obtains when for each time point in the life span there exists a data point. (Not every beat in a measure needs to have a note.) Most digital acoustic music signals, thus, are regular.

4. *Type* is one of

a. Step-wise constant.

b. Continuous (interpolation is possible); this corresponds to the usual notion of time in a sampled system.

c. Discrete (this is not the same as "discrete" in engineering applications); a TS is discrete when each value is *unrelated* to other values and therefore it makes no sense to interpolate missing values.
d. User defined: missing values can be calculated from arbitrary, user-specified interpolation functions.

Segev and Shoshani define a group of useful operators as well: Select, Aggregate, Accumulate, Restrict, Compose. All operators obey the following two principles: (1) Every operation on a TSC returns a TSC, this is a requirement for a functional semantic as well; (2) Every operator has three functional parts: a target specifying valid points, a mapping of source to target points, and specification of the function to be applied.

## A Proposed Signal Model

From the preceding discussion, it may be clear that the applicative model provides efficiency and conceptual clarity well suited to many of the computational needs of music signals; the object-oriented approach with its intrinsic support for independent programming modules satisfies many of the needs of highly parallel systems, with inheritance and abstract data types providing basic support for many kinds of knowledge representations; and the logic approach is well is suited for reasoning about the temporal relations of signals. Recent work in unifying functional models, object-oriented programming, and logic programming would therefore seem to provide a useful approach to modeling and manipulating digital music signals.

The most familiar logical programming languages are the functional and relational languages, based (respectively) on the equational and Horn Clause logics. This paper shows that object-oriented programming [OOP] can also be logical, and in fact gives the first precise semantics for OOP of which we are aware. Although the notion of deduction involved is more complex than for functional programming, we still get all the benefits of logical programming, and the resulting languages are remarkably simple and unified. (Goguen and Meseguer 1987)

But the authors state their semantics "do not work equally well for traditional object-oriented languages, since these also have many imperative features, are quite complex, and are not very unified" (p. 419, note 3).

With this in mind, I will outline a proposed model for music signals based on functional computation, object-oriented events, and logical time. First

I will examine a simple model using objects and functional programming, finally, I will expand that model to include relational logic in the manner of Segev and Shoshani (1987).

A key idea here is the definition of separate types, or domains, on which functions are defined. This is taken from the object-oriented semantics of abstract data-types. We therefore need to define separate domains for time and for values (and, in an implementation, for other general attributes as well). Functions applied to signals return signals, but time functions operate on the time of signals, value functions operate on the value(s) of signals. All functions return a new signal, they do not alter the existing signal. Thus, signals, as in Kopec (1985b) and Scaletti and Hebel (see chapter 11) are immutable.

First I define a set of objects that incorporate time. I call these *events*. To be concrete. I say that events use an interval model of time. For example, some event may occur during the interval from 1 unit (seconds, minutes, beats, and so on) to 5 units. The time of this event would then be represented by the pair [1, 5]. It is hoped that this specification can be expanded later to include the varieties of relative and imprecise time needed for music signals. These might be handled with relations between signals such as MEETS and BEFORE as discussed previously in the section on time models. While this substantially complicates the model, it may be possible to factor the interface to the time component into two separate subclasses: one representing explicit times, the other representing indefinite and relative times. It is not yet clear whether an abstract type can be defined specifying an interface that might be common to these two types.

Next I define a set $T$ of functions that operate on the time aspects of these events. These functions are at least: shift and stretch (unary functions), append, and inset ($n$-ary functions). Shift and stretch are the same as in Arctic. The operation **append** takes two or more signals and concatenates them into one by shifting the time of each to the end of the previous. If time is represented as an interval [2, 10], for example, we can show the working of append this way. The event $e_1$ has time [2, 10], the event $e_2$ has time [3, 5]. We apply append to them

**append:** $\langle e_1, e_2 \rangle$

Assuming **append** puts the rightmost argument on the end of the argument on its left, the above results in a new signal with time [2, 12].

The **insert** operator takes two or more signals and an insertion point for

each. It then shifts each successive signal to the insertion point and shifts
the portion of the original signal from the insertion point on to the end of
the new signal. Thus, effectively inserting the entire second signal into the
middle of the first signal. An example of this is inserting $e_2$ (with time [3, 5])
into $e_1$ (with time [2, 10]) at time 3.

**insert**(3): $\langle e_1, e_2 \rangle$

This application results in a new signal with time [2, 12] but in this case,
$e_2$ now begins at time 3 and is followed by the part of $e_1$ that was originally
at time [3, 10]. Both these operations, append and insert, are useful, for
example, in editing sampled sound.

A *signal* is a subclass of event (hence it has a time component and
responds to all the functions in $T$) but it has an added component called
*value*. The value is any object that is a subclass of magnitude type or
collections of magnitude-type objects. Signals, in addition to the interface
inherited from event, need only respond to the **valueAt** accessor function
to ensure uniformity of response. The argument to **valueAt** can be any
nonnegative number (hence, each signal must decide how to respond to 0,
to real numbers, to integers, and so on). A *dynamic-stream*, which is a
representation of the dynamic stream discussed in the secton on implicit
time, is a subclass of signal that has a single value, its length is one. A signal
can use a function to calculate **valueAt**, and the domain of that function
must include all nonnegative numbers. A static-stream can either interpolate to satisfy a requested value between its samples, or it can truncate
or round its argument. Probably a separate class would be constructed to
handle each of these different responses.

Next I define $V$, a set of functions that operate on the values of the signals.
These include all the standard unary, binary, and $n$-ary vector operations
($+$, $-$, $*$, $/$, **abs**, etc).

There are three ways the binary and $n$-ary operations on values could
work. First, they could be entirely independent of the time values, that is,
as if both signals started at time zero, with the resultant signal having either
the time of the first component, or a default element for time (presumably
0). Second, the operations could take the time of the operands into account.
Binary multiplication could, for example, multiply two sections of each
signal that have value elements at the same time; at all other times it would
return 0. In this case, multiplication results in a new signal whose begin time
is the minimum of the begin times of the original signals and whose end

time is the maximum of the end times of the original signals. Finally, the operation could also proceed by specifying an identity operation (such as 1 for multiplication) to be used anywhere outside of either signal's domain. Thus an envelope could be applied to a portion of a signal and the result would have the values of the original signal outside of the envelope. This last solution would seem to be most useful for music signals.

Now, since each operation returns a new signal event, we can use all of Backus's algebra of functional forms to define new functions. For example (using vector multiply "*" to multiply the values of two signals $s_1$ and $s_2$):

$$*: \langle s_1, s_2 \rangle.$$

To construct a new operation $f$ composed of a vector multiply operation followed by a time-shift operation would be:

$$\mathbf{def} f(\ ) \equiv @(\ ) \circ *.$$

Then we can take two signals $s_1$ and $s_2$ and apply our new function:

$$f(1 \cdot 0): \langle s_1, s_2 \rangle,$$

meaning:

$$@(1 \cdot 0): (*: \langle s_1, s_2 \rangle).$$

This results in a new signal that is the product of $s_1$ and $s_2$ time shifted by one.

To this object-oriented signal event with its added functional-programming semantics I can now add a mechanism for temporal reasoning as follows. I define the logical-time operations based on Segev and Shoshani (1987) to allow reasoning about signals and their time relations. I will again use the notation of Backus to clearly display the applicative nature of these operations and their algebra.

Segev and Shoshani use the triple $\langle s, t, a \rangle$ to specify a time sequence (TS) for the surrogate $s$, the time $t$, and the attribute $a$. Adopting this model, a *signal* would have a unique identifier $s$ and a set of time and attribute pairs. (If the signal consists of equal-spaced samples it is possible to specify the $t$ component only for the first member and leave it implicit for the remaining samples.) Relational operators are defined not on the domain of signals, but on the domain of time sequence collections (TSCs). By defining the relational operators on collections rather than on individuals, we can maintain an applicative style: all operations on TSCs return TSCs. Because the result of an operation can always be used as the input to the next operation, we can build compound operations out of simpler ones using functional forms. As an example, I now define three operators, one for each of the classes of surrogates, times, and attributes. The arguments to these can be taken as similar to a Structured Query Language (SQL).

$Select_s$ takes an argument $s$ specifying a set or range of surrogates to operate over.

$Select_t$ takes an argument $t$ specifying a set or range of times to operate over.

$Select_a$ takes an argument $a$ specifying a set or range of attributes to operate over.

Let $S$ denote a particular class of signals with attributes (for example, sampling-rate, number-of-channels, samples). $S$ consists of $\{s_0, s_1, \ldots, s_n\}$.

We can now apply any of the selection operations to $S$ (the entire collection of signals) or to a subset of $S$:

**Select$_s$ (s = "flute"):** $\langle s_0, \ldots, s_n \rangle$

or

**Select$_s$ (s = "flute"):** $\langle S \rangle$.

This returns a new collection of all the TSs that have a surrogate that matches "flute." Call this new collection $S_{flute}$. Since this is guaranteed to be a member of the domain of TSCs, we can apply a different select operation to this in turn:

**Select$_t$ (t > 5 AND t < 100):** $\langle S_{flute} \rangle$.

Similarly, we can use an algebra of functional forms for building new functions.

**def ST( )( ) $\equiv$ Select$_t$( ) $\circ$ Select$_s$( ),**

then the above function could be applied to a set of signals:

**ST(t > 5 AND t < 100) (s = "flute"):** $\langle S \rangle$.

Since the time representation is based on an interval model, as in Allen and Hayes 1985, it is possible to define operations such as MEETS, and all the temporal relationships that can be defined in terms of it, on the time domain of the model.

This representation goes a long way to fulfilling the requirements of music signals adumbrated above. It supports many types of specification and complex relationships and referencing. Its functional programming style of operations, particularly on the values of music signals, should provide support for efficient implementations based on one or the other block-computation models. It is, however, still weak in the area of indefinite time specification.

## Conclusion

In computer music applications, digital signals represent the information content of the acoustic waveform and analyses of that waveform, and they can be used as parameters of various models of sound production. In addition to this, the temporal dimension of these music signals varies from totally undefined, through implicitly defined and relatively defined, to absolutely defined with respect to one of several different types of clocks (program clock, computer clock, real-world clock).

The amount of data in a signal varies from negligible to enormous (a signal representing two channels of an acoustic waveform, with a sampling frequency of 44.1 KHz, and 16-bit datasize, needs about 10.5 Megabytes per minute of sound). Finally, many composers and performers would like to have the capability of manipulating these signals on a higher conceptual level, specifying properties and relationships at the perceptual or cognitive levels rather than the often unobvious, unintuitive, but nonetheless corresponding physical properties.

A framework including various models of time and signals has been presented in terms of which some of the literature of signal processing and computer music has been examined. The general outline of a new, hybrid model has been presented. Further work is of course necessary to adequately define this admittedly complex model and to test its properties in a real-world implementation.

## Acknowledgment

I thank Curtis Roads for inviting me to set down these ideas and for providing a vehicle for them. David Wessel has provided not only a sounding board for ideas and personal encouragement, but he has also given me use of the facilities of the Center for New Music and Audio Technologies (CNMAT) at the University of California, Berkeley. He has my lasting gratitude. I also thank Bernard Mont-Reynaud for clarification of many of my ideas on streams and blocks. Lastly, I thank Sherry for all her support and encouragement.

# References

Agha, G., and C. Hewitt. 1987. "Concurrent programming using actors." In A. Yonezawa and M. Tokoro, eds. *Object-Oriented Concurrent Programming.* Cambridge, Massachusetts: MIT Press. pp. 37–53.

Allen, J. 1983. "Maintaining knowledge about temporal intervals." *Communications of the Association for Computing Machinery* 26(11): 832–843.

Allen, J., and P. J. Hayes. 1985. "A commonsense theory of time." In A. Joshi, ed. *Proceedings of the International Joint Conference of Artificial Intelligence* 85: 528–531.

Backus, J. 1978. "Can programming be liberated from the Von Neumann style? A functional style and its algebra of programs." *Communications of the Association for Computing Machinery* 21(8): 613–691.

Bolour, A., T. L. Anderson, L. J. Dekeyser, and H. K. T. Won. 1982. "The role of time in information processing: a survey. *Association for Computing Machinery*, SIGMOD Record 12(3): 27–50.

Byte, 1986. Special Object-Oriented Programming Issue. *Byte* 11(8).

Claasen, T. A. C. M., and W. F. G. Mecklenbraüker. 1980. "The Wigner distribution–a tool for time-frequency signal analysis." *Phillips Journal of Research* 35 (3, 4/5, and 6).

Dannenberg, R., P. McAvinney, and D. Rubine. 1986. "Arctic: a functional language of real-time systems." *Computer Music Journal* 10(4): 67–78.

Dennis, J. B. 1980. "Dataflow supercomputers." *IEEE Computer* 13(11): 48–56.

Dodge, C., and T. A. Jerse. 1985. *Computer Music: Synthesis, Composition, and Performance.* New York: Schirmer.

Dutta, S. 1989. "Generalized events in temporal databases." *IEEE Proceedings of the 5th International Conference on Data Engineering.*

Flanagan, J. L. 1972. *Speech Analysis, Synthesis, and Perception.* New York: Springer-Verlag.

Garnett, G. E., and B. Mont-Reynaud. 1988. "Hierarchical waveguide networks." *Proceedings of the 1988 International Computer Music Conference.* San Francisco: Computer Music Association, and Köln: Feedback Studio Verlag. pp. 297–312.

Goguen, J., and J. Meseguer. 1987. "Unifying functional, object-oriented, and relational programming with logical semantics." In B. Shriver and P. Wegner, eds. *Research Directions in Object-Oriented Programming.* Cambridge, Mass.: MIT Press. pp. 417–477.

Goodman, N. 1976. *Languages of Art.* Indianapolis: Hockett Publishing.

Harrison, P. G., and H. Khoshnevisan. 1985. "Functional programming using FP." *Byte* 10(8): 219–232.

Israel, D. J. 1983. "The role of logic in knowledge representation." Special Issue on Knowledge Representation. *IEEE Computer* 16(10): 37–41.

Jaffe, D., and L. Boynton. 1989. "An overview of the sound and music kits for the Next computer." *Computer Music Journal* 13(2): 48–55.

Kelly, J. L., Jr., C. Lochbaum, and V. A. Vyssotsky. 1961. "A block diagram compiler." *The Bell System Technical Journal* 40(3): 669–676.

Kopec, G. E. 1984. "The integrated signal processing system ISP." *IEEE Transactions on Acoustics, Speech, and Signal Processing* ASSP-32(4): 842–851.

Kopec, G. E. 1985a. "An overview of signal representations in programs." In S. Y. Kung, H. J. Whitehouse, and T. Kailath, Eds. *VLSI and Modern Signal Processing*. Englewood Cliffs: Prentice-Hall. pp. 241–256.

Kopec, G. E. 1985b. "The signal representation language, SRL." *IEEE Transactions on Acoustics, Speech, and Signal Processing* ASSP-33(4): 921–932.

Loy, G. 1985. "Musicians make a standard: the MIDI phenomenon." *Computer Music Journal* 9(4): 8–26. Reprinted in C. Roads, ed. 1989. *The Music Machine*. Cambridge, Massachusetts: MIT Press. pp. 181–198.

Loy, G. 1989. "Composing with computers—a survey of some compositional formalism and music programming languages." In Mathews, M., and J. Pierce, eds. *Current Directions in Computer Music Research*. Cambridge, Massachusetts: The MIT Press.

Mathews, M. 1969. *The Technology of Computer Music*: Cambridge, Massachusetts: MIT Press.

Mathews, M. V., and F. R. Moore. 1970. "GROOVE—a program to compose, store, and edit functions of time." *Communications of the Association for Computing Machinery* 13(12): 715–721.

McCalla, G., and N. Cercone. 1983. Special Issue on Knowledge Representation. *IEEE Computer* 16(10).

McDermott, D. 1982. "A temporal logic for reasoning about proceses and plans." *Cognitive Science* 6: 101–155.

Messerschmitt, D. G. 1984. "A tool for structured functional simulation." *IEEE Journal on Selected Areas in Communications* SAC-2(1): 137–147.

Meyer, B. 1988. *Object-Oriented Software Construction*. New York: Prentice-Hall.

Meyers, C. 1986. "Signal Representation for Symbolic and Numerical Processing." Ph.D. diss.. Cambridge, Massachusetts: M.I.T.

Moore, F. R. 1988. "The dysfunctions of MIDI." *Computer Music Journal* 12(1): 19–28.

Moorer, J. A. 1977. "Signal processing aspects of computer music: a survey." *Proceedings of the IEEE* 65(8): 1108–1137.

Quine, W. 1970. *Philosophy of Logic*. Englewood Cliff: Prentice-Hall.

Rabiner, L., and B. Gold. 1975. *Theory and Application of Digital Signal Processing*. Englewood Cliffs: Prentice-Hall.

Rabiner, L. R., and R. W. Schafer. 1978. *Digital Processing of Speech Signals*. Englewood Cliffs: Prentice-Hall.

Segev, A., and A. Shoshani. 1987. "Logical modeling of temporal data." In U. Dayal and I. Traiger, ed. 1987. *Proceeding of the Association for Computing Machinery-SIGMOD International Conference on the Management of Data*. New York: Association for Computing Machinery. pp. 454–466.

Shannon, C., and W. Weaver. 1949. *The Mathematical Theory of Communication*. Urbana, Illinois: The University of Illinois Press.

Shaw, A. C. 1989. "Reasoning about time in higher-level language software." *IEEE Transactions on Software Engineering* 15(7): 875–889.

Shriver, B., and P. Wegner, eds. 1987. *Research Directions on Object-Oriented Programming.* Cambridge, Massachusetts: MIT Press.

# 11 An Object-based Representation for Digital Audio Signals

Carla Scaletti and Kurt Hebel

Ten thousand years ago the Sumerians kept track of agricultural goods by maintaining small clay tokens in one-to-one correspondence with actual animals or bushels of grain. About 4,000 years later, more sophisticated tokens came into use—small replicas of processed or manufactured goods (for example, figure 11.1A). Sumerian clerks recorded contracts, receipts, and IOUs by baking collections of tokens into clay globes or envelopes. In order to remember the contents of an envelope, the clerk first made an impression of each token on the soft clay surface of the envelope before sealing the tokens inside and baking the envelope. From here it was a small step to simply make impressions of tokens onto flat clay tablets, not bothering to actually store the tokens at all (figure 11.1B). Archeologist Denise Schmandt-Besserat has identified these clay tokens as the precursors of Sumerian script (Peterson 1988). By 3,000 B.C. pictograph versions of the tokens were being drawn directly onto the clay tablets using a stylus, and this pictograph writing evolved into Sumerian cuneiform (figure 11.1C), a system of writing that was to remain in use for the next 3,000 years.

## Defining the Problem

A "representation for musical signals" could mean many things. It could be interpreted to mean the representation of time-based signals in different *domains* in order to gain more information or computational efficiency (as, for example, through the Fourier and wavelet transforms). It might be interpreted to mean the representation of an *instrument* that produces the signal, as is the case with physical modeling or sine wave resynthesis from short-time Fourier analysis. One might even choose to represent the *intelligence* that produces the signal either by modeling human intelligence or by creating "artificial intelligences" in the form of complex dynamic systems.

We interpret the invitation to discuss a "representation for musical signals" as an opportunity to describe a *data structure* for representing digital audio signals on the computer. Our specifications for this representation are:

• It must be flexible enough to represent any sound, not only those sounds that can be represented in standard musical notation and produced on traditional musical instruments.

(a)

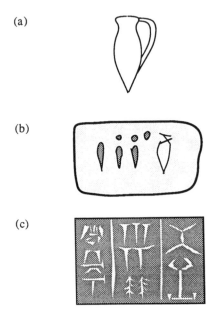

(b)

(c)

**Figure 11.1**
Ancient symbolic representations. (A) Small clay tokens were used in ancient Mesopotamia
to keep track of goods. (B) Contracts were recorded by impressing tokens into soft clay
surfaces. (C) This evolved into Sumerian cuneiform—a written language.

- It should be amenable to symbolic manipulation in the way that algebraic
expressions can be manipulated symbolically.

- It should allow the person using it to describe and manipulate sound at
a conceptual level and not be forced to always work at the level of sample
streams or assembly language programs.

Our goal is to come up with a data structure that is flexible enough and
complete enough to serve as the basis for a language of sound.

## An Object-based Approach

We begin our development of a language of sound in the same way that
the inhabitants of ancient Mesopotamia began the development of their
written language—by using tokens, or objects, to represent sounds. Rather
than use clay tokens, we use a drawing of a box to represent a sound (figure
11.2A). To make new, composite sounds out of existing sounds, we con-

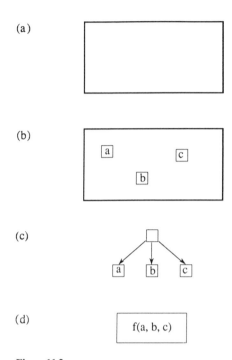

(a)

(b)

(c)

(d)

**Figure 11.2**
Sound object representation. (A) A token representing a sound object. (B) An "envelope"
containing other sound objects. (C) Internal sound objects shown below the container
object. (D) An "inscribed envelope" obviates the need for displaying the internal objects.

struct the equivalent of the Sumerian clay envelopes—a sound with other
sounds inside of it (figure 11.2B). If we substitute the relation *below* for
*inside*, we can draw the new sound as in figure 11.2C. If we, like the
Sumerians, inscribe the container sound with representations of each sound
within it, we can dispense with displaying the internal sounds and represent
the new sound as a single object (figure 11.2D).

We call this representation of a digital audio signal a *sound object*. A
sound object represents a *stream of samples*. This object-based representation enables us to deal with the large amounts of data necessary for digital
audio by hiding the details within a single object. We can design and
manipulate these objects in a high-level symbolic fashion, as human beings
are inclined to do, descending to greater levels of detail only when necessary.

In this paper, we will come up with a formal definition for sound objects,
describe how time and memory are represented in them, and show how the

introduction of variables allows us to define entire *classes* of sound objects. Next we will show how sound objects can be manipulated and transformed, how one might use them in signal analysis and musical analysis, and how they can be coordinated with other time-based signals such as animated computer graphics. Finally, we describe how some of these ideas can be implemented on the computer, and we offer several examples of languages for digital signal processing and computer music that employ data structures similar to the one described here.

## Definition of an Object-based Representation

A sound object is either atomic (a constant, a variable, or a stream of samples), or it is a function of one or more other sound objects. From this definition, it follows that we can represent a sound object on paper as either a directed acyclic graph or as a function (figure 11.3).

A sound object is, in essence, a mathematical expression, and it is evaluated in the same way that a mathematical expression is evaluated. For example, to evaluate the function shown in figure 3B, we would evaluate $a$, then $b$, then $d$, then $g(b, d)$ and finally we could use all of those values in determining the value of the function, $f$.

Each sound object has a duration and an algorithm for returning its next sample. For a compound sound object, the next sample is defined in terms of its constituent sounds' next samples; for an atomic sound object, the next sample is defined in terms of a sound synthesis algorithm.

(a)

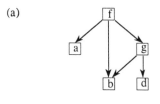

(b)

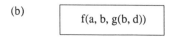

**Figure 11.3**
Graph and functional representations of sound objects. (A) Directed acyclic graph of a sound object. (B) The same object represented as a function.

Consider the following example of a compound sound object named *mixer*. The next sample of *mixer*,

nextSample $[\text{mixer}(s_1, s_2, \ldots s_n)]$

is defined as

nextSample $[s_1]$ + nextSample $[s_2]$ + $\cdots$ + nextSample $[s_n]$,

in other words, the next sample of *mixer* is the sum of its constituent sounds', or *subsounds'*, next samples. The duration of *mixer* is defined to be

max $[\text{duration}(s_1), \text{duration}(s_2), \ldots \text{duration}(s_n)]$,

that is, the maximum of its subsounds' durations.

## Time

A sound object has no absolute start time; relative displacements in time are indicated by *delay nodes* (where a delay node is just another type of sound object). Suppose we have three sounds $s_1$, $s_2$, and $s_3$ with durations

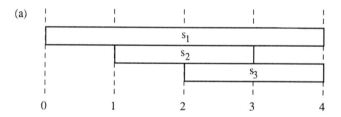

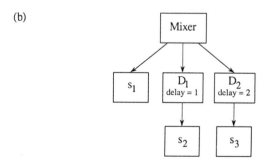

**Figure 11.4**
Temporal relationships among sound objects. (A) $s_1$ starts at time 0 and lasts for four samples; $s_2$ starts at time 1 and lasts for two samples; $s_3$ starts at time 2 and lasts for two samples. (B) The relative time offsets in (A) specified by delay nodes in a graph.

of 4, 2, and 2 samples, respectively, and suppose that we want to assign to them the absolute start times of 0, 1, and 2 samples (figure 11.4A). We indicate this by making $s_2$ and $s_3$ arguments to delay sound objects as shown in figure 11.4B.

Times within a sound object must be relative in order to maintain the uniformity of sound objects and to allow for shared nodes within the graph. Since a sound object has no absolute start time associated with it, a single sound object can have any number of transforming super-sounds. The idea of a single sound object appearing under different transformations at different times (that is, repetition with variation) is a powerful one in the realm of music composition.

## Memory

One interpretation of a sound object graph is that it is a signal flow diagram in which the signal moves in only one direction from the leaf nodes up to the root. Despite the fact that sound object graphs are directed *acyclic* graphs, they can still represent the feedback loops often used in signal flow diagrams as long as we define functions for reading and writing memory. For example, the graph in figure 11.5A is equivalent to the signal flow diagram of figure 11.5B and the function,

$$\text{write}\{\text{mixer}[x, \text{read}(z^{-1})], z^{-1}\}$$

where $x$ is some sound object, and $z^{-1}$ is a memory location. This simply makes explicit a fact that is not so obvious in a signal flow diagram—that feedback cannot occur without a time delay and memory of some kind.

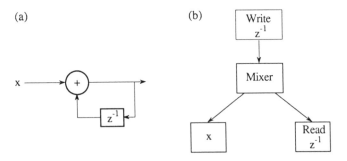

**Figure 11.5**
Representations of signal flow. (A) Schematic representation shows feedback with delay. (B) Sound object graph of the same signal processing circuit, showing nodes for reading and writing memory.

**Substitution**

Any sound object can be substituted for any other, and the substitution is itself a sound object. For example, we can substitute the sound object in figure 11.6A for $s_1$ in figure 11.6B to obtain the sound object shown in figure 11.6C. Figure 11.7 shows this substitution as a sound object.

**Variables**

Thus far, we have confined our discussion to specific sound objects. By introducing variables, we can generalize the definition of a specific sound object to a definition of an entire class of sound objects. A sound object with variables is called a *lifted sound object*, because it is, in a sense, at a *higher* level of abstraction than are specific sound objects (figure 11.8). By substituting specific values for variables in a lifted sound object, we obtain a particular instance of the class of objects defined by the lifted sound object. With variables and substitution we now have the necessary ingredients for doing pattern matching and symbolic manipulation of sound objects.

## Manipulating Sound Objects

A sound object represents a particular sample stream, but a given sample stream can be represented by any of an infinite number of sound objects. We can transform a sound object's structure while maintaining the same sample stream, or we can transform a sound object in such a way so as to alter both its structure and its sample stream.

**Equivalence Classes**

Two sound objects are defined to be *acoustically equivalent* if they represent the same sample stream. The set of all sound objects that are acoustically equivalent to a given sound object is its *acoustic equivalence class*. Each acoustic equivalence class consists of a single sample stream and an infinite number of acoustically equivalent structures (figure 11.9).

**Transformations**

A transformation is a change in the structure of a sound object. An *equivalence transformation* is one that takes one sound object to another in the same acoustic equivalence class. A *compositional transformation* is

(a)

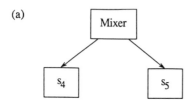

(b)

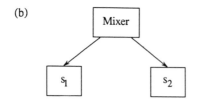

(c)

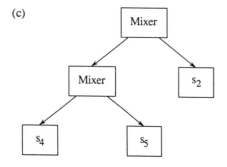

**Figure 11.6**
Sound objects are uniform and therefore interchangable. Graph (C) is the result of
substituting graph (A) for the node $s_1$ in graph (B).

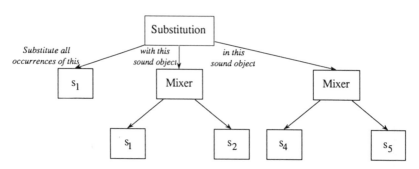

**Figure 11.7**
The substitution shown in figure 11.6 can itself be represented by a sound object.

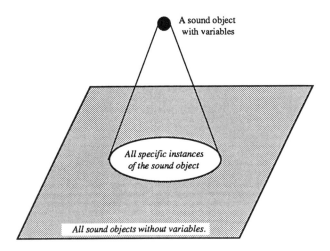

**Figure 11.8**
A "lifted" sound object. That is, a sound object with variables, which represents an entire class of specific sound objects.

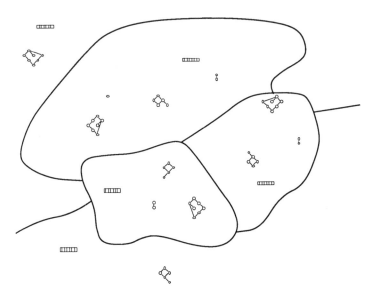

**Figure 11.9**
The universe of sound objects is partitioned by equivalence classes. Each equivalence class consists of one sample stream and an infinite number of sound objects that represent the same sample stream.

defined as one that changes both the structure and the acoustic equivalence class of a sound object.

Both kinds of transformation can be applied to sound objects. In the process of proving that one structure is acoustically equivalent to another, one might use a series of *equivalence* transformations. The process of composing music could be thought of as a series of *compositional* transformations.

### Analysis/Synthesis

Analyzing a sound object can be defined as applying a series of equivalence transformations until obtaining an object having the desired structure. The desired structure may be one that is simpler, or it may be one that yields more information. In figure 11.10, a search of a sound object's acoustic equivalence class turns up a structure that represents the same sample stream but that is more computationally efficient.

Synthesis is a specific case of analysis. Synthesizing a sound object can be defined as applying a series of equivalence transformations until obtaining its (unique) sample stream. A sound object can be synthesized via purely symbolic transformations, or it can be synthesized numerically by extracting and executing a program from the original structure and sound object definitions (figure 11.11). In practice, some combination of the two techniques is used; a sound object is transformed symbolically until it consists only of "primitive" sound objects, then a program is generated from the simplified structure.

### Interpretive Nodes

The graph of a sound object can also include nodes that are purely interpretive. These interpretive nodes have nothing to do with the production of the sample stream; they *identify* or *describe* a subgraph of the sound object. Interpretive nodes can include semantic information (such as the meaning of a digitized speech fragment), musical analyses (such as labeling a motive), or psychoacoustic attributes (such as "bright"). By extending the use of variables and substitution to interpretive nodes, we can use them to do automated reasoning about sound objects or to retrieve sound objects from a large database using partial descriptions.

### Coordination with Other Time-based Signals

The problem of specifying sound objects can be reduced to the problem of specifying what things should happen simultaneously and what things

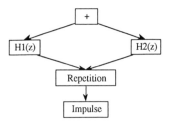

If the impulse response of H1(z) and H2(z) is shorter than
the duration of a single impulse:

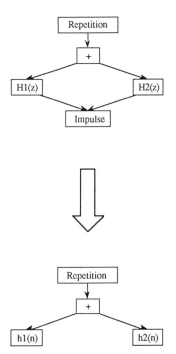

**Figure 11.10**
Analysis is the search for alternate structures that represent the same sample stream. In this
example, a sequence of acoustically equivalent structures illustrates Rodet's FOF synthesis
technique.

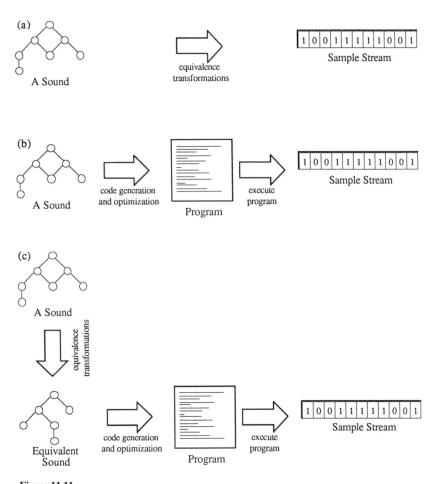

**Figure 11.11**
Sample generation can performed in three ways. (A) Symbolically. (B) By generating a
program and then executing it. (C) By rewriting the structure until it consists only of
primitives and then generating a program from the simplified structure.

should happen serially. The same problem arises in the specification of any time-based signal. In a graphics animation, for example, one might want to specify that $X$ moves from the upper left to the middle of the display while $Y$ moves from the bottom center up to the middle of the display, and after a short delay that another copy of $Y$ should move from the left center to the middle of the display. This mixture of concurrent and serial movements could be specified by a graphics object analogous to a sound object (for example, figure 11.12).

Instead of representing a stream of samples, a graphics object represents a stream of frames, and each type of graphics object includes a definition for its next frame. Like a sound object, a graphics object has a duration; a graphics object also has a size. In figure 11.12, $X$ an $Y$ could represent atomic graphics (e.g., a point or a line), or they could represent combinations of other graphics objects. In graphics objects, neither time nor location is absolute; displacements in time are indicated with delay node just as they are in sound objects, and displacements in two-dimensional location are specified with offset nodes. A single graph consisting of both sound nodes and graphics nodes could be used to represent synchronized sound and graphics.

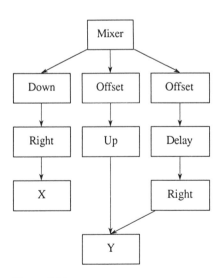

**Figure 11.12**
A graphics object is analogous to a sound object. Instead of a stream of samples, it represents a stream of frames—an animation.

## Implementation

Synthesizing a sound object by searching its equivalence class for its unique sample stream is a useful concept, but time and memory constraints make it impractical. In this section we outline alternative methods for synthesizing sound objects through interpretation and compilation.

We can express the sound object shown in figure 11.13A in functional notation as

$$\text{Mixer}(s_1(4), D_1(1, s_2(2)), D_2(2, s_3(2))),$$

where $s_1$, $s_2$ and $s_3$ are functions that take a duration as an argument, and $D_1$ and $D_2$ are functions that take a delay time and another function as arguments. One way to compute this time-varying function is with an interpreter that would rewrite this functon, evaluate it, and output a sample once for each sample period. In pseudocode,

newSound ← Sound;
while (newSound ≠ nil)
    Output nextSample(newSound)
    newSound ← Rewrite(newSound)

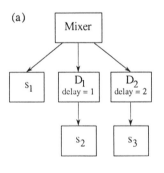

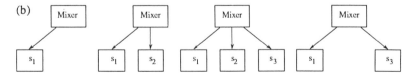

**Figure 11.13**
Execution graphs for a sound object. (A) The same sound object as in figure 11.4. (B) Execution graphs for the sound object in (A) for the time intervals 0–1, 1–2, 2–3, and 3–4, respectively.

Each sample period, the function is rewritten to reflect the fact that time has been incremented by one sample. This can be done by encoding the following rewrite rules in the interpreter:

| | |
|---|---|
| Rewrite($S(n)$) | $\Rightarrow S(n-1)$ |
| Rewrite($S(1)$) | $\Rightarrow$ nil |
| Rewrite($D(n, X)$) | $\Rightarrow D(n-1, X)$ |
| Rewrite($D(1, X)$) | $\Rightarrow X$ |
| Rewrite(Mixer($X, Y, Z$)) | $\Rightarrow$ Mixer(Rewrite($X$), Rewrite($Y$), Rewrite($Z$)) |
| Rewrite(Mixer($X, Y$, nil)) | $\Rightarrow$ Mixer(Rewrite($X$), Rewrite($Y$)) |
| Rewrite (Mixed($X$, nil, $Z$)) | $\Rightarrow$ Mixer(Rewrite($X$), Rewrite($Z$)) |
| Rewrite(Mixer(nil, $Y, Z$)) | $\Rightarrow$ Mixer(Rewrite($Y$), Rewrite($Z$)) |
| Rewrite(Mixer($X, Y$)) | $\Rightarrow$ Mixer(Rewrite($X$), Rewrite($Y$)) |
| Rewrite(Mixer($X$, nil)) | $\Rightarrow$ Rewrite($X$) |
| Rewrite (Mixer(nil, $Y$)) | $\Rightarrow$ Rewrite($Y$) |
| Rewrite(Mixer($X$)) | $\Rightarrow$ Rewrite($X$) |
| Rewrite(Mixer(nil)) | $\Rightarrow$ nil |

The first rule states that a sound object whose duration is $n$ samples is rewritten to become a sound object whose duration is $n-1$ samples (since one sample has elapsed). A sound whose duration is one sample long is rewritten to nil, since its total duration has elapsed. Similarly, a delay node whose delay is $n$ samples is rewritten to one whose delay is $n-1$ samples. When a delay node's delay time is only one sample long, it is rewritten to its second argument—the sound object that it was delaying; in other words, the delayed sound object starts after the specified delay time has elapsed.

Recall that the next sample of a compound sound object is defined in terms of its subsounds' next samples. In this case, the interpreter might have the following rewrite rules defined for computing the next sample:

nextSample($D(n, X)$) $\Rightarrow 0$

nextSample(Mixer($X, Y, Z$)) $\Rightarrow$ nextSample($X$) + nextSample($Y$)

$$+ \text{nextSample}(Z)$$

$\text{nextSample}(\text{Mixer}(X, Y)) \quad \Rightarrow \text{nextSample}(X) + \text{nextSample}(Y)$

$\text{nextSample}(s_1(n)) \qquad \Rightarrow n$

$\text{nextSample}(s_2(n)) \qquad \Rightarrow 1$

$\text{nextSample}(s_3(n)) \qquad \Rightarrow 2$

The next sample of a delay node is the value 0. In other words, a delay node contributes nothing to the total output amplitude. As defined earlier, the next sample of a mixer is the sum of its subsounds' next sample. The next sample of $s_1$ is defined to be $n$, the current sample number. $s_2$ and $s_3$ are constants, always equal to 1 and 2 respectively. In this example, $s_1$, $s_2$, and $s_3$ are simple atomic sound objects. They could just as well have been composite sound objects defined in terms of other sound objects. All of the nextSample rewrite rules must eventually terminate as a number or an expression with variables. When the stream of samples consists of numbers, it represents a realizable acoustic event. A stream that includes variables represents a (possibly infinite) *set* of acoustic events.

Using the stated rewrite rules, our interpreter would come up with the sequence of expressions and samples shown in table 11.1. If we implement our interpreter this way, sample computation is symbolic right up until the point where the expression is rewritten into a sum of integers; at that point, arithmetic primitives perform the addition. We would like to stay with symbolic manipulations for as much of the computation as possible because symbolic computation is more flexible; the rules can be easily changed, and they can include variables. However, it is clear even in this simple example that while purely symbolic computation may be the most flexible way to do things, it is certainly not the most efficient.

In the digital signal processing environment Javelina (Hebel 1989a, b), expressions are rewritten into a machine-independent register transfer

**Table 11.1**
Expressions for Realizing a Mixer

| Expression Sequence | Sample Stream |
|---|---|
| $\text{Mixer}(s_1(4), D_1(1, s_1(2)), D_2(2, s_3(2)))$ | $\text{next Sample}(s_1) \rightarrow 0$ |
| $\text{Mixer}(s_1(3), s_2(2), D_2(1, s_3(2)))$ | $\text{next Sample}(s_1) + \text{next Sample}(s_2) \rightarrow 1 + 1 = 2$ |
| $\text{Mixer}(s_1(2), s_2(1), s_3(2))$ | $\text{next Sample}(s_1) + \text{next Sample}(s_2) + \text{next Sample}(s_3)$ $\rightarrow 2 + 1 + 2 = 5$ |
| $\text{Mixer}(s_1(1), s_3(1))$ | $\text{next Sample}(s_1) + \text{next Sample}(s_3) \rightarrow 3 + 2 = 5$ |

language program. After optimization, this register transfer language program is rewritten into a microcode or assembly language program for any of several digital signal processors.

In the music composition environment Kyma (Scaletti 1987, 1989), sound object synthesis is a three-step process. The first step is to rewrite the sound object into a new sound object consisting of only signal processing primitives. The second step is to obtain a sequence of *execution graphs*; the execution graphs are computed by iteratively applying structure rewrite rules to the sound object and keeping track of the time intervals over which there are no changes to the structure. At the end of the second step, each execution graph in the sequence contains only those nodes of the original sound object that are contributing to the output over that interval of time. The sound object in figure 11.13A, for example, would be rewritten into the sequence of execution graphs shown in figure 11.13B. In the final step, the sequence of execution graphs is executed by a digital signal processor in real time.

At some point, inexpensive personal computers will be fast enough to allow us to do all sample computations symbolically on a single machine. For the time being, interactive implementations of sound objects require digital signal processors and combinations of symbolic and numeric computation.

**Discrete Sound Objects**

The idea of discrete sound objects forms the basis of several languages for music and signal processing. In Kyma these objets are called *Sounds*, in FORMES (Cointe, Briot, and Serpette 1987) they are called *processes*, in Herbert Brun's SAWDUST (Grossman 1987) they are called *links*, in HMSL (Polansky, Rosenboom, and Burk 1985) they are called *morphs*, and in Forest (Deiner 1989) they are called *T Trees*. Other systems based upon sound objects include SSSP (Buxton et al. 1985), Arctic (Dannenberg, McAvinney, and Rubine 1986), Sound Kit (Lentczner 1985), SRL (Kopec 1985), E-SPLICE (Meyers 1987), and QuickSig (Karjalainen, Altosaar, and Alku 1988).

**Conclusion**

The sound object representation of digital audio signals is simple, yet flexible enough to be used in a variety of contexts: software sound synthesis, signal analysis, algorithmic composition, and musical analysis. Sound objects are essentially functions, and they can be compiled into programs to run on particular computers. By packaging up details into higher level objects, we can deal with digital audio signals symbolically rather than as streams of samples or as low-level programs. Several music composition and signal processing languages employ some sort of object or function-based representation; they are offered as proofs of the viability and expressive power of such a representation.

Perhaps these sound objects, like the clay tokens of Sumerian commerce, can become the basis for a language—in this case, a language of sound.

## References

Buxton, W., W. Reeves, R. Baecker, and L. Mezei. 1985. "The use of hierarchy and instance in a data structure for computer music." In C. Roads and J. Strawn, ed., 1985. *Foundations of Computer Music*. Cambridge, Massachusetts: MIT Press. pp. 443–466.

Cointe, P. J. P. Briot, and B. Serpette. 1987. "The FORMES language: a musical application of object oriented concurrent programming." In A. Yonezawa and M. Tokoro, ed., 1987. *Object-Oriented Concurrent Programming*. Cambridge, Massachusetts: MIT Press. pp. 221–258.

Dannenberg, R., P. McAvinney, and D. Rubine. 1986. "Arctic: a functional language for real-time systems." *Computer Music Journal* 10(4): 67–78.

Deiner, G. 1989. "TTrees: a tool for the compositional environment." *Computer Music Journal* 13(2): 77–85.

Grossman, G. 1987. "Instruments, cybernetics, and computer music." In J. Beauchamp, ed., *1987 Proceedings of the 1987 International Computer Music Conference*. San Francisco: Computer Music Association. pp. 212–219.

Hebel, K. 1989a. "Javelina: an environment for digital signal processing." *Computer Music Journal* 13(2): 39–47.

Hebel, K. 1989b. "An environment for the development of digital signal processing software." Ph. D. diss. Urbana: University of Illinois.

Karjalainen, M., T. Altosaar, and P. Alku. 1988. "QuickSig: an object-oriented signal processing environment." in *Proceedings of the International Conference on Acoustics, Speech, and Signal Processing*. New York: IEEE Press. pp. 1682–1685.

Kopec, G. 1985. "The Signal Representation Language SRL." *IEEE Transactions on Acoustics, Speech, and Signal Processing* ASSP-33(4).

Lentczner, M. 1985. "Sound Kit: a sound manipulator." In B. Truax, ed., 1985. *Proceedings of the 1985 International Computer Music Conference*. San Francisco: Computer Music Association. pp. 237–242.

Meyers, C. S. 1987. "Signal representation and manipulation of signals." In *Proceedings of the International Conference on Acoustics, Speech, and Signal Processing*. New York: IEEE.

Peterson, I. 1988. "Tokens of plenty: how an ancient counting system evolved into writing and the concept of abstract numbers." *Science News* 134(26–27): 408–410.

Polansky, L., D. Rosenboom, and P. Burk. 1985. "HMSL (Hierarchical Music Specification Language) a real-time environment for formal, perceptual and compositional experimentation." In B. Truax, ed., 1985. *Proceedings of the 1985 International Computer Music Conference.* San Francisco: Computer Music Association. pp. 243–250.

Scaletti, C. 1987. "Kyma: an object-oriented language for music composition." In J. Beauchamp, ed., *Proceedings of the 1987 International Computer Music Conference.* San Francisco: Computer Music Association. pp. 49–56.

Scaletti, C. 1989. "The Kyma/Platypus computer music workstation." *Computer Music Journal* 13(2): 23–38.

# 12 New Generation Architectures for Music and Sound Processing

Sergio Cavaliere

Novel techniques for the analysis and synthesis of signals in the time domain such as granular synthesis, wavelets, formant synthesis, and others are emerging as new tools to be added to more established synthesis techniques.

Even if they are in their infancy from the viewpoint of theory and computational efficiency, some digital signal processing (DSP) applications as well as some musical realizations are provoking the idea that these techniques can be powerful in the manipulation and generation of sounds. This is because they provide new tools for unsolved problems in acoustic DSP (for example, granulation of sound for time compression and spectral transformation, analysis of transients, and others).

One problem with these time-domain techniques is that they are more computationally intensive than other established techniques, such as frequency modulation (Chowning 1973). Moreover, they force us to continuously update the parameters of the computation at short time intervals. This requires a high communication bandwidth, both for the controlling computer and for the specialized hardware.

In any case, the real-time production of a large number of acoustic events, which approaches the variety and richness of natural sounds using a wide class of algorithms, is a computational task that goes well beyond the computational power of traditional architectures. Even the most recent DSP chips are inadequate for flexible multichannel sound production and processing.

Therefore in this field, as well as in the broader field of DSP and general purpose computing, the demand is growing for highly parallel architectures, large-scale multiprocessing, fine grain machines, connection machines, and data flow models of computation.

In what follows we describe developments in these directions and the architectural issues involved in order to deduce the magnitude of computational complexity that they entail.

## Increasing the Computational Power of Machines for Acoustic DSP

To increase computational power, we can pursue various approaches. A first approach is to look for technology improvements, for example, increasing the operating speed of the *very-large-scale integration* (VLSI) circuits, together with their complexity and size. Even at this level however, the increased complexity requires architectural research aimed at devising optimized computational units in the form of *reduced instruction set computers* (RISCs).

Also promising for the future is *wafer scale integration*, which builds an entire system on a wafer, using redundancy and discretionary interconnect technology. The overall system is divided into a number of modules placed over a regular grid on the wafer. Then the modules that work well are connected in the chosen topology using laser techniques. This technique leads to powerful and compact systems, but unfortunately it is currently confined to laboratories where the cost of producing each circuit is high.

In the direction of the technologic approach advances in VLSI as well as more powerful silicon compilers are providing tools that render practically feasible complex architectural solutions.

A second approach to increasing computational power calls for architectural innovations to provide parallel processing. It is this approach that we discuss in more detail in this chapter.

Departing from a conjecture made in the 1960s, stating that the efficiency of parallel computers could only approach a logarithmic dependence from the number of processing elements, several advances have been made. This includes realizations providing up to a one million processing elements (PEs) and computational efficiency approaching a linear law for a wide class of digital computations.

Here it must be emphasized that in this general framework DSP applications play a major role. DSP can even be a paradigm for the more general problem of digital computing, for at least two reasons. First, DSP algorithms often show regularity and repetitiveness that suggest large parallel single-instruction multiple-data (SIMD) architectures (such as wavefront and systolic arrays). Second, in DSP algorithms data dependencies can be systematically and automatically revealed (by means of the *signal flow graph* [SFG] representation of algorithms). This allows a straightforward implementation of the *data flow* model of computation, which promises to be a solution for the scheduling of proceses on large parallel machines. (This issue will be developed later.)

In what follows we emphasize architectural methods for performance improvement because they are recognized as the starting point for dramatic changes.

## Architectural Issues in Individual Processing Elements (PEs)

Architectural issues are concerned with two main topics: the organization of low-level processing systems and the organization of large multiprocessor systems (often based on powerful interconnection networks), together with task scheduling and communication protocols.

As to the first topic—the architecture of the single processor—our aim is to devise the most efficient organization, not only to handle its complexity but even more for computation speed and throughput. This implies a RISC architecture, in analogy with the RISC strategy widely explored for general computation. A common RISC organization is the so-called Harvard architecture or its variations (e.g., the Texas Instruments TMS 320xx). In contrast to the Von Neumann architecture, data and instructions are separated, meaning that the fetch and the execution of an instruction overlap. Seen another way, the instruction sequence has a two-level *pipeline* (three levels if decoding and operand fetch have a separate pipeline stage, as in the Western Electric DSP1-20-32 and TMS320xx).

This mechanism is shown in figure 12.1. While the current instruction is executed in the execution block, the next instruction is fetched. Therefore the two operations take place in parallel. Also, while the current instruction is being decoded, the next instruction is being fetched from memory. Instruction execution is also pipelined, since each execution step Op 1 to Op $n$ works in parallel on its own data set, producing an $n$-times faster output data stream than a nonpipelined version of the same circuit.

Another widespread feature is a *three-address architecture*, which specifies two sources and a destination in a single instruction, allowing two simultaneous operand fetches, along with a one-cycle execution and easy pipelining. Data-dependent execution (jumps and branches) can also be managed with modifications to the Harvard architecture, allowing communication between data and program memory, as well as using direct data values from program segments. The TMS320xx allows these operations, for example.

Another common feature of RISC DSP chips is the parallel operation of different subunits (e.g., adder, multiplier) each on its own operands.

The last important aspect of processor design to be taken into account is a provision for parallel processing. This implies that part of the hardware resources are devoted to communication, synchronization, and coordination of connected PEs intended to work together. Communication and

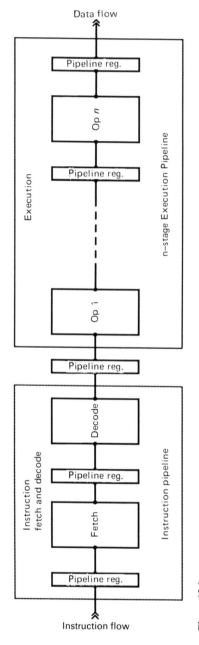

**Figure 12.1**
Pipelining the instruction and execution flow (two-level pipeline). In addition, both instruction fetch and execution are pipelined.

control strategies can even become more important than numerical processing power of each PE.

**PE Design: Two Case Studies**

A general model for DSP processor design can be illustrated starting from two example architectures. One is a high-performance design developed at the M.I.T. Lincoln Laboratory (Paul, Feldmann, and Sferrino 1980), which evolved from experience with several previous architectures for signal processing. The other one is an architecture developed at the Institut de Recherche et Coordination Acoustique/Music (IRCAM) by G. DiGiugno in various versions (4X, 4U, 4I). The $4n$ systems are well suited to general DSP tasks but are optimized for the production of high-quality audio signals with a large amount of control over the parameters of the computation for real-time performance (Asta et al. 1980).

Both systems were implemented around 1980 using discrete logic parts, but because of their high performance, we can use them to illustrate several techniques that can be applied to a VLSI design.

The "Lincoln Laboratory" architecture (figure 12.2) has three buses to interconnect the data registers, ALU, and other functional units as well as three additional buses to connect the data registers to the data memory. The instruction memory is separate so that instructions can be accessed in parallel with other operations. Operands from the memory are first brought to data registers and then used by the ALU. Results are then either utilized further within the processor or returned to data memory.

The architecture is of the three-address type and there is provision for immediate operands from the instruction. Two operands can be read simultaneously from the register file. Another feature of this design is the ability to carry out address arithmetic (indexing, incrementing with the proper step, and bit reversal) in parallel with other activities.

As a consequence of the organization of the processor, the following operations can be carried on simultaneously: (1) two reads from memory into registers, (2) an operation on two operands within the ALU, (3) the result can be returned to one of several registers, and (4) the contents of a register can be written back to the data memory. With the five-stage pipeline, a continuing stream of these operations can be performed once every 40 nsec (using emitter-coupled logic [ECL] discrete parts).

In this kind of pipelined structure, a problem arises when an instruction must read a datum computed by the preceding instruction and the datum

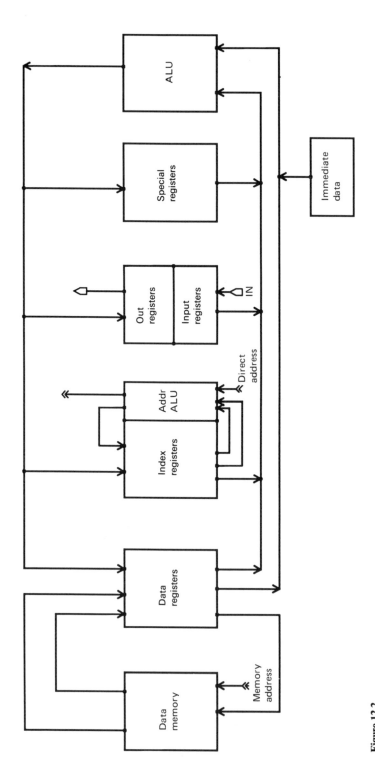

**Figure 12.2**
The architecture of the Lincoln Laboratory architecture for DSP (after Paul et al. 1980)

has not yet been written back to data memory. In such a case, the datum is read from a write queue where the datum is written together with the destination address. Similar problems are solved for other cases where conflicts can arise, thus preserving the functional correctness of memory reads and writes.

The second example architecture is the 4n series by DiGiugno (figure 12.3). The main feature of the 4n series in comparison with the Lincoln Laboratory system processors is the provision for multiprocessing: up to eight can be easily coordinated in a task of synthesis or analysis, exchanging data under program control. This occurs at a rate slower than the exchange rate in a single processor. The resulting interconnection network is powerful since it behaves as a virtual complete crossbar switcher by means of time-division multiplexing.

The other characteristics of the 4n machines include: a three-address architecture (even if data memory has only one access port), deep pipelining, and a hardware structure that is dynamically reconfigurable by software.

The 4n series architecture evolved over a number of years, with several iterations in the design. Each new version was a refinement of the earlier designs (Alles and DiGiugno 1977, Moorer et al. 1979). These systems were extensively used in applications such as analysis and resynthesis of sound, sound processing, and sound spatialization, and were tested in laboratory, studio, and live concert situations (Boulez and Gerzso 1988).

The 4X system (Asta et al. 1980) contains a 24-bit multiplier, large wavetable memories for lookup operations, and efficient hardware algorithms for generating envelopes. The 4X was designed with flexible real-time operation in mind, which is a mandatory requirement of an audio processor for music.

Apart from the features easily recognizable from figure 12.3, another useful capability of the 4X is the extensive use of "shortcircuits." Whenever data coming from a subunit (multiplier, adder) is to be used by another unit (as is often the case for DSP) a register is used to deliver the result to the following unit instead of writing it back to the memory and then reading it again (this is the case of multiply/accumulate for convolutions). These shortcircuits, carefully arranged on the basis of their frequency of occurence in the most common algorithms, and always controlled by the microprogram, allow dramatic improvements in operating speed. Careful programming strategies, developed in the same project, make full use of the pipelining built into the 4X design.

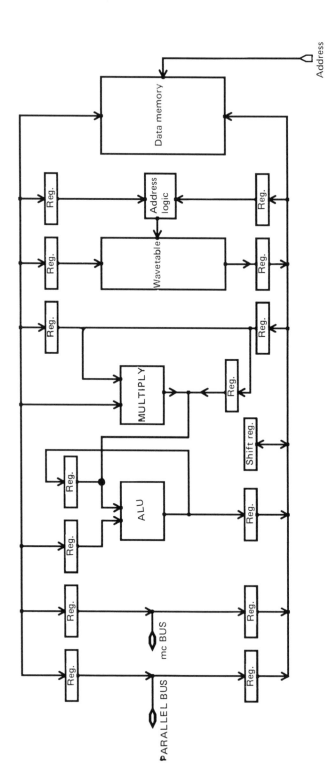

**Figure 12.3**
The 4X architecture (after Asta et al. 1980)

## New Ideas about Pipelined Structures: Pipeline Interleaving

To conclude these considerations on the low level organization of PEs for DSP, we must recall that the relatively old practice of pipelining is receiving renewed attention.

Deeply pipelined designs such as the ones described previously or the one used for some DSP chips are efficient only when the pipeline stream is steady. Filling and emptying the pipeline wastes time and reduces the operational speed to the worst-case speed of the nonpipelined structure. For data-dependent computations or recursive computations (e.g., infinite impulse respone filters) where data are needed immediately for further computation, these "pipeline bubbles" must be expected. In some cases, if the programmer makes careful use of the pipeline the operational speed can be very high. This requires time-intensive programming efforts and difficult checks for program correctness. A mechanism called *pipeline inter-leave* has been proposed (Lee and Messerschmitt 1987b, 1987c) as a way to avoid hazards, through interleaving the execution of independent tasks in a pipeline.

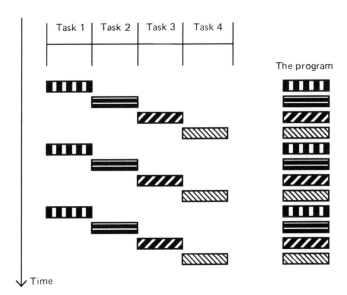

**Figure 12.4**
Pipeline interleaved programs (after Lee and Messerschmitt 1987b)

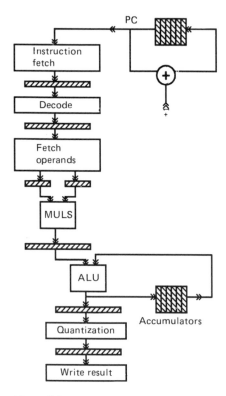

**Figure 12.5**
Duplicated program counters and data registers for a pipelined machine

Referring to the architecture of the Western Electric DSP32 chip, the provision for multiple accumulators and a large set of address registers allows four tasks progressing at once, each using its own set of registers. Therefore each of the four streams of operation can be scheduled without any concern for coherence, since for each of the four contemporaneous tasks in progress the execution is strictly sequential (figure 12.4). This, however, is only a limited form of interleaving. It has the limitation that the control flow of the four tasks in progress is far from independent, since branches, which alter the control flow, compromise the efficiency of the pipeline flow.

The solution proposed by Lee and Messerschmitt is to provide a separate program counter for each task (figure 12.5). Seven programs are interleaved in the same pipeline, each having its own program counter. After a program counter supplies an address for an instruction fetch it is incremented by one and returned to the back of a queue (or delay line). No pipeline is visible to the programmer for each of the independent tasks. The pipeline interleaved processor appears to the user as seven parallel processors sharing memory without contention.

A final design for the described principle is given by Messerschmidt and Lee to be embodied in the *synchronous data flow* high-level organization. They also provide proof that no data or branching conflict can occur in the proposed realization. This system starts from a general PE architecture similar to the Western Electric DSP32 and achieves significant speed with few hardware add-ons, while allowing easier programming under the paradigm of interleaved processing slices.

## Organization of Large Multiprocessor Systems for Acoustic DSP

Recent advances in large multiprocessor systems have been made in various directions, which can be schematically grouped into three categories: data flow architectures, systolic and wavefront array architectures, and connection architectures.

When organizing a set of processors cooperating on the same task two broad approaches can be devised.

One is the *explicit* appraoch: the system designer and the programmer must schedule in advance all processing steps to be executed at the same time by different processors (in the general case of multiple-instruction, multiple-data [MIMD] structures).

Therefore all possible parallelism must be detected in advance in order to increase the efficiency of execution. Also, all possible conflicts that compromise the coherency of the processing must be scheduled in advance. As a consequence of this increasing control complexity, the number of processors that can be efficiently controlled in a cooperating process remains relatively low. Efficiency in this case is achieved by increasing the computational power of each PE. This strategy works very well indeed in a large number of cases ranging from personal superworkstations to supercomputers.

Advances in VLSI make possible another approach to multiprocessor organization, namely that of increasing the number of PEs up to hundreds of thousands and even millions, provided that the resulting complexity can be managed. In some cases this approach, based on the inherently parallel structures of data, is the most efficient approach possible. This is the case, for example, in image processing, where the locality of data dependence suggests a topology in which each pixel has its own PE and memory. This PE and memory are assigned the task of storing and processing the information for the pixel and its immediate neighbors.

The case of difference equations for the simulation of bidimensional or three-dimensional physical systems (such as simulations of musical instruments) is for the same reason amenable to such a parallel solution.

In both cases, the regularity of the data structure suggests a SIMD architecture. Indeed, for machines built up from the same PE, which is replicated in space following the physical topology of the problem, the same instruction runs in the same time slot on a large set of data. Therefore the nature of the control, roughly speaking, remains strictly sequential. Actually, data-dependent execution can also be handled (as in the Connection Machine [Hillis 1987]). This means that the execution of the current instruction (the same for all PEs) can be either unconditional or subject to a conditional test before it is executed.

The principle of mapping the data structure directly onto hardware is also used in systolic/wavefront arrays where several PEs, arranged in a matrix or other fixed topology, carry on the same computation. The PEs also deliver data to their neighbors in some direction. These architectures are well-suited to computations that can be mapped from physical structures, such as matrix operations and convolutions.

The "fine-grain" parallel machines suggests a straightforward VLSI approach to sound synthesis, based on the modeling of musical instruments as large systems of difference equations (Wawrzynek and Mead 1985). A general elementary building block was defined (Universal Processing Element, or UPE) and replicated on a chip (containing 40 such serial processors) togehter with an interconnection matrix. A large set of sound synthesis and analysis techniques were implemented in a system using a number of chips whose UPEs were properly connected. The principle of modeling the hardware resources on the specific computation to be carried out is emphasized in this realization (Wawrzynek 1986).

The same principle is used in high-performance parallel architectures for image processing. Most algorithms in this field make use of simple two-dimensional convolutions. For example, values for a pixel's intensity are derived as a weighted sum of its north, south, east, and west neighbors;

therefore each pixel needs to exchange data only with its immediate N, S, E, W neighbors. This algorithm suggests an organization of an array of PEs, one for each pixel, arranged in a matrix with an interconnection grid. The hardware, in this case, is modeled completely after the algorithm.

## Data Flow Architectures

When parallel processing must execute different instructions in the same time slot, as in the case of digital audio signal processing, other solutions may be more efficient. An *implicit* control strategy can be appealing. An example of this kind of control is the *data flow* model of computation (Dennis 1980). In this model, the triggering of an instruction is not decided by a central program counter but is decided by the availability of all the instruction's operands or, in a similar model, by a request made from an instruction calling for its successor.

In a conventional computer architecture, an instruction is executed when the program counter of the machine points to it. This event is usually under the direct control of the programmer, who must stipulate the proper sequence of instructions for program correctness. A *control flow program* is a sequential listing of instructions, while a *data flow program* can be represented by a graph in which the nodes are the instructions (so-called *actors*) that communicate with other nodes through connection paths called *arcs*.

In the data flow model, an instruction is executed when all its operands have been delivered to it. In the graph representation this means that all the input arcs to an actor must carry data values (*tokens*) in order to trigger the operation of the actor. This operation, when completed, produces a *result token* for the cascaded actors.

In a sequential program the sequence of instructions cannot be modifed without affecting its functionality. In the corresponding flow graph, under the token mechanism the sequence of instructions is decided at run time without a schedule in advance, except for the interconnection graph. Only when a functional unit has produced its output token will the cascaded unit be enabled to work, thus respecting the data dependencies for correctness.

In a general model precedence relationships may exist between complex operations or even aggregates of complex operations; in this case the data flow mechanism can be stated at a higher level of abstraction.

## DSP Applications of Data Flow

DSP applications are well-suited to the data flow model of computation. For example, the regularity of the convolution operation acting on a steady stream of input data suggests the use of localized control mechanisms, which the data flow model embodies. Moreover, well-established algorithms have been devised in order to reveal data dependencies between computations. Indeed, when a *signal flow graph* (SFG) representation of a DSP algorithm is used, a precedence graph is easily constructed by a simple method. This reveals the amount of inherent parallelism in the algorithm.

Such parallelism detection is much more difficult for non-DSP applications if it must be detected completely automatically. With the spread of parallel computers, (table 12.1), compilers have been developed that try to allocate tasks to different processors that work in parallel. In order to preserve the functional correctness of the overall operation, tasks must exchange data properly and they must be synchronized on the basis of data precedences. However, no general algorithms for this complex task exist.

Starting from the signal flow graph representation of a digital network, node values can be evaluated as a linear combination of the inputs and past values of the nodes. If we do not order the computation of the nodes, it may happen that the computation of one node signal requires other node values not yet evaluated. Thus there is an implied set of precedence relations associated with the scalar system of equations describing the network. Sequential execution requires that we detect the precedences and embody them in the form of an ordered set of operations.

A procedure can order the nodes on the basis of these precedence relationship (Crochiere and Oppenheim 1975). Nodes in each of the resulting node sets can be computed without knowledge of any of the node values for following node sets. The resulting configuraton is referred to as the *precedence form* of the network, since it embodies all the precedence requirements in terms of node evaluation.

As regards parallelism, nodes in the same set can be evaluated together while precedences among a set of nodes must be observed for correctness. Therefore the precedence graph gives an exact evaluation of the maximum parallelism that can be achieved in the computation. A larger amount of parallel resources cannot achieve any further improvement.

Hence, the advantage of the SFG representation is that it embodies implicitly these precedences and under the data flow principle guarantees program correctness without the intervention of a central scheduling unit.

**Table 12.1**
Parallel Architectures for Signal Processing

| System | Characteristics |
| --- | --- |
| ESL<br>Polycyclic<br>Architecture | Made of several functional units (adders, multipliers, storage units) connected by a crossbar interconnection network. One of the system features is that it is provided automatic task assignment for optimal resources allocation even in deep pipelines. |
| Hughes<br>Data Flow Machine | A maximum of 512 PEs can be organized in a cube network and interconnections are made through a routing algorithm. Each PE shows a throughput of 2–4 MIPS while a 64 PEs could produce 64 MIPS (Gaudiot 1987). |
| USC TX16 | Based on the Inmos Transputer. Sixteen of these are connected using the point-to-point serial communication feature of the transputer. Task scheduling is based on the principle of data availability. Due to the power of the individual PE this is a less fine-grain machine than others. Parallelism therefore is shown at higher level of computation (Gaudiot 1987). |
| DSP*<br>AT&T Bell<br>Laboratories<br>(New Jersey) | Developed at AT&T Bell Laboratories (New Jersey) and based on DSP32 chips by Western Electric connected via a virtual crossbar realized on the basis of serial communication facilities of the chip and an external memory to buffer data from and to individual PEs (Kahrs, Killian, and Mathews 1986). |
| MUSEC<br>AT&T Bell<br>Laboratories<br>(Illinois) | Connects a set of heterogeneous chips and boards through a central switch. When the switch is under the control of a worklist, the switch makes the required connection between units using serial ports (Knudsen 1984). |
| ALPS<br>NRL/Imperial<br>College of Science<br>and Technology<br>(London) | Developed at NRL/Imperial College of Science and Technology (London) based on a ring pathway for data, messages, and monitors. The circus controller is responsible for the overall operation on the basis of a task table (Wu 1983; Wu and Wu 1984; Lanfear and Fernando 1985; and Yu, Wu, and Wu 1989) |
| MUPSI | Task processors connected via a ring parallel bus. Speed reaches some 50 Mflops (Bolch et al. 1987). |

## Systolic Array, Wavefront Array, and Connection Architectures

Many DSP machines have been built using the SFG paradigm. In some of these designs, the data dependencies have been frozen at design time. In these the hardware organization reflects directly the structure of the algorithm. Maximum parallelism is displayed by making use of replicated processing elements. These *systolic arrays* exhibit little flexibility and can be considered *application-specific* machines. Their efficiency relies also on the fact that they are well suited to VLSI realizations, owing to the regularity and repetitiveness of the structure and the locality of the interconnections. Each PE in the array starts working upon arrival of its arguments.

*Wavefront array processors* (WAPs) can be seen as programmable systolic arrays. They exhibit the phenomenon of the *computational wavefront*, in which an entire set of processors in the same wavefront can be programmed for the same operation. WAP machines are well-suited for matrix operations, image processing, and other multidimensional signal processing applications.

As regards control strategy, systolic arrays take advantage of their SIMD organization and they are completely synchronous. Wavefront arrays, on the contrary, are self-synchronized because the operation of the PEs is data-driven. This gives rise to the computational wavefront effect.

*Connection architectures* can be seen as an extension of systolic arrays in that the interconnections among the PEs are not frozen at design time. Rather, they can be programmed using routing technologies suited to the underlying connection machine architecture. In connection architectures, the need for a high communication bandwidth between a large number of PEs is a paramount concern. Another important feature of connection machines is the ability to dynamically reconfigure the hardware in order to match different algorithms. Whereas an array processor approach uses a fixed pattern of physical interconnection, connection architectures rely on a general interconnection topology (such as a cube, butterfly, shuffle, or ring). This general topology allows a program to interconnect, in theory, any number of PEs to each other.

Connection machine architecture are suitable for problems in which thousands of PEs can work in parallel on parts of a task. These applications include weather forecasting, models of fluid dynamics, simulations of room acoustics, cellular automata simulations, and database search operations.

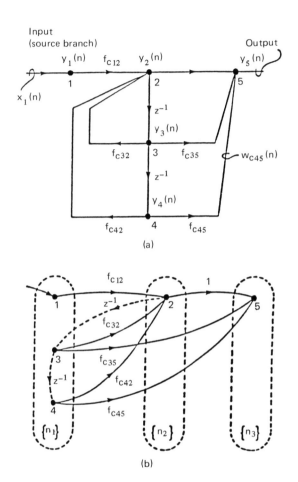

**Figure 12.6**
Graphic representation of a second-order difference equation (A) and its data flow
precedence graph (B)

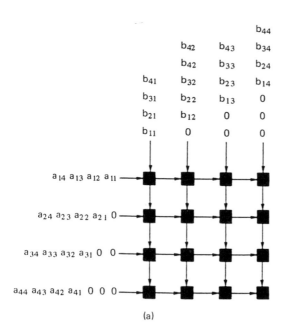

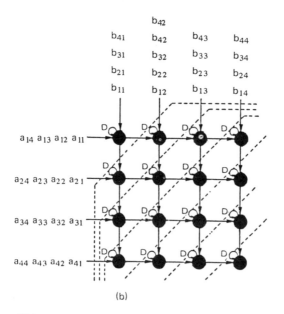

**Figure 12.7**
Comparison of systolic and wavefront array organizations. (A) Systolic array for matrix multiplication. (B) Wavefront array for the same task.

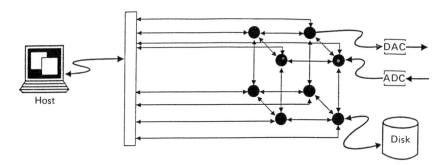

**Figure 12.8**
Small-scale connection architecture for signal processing based on a cube interconnection

We can illustrate the distinction between the data flow, systolic, wave-front array, and connection architectures by means of a series of diagrams.

Figure 12.6A shows a second-order difference equation, while figure 12.6B shows its data flow precedence graph. These data dependencies can be revealed algorithmically.

Figure 12.7A shows a systolic array architecture, while figure 12.7B shows a wavefront array organization for the same task (matrix multiplication). In these architectures, the physical structure of the array of PEs reflects the specific algorithm to be computed by the array.

Figure 12.8 shows a small-scale connection architecture for signal processing based on a three-dimensional cube interconnections network. A cube of order three guarantees that any vertex can communication with any other vertex in at worst three steps.

## Conclusion

As we have seen, many classes of DSP architectures can be applied to the synthesis and transformation of high quality digital sound. After a period of experimentation, in which many alternative approaches were proposed, we now see a trend toward standardization and concentration into fewer and more uniform classes of machines (Roberts 1989).

At the same time, the most recent research in sound analysis and synthesis in the time frequency domain, like granular synthesis, wavelets, and others, can be matched with technologic developments and architectural innovations, thus providing new tools for music production.

On the one hand, we could assert that existing machines and commerical synthesizers have almost completely met the processing needs of "classical" synthesis techniques, like additive synthesis. On the other hand, this technical result, which is the outcome of a more than ten years of research effort, has not yet met all the musical needs of researchers and musicians. Much room is left for experimenting with the production of new sounds and music. These artistic needs seem to call for innovations and further scientific research and experimentation.

Novel time-domain techniques have opened up new directions for music production (e.g., granular synthesis) and sound processing (e.g., time modifications). This has been demonstrated from a theoretical point of view and only occasionally with the evidence of acoustic experiments. Digital music practice, however, requires real-time implementation, interactivity, and ease of control, allowing us to identify relevant parameters from the acoustic and perceptual points of view. These requirements mandate that we turn theoretical tools into acoustic and musical experiences.

## References

Allen, J. 1985. "Computer architectures for digital signal processing." *Proceedings of the IEEE* 73(5).

Alles, H., and G. DiGiugno. 1977. "The 4B: a one-card 64-channel digital synthesizer." *Computer Music Journal* 1(4): 7–9. Revised version in C. Roads and J. Strawn, eds. 1985. *Foundations of Computer Music*. Cambridge, Massachusetts: MIT Press. pp. 250–256.

Asta, V., A. Chauveau, G. DiGiugno, and J. Kott. 1980. "Il sistema di sintesi in tempo reale 4X." *Automazione et Strumentazione* 28: 119–133.

Bolch, G., et al. 1987. "MUPSI: a multiprocessor for signal processing." *Proceedings of the IEEE* 75(9): 1211–1219.

Boulez, P., and A. Gerzso. 1988. "Computers in music." *Scientific American* 258(4): 44–50.

Chowning, J. 1973. "The synthesis of complex audio spectra by means of frequency modulation." *Journal of the Audio Engineering Society* 21(7): 526–534. Reprinted in C. Roads and J. Strawn, eds. 1985. *Foundations of Computer Music*. Cambridge, Massachusetts: The MIT Press. pp. 6–29.

Crochiere, R., and A. Oppenheim. 1975. "Analysis of linear digital networks." *Proceedings of the IEEE* 63(4).

DiGiugno, G. 1976. "A 256 digital oscillator bank." Presented at the 1976 International Computer Music Conference. Cambridge, Massachusetts: M.I.T.

Dennis, J. 1980. "Data flow supercomputers." *IEEE Computer* 13(11): 48–56.

Gaudiot, J. 1987. "Data-driven multicomputers in digital signal processing." *Proceedings of the IEEE* 75(9): 1221–1234.

Gordon, J. 1985. "System architectures for computer music." *ACM Computing Surveys* 17(2): 193–233.

Hillis, D. 1987. *The Connection Machine*. Cambridge, Massachusetts: The MIT Press.

Kahrs, M., T. Killian, and M. Mathews. 1986. "Computer music research at Bell Labs." In P. Berg, ed. 1986. *Proceedings of the 1986 International Computer Music Conference*. San Francisco: Computer Music Association. pp. 199–201.

Knudsen, M. J. 1984. "MUSEC, a universal signal-flow-graph network of digital signal processors." In V. Cappellini and A. G. Constantinides, eds. *Digital Signal Processing* 84. Amsterdam: Elsevier Science Publishers.

Kung, H. T., and C. E. Leiserson. 1978. "Systolic arrays (for VLSI)." *Sparse Matrix Symposium* 1978. SIAM.

Kung, S. Y., 1984. "On supercomputing with systolic/wavefront array processors." *Proceedings of the IEEE* 72(7).

Kung, S. Y. 1985. "VLSI array processors." *IEEE ASSP Magazine* 7.

Lanfear, T. A., and M. Fernando. 1985. "Simulation of signal flow graphs for signal processing systems." *Proceedings of the 1985 IEEE ICASSP*. New York: IEEE.

Lee, . A., and D. G. Messerschmitt. 1987a. "Synchronous data flow." *Proceedings of the IEEE*. 75(9): 1235–1245.

Lee, E. A., and D. G. Messerschmitt. 1987b. "Pipeline interleaved programmable DSPs: architecture." *IEEE ASSP Magazine* ASSP-35(9).

Lee, E. A., and D. G. Messerschmitt. 1987c. "Pipeline interleaved programmable DSPs: synchronous data flow programming." *IEEE ASSP Magazine* ASSP-35(9).

Lim, J., et al. 1984. "A programmable signal processing element designed for an efficient data-driven signal processing architecture." *Proceedings of the 1984 IEEE ICASSP*. New York: IEEE.

Loeffler, C., A. Ligtenberg, H. Bheda, and G. Moschytz. 1988. "Hierarchical scheduling system for parallel architectures." In J. Lacoume et al., eds. 1988. *Signal Processing IV*. Amsterdam: Elsevier Science Publishers.

Mason, S. J. 1953. "Feedback theory—some properties of signal flow graphs." *Proceedings of the IRE* 41.

Mason, S. J. 1956. "Feedback theory—further properties of signal flow graphs *Proceedings of the IRE* 46.

Mead, C., and L. Conway. 1980. *Introduction to VLSI Systems*. Reading, Massachusetts: Addison-Wesley 1980.

Moorer, J., A. Chauveau, C. Abbott, P. Eastty, and J. Lawson. 1979. "The 4C Macine." *Computer Music Journal* 3(3): 16–24. Reprinted in C. Roads and J. Strawn, eds. 1985. *Foundations of Computer Music*. Cambridge, Massachusetts: MIT Press. pp. 261–280.

Nishitany, T., et al. 1984. "CMOS floating point signal processor." In V. Cappellini and A. Constantinides, eds. *Digital Signal Processing* 84. Amsterdam: Elsevier Science Publishers.

Paul, D. B., J. A. Feldmann, and V. J. Sferrino. 1980. "A design study for an easily programmable, high-speed processor with a general-purpose architecture." Lincoln: MIT Lincoln Lab. Tech. Note 1980-50.

Roberts, J. B. 1989. "Recent developments in parallel processing." *Proceedings of ICASSP 89*. New York: IEEE.

Santos, J., et al. 1988. "A hypercube multiprocessor for digital signal processing algorithm Research." In J. L. Lacoume, et al., eds. *Signal Processing IV*. Amsterdam: Elsevier Science Publishers.

Steinmetz, R., et al. 1983. "Realization of digital filter algorithms by use of a high speed parallel processing architecture." *Proceedings of the* 1983 *IEEE ICASSP* New Nork: IEEE.

Wawrzynek, J., and C. Mead. 1985. "A bit serial architecture for sound synthesis." In P. Denyer and D. Renshaw, eds. *VLSI Signal Processing: a Bit-Serial Approach.* Edinburgh: University of Edinburgh.

Wawrzynek, J. 1986. "A reconfigurable concurrent VLSI architecture for sound synthesis." In S. Kung, R. Owen, and J. Nash, eds. *VLSI Signal Processing II.* New York: IEEE Press.

Wu, Y. S. 1983. "A common operational software (ACOS) approach to a signal processing development system." *Proceedings of the 1983 IEEE ICASSP.* New York: IEEE.

Wu, Y. S., and L. Wu. 1984. "An architectural framework for 'signal flow'." In V. Cappellini and A. G. Constantinides, eds. *Digital Signal Processing* 84. Amsterdam: Elsevier Science Publishers.

Yu, C., L. J. Wu, and Y. S. Wu, 1989 "Constant capacity—an information theoretic approach to VLSI/DSP architecture." *Proceedings of the ICASSP 89.* New York: IEEE.

# V  PARALLEL DISTRIBUTED PROCESSING REPRESENTATIONS OF MUSICAL SIGNALS

# Overview

## Aldo Piccialli

Rapid advances in the neurosciences and in computer science are leading to renewed interest in computational models that link animal brains and behavior (Hebb 1949, McCulloch and Pitts 1943). The idea of using massively parallel realizations of intelligence activity promises to be fruitful for the study of both natural and artificial computation.

Parallel distributed processing (PDP) models go by many names, such as connectionist models, neural nets, and neuromorphic systems. Whatever the name, all these disciplines model cognitive phenomena as the product of densely interconnected communications of simple computational elements. This approach seems to be particularly interesting in music research (Loy 1989, Dolson 1989). All musical activities, like composing, listening, and performing, rely to a great extent on specific cognitive capabilities that can be modeled by PDP systems.

In chapter 13, Lischka describes his research aimed at applying models of specific cognitive processes in order to achieve constructive hypotheses for theory formation. After a critical study of the present methods of research in music cognition, he points out that philosophy, psychology, and biology provide strong evidence that cognitive systems are necessarily biological systems, which can be modeled using modern neural network software.

As a case study, the author examines the well-known exercise of harmonizing Bach chorales and contrasts two different strategies: the procedural paradigm (decomposition into subtasks), and the connectionist paradigm. Following Piaget's lead, he then explains how music cognition could be studied by constructing artificial organisms in which behavior emerges by the interaction of organic *schemata*, which can be modeled as neural nets.

In chapter 14, authors D'Autilia and Guerra propose to exploit complex dynamic systems that are similar to neural networks for the purpose of musical signal processing. Input signals are encoded as external fields acting on the system, which affect the system's behavior in time. Output signals are decoded by measuring the average properties of the dynamic variables. Edge detection in vision and rhythmic recognition in music are primary applications of this new signal processing model.

# References

Dolson, M. 1989. "Machine tongues XII: neural networks." *Computer Music Journal* 13(3): 28–41.

Hebb, D. O. 1949. *The Organization of Behavior*. New York: Wiley.

Loy, D. G. 1989. Special issues on parallel distributed processing. *Computer Music Journal* 13(3), 13(4).

McCulloch, W., and W. Pitts. 1943. "A logical calculus of the ideas immanent in nervous activity." *Bulletin of Mathematical Biophysics* 5: 115–133.

# 13 Understanding Music Cognition: A Connectionist View

Christoph Lischka

The objective of this contribution is to discuss some questions concerning the application of artifical intelligence concepts, representations, and methods to the understanding of music cognition. In particular, we will sketch some arguments that support an alternative view of how music cognition could be studied by constructing artificial models.

For that reason we will start with a short overview of current research paradigms. A principal critique of their basic assumptions is then articulated; it relies on arguments derived from disciplines as different as philosophy, biology, and psychology. Finally, this allows an alternative approach to be formulated on which a research agenda on music cognition could be based.

## Preliminary Philosophical Remarks

In order to focus on the crucial points several philosophical remarks are necessary. Obviously, we will not be able to give here a comprehensive account of the entire argument; thus our discussion will seem sometimes rather subjective—which often implies (for certain people) that it will be completely irrelevant. But we think that in multidisciplinary fields such as this, such an argument is not only useful but even necessary to avoid blind "object-level junk" without any conceptual or methodological reflection. (It is easy to produce just anything, but it is much more difficult to produce something useful that serves several disciplines.)

### On Music Cognition

*What is music cognition?* We hope that nobody really expects an answer. Both concepts, music as well as cognition, involve such complexities that it seems hopeless to clarify their mutual interaction. But remembering that *what*-questions typically are delegated to philosophy, we should at least cast a quick glance at existing philosophical discourses—we might find some useful insights that eventually reveal at least some aspects of music cognition.

To start with, let us assume for the following that all discussions and reflections on music are always in relation to a general frame of reference: There exist specific music worlds even within one and the same cultural context, which constitute a web of different activities centered around production, reception, and interpretation of what we call "music." This concept is in some analogy to the *artworlds* of Arthur Danto (1964), which in turn provides a conceptual link between art and the "paradigms" of science. Or, by picking up a similar notion of Wollheim (1980): Music is a "Lebensform" in the sense of Wittgenstein.

In order to understand music cognition we are in particular interested in the music-oriented discourses within these "worlds," or, as we will call it, *folk musicology*. In western music these musicologies developed scientifically such as in music theory, music aesthetics, history of music and so on; often in strong dependence on related scientific disciplines (e.g., history and philosophy). Folk musicology thus plays a role in scientific discourses on music similar to *folk psychology* in scientific psychology or "cognitive science": It is the very basis for all the semantics of those concepts that characterize scientific discourse.

Now, music cognition can be located at the center of (at least) two interacting "folk discourses": musicology and psychology. The reason for combining both seems to be rooted in the idea that specific music activities, such as listening and composing, involve "cognitive" processes; moreover, there is evidence that in music very special processes, like auditory imagery, can be identified. But—what is music cognition? An absolute definition of music cognition seems to be impossible, or even senseless; it depends on the very idiosyncrasies of cultural contexts that determine both the concept of music as well as cognition. What cognition "really is" evolves (implicitly) from the games played in these contexts. Obviously the concept of cognition influences strongly the notion of music cognition, particular in determining which musical phenomena count as cognitive and which not. Moreover, it determines what could be "observed" about music cognition, and how "theories" and "empirical data" could be correlated (if at all).

### Artificial Intelligence and Music Cognition

Recently, increasing interest has been shown in the application of artifical intelligence (AI) methods and concepts to music, especially to problems of music cognition. Recent surveys include Roads (1985), Laske (1986), Leman (1989), AIM (1988a, 1988b, 1989). In order to understand the underlying appeal we should first look closer at AI.

**AI Objectives**    From a very general point of view, AI aims at the (methodical) construction of artificial systems exhibiting some kind of *intelligence*.

We can identify two principal approaches:

• Construction from a purely *engineering point of view* (e.g., in order to achieve an automatic language generator—for whatever reason); "natural" cognition is used as a heuristic to guide the engineer.

• Construction from a *theoretical point of view*. We become inspired to build some artificial cognitive systems by theoretical questions about cognition; "natural" cognition is the main reference point.

The second point of view will be adopted in this paper, for the following reasons:

• First, we could try to model natural cognitive processes by artificial systems, in order to obtain constructive explications of our theoretical understanding of (human) cognition.

• Second, we can build such systems in order to obtain instances of *artificial* cognitive systems. These are regarded as realizing some abstract concept of a cognitive system, and could be used to develop general theoretical principles that govern intelligent systems as such.

This research agenda is intimately connected to traditional (cognitive) psychology, and both are joined in the so-called cognitive science.

**Understanding Music Cognition**   This general idea to approach the understanding of cognition could be formulated in particular as a research agenda for the understanding of music cognition as well. How this could be accomplished will be outlined in the rest of this chapter, where the focus is on a reconstruction of current lines of AI and music research from a relatively abstract point of view. Pointers to more detailed work can be found in the references. Basically, we are concerned with the different attempts to build working models of music cognition, and why these seem to fail. This leads us finally to a criticism of the underlying paradigmatic assumptions of AI, and we will sketch an alternative approach.

## Cognition as Information Processing

Obviously, every AI assumes a specific semantics for such underlying paradigmatic concepts as *artifact*, *construction*, and *cognition*. The current AI paradigm regards cognition as *information processing* (IP).

## Basic Assumptions

According to this IP view, cognitive systems are retrieving, storing, and manipulating *representations* (of the external world). The basic activity is to accomplish a task: mapping (given) input-information to output-information by some information manipulating process.

In order to analyze the complex behavior of human IP systems, different levels of description can be distinguished:

• Specification of the IP function: What functionality is (to be) realized by the system, what is its input/output relationship? There exist slightly different terminologies, for this level, for example, the *computation level* of Marr (1982) or the *information processing analysis* of Chandrasekaran, Goel, and Allemang (1988).

• Specification of the IP process: What exactly is the internal structure of the process?

• Description of implementation: How are these processes realized? This is often called the *implementation level*.

• Physical realization: How are the representations and processes mapped onto existing physical devices?

See also Newell 1982 and the KADS approach (Wielinga and Breuker 1987) for a related account.

## Methodologic Aspects

The main research goal of an IP model is the (re-)construction of the overall behavior of a cognitive system by decomposing the complex behavior into different IP tasks, modeling them, and then feeling confident that all will fit together and the intelligence of the system will emerge.

According to the different levels of description this will be achieved by the following methodology:

• Trying to specify the functionality of the system; in the special case of the modeling of natural systems this specification serves as a rough theory of the behavior.

• Trying to implement the desired behavior (by some method).

• Checking the performance. Two criteria are normally considered: *weak equivalence* and *strong equivalence* (Pylyshyn 1984). Weak equivalence means: the "external" performance is adequate, that is, their input/output the (I/O) behavior is correct. Strong equivalence requires additional cor-relations: there must exist some *structural isomorphism* between the model and the system being modeled. See Pylyshyn's paper for more details.

**Performance Evaluation**    Whether weak or strong, how can the perfor-mance of artificial systems be compared with human performance? What are the criteria of "equivalence"? We do not want to discuss deep philoso-phical questions here (which are of great relevance to the so-called *knowl-edge acquisition* process [Becker 1888]). Rather, we state (as a working hypothesis) that an artificial problem-solving process could not be evalu-ated on an empirical basis alone: The problem-solving behavior must be matched against normative knowledge also. To give an example, whether an interval of a tritone is to be resolved into a major third in a given context cannot be decided by asking a statistically relevant sample of test persons; rather, this question can only be decided on the basis of deep acquaintance with the cultural context of a specific music world (normally conceded to the "expert"). Hence, it is a normative question. See (Apel 1976) for a similar analysis with regard to linguistics.

As a result, performance evaluation turns out to be based on *hermeneutic processes*, and for that reason it is difficult, if not impossible, to find hard intersubjective criteria that could be used to give these evaluations a more objective appearance. We should bear this in mind. But despite these difficulties we are convinced that there often exists a strong consensus among the expert members of music communities whether a given problem-solving process fails; this means that it seems to be easier to falsify a proposed solution than to argue for overall acceptance.

**Remarks on Implementation**    According to the above mentioned meth-odologic guidelines, we have—beyond the IP task specification—the problem of how to implement this task on physical devices. Two main paradigms are currently en vogue with regard to implementation: the *symbolic* (or *computational*) versus *subsymbolic* or *connectionist*.

## Music Cognition as Information Processing

If cognition is seen from an information processing point of view, then music cognition turns out to be a kind of (intelligent) problem solving, and we should look for suitable task decompositions and try to model each task: listening, performing, memorizing, composing, teaching. That is, we should aim at developing *artificial music problem solvers* so as to get a better understanding of how music cognition works. For a related account from the point of view of psychology, see Sloboda (1985) or Dowling and Harwood (1986).

**A Case Study: Harmonization of Bach Chorales**    In order to provide a more detailed background for our critical analysis of current AI research strategis, we should analyze a sample application. As a case study we choose a relatively well-known musical task: harmonization of Bach chorales. This choice combines several advantages:

• There exist competent experts in this field.

• There exists a literature of theoretical analysis.

• Harmonizing is a routinely performed task, normally involving no ingenious creative efforts.

The first two aspects reduce enormously the complexity of knowledge acquisition, whereas the last one implies relatively simple types of problem solving, which in turn reduces the complexities of the model building process.

**Harmonization as Design Problem Solving**    Naturally, if we try to analyze the IP task of harmonizing, completely different results are possible. An extensive study based on Schenkerian theory (and relying on a *logical* variant of symbolic processing, for instane), is reported by Ebcioglu (1988).

Our approach is guided by one main decision: Harmonization of chorales is conceived as a design problem-solving process. From a most general point of view, design is the specification of a set of basic (primitive) elements and relations such that some basic constraints are fulfilled (Brown and Chandrasekaran 1989). Thus, harmonizing turns out to be the generation of the description of an audible structure, consisting of a set of *tones* and (melodic, rhythmic, metric) *relations*, which matches specific stylistic constraints (in this case, derived from J. S. Bach).

To some extent typical design *strategies* can be identified. According to Brown and Chandrasekaran (1989) we can distinguish at least the following:

• *Decomposition* of tasks, for example, decomposition into the subtasks of melody-making, rhythm-making, harmony-making, text-making specification. In this way tasks are modularized, specific constraints between the subtasks are formulated, and after going into particulars eventually for each subtask (which is normally less complex) a solution is found. These partial solutions are glued together and matched against the constraints, thus forming an overall solution.

• *Case-based reasoning.* Typical for this strategy is the following sequence of steps: *identification* of situations similar to already solved cases (*matching*), *retrieving these cases, and modifying* them until a solution of the new problem is achieved.

• *Constraint satisfaction.* Because each design process aims at the satisfaction of some posted constraints, it could be conceived directly as a constraint satisfaction process. For most situations this is probably too abstract a point of view, but for some relatively simple subproblems this approach might be useful.

A real design process normally includes more or less all of these strategies; in particular, after a suitable decomposition we would expect that for these subproblems alternative strategies could be attained.

In the following we examine two approaches to design problem solving. Both (scenarios) are motivated by introspection and common verbalizations of this specific problem-solving task, and both emphasizing different viewpoints of the expert's behavior. The goal is not to give a detailed account of an exhaustive expert system design; rather the focus will be on prototypical strategies in order to project a basic understanding of how AI currently addresses music cognition.

## Scenario 1: Harmonization by Decomposition

### Analysis of the Harmonization Task

If musicians try to analyze the harmonization task, one might get the following (rather informal) picture as one possible, more or less plausible explication of this problem solving process.

**TASK**: Design Chorale
  Loop
    Separate melody into chorale phrases
    Post constraints between chorale phrases
      For each phrase: Design chorale phrase
    Check whether the subsolutions fit together
    If TRUE exit {Loop}
  End Loop

**TASK**: Design Chorale Phrase
Loop
   Design cadence
   Design bass line
   "Fill" in the remaining voices
   Do they fit all together?
   If TRUE exit {Loop}
End Loop

This strategy pursues a straightforward approach to decomposition. The posted constraints concern mainly such things as dependencies between the keys of the phrase cadences, the leading of voices, or (strongly) interacting constraints between choice of cadence and choice of bass line.

While decomposition is the main design strategy for the overall chorale design problem, the particular problem of cadence design seems to be approached (by student musicians) in a more case-oriented manner. Intuition might suggest that, for the purpose of harmonizing, melodies are split up into short, simple (possibly overlapping) phrases; that for each of these "melodic chunks" already known, possible harmonizations exist, and that these partial solutions are glued together by a kind of constraint relaxation process very similar to the Waltz algorithm known from object recognition in computer vision. To be more specific, let us analyze this task in more detail:

**TASK**: Design Cadence
   Analyze melody into subphrases
      For each subphrase:
      Match against keys in the library
      Select (locally) possible harmonizations from library
      Associate with the notes of the subphrase
   Post constraint net
   Filter out locally consistent labelings
   Return these as solutions

Figure 13.1 gives an impression of how this process should work. For both subphrases, we have a set of (locally) possible harmonizations. Each of these sets could be regarded as a specific constraint on the possible labelings for the given subphrase. Often there exist notes with inconsistent labelings (in our example the second note); a constraint satisfaction process

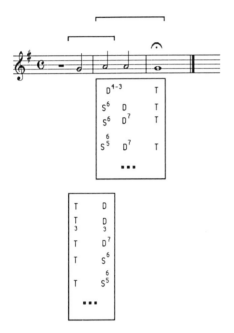

**Figure 13.1**
Two sets of possible labels generated by a cadence design task

should filter out exactly all these inconsistencies and yield locally consistent solutions.

## Implementation: The Computational View

**Physical Symbol System Hypothesis**   With regard to implementation, one of the most prominent accounts of the information processing view of cognition is the so-called "physical symbol system hypothesis" (Newell 1980), which is based on a computational view of information processing. According to this hypothesis, we should think of cognition essentially as a rule-governed manipulation of symbols. In particular, these manipulations could be explicated as precise algorithms and instantiated by physical systems. Thus we get an equivalence of *cognitive* and *physical symbol* systems. Hence, we can think of cognitive systems as *automatic formal system* (Haugeland 1981).

**A Computational Model of Cadence Design**   How would an implementation of our cadence design task run within the aforementioned symbolic framework? The decisions are:

• How should we represent the current problem state, what are the appropriate data structures for implementing note structures, melodies, chords, cadences? (See, for example Balaban 1989.)

• How should we represent problem-specific knowledge, in particular the library of possible harmonizations?

• How could we implement the matching of melodies and library keys, and the association of harmonic constraints with melodic subphrases as processes operating on symbols?

• Finally, how should we implement the constraint satisfaction process?

There are numerous tools available now to support the implementor during the system design process. For our sample application we choose a simple object-oriented formalism that allows a straightforward implementation of common symbolic structures and processes. Thus note structures, for example, are realized as primitive objects with properties that essentially represent an audible pattern as a set of melodic, rhythmic, and metric primitives in relation to some reference values. More precisely, note structures are *instances* of the following *generic* class:

```
(DEFFRAME note-structure
  (slots (list-of-notes nil
    :doc "notes of the melody")
    (reference-note nil)
    (melodic-structure nil
    :doc "intervals relative to reference-note")
    (reference-duration nil)
    (rhythmic-structure nil
    :doc "proportions relative to reference-duration")
    (metric-structure nil
    :doc "metric weights")))
```

In a similar way we can build up the library, using sets of possible labelings (the constraints) as entry and some note structure as key. The following is an example of a three-note constraint (called *constraint-1*):

```
(DEFCONSTRAINT
  (:type primitive)
  (:name constraint-1)
  (:variables note-1 note-2 note-3)
```

```
(:relation
  (:tupel (D S D3))
  (:tupel (D S3 D))
  (:tupel (T S3 D))))
```

Within the library, it is associated with the following note-structure and yields *figure-3*:

```
(make-figure figure-3
  3
  '(Prim SecondMajDown Prim)
  '(4 2 4)
  '(0 1 0.5)
  'constraint-1)
```

As such, these data structures represent a prototypical case:

If a 3-note sequence of such and such a structure is found in the chorale phrase, then typically the encoded harmonizations are possible.

Finally, both the matching as well as the constraint satisfaction process are well-known inference patterns in symbolic AI, and can be easily implemented. For more details see (Lischka and Güsgen 1986).

**Discussion of Harmonization by Decomposition**

What does this model show, in particular if it is used as a theoretical model? Subject to the difficulties of evaluating performances reliably, we could say that the model works somehow. Our result shows that it is possible—at least in principle—to specify the harmonization of Bach chorales as task decomposition and to implement this as a symbolic process. Our implementation exhibits interesting behavior; the proposed harmonizations, for instance, are (in a sense) correct. But they are not exciting. What is lacking, for instance, is some kind of global coherency. Also, the examples are not very specific to J. S. Bach's practice.

Obviously, there is no absolute argument to support the conclusion that just our particular system analysis and design failed. Nonetheless we think that there exist problems inherently connected with this approach.

• *Decomposition.* There is evidence that experts approach the harmonization task in a completely different way. In particular, the problem of resolving interacting constraints is counterintuitive: The artificial separation of different aspects of the problem-solving process neglects the mutual conditioning of all of them.

• *Knowledge acquisition.* As already mentioned, there exist difficulties in gathering relevant information—the well-known knowledge-acquisition problem. No common approach (protocols, repertory grids, and so on) works very well. The strategies recommended by textbooks turn out to be, at best, approximate. Even "introspection" does not help very much—it is nearly impossible to reconstruct how solutions arise spontaneously. Probably the main difficulty is the *perception-like* or *analogical* character of most interesting cognitive processes. In particular, there is strong evidence for a rejection of *cognitivism*, since all proposed symbolic explications for "unconscious" inference processes remain highly hypothetical and speculative.

Thus we reach as our main conclusion that it does not seem possible to model "really good" solutions (from an aesthetic point of view) by this kind of approach, because, esentially, knowledge acquisition fails. This result is very similar to the findings of, for example, Ebcioglu (personal communication).

## Scenario 2: Toward Case-Based Reasoning

Thus, we are led to the following considerations as one possible way out of these difficulties: First, we should try to generalize the *case-oriented* aspect. Experts often report that they solve most of the harmonization task by retrieving prototypical cases and transforming them to solutions of the current problem. Thus, we should try to expand this strategy from the labeling problem to the overall design task. Second, we should accompany or even substitute the knowledge acquisition process by some kind of learning.

Recently an alternative approach to the traditional symbol-processing view has arisen: *connectionist* modeling. (for a comprehensive introduction to this field, see Anderson and Rosenfeld 1988.) Because it seems to combine many interesting properties that match some of our problems with the symbolic approach, we choose this as a promising alternative to realize both the case-based reasoning aspect of our design task as well as the learning facilities.

## Implementation: The Connectionist View

Completely within the IP view of cognition, connectionists treat information processes in a different way. The mappings between different representations are not realized by algorithmic processes, they are rather seen as types of spreading activation, relaxation, or some other kind of dynamic process. States of the system (artificial *neural nets*) are interpreted as representing something, and the dynamics can be considered as realizing an information processing function: pattern completion, association, classification, or constraint satisfaction. In particular, most connectionist approaches involve some kind of learning procedure, which implies that the functionality of these systems must not be programmed explicitly; rather these systems are *trained* with a suitable set of training samples.

One of the more representative models is the *Boltzmann machine* (BM) (Aarts and Korst 1989), which belongs to the class of the so-called *thermodynamic models*. BMs are trainable and their dynamics could be interpreted as *constraint relaxation* process. This makes them a suitable candidate for modeling our harmonization problem.

In order to project a feeling for how this approach works we will give first a simple example.

**A Simple Example: Chord Classification**   A BM is a network of binary *units* and *links* between these units. To each state of the machine there is assigned a so-called *consensus* which is computed from *weights* on the links. Two main processes can be found:

• *Consensus maximization.* From a randomly selected state the machine "relaxes" into a state with globally maximal consensus (by "simulated annealing")

• *Learning.* This is procedure that modifies the "consensus-landscape" such that it reflects the statistical structure of the training samples (and generalize their probability distribution).

To demonstrate its capabilities let us state a simple music problem and show how it could be mapped onto this machine model. Suppose we give a set of pitch classes and a specific key: What harmonic *function* is realized by these classes? (map, for instance, C E G onto "tonic" in C major). Obviously, this is a classification problem. But suppose we provide incomplete information to this classification task. How can a pattern be com-

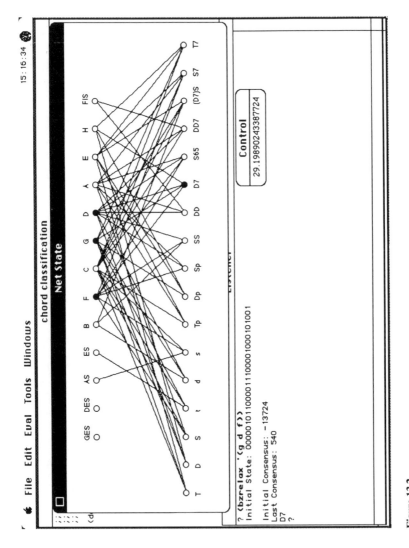

**Figure 13.2**
The structure of a Boltzmann machine for chord classification. Only excitatory links are visible.

pleted in a "meaningful" way (e.g., map E B-flat G onto "dominant-seven of subdominant")? Or suppose we specify a harmonic function, what is a prototypical realization of this function (the inverse mapping)?

We could map these problems onto a BM in the following way (figure 13.2 shows the basic structure of the corresponding machine):

• We have two layers of binary units.

• Each input unit encodes a pitch class (1 means the class is present, 0 means it is not present).

• Each output unit encodes a harmonic function.

• If a (harmonic) function is supported by a pitch class, an *excitatory* link is drawn between both units; otherwise we have *inhibitory* links.

• All output units are mutually exclusive. They are connected by strong inhibitory links (this ensures, that just *one* solution is obtained).

The performance of this machine can be described as follows. If we "clamp" some input units (set them to 1), say "G D F," we set the corresponding output unit (in our example, D7). Conversely, if we clamp an output unit we set the corresponding input units. Furthermore, the weights can be programmed or learned (by example).

What we have is essentially an instantiation of a simple classification problem. For more details, see (Aarts and Korst 1989), where a proof is given that the machine must perform in exactly that way.

With respect to our theoretical point of view, we see as a first result that this IP task can be implemented by such a machine. Second, the performance exhibits capabilities that cannot or can only with great difficulty be achieved by symbolic approaches. These include, for example, associative capabilities that reflect the music-theoretical requirements. Moreover, the machine need not be programmed but can be trained. These results, among others, convinced us to extend this kind of approach to the overall harmonization problem.

**Application to the Harmonization Problem**    As mentioned previously, from the point of view of IP specification we assume that the task of harmonization can be described as a case-based reasoning process. Furthermore, we would like to try to overcome the difficulties of the knowledge-acquisition process by designing suitable training strategies such that the machine could grasp the relevant structures of the underlying domain.

Thus the current research goal is the design of a connectionist machine which could be trained in such a way that it exhibits a behavior similar to the problem-solving process of an expert in Bach-style harmonization. We have proposed a scenario of how such a goal could be accomplished (Lischka 1987). The underlying idea is to use a BM-like architecture for memorization of typical solutions (including partial solutions as well) that a musician normally creates during problem solving. Moreover, we intend that the generalization capabilities of the machine could model the expert's transformation of cases into new solutions in the presence of new problems.

Basically, the following problems have to be solved:

• *Encoding.* How can the harmonization problem be mapped onto this formalism such that a suitable performance is achieved?

• *Parallelization.* Even our simple example takes a lot of time for performance (and learning) if it is implemented sequentially (whether Lisp or C does not matter very much); therefore, an efficient parallel implementation seems necessary, at least if we are concerned with a "real-world" problem.

• *Learning.* BM learning, based on an estimation of (implicitly) given probability distributions just by collecting statistics, should be modified in a way that it accepts explicit subjective probabilities also. The reason is that a musician normally evaluates solutions from an aesthetic point of view, and that "good" solutions are not at all the most frequent. For an analysis of BM learning that is concerned with these problems, see Paass 1989.

• *Training.* Different training strategies result in different performance results. How can machine training be oriented at common curricula?

**Evaluation**

Research in this direction is currently under way. Therefore, a conclusive evaluation is not yet possible. Learning is not very fast; we have to finish our transputer implementation for parallel processing. Encoding, which influences strongly the generalization capabilities, is difficult. We are experimenting with simple examples; we expect that analogical representations will yield the best generalization behavior.

In general, we can corroborate the impression that the connectionist approach is a serious alternative to a symbolic approach, especially in applications concerned with perception-like processes. This is mainly due to the learning facilities, which avoid that we become involved into knowledge acquisition processes in areas where almost no knowledge is extractable. Probably the most effective design strategy (within the current AI paradigm) would be a combination of both the symbolic and connectionist approach within a *hybrid system*, as proposed by Steels (1989b), for example.

## Cognition: Beyond Information Processing

So why should we bother with this kind of approach at all? What are the reasons that could force us to shift to a completely different paradigm? In order to understand our motivation it seems useful to go back in history and recall why we are basically concerned with cognition.

Originally, a main objective of psychology was to explain complex "intelligent" behavior. Since pure behaviorist approaches failed, and traditional mentalistic theories resisted more formal explications, it was difficult to take cognitive behavior into account. Therefore the notion of an information processing system, in conjunction with the availability of artificial information processors, had a great appeal to psychologists. It became possible to talk about cognitive states and processes without losing scientific respectability. And the interesting question of how cognition enables organisms to behave intelligently could be asked from a new and (seemingly) promising perspective.

### Cognition as Information Processing Revisited

Unfortunately, the concept of cognition as information processing conceals some deep philosophical and methodologic problems. What is explicated within the IP paradigm is due to a long empiricist tradition which, for instance, suggests that cognition is a kind of mirroring: There exists an external world, and through our sense organs we receive information about this world. A more naive view considers these internal representations as simple (more or less successful) "images" of the environment. A more advanced view meets some objections from the rationalist tradition, it concedes subjective influences during the construction of these images. In modern terms, our input is information about the world; this information is represented by *data structures*, and is stored, processed, and used for planning and action. Thus, complex intelligent (that is, adaptive) behavior is achieved by creating internal models of the environment, manipulating these representations, and performing actions in accordance with (internal) predictions. See, for example, Miller, Galanter, and Pribram 1960 or Neisser 1967.

Despite its popularity, there is strong evidence that this conception undermines all our efforts to build artificial cognitive systems, at least if we are concerned with systems whose performance equals (or even succeeds) biological standards. In order to see this we will enter somewhat into the details and sketch the criticism motivated (mainly) by philosophy, biology, and psychology.

**Representationalism**   A first objection concerns the *representationalist* view of cognition. The criticism focuses on the following points. First, there exist broad (empirical) data indicating that cognition is possible without representation. In particular, so-called sensorimotor intelligence does not rely on "symbols" (or any other kind of representations) to achieve its goals. Furthermore, highly advanced intelligent behavior like skilled chess playing doesn't seem to be based on the use of symbols, either (Piaget 1947; Dreyfus 1988).

Second, ethology suggests a kind of *constructivism*: At least from the point of view of the organism the environment is (more or less) unstructured at birth. Therefore, in order to explain cognition, it seems necessary to adopt a *developmental* approach. How, exactly, do cognitive capabilities, such as categorization, evolve during postnatal development? How is the world of an organism constructed? (Piaget 1970, Lorenz 1981, Edelman 1987).

Third, philosophical phenomenology shows that cognition in the sense of theorizing about the world is grounded on more basic modes of "being-in-the-world." It turns out that the information processing concept of cognition reduces all the highly different ways of recognizing the world to a narrow rationalistic point of view (Heidegger 1972, Winograd and Flores 1986, Lischka 1989). Also coupled with this rationalistic approach is the dominance of propositional representations. Even if alternative constructs (like analogical representations) are considered, they are almost always seen as deficient modes of "true" propositional representation (Pylyshyn 1984).

Finally, much philosophical analysis results in the rejection of the representationalist view of cognition completely. Either it is argued that this conception will lead to inconsistencies (such as the *homunculus* problem), or that it is simply naive and useless (Rorty 1980, Richards and Glasersfeld 1979).

**Cognitivism**   Further criticism examines more closely the functional role of cognition within mental life. Most AI reseachers seem to believe that all mental processes, like perception, motivation, learning, or action, could be considered, at least in principle, as inference processes or a form of problem solving. Thus they are inclined to treat all mental activities as cognitive processes, and resulting in a kind of cognitivism. In contrast, a vast amount of intelligent behavior does not seem to be based on inference or similar processes at all; rather, there is much evidence that it results from extensive practice without any intermediation by cognition (in that restricted sense of problem solving). A typical example is perception; but, see Dreyfus (1988) for a recent analysis of skilled behavior as well.

**Functionalism**   Another central assumption of the current AI paradigm is so-called *functionalism*: the belief that function (behavior) and the underlying machinery that realizes this functionality can be separated and analyzed independently. This view assumes that a given functionality can be implemented on fundamentally different systems (for example, biological systems, and digital computers).

But is it really possible to separate function and the underlying physical system and treat behavioral organization independently? Cognition stands in an intimate relationship to adaptation to the environment; therefore, it is mediated by "lower" forms of behavioral organization. Furthermore, cognition is linked with the organization of behavior, which in turn is inevitably bound to organisms. Thus this kind of functionalism seems implausible. Moreover, some neurologists suggest that brains are not capable of implementing information-processing algorithms; therefore, at least the computational version of functionalism becomes unlikely (Edelman 1987).

**Extensionalism**   Yet another underlying assumption leads to serious difficulties: The belief that a given functionality can be analyzed in terms of (primitive) parts and their additive (linear) composition (which is essentially a mechanistic approach). This idea is intimately connected with Western rationalism: Structures can be decomposed into parts, each part investigated separately, and then they can be recomposed by a transparent procedure to obtain an understanding of the whole; that is, the parts are independent of the whole.

On the contrary, human beings use organic thinking. The functioning (and understanding) of the parts is not possible without reference to the overall structure; there exist no clear monocausal relations, rather we have mutually dependent causes and effects. This kind of approach is often labeled as *holistic*, *organic*, or *structuralistic*, and we discuss it in more detail later.

**Conclusion**    Thus, if we are interested in building truly cognitive systems there is strong evidence to pursue a general paradigm shift. The usual consequence drawn from the previously mentioned insights is to yield to resignation concerning the possibility of AI. The argument runs more or less as follows: Because cognition seems to be inevitably bound to biological organisms, there will be no way to construct artificial systems that exhibit comparable functionality.

On the contrary, we think that there exists a much weaker conclusion: Because cognition is probably bound to biological organisms, the only possible way to build artificial cognitive systems is to ground them on artificial organisms. To make this point more precise we will present some very preliminary theses that should suggest the basic direction of this research.

## A Basic Paradigm Shift

First, this AI is built around a somewhat different concept of cognition. Taking into account both the critique of philosophy on the role of representation, as well as the insights formulated in the psychology of, for example, Merleau-Ponty (1942) and Piaget, we would argue for a concept that focuses on the specific structure of behavior: not complex behavior as it manifests intelligence, but the specific organization of this behavior, in particular its adaptiveness to the enviroment. Thus, we resume a basic theme of the early beginnings of AI.

Representation is not crucial for cognition, in principle. Rather, the opposite is true: A necessary condition for the evolution of symbol usage seems to be the existence of highly developed sensorimotor schemata, which enable organisms to categorize perceptually the environment. Thus, instead of presupposing the existence of representations, we have to ask how the use of symbols evolves during phylogenetic and ontogenetic development: what the underlying conditions are, and so on. Moreover, even if we would restrict our concept of cognition to those parts of mental activity that involve a kind of representation, we have to clarify the conditions under which representation is at all possible.

Next, what also has to be taken into account is the pragmatic dimension of symbols (and representations in general). Representations are always embedded in social interactions; their semantics is inescapably bound to subjects that use objects as representations. Thus, beyond a reconstruction of the biological basis of "symbolic behavior" we have to recognize its social and pragmatic roots.

Finally, we have to reject functionalism in so far as it implies an abstraction from the organic substrate of complex behavior. As pointed out in the last subsection, there is no clear-cut separation of behavior and biological processes; cognition as an organizational principle of complex behavior relies definitely on biological properties of the underlying machinery.

Second, because complex intelligent behavior—from a phenomenological point of view—has very strong structural similarities to organisms, it would be more appropriate if AI were to analyze this behavior in an organic instead of a mechanistic way; in particular, it seems doubtful that an algorithmic analysis (the mechanistic approach par excellence) will yield positive results.

There have been very preliminary attempts to explore the concepts of organism and life in order to get a more formal and precise account of what distinguishes living systems from common artificial mechanisms; see the next subsection for some details. In spite of this preliminary state, it seems possible to apply this conceptual framework to the phenomenological analysis of behavior as well. In particular, it becomes possible to give a new formal explication of the structuralist approach mainly due to Piaget. According to Piaget, complex intelligent behavior emerges from the interaction of specific schemata; these schemata are treated as so-called structures, with analogy to organisms. Thus, if we try to model schemata by means of organic formalisms, this could result in a new and interesting description of intelligent behavior.

Summing up, a basic research goal within this new paradigm arises: To build artificial organisms with emergent complex behavior that matches a phenomenological specification describing this behavior as a system of intelligently interacting (organic) schemata.

### Steps Toward Methodology

In order to achieve this goal, we suggest the following straightforward methodologic approach:

• *Specification* of complex behavior as interaction of specific schemata.

• *Implementation.* Build an artificial organism that exhibits the analyzed behavior as an emergent property: Emergent in the sense that the global behavior of the system is implicitly defined by locally interacting simple *elements*.

• *Verification.* Match this artificial behavior against the specification.

Let us comment on these basic aspects from two viewpoints.

**Artificial Life**   One of the most important problems that we have to solve is to find an adequate description level where we can abstract the relevant features of living systems (organisms) without becoming dependent on their specific implementation by biological means. Promising starting points are

• *Conceptual analyses.* On an abstract conceptual level there are surprising parallels between, for example, the concept of *structure* by Piaget (1968), and, on the other hand, the concept of *autopoetic system* by Maturana and Varela (1979). Both are centered around the concept of *homeostasis*.

• *Dissipative systems.* Modern physics, in particular *complex dynamics*, developed interesting theories of *nonequilibrium* states of physical systems. It turns out that these theories are especially well-suited to describe self-organizational processes of pattern formation, in particular those of living systems. See Haken 1977 or Babloyantz 1986 for references.

• *O-style and M-style systems.* Drexler (1989) makes an attempt to identify features that would distinguish *organic* (O-style) from *mechanical* (M-style) systems. As Drexler points out there exist different styles of structure, function, and development if we are looking at artificial mechines as well as living organisms. Organic-style systems exhibit features like *diffusive* (versus channeled) transport of energy (information, materials), *matching* (versus positional) assembly of parts, *topological* (versus geometric) structures, and *adaptive* (versus inert) parts. Up to now, both categories map simply onto the concepts of *natural* and *artificial*, respectively; that is, there exist currently no O-style artifacts.

In our view, these different (but related) approaches could lead to a working concept of living system that would enable us to implement artificial models of self-organization, or artificial organisms.

So as to see how this could be accomplished, let us focus on a second viewpoint.

**Complexity Engineering**   As is discussed by Wolfram (1986), traditional engineering approaches rely heavily on the transparency of the overall system design: Each aspect of the behavior must be, at least in principle, predictable, and often we have a complete analytical description.

Since organic systems seem to emerge from nonlinear interactions of many simple elements, an exact analytical treatment is unfeasible. Here is where modern *massive parallelism* (e.g., cellular automata, neural networks) comes into play. The computing capabilities of massively parallel machines allow an efficient simulation of these systems. This lets us avoid insurmountable analytical difficulties to pursue an experimental approach that eventually will lead to systems with the desired behavior. This form of complexity engineering (Wolfram 1986) is a three-step process:

- *Design goal.* Construct a complex dynamic system with given attractors showing the desired emergent behavior.

- *Method.* Implement a system of simple interacting units and explore the emergent global behavior. Here the engineer is guided both by theoretical insights like reaction-diffusion models (Steels 1989a) for example, as well as general heuristics that arise from previous attempts to model complex dynamics.

- *Verification.* Match this behavior against the specification.

Admittedly, this general outline remains highly abstract. Furthermore, since we are operating in a newly evolving field of research, these conceptions are, at best, first approximations, and subject to continuous change. Nonetheless, we think that a glance at the future makes sense, at least if we are interested in general prospects.

Thus, we arrive at the final topic of this paper: How can we build a research agenda on music cognition around this AI paradigm?

## Understanding Music Cognition: A Research Agenda

Most people would agree that musical activity involves some kind of cognition; thus we need no further justification for this research topic, in general. But, as mentioned earlier, it seems that there exists a very specific kind of cognitive process which is peculiar to music: *auditory imagery.* This impression is supported by the role which imagery plays in both theoretical and aesthetic discourse about music. See Lischka 1985 for references.

For this reason, a better understanding of this particular aspect of music cognition would broaden our understanding of such music activities as composition and listening as well. And thus we are led to long-term research goal, where we can exemplify a promising research strategy and are also concerned with a fascinating scientific problem. Let us present in this last section some preliminary ideas about how these questions could be addressed.

**Research Objective**

According to the general strategy sketched previously we need to perform two basic tasks:

• Explicate the phenomenology of auditory imagery as a system of interacting schemata.

• Implement this system through building an artifical organism.

**Auditory Imagery**    Our understanding of auditory imagery will be guided by the assumption that imagination is, following Piaget, based on the *interiorization of sensorimotor schemata*. To be more specific: Imagination is an internal activation of schemata, embedded into the general mimic activity of the organism. Or, to put it into more metaphorical terms: Auditory imagery is just listening to an inner voice.

Two main research areas emerge: (1) Analyzing and modeling how auditory perception and, in particular, how categorization works, and how it evolves. In more Piagetian terms: We have to describe the interaction and evolution of complex auditory sensorimotor schemata; and (2) Reconstructing the process by which these schemata are interiorized; in particular, showing how this interiorization emerges from the general accommodation aspect of sensorimotor schemata. In a sense, this second topic is at the very focus of high-level cognition: How, exactly does an organism acquire the capability to re-present objects or events; what are the "roots of reference"?

Obviously, there are strong commonalities between musical and *speech* perception and production, but it is an open question where their evolutionary paths branched. Moreover, a phenomenon such as bird songs indicates that it makes sense to study music perception and imagery at this stage in its own right. Thus we choose as starting points the following two points of departure.

**Speech Production as a Self-Organizing Process.** First, in Kelso and Scholz 1985 theoretical analysis shows how empirical data concerning speech production can be interpreted as realizing a *self-organizing process* of a large number of simple articulatory movements. Each meaningful syllable can be represented by a specific attractor in a dissipative system, and so-called *phase transitions* between different attractor states are achieved by changing an *order parameter*. This analytical approach has to be complemented by a *constructive* realization of these processes in order to obtain a working model of auditory pattern formation. Furthermore, the peculiarities of music pattern formation must be identified before this system will be a useful model for music cognition.

**Neuroethology of Bird Songs** A vast amount of empirical data describes the development and learning of bird songs; see, for recent accounts, Margoliash 1989 and Marler 1989. Main results include, for example, strong evidence for deep sensory and motor interactions, plasticity of learned songs, and identifiable stages of song learning.

**Basic Approach**

The modeling of auditory perception can start with a theoretical idea and an empirical background. Three different research strategies seem, with minor modifications, to be promising.

• *Dissipative systems.* The already mentioned studies in the field of cellular automata form the basis for designing artificial organisms as dissipative systems. How, for example can *atomic behaviors*, such as muscle contractions of the articulatory system, be mapped onto elements of cellular machines, and how must the interactions between these elements be defined in order to provoke cooperative phenomena exhibiting the desired global behavior?

• *Classifier systems.* The well-known classifier systems, due to the work of Holland et al (1986), possess features that match at least some of the O-style criteria of Drexler (1989). Thus one idea would be to explicate the Piagetian notion of structure by classifier systems; for example, interacting schemata are realized by cooperating classifier systems, and the accommodational aspect of structures is achieved by genetic algorithms operating on classifier populations.

• *Neural Darwinism.* A third starting point, in many aspects very close to our overall approach, in *neural Darwinism* (Edelman 1987). Again, Edelman's sets of neural groups have O-style characteristics; furthermore, his approach picks up the work of Kelso and Scholtz (1985) and pursues a line closely related to synergetics. In addition, a lot of research is already done, especially in the field of perceptual classification.

Thus there exist encouraging initial attempts to formalize complex behavior in the sense of interacting schemata, where these schemata are modeled organically and the global behavior emerges by their interaction. But how could this behavior, in turn, be grounded in physics?

**Artificial Birds**   At last, we arrive at the nucleus of our current research perspective: constructing and building artificial birds that "implement" the requirements we have sketched. The following activities describe current research topics:

• *Robotics.* Build artificial articulatory systems, exhibiting O-style properties to some degree. The latter seem necessary, because natural systems rely on flexibility and adaptive features of the organism as well. There is empirical evidence, for example, that movement is controlled by the neural system only to a limited degree; all the fine-tuning is performed by the organs themselves.

• *Artificial neural networks.* Design neural network modules and their mappings. It is obvious that homogeneous networks are probably not capable of complex behavior. On the other hand, reentrant mappings seem necessary for memory and categorization (Edelman 1987).

• *Genetic algorithms.* Model evolutionary aspects by genetic algorithms.

## Conclusion

An open question remains (and we currently do not have any concrete idea of how this could be realized by one of the proposed formalisms). How does interiorization occur? Of course, there are hints, for example by Piaget, ending in the idea that this is a byproduct of the evolution of the accommodation of sensorimotor schemata. But this is just a reformulation of the question, rather than an answer. Nonetheless, if AI is to succeed, then it must solve this problem in some way—even though it is one of the hardest.

# Acknowledgments

Thanks to Aldo Piccialli for inviting me to the fine conference in Sorrento; Peter Beyls and Luc Steels for their kindness during the AI and Music Workshop at the VUB AI Lab in Brussels, where I had the opportunity to discuss some of these dieas; Luc Steels for interesting conversation about AI and organic thinking, in general; Gerd Paass for several discussions on "statistical cooling"; and Jörg Prust for his support with the transputer implementation. Thanks also to Barbara Becker, Joachim Diederich, and Tom Gordon, who read an earlier version of this paper, for their useful comments. Thanks, above all, to Curtis Roads, who encouraged me to write this paper in the first place.

# References

Aarts, E., and J. Korst, 1989. *Simulated Annealing and Boltzmann Machines.* New York: Wiley.

AIM. 1988a. *Proceedings of the First Workshop on Artificial Intelligence and Music, AAAI-88,* Minneapolis/St. Paul, Minnesota.

AIM. 1988b. *Proceedings of the First International Workshop on Artificial Intelligence and Music,* GMD St. Augustin.

AIM. 1989. *Proceedings of the Second International Workshop on Artificial Intelligence and Music, IJCAI-89,* Detroit, Michigan.

Anderson, J. A. and E. Rosenfeld, eds. 1988. *Neurocomputing. Foundations of Research.* Cambridge, Massachusetts: The MIT Press.

Apel, K. O. 1976. "Noam Chomsky's Sprachtheorie und die Philosophie der Gegenwart." In *Transformation der Philosophie* Vol. 2. Frankfurt: Suhrkamp. pp. 264–310.

Babloyantz, A. 1986. *Molecules, Dynamics and Life.* New York: Wiley.

Balaban, M. 1989. "Music Structures: A temporal-hierarchical representation for music." Ben Gurion University, Technical Report FC-TR-021 MCS-313.

Becker, B. 1988. "Towards a concept for case-based knowledge acquisition." *Proceeding of the European Knowledge Acquisition Workshop (EKAW-88).* GMD St. Augustin, 1 September, 1988.

Brown, D. C., and B. Chandrasekaran. 1989. *Design Problem Solving.* London: Routledge.

Chandrasekaran, B., A. Goel, and D. Allemang. 1988. "Connectionism and information-processing abstractions." *AI Magazine* 9(4): 24–34.

Danto, A. C. 1964. "The artworld." *Journal of Philosophy* 61: 571–584.

Dowling, W. J. and D. L. Harwood. 1986. *Music Cognition.* New York: Academic Press.

Drexler, K. E. 1989. "Biological and nanomechanical systems: contrasts in evolutionary capacity." In C. Langton ed., *Artificial Life, SFI Studies in the Sciences of Complexity VI.* Reading, Massachusetts: Addison-Wesley.

Dreyfus, H. 1988. "The Socratic and Platonic basis of cognitivism." *AI & Society* 2: 99–112.

Ebcioglu, K. 1988. "An expert systems for harmonizing four-part chorales." *Computer Music Journal* 12(3): 43–51.

Edelman, G. M. 1987. *Neural Darwinism*. New York: Basic.

Fodor, J. A., and Z. W. Pylyshyn. 1988. "Connectionism and cognitive architecture: a critical analysis. Cognition 28: 1–71.

Haken, H. 1977. *Synergetics. An Introduction*. New York: Springer-Verlag.

Haugeland, J., ed. 1981. *Mind Design*. Cambridge, Massachusetts: The MIT Press.

Heidegger, M. 1972. *Sein und Zeit*. Tübingen

Holland, J. H., K. J. Holyoak, R. E. Nisbett, and Thagard, P. R. 1986. *Induction. Processes of Inference, Learning, and Discovery*. Cambridge, Massachusetts: The MIT Press.

Kelso, J. A. S. and J. P. Scholz. 1985. "Cooperative phenomena in biological motion." In *Complex System—Operational Approaches: Proeedings of the International Symposium on Synergetics 1985*, Springer, Berlin. pp. 124–149.

Laske, O. E., ed. 1986. "Cognitive musicology." *CC AI*. 3(3):

Leman, M., ed. 1989. "Models of Musical Communication and Cognition." *Interface. Journal of New Music Research* 18: 1–2.

Lischka, C. 1985. "Toward a theory of auditory imagery." *Proceedings of the 2nd Darmstädter Symposium on Mathematics and Music Theory 1985*. Darmstadt.

Lischka, C. 1987. "Connectionist models of musical thinking." *Proceedings of the International Computer Music Conference 1987*, Urbana-Champaign, Illinois. pp. 190–196.

Lischka, C. 1989. "Apophansis and Kognition." *Proceedings 5. Österreichische Artificial-Intelligence-Tagung* 1989, Igls/Tirol. pp. 340–345.

Lischka, C. and H. W. Güsgen. 1986. "Mvs|c—A constraint-based approach to musical knowledge representation." *Proceedings of the International Computer Music Conference 1986*, The Hague. pp. 227–229.

Lorenz, K. Z. 1981. *The Foundations of Ethology*. New York: Springer-Verlag.

Margoliash, D. 1989. "Neural mechanism and behavioral plasticity in birdsong learning." *Proceedings of the 2nd International Congress of Neuroethology 1989*, Thieme, Stuttgart. pp. 149–150.

Marler, P. 1989. "Sensory-motor interactions in song learning in birds." *Proceedings of the 2nd International Congress of Neuroethology 1989*, Thieme, Stuttgart. pp. 151–152.

Marr, D. 1982. *Vision*. New York: Basic.

Maturana, H. R. and F. J. Varela. 1979. *Autopoiesis and Cognition. The Realization of the Living*. Boston:

Merleau-Ponty, M. 1942. *La Structure du Comportement*. Paris.

Miller, G. A., E. Galanter, and K. H. Pribram. 1960. *Plans and the Structure of Behavior*. New York:

Neisser, U. 1967. *Cognitive Psychology*. New York: Prentice-Hall.

Newell, A. 1980. "Physical symbol systems." *Cognitive Science* 4: 135–183.

Newell, A. 1982. "The knowledge level." *Artificial Intelligence* 18: 87–127.

Paass, G. "Structured probabilistic neural networks." *Proceedings of the "Neuro-Nimes" 1989*, Nimes, France (forthcoming).

Piaget, J. 1947. *La Psychologie de l'Intelligence*. Paris.

Piaget, J. 1968. *Le Structuralisme*. Paris.

Piaget, J. 1970. *Genetic Epistemology*. New York: Columbia University Press.

Pylyshyn, Z. 1984. *Computation and Cognition*. Cambridge, Massachusetts: The MIT Press.

Richards, J. and E. Glasersfeld. 1979. "The control of perception and the construction of reality." *Dialectica* 33(1) 37–58.

Roads, C. 1985. "Research in Music and Artificial Intelligence." *ACM Computing Surveys* 17(2): 163–190.

Rorty, R. 1980. *Philosophy and the Minor of Nature*. Princeton, N.J. : Princeton University Press.

Sloboda, J. A. 1985. *The Musical Mind*. Oxford: Oxford University Press.

Steels, L. 1989a. "Cooperation between distributed agents through self-organization." *VUB AI Lab Memo 89-5*, Brussels.

Steels, L. 1989b. "Cooperation between symbolic and connectionist mechanisms." *Proceedings of the GMD Symposium "High-Level Connectionism" 1989*, GMD St. Augustin (forthcoming).

Wielinga, B. and J. Breuker. 1987. "Model-driven knowledge acquisition: interpretation models." *Memo 87, Deliverable task A1, Esprit Project 1098*.

Winograd, T., and F. Flores. 1986. *Understanding Computers and Cognition*. Erlbaum: New Jersey.

Wolfram, S. 1986. Approaches to complexity engineering. In S. Wolfram, ed. *Theory and Applications of Cellular Automata*. Singapore: World Scientific.

Wollheim, R. 1980. *Art and its Objects*. Cambridge: Cambridge University Press.

# 14 Qualitative Aspects of Signal Processing Through Dynamic Neural Networks

Roberto D'Autilia and Francesco Guerra

In recent years there has been great interest in the peculiar properties of complex systems in statistical mechanics, as represented for example by disordered systems, in particular the so-called *spin glasses* (Mezard, Parisir, and Virasoro 1986).

One of the most important properties of complex systems is their tendency to produce a multiplicity of states with spontaneous innate hierarchical organization, which is very sensitive to external conditions. This property makes complex systems a promising conceptual starting point for building models of phenomena where spontaneous self organization plays an important role, as in most biological problems. In particular, Hopfield and Anderson, in important pioneering works, have shown the relevance of complex systems for the problem of constructing models of associative memory (Hopfield 1982) and models of biological evolution (Anderson 1983).

A large body of literature (see for example Mezard, Parisi, and Virasoro 1986; Wallace 1986; Amit 1987; Sompolinsky 1987; Peliti and Vulpiani 1987) has applied the emerging complex systems theory to many problem of biological interest, such as brain activity, natural selection, perception, and learning.

Here, we must stress first of all that we exploit the notion of *complexity* in a well-defined technical sense, adapted to a particular class of models. Sometimes, in the literature, complexity is understood in vague terms, as for example in the definition: "A system is complex if it consists of a very large number of interacting elements that evolve in parallel over time." At this introductory level, we give an elementary example to show the technical notion of complexity.

Consider a very large number $N$ of interacting elements $i = 1, \ldots, N$. Assume that, for each couple $\{i,j\}, i \neq j$, a number $J(i,j) = J(j,i) = \pm 1$ has been independently defined. Moreover, let us suppose that the elements evolve in parallel over time, each with the same dynamic law that takes into account the state of the other elements and the values of $J$. Then, the complexity of the system is connected with the existence of a high number of *frustrated triples*, $\{i,j,k\}, i \neq j, i \neq k, j \neq k$, for which $J(i,j)J(j,k)J(k,i) = -1$.

Only if there are a high number of frustrated triples does the system show the interesting aspects of complexity, as for example spontaneous hierarchical organization. A system with all $J(i,j) = 1$ can be made "of a very large number of interacting elements that evolve in parallel in time," but cannot be considered complex in rigorous technical terms, since it shows no interesting consequences of complexity.

Our research on the application of dynamic complex systems, is partly motivated by previous work on the role of multilevel hierarchical organization in the analysis and simulation of musical structures (Baffioni, Guerra, and Tedeschini Lalli 1981, 1984).

We propose some simple models of stochastic dynamic systems. The systems are characterized by a large number of degrees of freedom, and incorporate two classes of dynamic variables (fast and slow). The fast and slow variables evolve at different time scales on the microscopic level. These models are not complex in themselves (in the previously described technical sense); in particular they have a quite trivial thermodynamic behavior. However, the fast variables move in the general landscape of the slow variables, which, according to the previous history of the external influences, may show features of complexity. In other words, fast variables can be considered to form a subsystem with time changing complexity, while slow variables retain a memory of external influences and may change the complexity.

While our models are interesting in many other fields, as general dynamic models for systems with time changing complexity (D'Autilia and Guerra 1990), in this report we would like to stress their relevance as specialized signal processors, able to take into account, in principle, very complicated multiple correlations, even at delayed times, between the input signals.

The rest of this report is therefore organized as follows. In the next section we recall the main properties of the Hopfield model (Hopfield 1982) of associative memory. After that we introduce our class of models, taking into account only the simplest formulation, and compare them with the Hopfield class of models.

The core of this report is devoted to a simplified treatment of the models, based on the mean field approximation, a well-known tool in statistical mechanics. We show how to exploit our models as general signal processors.

Then memory phenomena and the ability to take into account signal correlations are shown in some simple but significant cases. In particular, we deal with features related to conditioned reflex, rhythm recognition, and time edge detection. For each phenomenon, we isolate the minimal structure in the neural network relevant for the appearance of the effect. The final section is devoted to some conclusions and the outlook for future developments.

## The Hopfield Model of Associative Memory

Here we give only a very short description of the Hopfield model, just enough, for the introduction of our model in the next section. For more details, refer to Hopfield (1982).

Let us consider the set $\{1, \ldots, N\}$. Conventionally, we call *neuron* each of its elements $i$, $1 \leq i \leq N$. We assume that each neuron can assume only two states denoted by $\pm 1$. Therefore, a generic configuration of the system is given by the function

$$\sigma: \{1, \ldots, N\} \ni i \rightarrow \sigma_i \in \{1, -1\}. \tag{1}$$

Notice that, for a system made by $N$ neurons, there are $2^N$ configurations. The other variables of the system are called *synapses*. They are symmetric variables, $J_{ij} = J_{ji}$, defined for each couple of neurons, $i, j = 1, \ldots, N; i \neq j$.

The Hopfield model is meant to be a model of associative memory, or content addressable memory, more similar to the working of human brain, in contrast with the memory of ordinary computers, which is addressed through locations.

The *words* to be stored, and later remembered, are given by $K$ generic configurations

$$\xi_i^\alpha \in \{1, -1\}, \qquad \alpha = 1, \ldots, K, \qquad i = 1, \ldots, N. \tag{2}$$

The model works on the basis of two regimes. In the first regime (learning), given the $K$ words, $\alpha = 1, \ldots, K$, the synapses are defined as

$$J_{ij} = \sum_{\alpha=1}^{K} \xi_i^\alpha \xi_j^\alpha, \tag{3}$$

in agreement with Hebb's rule of learning (Hebb 1949).

In the second regime (retrieval), the system synapses are kept fixed, while the neuron configuration is allowed to evolve from some initial configuration $\sigma^0$, which can be understood as a deformation of some word $\xi$, that is, $\sigma^0$ differs from some word $\xi^\alpha$ by the change of some bits. The evolution law is cycled according to

$$\sigma_i' = sign\left(\sum_{j=1}^{N} J_{ij} \sigma_j\right), \tag{4}$$

where $\sigma$ is the old configuration and $\sigma'$ the new one at each cycle. The function *sign* can be defined as

$$sign(x) = \begin{cases} +1, & \text{if } x \geq 0, \\ -1, & \text{if } x < 0. \end{cases} \tag{5}$$

It is impressive to see, in computer simulations, that the initial neuron configuration evolves very rapidly, in most cases, to some of the learned words, considered as the "nearest" to the initial configuration $\sigma^0$. We can consider $\sigma^0$ as a deteriorated or incomplete piece of information and the final $\sigma$ as the restored one. The learned words act as attractors for the cycled evolution.

There is a large body of literature about the analysis, applications, and extensions of this interesting model (Wallace 1986; Amit 1987; Sompolisky 1987). We would like to highlight two important features of the model. First of all, it can happen that the system relaxes to a final configuraton that is not one of the learned words, but, for example, a mixture of some words (chimera states). This is a serious defect, if the objective of stored information retrieval is the only one involved. But it can be an attractive feature if the model is considered as a kind of zero order simulation of brain activity, because in this case we have the emergency of a kind of "creativity," based on the elaboration of the stored information to produce new attractors.

Moreover, there is an upper bound to the number $K$ of the words to be stored and retrieved. This number is estimated to be $\simeq 0.14N$, enormously smaller then the number of states $2^N$. However, in contrast with location addressable memory, this model shows some robust features, in the sense that one can make changes in some of the $J$s without affecting the attractors.

If the number of stored words increases beyond the capacity of the system, then retrieval becomes less and less reliable and chimera states begin to be very different from learned words ("the more you learn, the more you get confused"). Some interesting proposals have been made in order to avoid the state of total confusion characteristic of the Hopfield model, by exploiting unlearning procedures, where old words are automatically forgotten and the memory recalls only the most recent ones (Parisi 1986).

In the next section we introduce our model as a stochastic dynamic generalization of the Hopfield model. The main differences are the following. The learning regime, given by equation 3, and the cycled retrieval regime, given by equation 4, will be unified in a stochastic evolution in continuous time, ruled by two time scales, a faster one for the neurons and a slower one for the synapses. Moreover, the influence of the "external world," represented by the learned words $\xi$ and the initial conditions $\sigma^0$ in the Hopfield model, will be replaced by external fields continuously acting in time on the neuron evolution.

## Stochastic Dynamic Models of Neural Networks

This section has quite technical content. For those interested only in signal processing we suggest that you might skip to the next section. In the simplest formulation our model can be described as follows.

We consider a Markov stochastic process, evolving in continuous time $t$, characterized by the dynamic variables

$$\sigma_i, J_{ij}(t) \equiv J_{ji}(t), \qquad i, j = 1, \ldots, N, \qquad i \neq j, \tag{5}$$

all jumping between values $\pm 1$, according to well defined probabilistic laws (Glauber dynamics [Glauber 1963]). We call $\sigma$ the neurons and $J$ the synapses.

In order to describe the probabilistic laws of Glauber dynamics, let us start from a system made by a single neuron $\sigma(t)$. Introduce a time constant $\tau > 0$ and a given function $M(t)$, $|M| \leq 1$. Then, the probability that $\sigma(t)$, starting from the state $x$ at time $t$, will be found in the state $x'$ at time $t + \Delta t$, with $\Delta t$ positive and small, is assumed to be given by the basic definition

$$P(\sigma(t + \Delta t) = x' | \sigma(t) = x) = \delta_{x,x'} + \frac{x'}{2\tau}(M(t) - x)\Delta t + R, \tag{6}$$

where $R$ is a small correction of order $(\Delta t)^2$, and $x$, $x' = \pm 1$. In our notations, the conditional probability $P(A|B)$ is the probability of the event $A$, conditioned to the event $B$. Moreover, $\delta_{x,x'}$ is the Kronecker symbol, $\delta_{x,x'} = 1$ if $x = x'$, $\delta_{x,x'} = 0$ if $x \neq x'$.

In the case of a single neuron $\sigma(t)$, the stochastic system evolution is fully described through the average

$$m(t) = \langle \sigma(t) \rangle, \qquad |m(t)| \leq 1. \tag{7}$$

In fact, as immediate consequence of equation 6 we have

$$\tau \frac{d}{dt} m(t) = -m(t) + M(t). \tag{8}$$

The constant $\tau$ fixes the time scale of the dissipative evolution for $m(t)$ driven by the given $M(t)$.

The assumed stochastic evolution for the system $\{\sigma_i(t), J_{ij}(t)\}$ is defined as a simple generalization of the single neuron evolution. In fact, for given $M_i(t)$, $M_{ij}(t)$, we assume that each separate variable $\sigma_i(t)$, $J_{ij}(t)$ evolves stochastically according to the respective law analogous to equation 6. Only we assume a time scale constant $\tau$ for all $\sigma_i$ and a different, and longer, time scale constant $T$ for all $J_{ij}$. Of course, each $M_i(t)$, $M_{ij}(t)$, will depend, in general, on the actual values of the other variables. Therefore, each variable will make jumps with probabilities continuously depending on the actual values of the other variables, which are also jumping.

Now we must specify $M_i(t)$, $M_{ij}(t)$. We assume a generic external signal $s(t) \equiv \{s_i(t)\}$ acting on the neurons, and for a given positive constant $\beta$ we define

$$M_i(t) = \tanh\left(\beta \sum_{j:j\neq i} J_{ij}(t)\sigma_j(t) + s_i(t)\right),\tag{9}$$

$$M_{ij}(t) = \sigma_i(t)\sigma_j(t)\tanh\beta.\tag{10}$$

Stochastic systems of this kind are well known in statistical mechanics for dissipative behavior under the influence of external fields. Their mathematical treatment is quite complicated, because one must take in account all the correlations between the stochastic variables.

For the sake of completeness we will briefly describe the evolution of equal time correlations, referring to D'Autilia and Guerra 1989 for a more complete treatment.

Let $A$ be a generic subset of neurons with $|A|$ elements, and $B$ a generic subset of synapses with $|B|$ elements. Define

$$\sigma_A(t) = \prod_{i:i\in A} \sigma_i(t),\qquad J_B(t) = \prod_{(i,j):(i,j)\in B} J_{ij}(t).\tag{11}$$

Then, as a consequence of the assumed dynamic laws, we have the time evolution for the correlations

$$\frac{d}{dt}\langle \sigma_A(t)J_B(t)\rangle = \frac{1}{\tau}\sum_{i:i\in A}\left[-\langle\sigma_A(t)J_B(t)\rangle + \langle\sigma_{A'}(t)J_B(t)M_i(t)\rangle\right]$$

$$+\frac{1}{T}\sum_{(i,j):(i\cdot j)\in B}\left[-\langle\sigma_A(t)J_B(t)\rangle + \langle\sigma_A(t)J_{B'}(t)M_{ij}(t)\rangle\right],$$

$$\tag{12}$$

where, in the sums, $A'$ denotes $A$ with $i$ subtracted out, an $B'$ denotes $B$ with the couple $(i, j)$ subtracted out.

In principle, equation 12, together with the definitions 9 and 10, give a complete characterization of our model.

A drastic simplification can be made by using the mean field approximation, well known in statistical mechanics. It is important to remark that the mean field approximation preserves all the qualitative features of our model, and is very useful for the purpose of interpreting our model as a signal processor.

Let us introduce the averages

$$m_i(t) = \langle \sigma_i(t) \rangle, \qquad w_{ij}(t) = \langle J_{ij}(t) \rangle. \tag{13}$$

Consider the particular cases where $A$ is made by the single element $i$ and $B$ is empty, and $A$ is empty and $B$ contains only $(i, j)$. Then equation 12 reduces to

$$\tau \frac{d}{dt} m_i(t) = -m_i(t) + \langle M_i(t) \rangle,$$

$$T \frac{d}{dt} w_{ij}(t) = -w_{ij}(t) + \langle M_{ij}(t) \rangle, \tag{14}$$

with $M$s defined in equation 9 and 10.

The mean field approximation consists in the bold assumptions

$$\langle M_i(t) \rangle = \left\langle \tanh\left( \beta \sum_j J_{ij}\sigma_j + s_i \right) \right\rangle$$

$$\simeq \tanh\left( \beta \sum_j \langle J_{ij} \rangle \langle \sigma_j \rangle + s_i \right)$$

$$= \tanh\left( \beta \sum_j w_{ij} m_j + s_i \right), \tag{15}$$

$$\langle M_{ij}(t) \rangle = \langle \sigma_i(t) \sigma_j(t) \rangle \tanh \beta$$

$$\simeq \langle \sigma_i \rangle \langle \sigma_j \rangle \tanh \beta$$

$$= m_i(t) m_j(t) \tanh \beta. \tag{16}$$

In this way higher correlations are destroyed and equation 14 reduces to equation 17 of the next section, which will be taken as the basic equations of our model.

We end this section with a warning. As is well known in statistical mechanics, the mean field approximation tends to develop spurious spontaneous magnetization in models of the type introduced here. This happens if $\beta$ is too large in equation 17. Then the system will have the tendency to stick to some states, even when external fields are absent. These unpleasant features are avoided by taking a small enough value for $\beta$ in equation 17.

## Dynamic Models of Neural Networks

In order to keep this section completely independent from the previous one, let us briefly recall the basic structure of the dynamic models of neural networks, obtained through the mean field approximation from the stochastic models introduced before.

For a system of $N$ neurons, the neuron activity in time is described through the functions $m_i(t)$, with $|m_i(t)| \leq 1$, while the synapsis status is described through the functions $w_{ij}(t) \equiv w_{ji}(t)$, with $|w_{ij}| \leq 1$.

There are two time constants, $\tau$ and $T$, with $\tau \ll T$. The first is connected to the fast neuron evolution, the second to the slow synapse evolution. We must also introduce a positive constant $\beta$, which represents the coupling between neurons and synapses.

We assume that the system is under the continuous influence of external fields $s_i(t)$, which can be interpreted as signals to be processed (some can be identically zero, of course), while $m_i(t)$ will be interpreted as outputs (in some cases it is interesting to consider also $w_{ij}$ as outputs).

The assumed time evolution is given by

$$\tau \frac{d}{dt} m_i(t) = -m_i(t) + \tanh\left(\beta \sum_{j:j \neq i} w_{ij}(t)m_i(t) + s_i(t)\right),$$

$$T \frac{d}{dt} w_{ij}(t) = -w_{ij}(t) + m_i(t)m_j(t)\tanh \beta, \qquad (17)$$

$$i, j = 1, \ldots, N, \qquad i \neq j, \qquad w_{ij}(t) = w_{ji}(t), \qquad \tau \ll T,$$

with $\tanh(x) = (e^x - e^{-x})/(e^x + e^{-x})$.

These equations are typical of a dissipative dynamic system. Notice that, in general, the variables $m_i(t)$, $w_{ij}(t)$ depend on their initial conditions, but, after a transient period, they forget completely the initial conditions and evolve taking into account only the external fields $s_i(t)$.

It is also important to point out the causal structure, given by the fact that, for some assumed initial conditions, the variables $m_i(t)$, $w_{ij}(t)$ are affected only by the external fields $s_i(t')$, with $t' \leq t$.

It is easy to understand the qualitative features of the system. First of all, we see that the evolution equation for the synapses can be easily solved in the form

$$w_{ij}(t) = \tanh \beta \int_{-\infty}^{t} e^{-(t-t')/T} m_i(t') m_j(t') \, dt', \qquad (18)$$

where we have put a forgotten initial condition at time $t = -\infty$.

We can compare this equation with the analogous equation 3 in the Hopfield model. In equation 3 the synapses learn through a sum over correlations among the specifications of the words to be learned. Here the synaptic status is ruled through a continuous time integral over the correlations between past neuron activities.

Notice also that the time contributions have an exponential damping with time $T$. Therefore, neuron activities in the distant past have a smaller influence over the present synaptic status, then respect to recent ones (compare also with a similar idea in Parisi 1986).

However, it would be wrong to conclude that memory effects have a persistence lasting for average time $T$. Actually, in models of this type, collective phenomena develop with very long persistence times. Therefore, there can be memory effects lasting much longer time than $T$.

The equations for the neuron activities $m_i(t)$ are of a kind very similar to equation 4. Here the state variables $m_i(t)$ are continuous, and not restricted to the discrete values $\pm 1$ as in equation 4. Moreover, the cycled evolution has been replaced by a continuous evolution and the sharp *sign* function has been replaced by a smooth hyperbolic tangent. The external signals $s_i(t)$ act continuously on the evolution of $m_i(t)$. However, the qualitative influence of the variables $m_j(t)$ on the evolution of $m_i(t)$ is very similar to the analogous influence of $\sigma_j(t)$ on the changes of $\sigma_i(t)$. In fact, in both cases, the synaptic levels act as weights for the influence of the neuron $i$ coming from the neuron $j$.

As we have explained before, these dynamic neural networks can be exploited as specialized signal processors, with $s_i(t)$ interpreted as inputs, and $m_i(t)$ [and $w_{ij}(t)$] as outputs (figure 14.1).

Signal processing of this kind has some interesting features. First of all, there are long-term memory effects, which can keep track of instantaneous and delayed correlations between input signals.

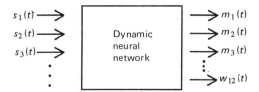

**Figure 14.1**
A dynamic neural network acting as a signal processor, accepting input signals and emitting processed output signals

For example, suppose that the system has been subject to a long train of input bursts of some specific nature, which has enforced some synaptic status. Then the arrival of a signal with features partially similar, but not identical, to the previous bursts will produce a neural activity of the same kind as the activity produced by the previous bursts. In a sense, the system is able to perform a kind of categorization, by putting together signals of similar nature, on the basis of previous experience, and giving roughly the same output for all inputs in the same category.

Moreover, all these features tend to be organized in hierarchical fashion, according to different time scales.

We began a systematic investigation of the general properties of the signal processing performed by dynamic neural networks of this kind, through computer simulation. Applications run from prediction and forecasting, to intelligent control, model identification and topics falling in the scope of artificial intelligence programs.

While we refer to D'Autilia and Guerra (1989) for a more detailed treatment, here we would like to report three simple examples related to conditioned reflex, rhythm recognition, and time edge detection, by isolating the essential elements of the neural networks able to reproduce the effects.

## Conditioned Reflex, Rhythm Recognition, and Time Edge Detection

For the conditioned reflex we employ the terminology borrowed from physiology. However, the main underlying concept is completely independent from physiologic considerations and can be described as follows.

Suppose that we have two independent channels, with respective signals $s_1$ and $s_2$ and outputs $m_1$ and $m_2$. For the sake of simplicity, assume that

$s_1$, $s_2$ can take only the values zero (no signal) and one (signal). When a signal is present in one of the channels, then there will be some subsequent output in the channel.

Neural networks can realize a coupling between the two channels. If signals are simultaneously applied, then the system will learn that there is a correlation between the two channels. After some learning period (training) the system will be able to reproduce answers in the two channels, even if signal is applied only in one channel.

The essential elements of the neural network able to reproduce this conditioned reflex phenomenon can be taken as two neurons coupled through a synapse. The basic equations are therefore

$$\tau \frac{d}{dt} m_1(t) = -m_1(t) + \tanh(\beta w_{12}(t)m_2(t) + s_1(t)),$$

$$\tau \frac{d}{dt} m_2(t) = -m_2(t) + \tanh(\beta w_{21}(t)m_1(t) + s_2(t)),$$

$$T \frac{d}{dt} w_{12}(t) = -w_{12}(t) + m_1(t)m_2(t) \tanh \beta,$$

$$w_{12}(t) = w_{21}(t).$$

(19)

A typical computer output is as in figure 14.2. One can easily recognize an untrained regime where the signal in channel two ($s_2$) produces an answer only in the same channel. Afterwards, there is a training period, where signals are applied in both channels and produce answers in $m_1$ and $m_2$. After the training period, the coupling $w_{12}$ between channels increases to some significant level. Therefore, if now a signal is applied in channel two, there will be an answer both in channel two and in channel one. If the correlation is not enforced, the coupling decreases in time.

A picturesque interpretation of the effect can be realized through the following input-output coding. The signal in channel two is bellringing while signal in channel one is food showing. The answer in channel one is dog salivation.

Of course, much more elaborate correlation effects can be obtained through more complicated architectures.

Let us now turn to rhythm recognition. It is defined by the following effect. We assume a regular rhythmic signal in the input channel $s_1$, for example, given by $s_1(t) = A \cos \omega t$. The output $m_1$ will reproduce the effects

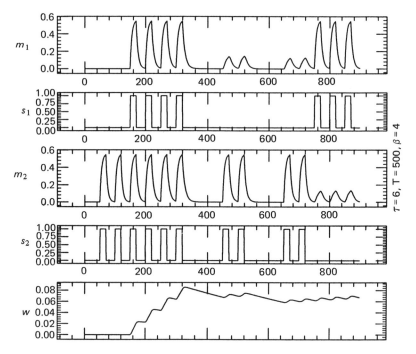

**Figure 14.2**
Conditioned reflex processing. The input signals are $s_1$ and $s_2$, and the output signals are $m_1$ and $m_2$. The coupling between channels is shown in $w$.

of the input with the same rhythmic regularity. Suppose that, after some training period, the external signal disappears. We would like that the output $m_1$ continues for some time to oscillate with the same learned period, even if no signal is applied.

The minimal neuron subset able to reproduce this kind of rhythm recognition can be described as follows.

Let us introduce a kind of delay line, made by neurons 1, 2, ... with fixed properly adjusted couplings between nearest neighbors $w_{12}$, $w_{23}$, $w_{34}$, .... If a periodic external signal is applied to the first neuron, then, as a consequence of the basic equations, all $m_i$ will oscillate with the same period. However, due to the dissipative nature of the system, there will be an increasing delay in the phase of the oscillation of each single $m_i$. The delay will increase with $i$. In particular, for the given external signal, some neurons, with large $i$, will oscillate with approximately one period delay with respect to the first neuron. Others will oscillate with a two-period delay, and so on.

Let us now introduce additional synaptic connections $w_{1j}$, between the first neuron and the others, and let them evolve according to the basic equations 17, while the external signal is applied. Among other things, a large value of $w_{1i}$ will build up during the training period, for those *i*s that have a one period delay with respect to the first neuron, or a two-period delay, and so on.

As a consequence, if the external signal disappears, the first neuron will be still under the influence of the neurons with delayed phases given by a multiple of the period. Exactly as in the previous example, a kind of delayed conditioned reflex can develop along the delay line. Therefore, the first neuron will continue to oscillate even in the absence of a signal.

A typical computer output is shown in figure 14.3. One can recognize the training period, with applied external signal, and the delay effects. Then the external signal is suppressed. After a transient period, there is a clear continuation of the rhythmic behavior, with continuously decreasing intensity.

The third elementary phenomenon is the time edge detection. This is the time analog of the usual edge detection in physiological optics. Time edge detection, in the simplest case, can be described as follows.

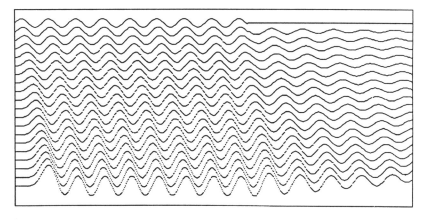

**Figure 14.3**
Rhythm recognition. The pattern shows neuron activities in the delay line following the action of the signal traced at the top of the figure.

A system is subject to some constant external signal $s(t) = s$. Due to the dissipative nature, there will be a constant equilibrium output $m_1, m_2, \ldots$. Suppose that, at some time $t_1$, the external signal changes suddenly from the value $s$ to $s'$, so that $s(t) = s$ for $t \leq t_1$, $s(t) = s'$ for $t > t_1$. Clearly, after some relaxation period, the system will reach the new equilibrium values $m_1', m_2', \ldots$. In most cases, the new equilibrium values are reached monotonously from the old ones. We say that there is time edge detection, if, in some channel, let us say $m_1$, the output signal shows a large quantitative change after the external signal variation, and then relaxation follows. In a sense, the output channel must emit a large signal as a consequence of the external signal variation. So the time edge (in the shape of the external signal) is detected.

There is an interesting biological analog of this phenomenon, because perception processing in the brain is very sensitive to abrupt changes of

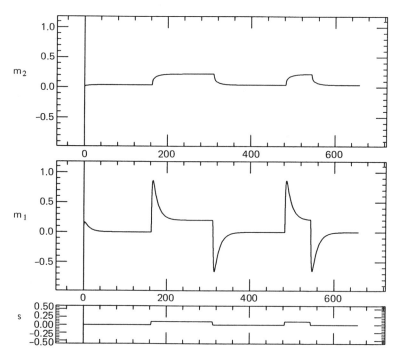

**Figure 14.4**
Time edge detection. The input signal is $s$ and it produces the output signals $m_1$ and $m_2$.

sensation levels. Indeed, time edge detection, as described before, is an important prototype of first-order categorization.

The minimal neuron network structure able to reproduce time edge detection is made of two neurons with a synaptic connection of negative sign. The external signal is sent to both neurons with appropriate weights.

A typical computer output is shown in figure 14.4. One can see the drastic response in the output $m_1$, as a consequence of the variation in the external signal. On the other hand, the output $m_2$ shows a regular monotone relaxation behavior.

## Conclusions and Outlook

We have introduced models of statistical mechanics characterized by two different relaxation time scales. In the mean field approximation, these models can be interpreted as neural networks, where neuron activities change on a fast time scale, in the general correlational landscape of synaptic levels, under the influence of external fields. On the other hand, synaptic levels change on a slow time scale and continuously encode the learning activity.

These models of neural networks provide a very interesting new tool in signal processing, whose possibilities are worthy of intensive exploration. The attractive features of this signal processing technique are its memory effects, its sensitivity to instantaneous and time delayed correlations, and its ability to categorize.

We have given a detailed description of some elementary effects such as conditioned reflex, rhythm recognition, and time edge detection by isolating the minimal components of the neural networks able to reproduce them. These elementary effects should be understood, on a modular basis, as qualitative building blocks for the more complicated behavior of the full network.

## References

Amit, D. J. 1987. "Neural network, achievements, prospects, difficulties." In W. Guttinger, ed. 1987. *Tubingen Symposium on The Physics of Structure Formation.* Berlin: Springer-Verlag.

Anderson, P. W. 1983. "Suggested model for prebiotic evolution: the use of chaos." *Proceedings of the National Academy Sciences USA* 80: 3386–3390.

Baffioni, C., F. Guerra, and L. Tedeschini Lalli. 1981. "Music and aleatory processes." In *Stochastic Differential Equations, Proceedings of the "5-Tage Kurs" of the USP Mathematisierung at Bielefeld University.*

Baffioni, C., F. Guerra, and L. Tedeschini Lalli. 1984. "The theory of stochastic processes and dynamical systems as a basis for models of musical structures." In M. Baroni and L. Callegari, eds. 1984. *Musical Grammars and Computer Analysis.* Fienze: L. S. Olschki. pp. 317–324.

D'Autilia, R. and F. Guerra. 1990. "Dynamical models of neural networks." in preparation.

Glauber, R. J. 1963. "Time-dependent statistics of the ising model." *Journal of Mathematical Physics* 4(294): 294–307.

Hebb, D. O. 1949. *The Organization of Behavior.* New York: Wiley.

Hopfield, J. J. 1982. "Neural networks and physical systems with emergent collective computational abilities." *Proceedings of the National Academy of Sciences USA* 79: 2554–2558.

Mezard, M., G. Parisi, and M. A. Virasoro. 1986. *The Spin Glass Theory and Beyond.* Singapore: World Scientific.

Parisi, G. 1986. "A memory which forgets." *Journal of Physics* A19(L617): L617–L620.

Peliti, L. and A. Vulpiani eds. 1987. *Measures of Complexity, Lecture Notes in Physics, 314.* Berlin: Springer-Verlag.

Sompolinsky, H. "The theory of neural networks: the Hebb rule and beyond." In I. Morgenstern and J. L. Van Hemmen, eds. 1987. *Heidelberg Symposium on Optimization and Glassy Dynamics.* Berlin: Springer-Verlag.

Wallace, D. J. 1986. "Memory and learning in a class of neural models." In B. Bunk, and K. H. Mutter, eds. 1986. *Proceedings of the Workshop on Lattice Gauge Theory.* Wuppertal: Plenum.

# Name Index

# Subject Index